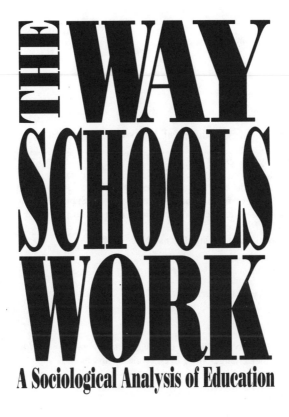

THE WAY SCHOOLS WORK

A Sociological Analysis of Education

KATHLEEN P. BENNETT

University of Tennessee

MARGARET D. LeCOMPTE

University of Colorado

Longman

New York & London

The Way Schools Work: A Sociological Analysis of Education

Longman, 95 Church Street, White Plains, N.Y. 10601

Associated companies:
Longman Group Ltd., London
Longman Cheshire Pty., Melbourne
Longman Paul Pty., Auckland
Copp Clark Pitman, Toronto

The first printing of this book was titled *How Schools Work: A Sociological Analysis of Education*. No other changes have been made to this book.

Executive editor: Naomi Silverman
Production editor: Judith Harlan
Cover design: Thomas Slomka
Production supervisor: Joanne Jay
Production coordinator: Camilla T. K. Palmer

Library of Congress Cataloging-in-Publication Data

Bennett, Kathleen P.
   [How schools work]
   The way schools work: a sociological analysis of education /
Kathleen P. Bennett, Margaret D. LeCompte.
     p.   cm.
   Previously published under title: How schools work. 1990.
   Includes bibliographical references and index.
   ISBN 0-8013-0687-6
1. Educational sociology–United States.   2. Education–Social aspects–United States.   3. Education–Social aspects–United States–History.   4. Educational sociology–History.   I. LeCompte, Margaret Diane.   II. Title.
LC189.B44   1990b   90-40579
370. 19'0973–dc20   CIP

4 5 6–MA–939291

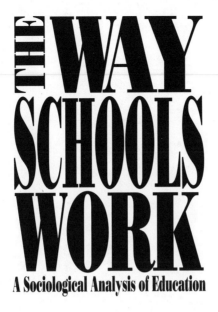

THE WAY SCHOOLS WORK

A Sociological Analysis of Education

Contents

Acknowledgments

No book is entirely the product of its named authors, and this one is no exception. Without the support and light-handed encouragement of our editor, Naomi Silverman, this book never would have seen the light of day. She dared us to do it. A number of our colleagues have contributed substantially to the improvement of the book, reading, editing, correcting mistakes, criticizing our arguments, and chasing down documentation when our own libraries failed us. To Virginia Cox, Donna Deyhle, Rosalind Dworkin, Nancy Edwards, Margaret Eisenhart, Judith Goetz, Linda Grant, Edith King, Joel Spring, and the unnamed reviewers commissioned by Longman, Inc., we are deeply grateful. We owe a very special thanks to Gary Dworkin, whose generous help and unfailing good humor in all of these areas exceeded all ordinary bounds of friendship and colleagueship.

To all of our colleagues whose research contributed to the depth and breadth of our analysis, we are thankful, and we take full responsibility for errors of omission, commission, and interpretation in citing their work. Without the enthusiasm and dogged research services of Lisa Plante and Roger White, the book would have been less timely and certainly less well-documented. We also must acknowledge the insights of our students. They were guinea pigs for our ideas, and their comments and lively criticism made the work much clearer. This book is intended for them.

Clinton B. Allison and Sergiu Luca are owed a special debt of gratitude for all manner of editorial help, but most of all for patience, understanding and moral support.

Finally, we would like to dedicate this book to the memory of our friend, colleague, student and peer, Laurie B. McDade (1950–1988). She was just beginning the work we hope to continue.

Introduction

This is a book about schooling, a process which differs from education. The term *education* broadly refers to the process of learning over the span of one's entire life. Much of it does not take place in formal institutions. Human beings begin their education at birth and continue it through life in a great variety of formal and informal settings. Education as a process is concerned with individuals and the psychological processes involved in learning and cognition. Psychology is the primary discipline which concerns itself with these processes, and psychologists specialize in the study of how individuals learn.

Schooling, by contrast, is a social or group process, and sociology is its associated discipline. Sociology is concerned with the study of social groups, and the sociology of education is the study of groups of people within educational institutions. Sociologists have named the process of learning through which people pass while attending school the "process of schooling." This process is concerned with the understandings which people, generally children, acquire as they participate in formal institutions whose specific function is the socialization of designated groups within society. Sociologists also study the characteristics of people and institutions which make up educational systems, as well as the dynamics of their interaction and operations.

Because no one book can cover all topics in a discipline, we have imposed some arbitrary limitations on this volume. First, we have concentrated our discussion on schools in America, although we draw to some extent on research carried out in other countries. We feel that this is appropriate, given that schools in America differ considerably in organizational and professional structure from schools in other countries. We hope that the book might prove useful to people interested in comparing the American system of education with those in other countries.

Second, we devote much of our discussion to elementary and secondary education, somewhat at the expense of pre-school and higher education. In truth, with the exception of studies evaluating the effectiveness of compensatory pre-school education, the range of research by sociologists on pre-school training is limited. We chose not to include a more extensive analysis of higher education *per se* simply because of limitations of space; we hope, however, that the insights contained in this book, particularly those pertaining to the training of teachers and the impact of race, class and gender on educational achievement—will generalize to your thinking about schooling in universities and colleges.

A special feature of this book is its strong historical bent, in terms of both the information presented and the way developments in theory over time have affected the way we look at and interpret the impact of schools. We have couched our discussion of contemporary schools within the context of their historical development because we believe the way schools currently are organized has been powerfully influenced by events and social policies of the past. Similarly, although our own interpretations of schooling and its effects, as well as the conclusions in this book, are informed by critical and feminist perspectives, they are, like the viewpoints of all social scientists, built upon and affected by the theoretical models and analyses of the past—especially functionalism and conflict theory. Because this text is an introduction to the way sociologists think about educational processes, we weave both classical and contemporary critical perspectives into each chapter. Each chapter usually begins with a descriptive, functional approach and concludes with a more recent critical analysis. We do this because we believe that it is easier to know where we currently are if we understand where we came from!

The chapters in this book derive from subfields in sociology: social theory, the sociology of organizations, the sociology of work and professions, the sociology of knowledge, and the study of class, race, and gender. Chapter One examines the theories which underlie how people conceptualize the purposes for which schools are organized, whose interests schools serve, and what should be taught. We have divided these theories into two categories: transmission theories of function and conflict, which posit that schools rather passively transmit the patterns of society unchanged from one generation to another; and transformation theories of interpretation and criticism, which describe the roles schools can play in transforming society.

Chapter Two examines the structure and dynamics of schools as social organizations. First, it presents an historical analysis of school organization, especially as it has been shaped by ideas and practices from business and industry. Then it examines both the internal organization and patterns of control within schools and districts, and the external matrix of local, state, and national agencies which impinge on their operation. It emphasizes both the apparent ambiguity of patterns of authority in school and the degree to which political, rather than strictly pedagogical, concerns direct their workings.

Chapter Three is a detailed discussion of a group whose participation in schooling often is overlooked—the students. In it, we examine the impact of societal change on the way children experience childhood, the special ways children relate to and resist the influence of schools and their teachers, and the evolution and impact of student peer groups and youth culture on schooling.

Chapter Four examines the characteristics of school participants—teachers, administrators, parents, counselors, and members of state, local and national agencies—and the work they do. It describes trends which have given more control over teaching and classroom management to administrators, at the expense of teachers, and questions the extent to which teaching really is a profession. Chapter Four also examines gender-bias in the educational work force and its impact on the social power and professional prestige of teachers.

Chapter Five is an analysis of the relationship between social class and education. It traces changes in social thinking about the origins of social class hierarchy, as well as what has led to the acquisition of social power in society. The chapter examines the impact of social class on the structure of society as well as on the educational and occupational attainment of individuals, and raises questions about the degree to which contemporary educational systems really are "fair," meritocratic, and egalitarian. Chapter Five sets the stage for similar analyses of the impact on educational achievement and occupational placement of minority status (Chapter Seven) and gender (Chapter Eight).

Chapter Six examines the curriculum, or what is both openly and covertly taught in school. It looks at the differences in power and prestige attributed to various kinds of knowledge, and examines how curricular differentiation, or tracking and ability grouping, serves to sort children into academic programs which prepare them for occupational niches roughly similar to those held by their parents.

Chapter Seven discusses the relationship between minority status and schooling. It examines the role of the federal government in attempting to provide equal opportunities for minority group students. It also analyzes various sociological explanations for the failure of minority students. This chapter concludes with a discussion of minority student responses in the form of assimilation, accomodation, and resistance.

Chapter Eight is an analysis of the relationship between gender and education. It looks at gender differences in both formal and informal curricula. In the formal curriculum, we provide a discussion of gender identified subject matter, engendered staffing of schools, and the portrayal of women in the context of curriculum materials. In the informal curriculum, we examine the hidden messages sent to females and males in school through class organization, instructional technology, and class interaction. This chapter concludes with a discussion of gender differences in academic performance and occupational outcome.

Chapter Nine presents a summary of the arguments in the book, as well as an examination of ways we feel sociological analysis and critical insights might be used to develop alternatives to the current system of education.

There are a few other special features in this book. At the end of each chapter you will find three sections.

First is a glossary of "key concepts" introduced in the chapter. They are listed sequentially—as they have been introduced in the text—rather than alphabetically, and are intended as both a memory aid and a reference. You will find that the textbook index is keyed to these concepts, so that referring to it will permit you to find all the places where the key concepts have been used.

The second feature is a group of exercises which challenge you to confirm the information presented in the book with your own first hand experience. We ask you to interview educators, observe in institutions, analyze textbooks and the media, and question your own assumptions. In so doing, we invite you to try out the critical analysis outlined in this book.

The final special feature is a list of suggested readings, which supplements the extensive bibliography of references listed at the end of the book. The suggested readings are divided into "classic works" and "modern works." These are, respectively, the books and articles which we feel are most typical of or seminal to the thinking reported in each chapter. We hope that you will turn to these volumes to deepen your understanding of specific subjects which interest you.

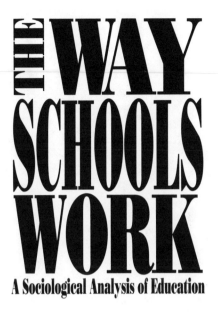

THE WAY SCHOOLS WORK

A Sociological Analysis of Education

CHAPTER 1

Theoretical and Historical Overview of the Purposes of Schooling

OVERVIEW

OVERVIEW (cont'd)

KEY CONCEPTS
EXERCISES
SUGGESTED READINGS
    Classic Works
    Modern Works

INTRODUCTION

- What is theory?
- What are the purposes of schooling?
- How does theory relate to these purposes?
- What are your own theories that explain the purposes of schooling?

This is a chapter about how sociologists, using different theories, explain the purposes of **schooling**. We begin with definitions of several key concepts, including the term **theory**, which we will use throughout the book. Because what one believes varies according to one's belief system or theoretical perspective, we then examine the various **theoretical frameworks** which have informed the sociology of education, showing how these frameworks alter the interpretations people have of the purposes and impact of schooling. We distinguish between theories of transmission and transformation. In our discussion of transmission theories we explain **functionalism** and **conflict theory**. In our discussion of transformation theories, we examine **interpretive** and **critical theories**. We conclude the chapter with a brief discussion of what we think may be future directions in the sociological theories informing education.

THEORETICAL APPROACHES TO THE SOCIOLOGY OF EDUCATION

What Is Theory?

In very simplistic terms, a *theory* is a world view, a way we organize and explain the world we live in. In social science research, we generally use theoretical models or perspectives to organize thought and inquiry. Theoretical models or perspectives are "loosely interrelated sets of assumptions, concepts, and propositions that constitute a view of the world" (Goetz and LeCompte 1984, p. 37) or some significant part of it. Gabarino (1983) describes theory as a "statement of the principles presumably regulating observed processes, or one that accounts for causes or relationships between phenomena" (p. 5). Human beings have created theories to explain the operation of the natural universe, such as theories stating the relationship between energy and mass, or between moisture and the growth rates of plants. We also have developed theories to explain the workings of the social world, such as why job satisfaction and job performance are related, why people seem to develop conservative social attitudes as they grow older, or why higher occupational status usually is associated with higher levels of educational attainment.

Both social theory and scientific theory evolve because both are affected by developments in their current historical and cultural context. While some kinds of speculation, especially in mathematics, generate theory independent of empirical, or observable data to confirm it, in general, theories change as we develop the need for more accurate interpretations of existing facts or to explain changes in what was previously believed to be true. Science, for example, has been affected for centuries by the beliefs of religious and philosophical thinkers who theorized that the sun revolved around the earth. Consequently, during that period all scientific inquiry was organized to support that belief. In time, however, as scientific observations were able to provide empirical support for a heliocentric view of our immediate planetary system, cultural and social beliefs also changed so that good science no longer was viewed as heresy.

In the realm of social science, people have observed throughout history that individuals who have higher levels of education tend to have higher social status. A number of theories or interpretations have been developed to explain this observation. At first people simply believed that the wealthy were smarter. Then, belief in the redemptory effect of education on human nature led first to a corresponding belief that acquiring education would ameliorate or eliminate baser human characteristics, including poverty, disease, and antisocial or immoral behavior. In practice, this belief justified the institution of schools for the poor, compensatory education programs, and a variety of social service practices. Later developments in social theory have altered our beliefs about the role and purpose of education. Now, rather than leading to elimination of poverty and social differences, it appears that educational experiences in schools may actually act to reinforce existing differences.

The theory about education described above is a social science theory. However, we all have acquired from various sources rather unscientific "pet theories" that we use to explain what goes on around us in the social world. For example, one of our students who had obviously been having difficulties with the men in her life sarcastically explained her favorite theory about them: "Men go through a series of adolescent stages and then they die." Obviously some theories are more valid than others in explaining phenomena, but all of them help us to organize and understand our worlds. Many govern what we think about our educational experiences. At this point, you might stop to consider some of your own theories. What theories do you use to answer the following questions?

- Why are some students or teachers more successful in school than others?
- Why are teachers generally so little respected as professionals?
- Why is the public so dissatisfied with the public schools today?

Sociological Theories of Education

One of the primary theoretical issues addressed in the sociology of education involves social transmission and socialization. By this we mean the process by which a society's ways of life, values, beliefs and norms, or standards for appropriate behavior are transmitted from one generation to the next. In the traditional functionalist view of social transmission, each elder generation passes on to each succeeding generation the rules and regulations, habits, and appropriate behaviors for operating in the society. The task of individuals is to learn and accept their roles within the society. We refer to the organization of social roles which people assume within society as the *social structure*.

Sociologists believe that society is understood by studying its structure, the way it is organized, and the roles people play within it. Theories of *transmission* are concerned with the description of the structural aspects of society and their transmission from one generation to the next (Parsons 1951, 1959; Weber 1947). The theories are more concerned with how existing social structures facilitate the general functioning of society than with the role of change or social transformation. For example, a sociological analysis based on transmission theory may examine the social system within a school to understand how the values and behaviors of the society are passed on. American values such as neatness, efficient use of time and obeying authority, for example, are evident in the daily routines of the classroom.

Social transmission frameworks examined in this book are (1) functionalism, and (2) conflict theory. In contrast to functionalist and conflict theories, a less static view of social transmission involves a contrasting "sociology of control," or "action." Its central concern is the *transformation*, rather than reproduction, of the society (Burtonwood 1986). Central to this perspective is a different view of the role of individuals. Whereas static models of social transmission view individuals as passive, the transformative model views individuals as active. They have the capacity to become "empowered," or to engage in the critical thinking which permits them to identify the forces which oppress and constrain them (Ellsworth 1988). Rather than to accept the world as it is, they become agents for social action and changes which potentially could improve their situation. Within this framework we will discuss (1) interpretive theory and (2) critical social theory. It is important to remember that it is difficult to make neat distinctions among these perspectives, because many of them overlap, and many borrow heavily from each other.

Differences between Theories of Transmission and Transformation

The primary difference between theoretical frameworks concerned with transmission and those addressing transformation is explained by Weiler (1988) in terms of *reproduction* and *production* of culture. Reproduction, or transmission, is concerned with an examination of the ways in which existing social structures are exactly copied from generation to generation, regardless of external forces such as the activities or desires of groups or individuals. By contrast, theories of production, or transformation, give the specific activities and desires of individuals an important role in the creation of culture. Weiler refers to "theories of production" as those which describe the ways in which

> both individuals and classes assert their own experience and contest or resist the ideological and material forces imposed upon them in a variety of settings. Their analyses focus on the ways in which both teachers and students in schools produce meaning and culture through their own resistance and their own individual and collective consciousness (p. 11)

SOCIAL TRANSMISSION THEORIES

Functionalism

The first theoretical frame we will discuss is called "functionalism." The language and analyses of functionalism use analogies from biology. Functionalism holds that, like living organisms, all societies possess basic functions which they must carry out to survive. Functionalism has been the prevailing theoretical framework in the social sciences throughout the twentieth century, and argues by analogy that society operates like the human body. For example, the human body is composed of many interdependent organs, each of which carries out a vital function. Each of the organs must be healthy and work together in order to maintain the health of the entire body. If the heart, liver, or any other organ malfunctions and is out of equilibrium with the other organs, the entire body is at risk of dying.

Similarly, societies must be able to carry out vital functions, such as cultural transmission, reproduction, distribution of goods and services, and allocation and control of power in order to survive. Families, churches and schools are the major social institutions which serve as transmitters of the culture. If one of these institutions is not fulfilling its function, another will take over more of that role to maintain the equilibrium of the society. For example, in today's society it can be argued that with the increasing need for both parents to work to support their families, schools have taken over many of the functions formerly accomplished within the home. Functionalists not only identify the various functions within a society, but also the connections between the component parts of societies and the relations of one society to another.

Structural Functionalism

The search for societal *functions* led to a search for *structures*, like bodily organs, which carry them out. This variation of functionalism has been called structural functionalism. Structural functionalists generally believe that social structures must function effectively and in cooperation with others in order for societal health to be maintained. This point of view often led social investigators to believe that any social structure found in a system *must* have some function, and probably one which serves to perpetuate the system and keep it healthy.

Some social scientists have used this argument to oppose any alterations of traditional societies, on the grounds that even practices they find morally offensive, such as the cremation of widows upon the death of their spouses, must have some reasonable utility within the given cultural context. They have argued that to remove such a structure might cause great harm to the system, and should, like surgery to the human body, be undertaken only with great care and in extreme circumstances.

Central to structural functionalism is the conviction that the natural healthy state of a system, like that of a living body, is to be in equilibrium or stasis. Conflict, like an illness, is felt to be an aberration which the normal healthy system avoids and seeks to resolve as quickly as possible. Change, as a consequence, takes place only gradually in healthy systems.

Functionalists view educational systems as one of the *structures* which carry out the *function* of transmission of attitudes, values, skills and norms from one generation to another. Sociologists such as Emile Durkheim (1961), Talcott Parsons (1951, 1959), Robert Merton (1967), and Robert Dreeben (1968) have described how educational systems and the process of schooling transmit culture. According to functionalists, educational systems perpetuate the "accepted," or dominant culture. The concept of "accepted culture" implies the existence of consensus on the values, attitudes and behaviors that should be transmitted by the schools to children. When conflict over values does occur, adjustments and adaptations are made to regain a state of consensus and to keep the entire system balanced. For example, in midtwentieth century America, conflict arose over whether school curricula should portray America as a white-dominated society in which immigrants were expected to assimilate completely, or a multicultural society in which accommodation to differences was celebrated. The past several decades have witnessed a variety of adaptations and adjustments in curricula, each reflecting what could be viewed as attempts to arrive at a new consensus.

Functionalism has been criticized because it assumes the existence of consensus or shared values and beliefs in society, especially with regard to the allocation and use of power. It presents a benign, unquestioning view of the social system and accepts existing class structures as appropriate. Critics of functionalism also contend that it rejects the notion—integral to conflict theories—that conflict and contradictions are inherent aspects of social system, which, in fact, serve to stimulate the system's adaptation to new conditions. Functional analysis has become an inescapable part of the training and worldview of all social scientists. Although social scientists may not accept all the tenets of traditional functional social theory, especially its rejection of conflict and change as viable and often valuable social processes, all social scientists use structural functional categories as basic analytic tools to describe social systems and the relationships among them.

Some practitioners of functionalism, called "methodological empiricists" (Karabel and Halsey 1977), also have been criticized both for their reliance on large-scale quantitative analyses and for their assertion that their results produce "objective," neutral or truly "scientific" unbiased findings. In part, they may assert this because their training may never have presented them with alternative theoretical perspectives. Under these circumstances, they may have become so steeped in functional analysis that it appears to be truth, rather than simply a particular way of looking at the world. Other theories, some of them variations of functionalism, are available however, and may provide more adequate and/or critical explanations. Later we will turn to these approaches.

Functional Theory and the Purposes of Schooling

Functionalists believe that schooling serves to reinforce the existing social and political order. Because they constitute the commonly held or conventional wisdom about schools, you probably will find that our descriptions of the **purposes of schooling** in the following paragraphs sound quite familiar. Following this discussion, we will examine other theories, showing how interpretations of the purposes of schooling alter according to which theoretical perspective you hold. Despite their theoretical orientation, social science theorists would not necessarily disagree with the reality of how schools are organized, but they do disagree with their functions in the society or the purposes they serve. They also disagree in their interpretations about the desired goals for schooling or what they think schools should be. Regardless of one's theoretical perspective, the purposes which the general public attribute to schools fall into four general categories: intellectual, political, economic, and social. The following discussion presents how these purposes would be interpreted by a functional theorist of education.

Intellectual Purposes of Schooling. The three primary intellectual purposes of schooling are:

1. To assist students in the acquisition of cognitive skills (reading, mathematics, etc.)
2. To assist students in the acquisition of substantive knowledge.
3. To assist students in the acquisition of inquiry skills (evaluation, synthesis, etc.)

If you were to ask an individual parent, student or teacher why children attend school, the most common response would be "to learn," which implies acquiring the skills enumerated above. In 1988, the United States Secretary of Education stated, "American parents want their schools to do one thing above all others: teach their children to read, write, and speak well" (W. Bennett, 1988). Businesses and industry also view schools as institutions whose job it is to impart to children both cognitive skills and a body of substantive knowledge in the natural and social sciences. The recent outcry over the lack of knowledge possessed by high school students (Ravitch & Finn 1987; Bloom 1987; E.W. Bennett 1988) has called to the attention of educators and the general public this purpose of education, and there has been an accompanying movement by neoconservatives toward a "core curriculum" which would provide the same basic liberal arts education to all students. A recent example is Bennett's (1988) proposal for a standard high school curriculum entitled "James Madison High". This plan, which relies primarily on an Anglo Euro-American literary and educational tradition, requires four years of literature, three years each of Anglo Euro-American history and democracy, science (astronomy, geology, biology, chemistry, physics, etc.) and mathematics (algebra, geometry, trigonometry, statistics, calculus, etc.), two years each of foreign language and physical education and one year of art and music history. This approach to education emphasizes only the acquisition of knowledge. However, schools also are viewed as places which must produce future citizens and workers. To that end, other purposes of schooling are important.

Political Purposes. Schools serve four major political purposes:

1. To educate future citizens for appropriate participation in the given political order.
2. To promote patriotism by teaching myths, history, and stories about the country, its leaders and government.
3. To promote the assimilation of immigrants.
4. To assure order, public civility, and conformity to laws.

Functionalists believe that schooling facilitates integration into and knowledge about the political system; it is a means by which common social and political values are transmitted to young people and others, like immigrants, who initially may not share them. The education of future citizens has been one of the most important goals of modern public schooling (Durkheim 1961; Spring 1988a).

Early American educational leaders believed that maintenance of a republican form of government required that citizens must be sufficiently educated to participate wisely in the political system. Individuals needed to know how to vote, how to run for public office, and how to make informed decisions about government. To do this, they had to be literate. Hence, all people—at least all white male people—had to attend school at public expense.

One of the earliest plans for a system of schooling that would provide free public elementary education to both male and female children was introduced by Thomas Jefferson to the Virginia legislature in 1779. In his "Bill for the More General Diffusion of Knowledge," Jefferson proposed that elementary schools be established in each locality so that all children would receive three years of free public education. There, they would learn reading, writing and computation. The most talented male child in each of these schools would then be selected for further education in regional grammar schools at public expense. A final selection process would determine the most talented male child from all the schools, who then would attend the College of William and Mary at public expense.

Jefferson's plan differed from those in the New England and other colonies, in that it envisioned an *articulated system* of schools, from elementary school to college. An articulated system links requirements from each lower level to prerequisites in each higher one; students must successfully master preceding levels before passing on to the next. Jefferson's plan specifically sought to elevate by means of education a few males from the lower classes to the ranks of potential leaders. However, other than teaching children to read, Jefferson's plan was not explicitly geared toward citizenship. This was evident from the dearth of courses in government or civics and the emphasis on a classical curriculum of Greek, Roman, English and American history. He believed that literacy and the existence of a free press were sufficient to permit individuals to make wise political decisions.

Jefferson's plan was limited; it did not provide equal opportunities for women, minorities, or the poor. Furthermore, it was never enacted. However, it did provide a catalyst for the idea that schools were critical to the development of leadership in a democracy. This type of thinking continues to characterize the way many people view schools today.

Horace Mann, often called the "father of American education," believed that schools not only should produce future leaders, but that they also should train citizens. Mann felt that a national political consensus could be developed by teaching common democratic values and beliefs in public schools. In this he foreshadowed John Dewey and other educational thinkers.

During Mann's tenure as Secretary of the Massachusetts Board of Education (1837–1848), political tension, mass immigration and class conflict caused great concern among civic and business leaders. Mann was active in school reform, advocating, as editor of the *Common School Journal,* the establishment of publicly supported elementary schools, open to children of all socioeconomic classes. Their purpose was to provide basic literacy and to instill in children social and political values for a common and unified American identity. Mann's concept of the "Common School" was presented as the key to reforming society and creating a more stable union. His plan was supported by leaders of the dominant culture—industrialists, church leaders and the business community— who felt that instilling respect for a common order would build a productive and complacent work force.

At the end of the nineteenth century, the influx of immigrants from southern and eastern Europe led educators to become involved in assimilating newcomers into the society. "Americanization" programs were established to teach the language, customs and laws of the land. Especially after World War I, schools not only were used to Americanize immigrants, but also to support an increased emphasis on patriotism for all children. Opening exercises in school included the Pledge of Allegiance and patriotic songs because allegiance and service to the school were viewed as training for later allegiance and service to the nation (Durkheim 1961; Spring 1988a). Participation in student government and competitive sports were encouraged in order to develop school spirit.

Current curricular trends differ little from those described above. High schools require courses in civics and economics, with special emphasis on the "free enterprise system"; children still learn political history and myths, as well as say the Pledge of Allegiance; and both political education and English as a Second Language classes are required for students who are new immigrants.

Economic Purposes. Schooling serves two major economic purposes:

1. To prepare students for later work roles.
2. To select and train the labor force.

The economic purposes of public schooling include preparation of students for the work force by teaching attitudes, technical skills and social behavior appropriate to the work place. Schools also act as "sorting machines" (Spring 1976). In this role, schools first categorize students by academic ability, then point them toward specific career goals appropriate to their ability. In this way, schools create a "meritocracy" (Young 1958), a hierarchial social structure organized by ability, and distribute individuals accordingly to fill the diverse roles required by a complex modern industrial work force. Such a meritocracy assumes that no major external impediments stand in the way of success for able, hard-working individuals (Young 1971). The attitudes and behaviors which schools teach students include traits such as cooperation, conformity to authority, punctuality, gender appropriate attitudes, neatness, task orientation, care of property, and allegiance to the team (Bossert 1979; Carroll 1975; Dreeben 1968; Jackson 1968; LeCompte 1978b).

Schools also serve as the primary agencies for the **stratification**—or creation of an ability-based hierarchical ranking—(see the glossary of Key Concepts for Chapter Five) of students for later work roles. As the United States industrialized near the turn of the century, the concept of "human capital" and "manpower planning" came to dominate educational thinking (Becker 1964; Blaug 1970). The human capital school of thought, which originated in the late 1950s, calculates the rate of return which people get by "investing" in years of schooling, measured by lifetime earnings—diminished by the total costs of education, including "opportunity costs", or the amount of money *not* earned while in school (Miles 1977; Schultz 1961). Human capital theorist view humans as economic resources. They treat the laboring ability of human beings much like facilities and natural resources (or physical capital) such as money, coal, steel or electrical power, which are needed for the industrial process. Physical capital can grow by being invested wisely; similarly, the value of human capital can be increased and enhanced by increasing the educational levels of the work force.

Young people are viewed as resources having future value and as commodities in the labor market. Schools were believed to increase the capacity of humans by increasing their levels of skill and knowledge. By supporting public education, canny industrialists invested in the development of human resources, or human capital, just as they invested physical capital and other kinds of resources. They also selected and trained students for later roles at various skill levels in the work force. Industrial growth was believed to be intimately linked to a nation's ability to increase its supply of skilled human capital. School-business partnerships like the "Adopt a School" programs in which community businesses invest in particular schools are current examples of the belief in human capital. This belief serves as one of the strongest catalysts for the growth of educational systems in underdeveloped countries. Ultimately, the process of selection and stratification of students in school links occupation to social class differences in society.

Social Purposes. Schools serve three major social purposes:

1. To promote a sense of social and moral responsibility in people.
2. To serve as sites for the solution or amelioration of social problems.
3. To supplement the efforts of other institutions of socialization, such as the family and the church.

In traditional societies, the family, churches and the community served to transmit to youth appropriate social and moral values for the maintenance of culture. As nations became more complex and industrialized, children did not always exactly follow the paths of their parents. The skills needed for work life became more complex, and schools were called upon more and more to assist in the training and socialization of children. Since the nineteenth century, schools also have been viewed as the primary institution for solution of social problems. In fact, in the 1890s, the sociologist, Edward Ross, argued that the school had *replaced* the church and family as the primary institution for instilling social values, and described education as an inexpensive alternative to the police (Ross, 1901).

In the twentieth century, schools have been called upon to solve problems like juvenile delinquency, poverty, child and drug abuse, teenage pregnancy, sexually transmitted diseases and highway safety. Our list could continue, but this should be enough to show the extent to which social goals are a very real component of schooling. We address some of these issues in more detail in Chapter Two, where we discuss what we have called the "social service" function of schooling.

Social services have been incorporated into schools on the basis that well-fed, rested and healthy children learn more readily and are not so likely to drop out of school. They also are supported by the belief that children are more easily influenced in reform movements than are adults. Service programs also facilitate American egalitarian notions of "equal opportunity" and fair play.

This discussion of the purposes of schooling is a backdrop for our discussion of the various theoretical frameworks which have informed the sociology of education, particularly in the United States in the twentieth century. It is important to keep in mind that people interpret the purposes of schooling in accordance with their theories about how schools relate to society. We have begun with the functionalist view, because it probably is the one with which people are most familiar. We now move to other views which, in our view, more closely correspond to the way schools and society actually are linked.

Conflict Theory

Conflict theorists such as Karl Marx, Lewis Coser, Georg Simmel, and Ralf Dahrendorf believed that structural functionalist analysis, with its emphasis on social equilibrium and maintenance of existing patterns, was inadequate to explain the dynamism of social systems. They addressed questions not raised by structural functionalists. These include:

1. What are the sources and consequences of conflict in social systems?
2. How do conflicting groups organize and mobilize?
3. What are the sources of inequality in society?
4. How do societies change and transform themselves?

Especially as developed by Marxists and neo-Marxists, conflict theory states that the organization of a society is determined by its economic organization, and in particular, the patterns of ownership of property. These theorists held that inequality of property or resource distribution in society, then, is the major source of conflict in societies. This, insofar as schools are intimately linked to the kinds of economic opportunities individuals will have in society, they, too, are institutions in which social conflict will be played out.

Conflict theory has led to a rethinking of the relationship between schools, social class structure, and patterns of economic opportunity. Having determined that the educational attainment of males is a good predictor of their ultimate socioeconomic status, Blau and Duncan (1967) then noticed that the educational and socioeconomic status of fathers tended to be the same as that of their sons, indicating that status seemed to be inherited, rather than transcended. Thus, the whole system of class status seemed much more inflexible than the egalitarian social ideology of America purported. While interpretations differ as to whether individuals themselves or the system dictate the ultimate destinies of specific individuals, it became clear that the process of schooling, because of its close ties to placement in the labor market, was linked as closely to the structure of inequality as it was to opportunities. We now move to a discussion of reproduction theories, which examine the variety of ways in which educational theorists explain how schools stratify—or rank order—opportunity.

Reproduction Theory

Reproduction theory questions the American belief that schooling in America promotes democracy, social mobility and equality. Rather, it views schools as socializing institutions which reproduce both the values and ideologies of the dominant social groups and the status rankings of the existing class structure. According to reproduction theorists (Carnoy 1972; Persell 1977; Bowles and Gintis 1976; Boudon 1974; Carnoy and Levin 1985), schools do so in several ways. First, schools and teachers exclusively use the formal language and associated expectations for behavior of the dominant culture. This disadvantages the lower classes because they cannot speak the formal language as well as members of the middle and upper classes, and they engage in different patterns of social behavior (Bernstein 1977; Bourdieu and Passeron 1977).

Second, schools tend to magnify class differences by sorting individuals into various occupational niches, not so much by their ability, but according to their social class origins. Thus, children are thought to be more able if they are from middle or upper class families, and as a consequence, they are pushed toward professional or more desirable careers. Similarly, lower class and minority children are viewed as less able and are placed in vocational curricula with lower job expectations. Children also are encouraged toward fulfillment of traditional gender roles.

Third, the *status quo* is reinforced by the fact that dominant groups control the major social and political institutions in society and assure that competition for control never threatens their power. Giroux (1983a) summarizes this process of reproduction in schools:

> First, schools provided different classes and social groups with the knowledge and skills they needed to occupy their respective places in a labor force stratified by class, race and gender. Second, schools were seen as reproductive in the cultural sense, functioning in part to distribute and legitimate forms of knowledge, values, language and modes of style that constitute the dominant culture and its interests. Third, schools were viewed as part of a state apparatus that produced and legitimated the economic and ideological imperatives that underlie the state's political power. (Giroux 1983a, p. 258)

There are three models of reproduction theory: economic reproduction, cultural reproduction, and hegemonic state reproduction. Researchers employ these different perspectives to explain how schools promote inequality of educational access and perpetuate social class distinctions. Each of these models can be used both at what we refer to as the macro level, or schooling in the larger societal context, and at the micro level, or the smaller, more individual, level of classroom and school practice. Some reproduction theorists use large-scale quantitative analyses to study schooling. Their methods are similar to the functionalists, but their interpretations differ because they employ different theoretical frames to explain their results. Following a discussion of the way in which reproduction theorists view the purposes of schooling, we will examine the different models of reproduction theory.

Reproduction Theories and the Purposes of Schooling

Let's return once again to our discussion of the purposes of schooling. It should be fairly clear by now that despite their differences, reproduction theorists feel that public schooling operates so that the dominant class can maintain its place in a stratified society. Schools serve to maintain and reproduce the class structure within the society through preparation for stratified roles in the work force, rewards for use of dominant language and **cultural capital** and state regulation over most aspects of school life. In this view they differ very little from the structural functionalists; they vary, however, in that rather than accept the *status* *quo* as normal and natural, they abhor the inequalities which reproduction perpetuates.

Economic Reproduction. The economic-reproductive model evolved from the work of Bowles and Gintis (1976). This view, informed by traditional Marxism, states that power is in the hands of dominant classes or groups who control all wealth and capital, and who maintain and reinforce traditional class, ethnic and gender inequalities. Work roles also are stratified by race, class and gender, and systematically leave certain groups, like women, blacks, Hispanics, Native Americans and other minorities, at a disadvantage. The schools facilitate this because their sorting and testing processes create a student body stratified by training and ability. This, in turn, inculcates students with skills, values and attitudes considered appropriate for their later roles in the hierarchically stratified occupational structure.

Schools tend to mirror the inequalities in society at large so that children learn through both a hidden curriculum and an explicit curriculum the skills and attitudes which will correspond to their later work roles. Jackson (1968) used the term hidden curriculum to describe those implicit messages about "appropriate", values, beliefs and behaviors conveyed to children. For example, by encouraging children to keep busy, finish their work, complete their work neatly, come to school on time, wait quietly, etc. schools teach children behaviors they are expected to need in the labor market.

What the hidden curriculum conveys differs according to the social class, ethnicity and gender of children. The structure of schooling socializes lower- and working-class children to accept authority, to be punctual, to wait, and to be compliant, while middle class children learn to assume roles of responsibility, authoritative modes of self-presentation, and independent work habits. Teachers anticipate that middle class children will need highly developed skills in verbal communication for later work roles but that lower class children will not. Research in primary classrooms has confirmed that middle class children are treated very differently from lower class children. For example, during "sharing time," when children are encouraged to talk about themselves, teachers give middle class children much more feedback to correct and enhance their self-presentation skills, while teachers of lower class children tend to accept passively the oral presentation of their students without correction or elaboration (Bernstein 1970; Rist 1970; Labov 1972).

Gender differences also are reinforced by schools. Studies show that males in schools are called on more frequently, asked questions requiring higher-order thinking skills, given more criticism (both positive and negative), given more responsibility for leadership, and generally provided with more teacher attention than are females (Sadker and Sadker 1985). The hidden message is that males are more capable and important than females.

The Concept of Correspondence in Economic Reproduction. Researchers have documented at the micro level the connection between the way social relationships in schools are organized and their implicit messages about roles in terms of authority, work and social roles and values of the capitalist society (Jackson 1968; LeCompte 1978b; Metz 1978; Borman 1987). Critical to this is the concept of *correspondence*. Correspondence means that the structure of society at large is mirrored in the school system and vice versa. Thus, if schools look like factories, it is because factory organization is a dominant form of social organization in modern industrial society (see Chapter Two for a more detailed discussion of correspondence between schools and factories). Bowles and Gintis summarize the correspondence principle which is central to their argument:

> The educational system helps integrate youth into the economic system, we believe, through a structural correspondence between its social relations and those of production. The structure of social relations in education not only inures the student to the discipline of the work place, but develops the types of personal demeanor, modes of self-presentation, self-image, and social class identification which are the crucial ingredients of job adequacy. (1976, p. 131)

The economic reproduction model provides insights into the relationships between social class, structural inequality in schooling, and reproduction of the social division of labor. It explains how initial social class differences are reinforced by the structure of the school, so that students from lower class backgrounds are relegated to lower level jobs while middle and upper class students are rewarded with more desirable positions in the work force.

Researchers within this tradition focus on system blame, placing responsibility for social inequality on the schools. They link the failure of schools to reduce poverty and disadvantage to inequities in the economic structure of capitalist society (Carnoy 1972). However, this model has been criticized for its mechanistic and one-sided assumption that structure alone determines outcomes for human beings. Economic reproduction theory allows no room for individuals to act in behalf of their own destinies. It fails to explain **resistance** or the conflict and dynamics of social relationships among students, teachers and staff within school settings. This theory has also been criticized for omitting forms of domination based upon ethnicity or gender. It is radically pessimistic in that it offers little hope for social change or alternative educational practices (Giroux 1983a, p. 266).

Cultural Reproduction. Another group of sociologists identify "cultural reproduction" as the link between schools and the class structure. Cultural reproduction goes beyond transmission of the class structure alone; it examines how class-based differences are expressed in the political nature of school knowledge, as well as in cultural and linguistic practices embedded in the formal school curriculum. Bernstein's work, *Class, Codes and Control*, Vol. III (1977), examines these issues, integrating both macro and micro levels of analysis. His studies of differences in social class and linguistic codes dissect structural as well as interactional aspects of social life, and demonstrate that inequalities of social class begin in class-based differences in the linguistic codes of the family. These are, in turn, reinforced by the schools.

According to Bernstein, the class structure of society causes each social class to develop a different family role system. Each role system tends to have its own unique mode of communication, which evolves as individuals participate in the shared assumptions and expectations of their class. Working class life is organized around a family structure limited to traditional roles and positional authority based on age, class and gender. It generates what Bernstein calls a "restricted" or "particularistic" code or meaning system, in which speakers use a "shorthand" form of communication, assuming their intentions and meanings are understood by the listener. This language code is described as closed or "restricted," because its practitioners do not use an elaborate and specific language system to make meanings explicit to their listeners.

By contrast, the family structure of the middle class tends to be more open and flexible, and to rely on individual personality characteristics and personal relationships, rather than traditional and stereotypic role relationships. Because roles are negotiable, members of the middle class do not assume that meanings always will be shared by listeners; hence, they use an elaborated language code to facilitate verbal communication. This facilitates what Bernstein calls an elaborated or universalistic language code. Differences between typical working class and middle class communication styles, as described by Bernstein, can be illustrated by the following example, in which a mother tells a child how to behave on a moving bus:

Working Class Code:

> MOTHER: "Hold onto the strap when the bus starts."
>
> CHILD: "Why?"
>
> MOTHER: "Because I said so!"
>
> CHILD: "Why?"
>
> MOTHER: "Sit down and do as you're told."

Middle Class Code:

> MOTHER: "Hold onto the strap when the bus starts."
>
> CHILD: "Why?"
>
> MOTHER: "Because when the bus starts up, you might fall down."
>
> CHILD: "Why?"
>
> MOTHER: "The bus jerks when it starts, and you might trip."
>
> CHILD: "Why?"
>
> MOTHER: "Sit down and do as you're told!"

Notice that the working class code is more direct and immediate. It relies on the authority of the mother to obtain compliance, while the middle class mother engages in dialogue with her child and tries to obtain its compliance by means of a rational explanation.

Bernstein suggests that the elaborated or universalistic language and communication patterns of the middle class predominate in schools. Children from middle class backgrounds are more able to participate in their own socialization processes in educational institutions because their language is congruent with, or similar to, the language of schools. The restricted language code of working class students, by contrast, is less flexible, more tied to traditional roles, and less congruent with "school talk." Since working class students have less competence in the language of the school (or in Bernstein's words, have limited access to the elaborated codes of the socializing agencies), they often fail to understand exactly what is expected of them, respond inappropriately, perform more poorly, and reap fewer rewards for their efforts. Their poor academic performance leads them overwhelmingly into preparation for vocational and blue-collar employment. By contrast, students from the middle and upper classes are prepared for skilled and professional careers. In this way, the class structure is maintained.

Pierre Bourdieu and Jean-Claude Passeron (1977) elaborated on Bernstein's notion of linguistic codes. Expanding on existing studies of class reproduction, they developed the concept of cultural capital to explain the function of schooling in the transmission of cultural and economic wealth. Cultural capital is more than language and social roles. It includes the general cultural background, knowledge and skills passed from one generation to the next and differs according to social class background. Some cultural capital has a higher "exchange rate," or is more valuable, than others. High culture—that concerned with the arts, literature, and languages, as well as interpersonal skill in verbal communication, cooperative work arrangements, creative endeavor, and what might be called "middle class manners and behavior"—characterizes the middle and upper classes and is the most highly valued. This type of cultural capital forms the basis of the overt and the hidden curriculum in schools.

On one hand, children go to school, ostensibly to add to their store of cultural capital. However, in the exchange of cultural capital, working class children find that their stock is undervalued. In fact, the capital they do have handicaps them. Since the schools embody the values and ideals—the cultural capital—of the middle and upper classes, children who come from those backgrounds will be more familiar with the linguistic and cultural codes or meaning systems used within the school system. Children from lower social class backgrounds who are not as familiar with these codes will have more difficulty in understanding the schooling process. The influence of cultural capital is especially pronounced in the first years of schooling when the understanding and use of language by students is a major point of leverage in assessments made by teachers. For example, students are more likely to be perceived by their teachers as less intellectually competent than their standard-English speaking middle class peers if they respond in single words—such as "yeah" or "nope"—or in short phrases, rather than in more complete statements; if they do not make direct eye contact with teachers; or if they use dialects such as Appalachian, Black English or the "village English" of Native Alaskan communities. These are the students who will be judged by teachers to be less academically able and placed in reading groups for the "less capable" (Bennett 1986).

By contrast, students whose cultural and linguistic competence is congruent with school expectations will be judged to be superior in their academic performance. Schools serve to reinforce the knowledge and competencies already acquired by middle class children. Since academic success tends to be associated with later success in the job market, the pattern of reinforcement acts to reinforce the existing class structure.

Hegemonic State Reproduction Model. The core concern of a third model of reproduction is the complex role of governmental intervention in the educational system. The term **hegemony** refers to a societal consensus or "organizing principle or world view (or views) that is diffused by agencies of ideological control and socialization into every area of daily life" (Boggs 1976, p. 39). In other words, the state and federal agencies which play key roles in the production and dissemination of knowledge determine the curriculum as well as the ways in which that curriculum is presented in the schools. States require that school districts comply with a standard curriculum and and some states require that they select textbooks from state textbook adoption lists. Teachers are required by state law to teach the skills and concepts established in the curriculum; and some states require that they must use the approved list when selecting their texts. Schools, therefore, reflect the ideology underlying the state agencies regulating the schooling process. For example, if state officials have mandated that sex education, AIDS education, driver education or gun safety be taught in schools, districts must comply with those regulations.

While researchers in the hegemonic tradition refer to control by "the state" rather globally, it is important to recognize that there are three kinds of "state" control in the United States—at the local, state and national governmental level. To some extent, these do not always coincide, though Marxists would argue that all are products of a similar dominant culture, and that the term "state" refers not to a political entity, but to the more general power structure in modern society.

Giroux (1983b, p. 197) explains that hegemony is reflected in schools not only in the formal curriculum, but also in routines and social relationships within the schools and in the way knowledge is structured. Theorists of hegemonic domination argue that economic and cultural models of reproduction fail to consider how powerful the political intervention of the state is in enforcing policies which direct the reproductive functions of education. The hegemonic model, by contrast, explains two functions which the state carries out in regard to schooling. The first involves the role of state and federal agencies in the actual production of knowledge taught in schools. The second involves the exercise of state control over schools through regulation of certification requirements, length of compulsory schooling, and guidelines for mandatory curriculum requirements.

The State Production of Knowledge. At the national and state level, government research reflects the interests of the current party in power. According to hegemonic theorists, the state intervenes in the production of knowledge by determining which types of research should be funded by the federal and state governments. One of the earliest examples of federal governmental involvement in educational research and the production of knowledge was in the 1950s. Following the Russian launching of Sputnik, federal officials believed that America was losing ground in the race to space. In order to encourage talented students to study science and math, the National Science Foundation channeled funds into math and science curriculum writing groups and later, into summer institutes to train teachers in the use of the materials these groups developed. In addition, the National Defense Education Act provided funds for college scholarships in science and mathematics, for new science and math equipment, and for purchase of curricular materials by local schools systems. Spring (1985) elaborates:

> . . . the National Institute of Education's main concern is the control of education by channeling of research interest into particular fields, which is accomplished by making available government funds for certain areas of research. The NIE, by designating priority areas for research, creates a potential situation wherein the production of knowledge about education is guided, by the means of attracting researchers into desired areas with offers of monetary support. (p. 196)

The work of Giroux (1983a and b), Anyon (1983, 1988), Apple (1979), Spring (1988b) and others illustrates the extent to which the production of knowledge is linked to the political sphere. We will provide a more detailed discussion of this process in Chapter Six, where we examine the school curriculum.

The Role of the State in Regulation. In addition to the political production of knowledge, state political influence is evident in the state control of teacher certification 'and assessment requirements, compulsory education laws, mandated curriculum requirements, and mandatory testing requirements. The trend today is toward more and more involvement by the states in the schooling process. For example, current teachers in Tennessee, Texas, Georgia, and many other states are required to teach prescribed sets of "basic skills" on which the students regularly are examined for mastery by standardized tests. Where they are mandated, these basic skills constitute the major portion of the curriculum to be taught by elementary teachers.

The regulatory function also exists in the state-mandated student exit examinations instituted by many states. These tests, in reading, mathematics, and written composition, are required for students to graduate from high school. Another state regulatory function is the requirement by many states that preservice teachers pass a National Teachers Examination before they can be certified to teach. Many states also are considering ongoing competency testing for experienced teachers to ensure that their skills are maintained. As we shall describe in Chapters Two and Four, many of these policies directly affect students, parents, teachers and schools, but are outside of their control (Giroux 1983a and b; Spring 1985).

Hegemonic state reproduction theory is important because it directs attention to the autonomy of national and state governments in exerting pressure on schooling. It has been criticized, however, because while it attempts to explain macro level structural issues in schools, it fails to consider the micro level, or daily life in classrooms. It neglects the social relations among teachers, students and school staff within the school and how these interactions work to help them accept, accommodate to, or resist the role of the state in the daily workings of the classroom.

Problems with Reproduction Theories. In summary, the three models of reproduction theory provide structural views of the relationship between the work place and the schools, the relationship between the dominant cultural and linguistic codes of the schools and that of the students, as well as an explanation of the effects of the government on school policies and practices. Reproduction theories offer views of schooling in which the repressive economic, sociocultural and political power of the dominant groups reign supreme. According to these theorists, the system, then, is to blame for the failure of students to succeed in schools and the failure of the schools themselves to act as meliorating forces for social problems. At the same time, these theorists claim, the hegemonic power of the state leads people to internalize the state's official explanation for their individual failures in school and consequently, to place the blame on themselves.

These theories have been criticized for their overly deterministic or one-sided view of schooling. Some researchers in this tradition have been criticized for their overreliance on quantitative research methods; their focus on social class and lack of attention to oppression of certain groups on the basis of ethnicity and gender (Delamont 1989; Ellsworth 1988; Eisenhard and Holland 1988); their lack of empirical data in their analyses and their disregard for the power of human agency (Giroux 1983b). Giroux explains that reproduction theorists have "overemphasized the idea of domination in their analysis and have failed to provide any major insights into how teachers, students and other human agents come together within specific historical and social contexts in order to both make and reproduce the conditions of their existence" (Giroux 1983b, p. 259). Giroux argues that by avoiding a focus on human activity within social relationships, reproduction theorists offer little hope for change or reforms. While they have offered a different and often useful way of looking at schools as sites for social and cultural transmission, their view is a pessimistic one. It describes the structure of schooling without considering how individuals within the schools could interact to ameliorate or alter the constraints of the system.

Summary of Social Transmission Theories

Several themes emerge from our discussion of cultural transmission theories. Functionalism and theories of reproduction all address the macro, or structural aspects of schooling and its role in cultural transmission. The major differences between functionalist and reproductive theories lie in their interpretation of cultural transmission. Functionalists believe in the existence of an underlying *consensus* regarding social beliefs and values and do not question its assumptions. Reproduction theorists are critical of this assumption, arguing that social attitudes and values reflect the stratification in the society as a whole. They are primarily concerned with how schools act to serve the interests of dominant groups in society by replicating the existing social class structure and maintaining the division of labor necessary for a society stratified by class, ethnicity and gender.

SOCIAL TRANSFORMATION THEORIES

In this section we discuss sociological theories whose central tenets are those of transformation, rather than transmission, of culture. We must emphasize that these have grown out of the work of previous theorists. Sociological thought is historical in that it continues to build upon, reject, change and reformulate what has come before. Interpretive and critical theories of education draw upon theories of production. Their commonality with each other and their difference with transmission theories is that they view actors within school settings as active, rather than passive, participants in the social construction of their own reality. We will discuss the differences between these and other theories and their limitations following an examination of the theories themselves.

Interpretive Theory

Interpretive theory views schools as places where meaning is constructed through the social interaction of people within the setting. Researchers working within this paradigm believe that the best way to understand the process of schooling is to study what goes on in schools, communities and classrooms through an interpretive approach. This means studying real-world situations using qualitative or descriptive rather than experimental methods of inquiry. Interpretive approaches are a major departure from the quantitative studies which once dominated educational sociology. Quantitative studies, using analysis of census data or survey research methods, relied on statistical analysis of demographic information.

Sociologists within the interpretive paradigm refer to themselves as phenomenologists, ethnomethodologists (Cicourel 1964; Garfinkel 1967), or symbolic interactionists (Blumer 1969). The common thread linking interpretists is their focus on the social construction of meaning in social interactions, elicited through descriptive methods heavily dependent upon direct observation and often participant observation in school settings.

The interpretive approach to the process of schooling gained prominence in the early 1970s when Michael F. D. Young in England announced the "new sociology of education." In so doing, he heralded an approach whose key concerns were classroom interaction, utilization of the analytic categories and concepts used by educators themselves, and sociological studies of the curriculum itself (1971). Questions to be explored in the new sociology of education included the social meaning of various kinds of knowledge, what its possession meant, and how it was distributed.

This approach developed from an interest in the work of the cultural reproduction theorists, particularly the work of Bernstein (1977), who was interested in describing exactly how the process of cultural reproduction took place. According to Karabel and Halsey, Bernstein's arrival at the London Institute of Education in 1963 "played a crucial role in stimulating the emergence of a new approach focusing directly on the content of education and the internal operation of schools" (1977, p. 45). It sparked the development of phenomenological studies of schools, wherein researchers attempted to uncover meaning within social settings.

Within the interpretive paradigm, the central concern of phenomenology is how people construct meanings in their interactions with one another. For example, the concept of what constitutes a "good reader" is developed through the interaction between teachers and students in classroom practice. In one classroom, children may learn that being a good reader means being able to sound words out quickly and efficiently. In another, children may learn that reading ability is assessed by how much of the text one comprehends (Bennett, 1986). Thus, meaning differs according to the actors and their social context.

Increased interest in phenomenological studies of knowledge, or the social meaning of knowledge and its possession, began with the writings of Schutz (1962) and Berger and Luckmann (1967), who viewed reality as something not given, but constructed within the social interactions of individuals. The interpretist emphasis moved sociology of education from the study of macrostructural concerns to micro level analysis of interactions of actors within schools and classrooms.

An early example of the use of interpretive approaches is the work of Nell Keddie (1971), who worked with Michael Young at the London Institute of Education in the late 1960s and early 1970s. She was interested in what teachers know about their students and what they consider suitable knowledge for discussion and evaluation in the classroom. Keddie examined the organization of the curriculum, teacher-student interactions, and the terminology, or categories into which educators divided their world. Careful use of observational techniques revealed that meanings constructed by educators resulted in differential treatment of pupils assigned to different ability categories. The teachers in the study, though denying that student ability was associated with social class, suggested in concrete cases that there was an intimate relationship between the social background and ability levels of their students. Thus, the categories of meaning (for example, "poor children are poor learners") used by teachers shaped the internal structure of the school and led to tracking of students. This, as well as the differentiated form and content of the curriculum (for example, poor learners use remedial books and receive less instructional time from teachers and more from aides than learners who are defined as more able [Bennett 1986]), facilitated the differential treatment of the students. Keddie's study illustrated how this differentiation of curriculum impedes the academic achievement of lower class students. You will remember from our previous discussion that the findings of the reproductionists were similar to these—different social classes of students received different schooling. However, researchers in a reproduction framework looked at the macrosocietal level using large-scale quantitative data as compared to the microlevel qualitiative studies completed by the interpretist researchers described here.

The field of interpretive inquiry has grown tremendously since the late 1960s. It has extended far beyond the discipline of sociology to include researchers from a variety of disciplines whose major concern is to understand the complex processes of schooling through studies variously known as naturalistic, qualitative, descriptive, and ethnographic. Anthropologists of education, cognitive anthropologists, sociolinguists and qualitative sociologists have begun to use the methods of interpretive inquiry. The methods used by these researchers include long-term participant observation in classrooms, analyses of curricular content, methods and strategies used by educators, and extensive open-ended interviewing of those involved in schooling processes.

Interpretive theorists have been criticized for their single-minded focus on microlevel analyses to the exclusion of macrolevel linkages to social, political and economic constraints—such as discrimination by class, ethnicity and gender—described by critical and reproduction theorists. Interpretive researchers were primarily concerned with demonstrating that qualitative methods would provide "objective" descriptions of classroom processes. Their research methods were drawn largely from the ethnographic literature of anthropologists. Researchers were trained to "bracket" or suspend their own beliefs and biases so as to describe classroom happenings from the point of view of the participants. Detailed descriptive analyses of microlevel interactions resulted from these studies. Many researchers who define themselves as symbolic interactionists, especially those in America, are careful to maintain this stance. Symbolic interactionism (Blumer 1969) is the study of the meanings people construct in their interactions with one another over time. Although these researchers may hold perspectives similar either to functionalism or reproduction theory, they do not explicitly address political issues. Apple describes this stance as follows:

> In the United States, England and France, it was argued that the questions most sociologists of education and curriculum researchers asked concealed the fact that assumptions about real relations of power were already embedded in their research models and the approaches from which they drew. As Young put it, sociologists were apt to 'take' as their research problems those questions that were generated out of the existing administrative apparatus, rather than 'make' them themselves. In curriculum studies, it was claimed that issues of efficiency and increasing meritocratic achievement had almost totally depoliticized the field. Questions of 'technique' had replaced essential political and ethical issues of what we should teach and why. (Apple 1982, p. 16)

In summary, interpretive theorists such as phenomenologists and symbolic interactionists study social meanings at the microlevel through qualitative or descriptive research methods. They are transformative in that they view the participants in their studies as actively engaged in the process of constructing culture through their daily interactions.

Critical Social Theory in Education

Critical theory in education has its historical roots in a number of theoretical traditions. First, it combines both macro and micro analyses of social phenomena. It uses the analytic basis and many of the concepts of both functionalism and conflict theory. It shares with conflict theory a concern for the existence of social and economic inequality, and a conviction that inequality is determined by the structure of economic organization, especially the ownership of property. Like conflict theorists, critical theorists believe that inherent in social organizations are contradictions which cause their opposite. For example, for every group of liberated people, there exists a group which is oppressed. Contradictions act as destabilizing agents and force the onset of change.

Because critical theorists are interested in the reponses of individuals to social, political and economic oppression, they are interested in locating contradictions. They see them as points of leverage within oppressive systems which individuals can use to change their condition for the better.

Critical theorists also borrow from symbolic interactionism and phenomenology; they believe that social reality is constructed and operates at multiple levels of meaning. Knowledge and understanding of meaning also serve as sources of inequality because they are stratified and distributed unequally. Questions which critical theorists ask include the following:

1. What are the sources of inequality and oppression in society?
2. How do individuals experience life in social organizations?
3. How can individuals achieve autonomy in the face of societal oppression?
4. How are language and communication patterns used to oppress people?
5. How do people construct positive and negative identities?

Historical Roots of Critical Social Theory

In addition to the reproductionists and interpretist theorists previously mentioned, the Frankfurt School of critical theory, the writings of Italian Marxist Antonio Gramsci, and the work of Brazilian educator Paulo Freire all have been influential in the development of current critical analyses of education. We will provide only a very brief glimpse at the works of several theorists whose research currently informs critical educators.

The Frankfurt School. The term Frankfurt School refers to social theorists and philosophers who worked at the Institute for Social Research in Frankfurt, Germany, in the 1930s. Max Horkheimer was the director of the Institute from 1931 until he retired in 1958. Theodor Adorno, who had served as codirector for three years, then assumed leadership. Among the best known of the theorists associated with the Frankfurt School was Herbert Marcuse, who joined the Institute in the 1930s.

The critical perspectives which Horkheimer, Adorno, Marcuse and others developed served as the foundation for critical theorists today. Much like the current work in critical theory, what emerged from their work was no single shared theory, but rather a perspective which had several common elements. One of these was the destruction of a deep faith in the efficacy of science accompanied by despair over current social and political conditions.

Social theorists had entered into World War I feeling that it was a necessary conflict, one which would eradicate existing social, political and economic aberrations. Once the war was over, the insights and methodological skills of social scientists could be turned to creating a new millennium. However, by the 1930s, it had become apparent not only that World War I had not changed things, but that the world was on the verge of another, equally terrible conflict. Clearly, existing social science theory and methods were faulty; they were in need of radical critique or wholesale elimination.

Horkheimer himself coined the term "critical theory" to contrast what they were doing with the traditional social theory of Descartes and Saint Simon (Tar 1985). The analysis of the Frankfurt School was a critique of traditional or bourgeois perspectives, which assumed that social phenomena could be understood by means of scientific methods of description, classification, generalization, and quantification. This traditional social theory view of science is patterned after that used in the natural sciences; the tradition is referred to as *positivism* (Popper 1968; Phillips 1987). Knowledge gained by means of this type of research is presented as objective, valuefree and "scientific." Frankfurt School theorists were critical of the positivistic model on the grounds that social, or human, phenomena could not be understood in the same way that natural, or physical, phenomena could. Social phenomena could not be separated from their social and historical context. They believed that research methods themselves, as well as the decision to use specific methods, were embedded in social values and therefore could not be considered objective. Rather, they were subjective, or expressive of a particular theoretical or philosophical position. Critical theorists advocate recognition of this subjectivity through a process of self-criticism and self-reflection. While positivistic research tends to ignore historical antecedents, critical theorists consider historical analysis central to understanding of social phenomena. In addition, critical theorists share a concern for injustice, oppression and inequality in society, looking toward the radical transformation of social arrangements in order to increase human freedom.

Antonio Gramsci. Gramsci was an Italian Marxist, both a theorist and activist, who is best known for his *Selections From the Prison Notebooks* which he wrote during eleven years of imprisonment for political activities during the 1930s. This book was translated into English in 1971. Gramsci was particularly concerned with the struggles of the working class in Italy and the ways in which dominant ideology of the state shapes individual consciousness. He used the term hegemony to describe the process by which the worldview of the dominant state is expressed within institutions and maintains control. You will recall our discussion of the hegemonic state reproduction model earlier in this chapter. Gramsci believed in the power of the state to oppress, but he also viewed individuals as active rather than passive learners who produce knowledge and culture in their interactions within institutions. Gramsci argued that the oppressed and subordinate classes could create alternative cultural and political institutions in order to resist and change the hegemony (or patterns of power and control) of the dominant groups. An example of this may be a group of female elementary teachers who resist the oppression of a male-dominated hierarchical administrative structure by working together toward an organizational structure in which they share in the governance of the school.

Paulo Freire. Freire is a Brazilian educator who has spent his life working with students and educators to challenge the constraints and inequities of traditional institutions. His work in teaching literacy skills to peasants demonstrated the need for teachers and students to engage in active dialogue using texts which are meaningful to their daily lives and experiences. Freire's work draws on the radical Catholicism of liberation theology, which emphasizes the role which individuals have in understanding and creating their own salvation, free from the mediation or definition of Church authority (Cleary 1985).

One of his central beliefs is that teachers must respect the culture of their students in providing liberating situations in which students can actively participate in their own learning processes. Teachers and students also must be self-reflective in discovering the ways in which state hegemony has structured their experiences. Freire views teachers and students as active agents in understanding, criticizing, resisting and transforming schooling practices which serve to maintain a society which oppresses large groups of people.

Critical Theory in American Educational Thought

Michael Apple and Henry Giroux are two major American educational theorists currently active in developing critical theory in education. Their work has been stimulated in part by the inadequacy of both reproduction and interpretive theories to encompass and explain the relationship between schooling and society. Apple and Giroux contend that reproduction theory examines only the structural concerns of schools and that interpretive theories are limited to microlevel examinations of classroom interactions, despite the fact that the methods used by interpretive researchers were a real breakthrough in our understanding of how educators and students interact to create social reality. The use by Apple and Giroux of critical theory attempts to unite these approaches—macro and micro—into one lens through which to view and understand the schooling process. Thus, critical theory is a way to integrate macrostructural and microinteractional approaches to the study of schooling.

Central to critical theory is the notion of power. It is critical of the current structure of society, in which dominant socioeconomic groups exploit and oppress subordinate groups of people. Critical social theory assumes that schools are sites where power struggles between dominant and subordinate groups take place. A major theme of their research is an analysis of how dominant groups maintain power in school, as well as how subordinate groups resist this domination.

Reproduction and Cultural Domination. On the macrostructural level, critical theorists view schools much as do reproduction theorists—as places in which a class-based society is reproduced through the use of the economic, cultural and hegemonic capital of the dominant social class. Giroux elaborates:

> Reproduction refers here to texts [language and communication patterns] and social practices whose messages, inscribed within specific historical settings and social contexts, function primarily to legitimate the interests of the dominant social order. I want to argue that these can be characterized as texts as social practices *about* pedagogy, and refer primarily to categories of meaning constructed so as to legitimize and reproduce interests expressed in dominant ideologies. (1983b, p. 157)

Informed by conflict theorists, critical theorists contend that the power of dominant groups is reinforced within schools, maintaining the power of the upper and middle classes. Hence, by means of academic selection, socioeconomic stratification, and a governmentally imposed system of regulations which prescribe specific curricular and pedagogical modes, dominant, white, male, and middle or upper-class cultural standards are imposed on children.

Human Agency and the Production of Culture. On the micro level, critical theorists view schools and classrooms as sites of cultural *production*, in which people interact to construct meaning, much like those working from the interpretist theories. Issues of power and control are worked out in classrooms by individual participants. Critical theorists refer to active involvement by participants as "human agency" and believe that despite the influence of oppressive reproductive forces on schools, it is through human agency that hope exists for transformation of society. If those involved in the schooling process are able to resist the oppressive practices of schooling, and if critical consciousness can be developed by teachers, administrators, and students, schools can become sites of social change rather than of social reproduction.

Pedagogy and the Critical Theorists. Critical educational theorists are deeply concerned with the art and practice of teaching. They argue that teachers must become "transformative intellectuals" and "critical pedagogues" in order to resist the oppression of the dominant ideology and to produce a liberating culture within schools. In other words, teachers must continue to be active, questioning learners. They must have knowledge as well as critical ability, so they can question and criticize not only their own practice but school structure as well. Students also must be taught to become active, critical and engaged learners in an environment made stimulating.

The work of critical theorists and researchers today is to uncover and to understand the ways in which dominant ideology is translated into practice in schools and the ways in which human agency mutes the impact of that ideology.

Critical Ethnography. We now will discuss the research methods used by those employing a critical approach to understanding the process of schooling. The guiding concept of these scholars is "collaboration," which means that they attempt to work with the people being studied to help them achieve release from oppressive conditions, especially in the workplace. In this stance, they resemble applied researchers everywhere, whose research questions are guided by the interests of the clients, rather than notions of pure science or the interests of the researcher.

Researchers who call themselves critical ethnographers both approach schools from a critical perspective and use qualitative research methods, much like those used by interpretive researchers. They, too, draw on the ethnographic methods of anthropology and qualitative sociology; however, they differ from interpretive researchers in their concerns and the questions they ask. Unlike interpretists, who "let the field talk" to them and try not to enter the field with preconceived notions of what they will find there, so-called critical ethnographers *assume* and *explicitly state* that schools contain both dominating, empowered groups and oppressed, disempowered groups of people. Many advocate abandoning the detachment of the scholar for active confrontation with situations and individuals they or their collaborators find to be oppressive (Gitlin 1988).

These researchers borrow from the sociology of the curriculum to explain how relations of power in school are maintained through control of the flow of information, and how dominant groups use the curriculum, methods of instruction and modes of evaluation to maintain their power. They, too, look at the way in which hegemonic state control at the macrolevel and the hidden curriculum of schools at the microlevel serve to maintain social inequalities. Using the methods but not the detached perspectives of ethnography, they study the curriculum in an attempt to determine how hierarchically arranged bodies of knowledge (ability grouping and academic tracks) facilitate the sorting of children into a stratified system. Since this system provides differential learning, it marginalizes, or disqualifies, certain groups of students, including women, minorities, and members of lower socioeconomic classes, from positions of power and influence in society. Critical ethnographers study interaction to understand how dominant structures and practices are resisted by subordinate groups and individuals. They hope to uncover 'some of the implicit and explicit ways in which school structures disempower groups, so as to propose transformative approaches to education.

Critical Theory and the Purposes of Schooling

Critical theorists and reproduction theorists interpret the purposes of schooling similarly. Both believe that schooling serves the interests of the dominant classes. However, critical theorists point to a way out by placing a strong emphasis on the power of individuals to structure their own destiny and to ameliorate the oppressive nature of the institutions in which they live. In many ways, the focus which critical theorists place on the liberating, democratizing qualities of critical thinking resembles that of John Dewey and other educational philosophers, who felt that an educated citizenry would facilitate the preservation of a democratic and egalitarian society.

Beyond Critical Theory

We have stressed throughout this chapter the fact that social theories change over time to reflect new ways of thinking and the impact of new information. The first challenge to accepted social science theories that is of concern to us in this book is conflict theory; the second began in the 1950s and gave rise to the application of phenomenological approaches and critical theory to educational, as well as other social and scientific issues. Called "post-positivism," it attacked the notion that scientific knowledge, especially as exemplified in classical physics, chemistry and mathematics, was the ideal toward which knowledge should strive, and that scientists were infallible "paragons of intellectual virtue and fortitude, worthy of emulation by lesser mortals" (Phillips 1987, p. 17). Post-positivists believe that knowledge no longer consists of true statements, but of "statements that have been rigorously tested-and-thus-far-not-rejected" (Bredo 1989, p. 4). As a consequence, reality cannot be immutable and fixed. Scientific truth and the reality it represents is neither verifiable nor completely falsifiable; it consists of whatever can, for the moment, be subjected to rigorous empirical testing, compared with the results of other tests, and warranted to be the most complete and accurate explanation yet obtained (Dewey 1929; Popper 1968; Phillips 1987).

Because it questioned infallibility of scientific inquiry, post-positivism facilitated an attack on the capability of science and individual scientists to be objective. No longer could scientific inquiry be viewed as "value-free"; researchers began to realize that their own points of view inevitably shaped the direction and results of inquiry. Critical theorists have used this position to question the methods, theories, and interpretations of functionalists. Further, post-positivism helped to legitimate the use of nonexperimental, qualitative and naturalistic research—the kind carried out in the real world, not the laboratory, by ethnographers, qualitative sociologists and symbolic interactionists.

In the middle and late 1980s, critical theory came under its own attack by social theorists such as post-structuralists, feminists (Delamont 1989; Lather 1986; Ellsworth 1988) and anti-rationalists (Ellsworth 1988). While these approaches differ in their emphases and are as varied as the researchers who espouse them, they all draw on the analytic constructs of earlier functionalist and conflict approaches, as well as the post-positivists' attack on "hard science." They also utilize the perspective of interpretive theorists, accepting the premise that reality is constructed of the sum of the realities of individuals interacting in any given setting. These approaches place great importance on presentation of the "multiple voices" (Geertz 1973, 1988) of all participants— especially less powerful participants such as women, members of minority groups, and students—in social interaction.

These critics of critical theory share a belief that critical theory has merely substituted another form of hegemonic domination—that of the white male working class—for the elitism of traditional capitalists or bureaucrats. Because critical theorists are primarily concerned with oppression of the working classes, and because their models are based upon analysis of conditions which prevail in western European societies, critical theorists are, whether consciously or not, biased toward a working class European perspective. Included in this perspective are acceptance of patriarchal, male-dominated aesthetic values and forms of social organization as well as individualistic, rather than collective, forms of human liberation. Critics of critical theory believe that models of resistance to oppression which are appropriate for working and middle class males of European descent may be totally inappropriate for non-European, nonworking class and nonmale individuals.

Perhaps most important, critical theory presents an oversimplified view of asymmetrical power relationships. Critical theorists assume that the end result of resistance, confrontation and open dialogue will be some kind of consensus. However, while paying lip service to the existence of unequal power relation— as, for example, those which exist between students and teachers—critical theorists have made no systematic examination of the barriers unequal power relations create to the kind of expression and dialogue they advocate. "Critical educators have defined 'student voices' in terms of . . . being different from but not necessarily opposed to the voice(s) of the teacher or other students" (Ellsworth 1988, p. 7). However, especially in matters of cultural difference, matters of truth, and questions of who is entitled to receive privileges, consensus may be impossible to achieve. Further, the emancipation advocated by critical theorists is predicated upon Western and European notions of power and group relations. Imposing this view on people who are not part of that tradition is no less authoritarian, say the critics, than other kinds of oppression (LeCompte and Bennett 1988; Burtonwood 1986; Ellsworth 1988).

SUMMARY

In this chapter we have tried to give you some idea of how the theories which underlie social science thinking affect our beliefs about the purposes and operation of schools. In the remaining chapters, we will talk about schools, their organization, participants, and purposes, presenting our discussion in the language of sociologists. In many places, you will find that we first present perspectives which will appear to you to be rather traditionally functionalist in their orientation. This is because we feel that the earlier works established the foundations and developed the vocabulary for analyses which followed. We end each chapter, however, with the critical analysis which is closer to our own thinking. You should keep this in mind throughout your reading and consider how you, or other social theorists, might explain or interpret what is being presented.

KEY CONCEPTS

A Theory is a statement of interrelated sets of assumptions and propositions which help us to explain our worlds. Theories are like mental road maps, guiding the way we perceive the world.

A Theoretical Framework is a set of related theories which serve as an overall way to explain, interpret, or investigate the social world. Some major theoretical frameworks which inform sociological perspectives in education include functionalism, conflict theory, interpretive theory, reproduction or transmission, and critical theory.

Functionalism is based on an analogy drawn from human biology. Like the interrelated organs of the human body, functionalism argues that all societies consist of systems which perform the basic functions necessary for the society to survive. Functionalism focuses on the identification of social functions and the description of their operations, as well as the relationships between different functions within a society. It assumes that change tends to occur through growth or outside forces rather than through internal conflict or contradictions. Thus, the natural state of a social system, and the one which it seeks, is equilibrium. Functionalism suggests that because society exists within a hostile external environment, it must continually face and solve problems which are a threat to its survival. Consequently, those elements in society which persist are those which have contributed to its continued viability. In other words, societies continue to organize formal schooling because doing so helps societies to survive (Parsons 1959; Merton 1967; Turner 1978).

Conflict Theory uses the same general systems analysis as does functionalism, but its emphasis is on conflict, change, and inequality, which it views as natural and inherent to social systems, rather than on equilibrium. Conflict is, in fact, a factor which contributes to the healthy adaptations of social systems. It is primarily created as a consequence of unequal resource distribution within society (Turner, 1978; Marx, 1955; Simmel, 1955; Coser, 1956).

Hegemony is a kind of domination which maintains the power of the existing social and political structure without the use of force. It does so by the existence of societal consensus, in which people agree that the *status quo* is satisfactory and fairly equitable. Consensus is created because dominant groups control institutions such as the media, schools, churches, and the political system, preventing alternative views from gaining an audience or establishing their legitimacy (McLaren, 1989).

Reproduction Theory is concerned with the passing of social and cultural forms from one generation to another. It views schools as institutions which help to reproduce both the values and ideologies of the dominant social class and the existing social class structure. It suggests that schools do not, as is widely believed and hoped in America, necessarily promote democracy, social mobility, and equality. Rather, reproduction theory views schools as institutions which help to perpetuate dominant culture values and ideologies as well as the existing social class structure. Conflict theorists state that reproduction takes place as members of disadvantaged groups resist or drop out of school as they realize that schools really serve the needs of elites, rather than their own. Conflict theorists place the blame for individual failures on system bias and inequity. Hegemonic theorists state that reproduction takes place as the disadvantaged come to blame themselves for their failure; they believe that the reason that they have had less success than members of the elites lies in their own inadequacy, rather than the system's inequity (Carnoy, 1972; Karabel and Halsey, 1977; Giroux, 1983b).

Cultural Capital is the knowledge base possessed by individuals. It consists of general cultural knowledge, language patterns, manners, and skills. Some kinds of cultural capital are more valuable than others, and people who possess valuable cultural capital have more social power.

Interpretive Theory states that meaning—and hence, reality—is constructed through the social interaction of people within a social setting. Meanings change in the course of interaction because the participants hold different perceptions; thus reality is flexible and based upon interpretations, rather than fixed. Many researchers working within this paradigm believe that the way to truly understand human interaction is by using qualitative or descriptive research methods. They have pioneered observational research in schools and classrooms.

Critical Theory historically was a reaction against the assumptions of most current and dominant philosophical or theoretical viewpoints. It subsumed two strands, both of which serve as a critique of the existing social order. One is pessimistic, viewing the hegemony of the existing order as inescapably rigid and inegalitarian, dooming most of the human race to slavery or rule by autocrats. The other, which emphasizes "agency" or selfdetermination of human beings in the face of institutional rigidity, is more hopeful. It views the critique as pointing out alternative means for people to escape the overpowering control of the dominant classes (Tar 1985). Like interpretists, many critical theorists are concerned with the power of language and control of information; as such, they often pay particular attention to curriculum and its content.

Resistance is behavior which takes a conscious, principled and active stand contrary to the dictates of authority figures or social systems.

Schooling is the social process by which members of a society, particularly youth, acquire norms, values and specific skills by participating in formal educational institutions.

The Purposes of Schooling can be viewed primarily as training in the cognitive, intellectual, political, economic, or social realms. Researchers, communities, politicians, educators, and others interested in schools vary in the way they believe these purposes should be slanted and how much emphasis should be accorded to each, depending upon their theoretical orientations.

EXERCISES

1. What do you think are the primary purposes of public schooling? How do these compare with the purposes of schooling discussed in this chapter?

2. Divide your class into four or five groups. Have each group choose a different category of people to interview to determine what they consider to be the primary purposes of public schooling. These categories could include parents, students, teachers, administrators, community professionals, religious leaders, blue and pink collar workers, etc. Compare your findings in a class discussion.

3. In this chapter we examined functionalism, reproduction, interpretive theory and critical theory as they relate to schooling. Choose two of these theories to compare and contrast. Which theory most closely resembles the way in which you view the schooling process? Explain.

4. Imagine a group of teachers who viewed schooling from the perspective of critical theory. If they had the freedom to make any changes they wanted in their schools and classrooms, what do you think they would do? What problems would they encounter and how would they be handled?

SUGGESTED READINGS

Classic Works

Apple, M. W. (1978). The new sociology of education: analyzing cultural and economic reproduction. *Harvard Educational Review 48* (4), 495–503.

Berger, P. L. and Luckmann, T. (1967). *The social construction of reality: A treatise in the sociology of knowledge.* New York: Anchor Books.

Bernstein, B. (1977). *Class, codes and control* (Vol. 3). London: Routledge and Kegan Paul.

Blumer, Herbert. (1969). *Symbolic interactionism: Perspectives and method.* Englewood Cliffs, N.J.: Prentice-Hall.

Bourdieu, P. and Passeron, J. (1977). *Reproduction in education, society and culture.* Beverly Hills: Sage.

Bowles, S. and Gintis, H. (1976). *Schooling in capitalist America: Educational reform and the contradictions of economic life.* New York: Basic Books.

Carnoy, M. (Ed.). (1972). *Schooling in a corporate society: The political economy of education in America.* New York: McKay.

Dreeben, R. (1968). *On what is learned in school.* Reading, Mass.: Addison-Wesley.

Durkheim, E. (1961). *Moral education.* Free Press Paperback Ed., Glencoe, Ill.: The Free Press.

Freire, Paulo. (1970). *Pedagogy of the oppressed.* New York: Continuum.

Garfinkel, H. (1967). *Studies in ethnomethodology.* Englewood Cliffs, N.J.: Prentice-Hall.

Karabel, Jerome, and Halsey, A.H. (Eds.) (1977). *Power and ideology in education.* New York: Oxford University Press.

Merton, R. K. (1967). *Social theory and social structure.* New York: Free Press.

Parsons, T. (1951). *The social system.* Glencoe, Ill.: The Free Press.

Parsons, T. (1959). The school class as a social system: Some of its functions in American society. *Harvard Educational Review, 29,* 297–319.

Turner, J. H. (1978). *The structure of sociological theory,* (rev. ed.). Homewood, Ill.: The Dorsey Press.

Young, M. F.D. (1971). *Knowledge and control: New directions for the sociology of education*

Modern Works

Burtonwood, N. (1986). *The culture concept in educational studies.* Philadelphia, Penn.: Nfer-Nelson.

Delamont, Sara. (1989). *Knowledgeable women: Structuralism and the reproduction of elites.* New York: Routledge.

Giroux, H. (1983a). Theories of reproduction and resistance in the new sociology of education. *Harvard Educational Review, 53*(3), 257–293.

Giroux, H. (1983b). *Theory and resistance in education: A pedagogy for the opposition.* South Hadley, Mass.: Bergin & Garvey.

Giroux, H. (1988). *Teachers as intellectuals: Toward a critical pedagogy of learning.* South Hadley, Mass.: Bergin & Garvey.

Lather, P. (1986). Research as praxis. *Harvard Educational Review, 56* (3), 257–277.

McCarthy, C. (1988). Rethinking liberal and radical perspectives on racial inequality in schooling: Making the case for nonsynchrony. *Harvard Educational Review, 58* (3), 265–279.

McLaren, P. (1989). *Life in schools.* New York: Longman.

Tar, Zoltan. (1985). *The Frankfurt school.* New York: Schocken Books.

Weiler, K. (1988). *Women teaching for change.* South Hadley, Mass.: Bergin & Garvey.

CHAPTER 2

The Social Organization of Schooling

OVERVIEW

INTRODUCTION

In Chapter One, we presented the theoretical basis for a sociological analysis of schooling. In this chapter, we present the organizational basis. We begin by defining key concepts used in a sociological analysis of organizations. Then we move to a descriptive and historical analysis of how school systems were organized and developed in America. We do this as a way of setting the stage for examining, in later chapters, the impact of schools on society and the people who participate in them. Following our presentation of the structure of school *systems*, we describe the internal organization of individual schools, as well the many different groups which participate in the schooling process. In this "micro" look at schools, we describe the varying levels of influences which participants have, given the differences in their social status and place within the organizational structure.

We first use a rather traditional analysis, describing school organization in terms of functions and the structures which carry them out. We then look more critically at how the organizational structure of schools has changed in response to conflicts among various community constituencies over whose interests should be served by the public schools. In this part of our discussion we have used the work of critical, or revisionist, historians because, like critical theorists in sociology, they have begun to question traditional interpretations of past events. These historians are especially interested in the degree to which these traditional interpretations helped to perpetuate cultural myths such as the belief that schools were organized to eliminate poverty and to promote equality and mobility. Among the themes which emerge in our discussion are the powerful impact which business and industrial ideologies have had on the supervision and organization of schools, the degree to which schools have been pressured to serve economic, social and political, rather than intellectual or cognitive goals, and how school organization facilitates resistance to perspectives different from those held by dominant groups in the system or society.

THE SCHOOL AS A BUREAUCRACY

When most people think about schools, they usually have in mind what goes on in classrooms or individual school buildings, usually the ones they attended. But contemporary schools are a great deal larger and more complex than classrooms and buildings. In fact, they are large, formal, social organizations, similar to other big organizations such as corporations or factories. These organizations are called bureaucracies. As we use it, the term **bureaucracy** is neither an insult nor a reference to the amount of red tape and frustration it creates. Rather, it is a term sociologists use to describe large, multileveled social organizations which are run by full-time professional people.

It is no accident that schools resemble many other kinds of bureaucratic organizations in modern society. Bureaucratization of organizations, industrialization and urbanization occurred together, and organizations assumed the shape they did because priority was given to order, uniformity, and efficiency (Katz 1971). Like large hospitals, governmental agencies, factories and other institutions, schools developed and changed in response to these priorities in ways that parallel changes in their parent society. Because schools and other institutions do not exist in isolation, their operation cannot be understood without considering the social and historical context in which they have developed. Their history and physical arrangements, as well the characteristics of the people within them, shape how people behave within them and the way their participants feel about themselves and others.

Schools are a special kind of organization. While they share similarities with other organizations, such as factories, prisons, and social service agencies with which they often are compared, other characteristics conspire to make them unique. These unique characteristics include the particular historical, cultural and economic context in which they developed and the type, specifity and number of their goals. Schools also are unique in the variety of ways people can participate in them, and their multiple lines of power and control. In the pages which follow, we shall discuss the special characteristics of school organization, how it affects the people who work in them, and some of the political and social forces which were critical to the development of contemporary schools.

A Formal Definition

A convenient way to begin to understand bureaucracies is in accordance with functional theory as we defined it in Chapter One. Examined this way, bureaucracies are formally defined in terms of the tasks they perform and the organizational structures which carry them out. These can easily be visualized if you imagine a typical organizational chart, in which the organizational president occupies a box at the top of the page, the lowest levels of workers are at the bottom, and other tasks and departments occupy the remainder. Organizational charts specify the goals of the **formal organization**, what jobs are required to achieve them, and who shall carry them out. In effect, organizational charts provide a visual functional analysis of formal structure.

One of the characteristics of bureaucracy is that each job or task (function) has an individual, department, or group of people (structure) to carry it out. The functional division of labor is typified by an automobile assembly line, where areas of responsibility generally are separate from each other and clearly defined. **Line offices** are arranged hierarchically, so that people lower in the organization are supervised by those higher up. **Staff offices** operate laterally. They are like design departments and quality control officials in the automobile industry, which advise line personnel, but are not involved with the direct production of cars.

According to Max Weber, who was the first theorist to completely delineate the characteristics of bureaucracy, workers in bureaucracies must be full-time workers, not volunteers or part-timers with divided loyalties. They must be paid or rewarded according to the amount of skill and training they have obtained. Often they receive merit pay for objectively assessed exemplary performance, and those with more training and responsibility usually are paid more and hold higher positions than those who do not (Blau and Scott 1962; Weber 1947; Dalton, Barnes, and Zaleznik 1968).

Bureaucracies operate by means of rules which establish rationally and systematically *what* each person is expected to do—and often just *how* they are to do it as well. These rules are the basis for systems of accountability; they apply to all jobholders without favoritism. The rules can be found in job descriptions, by-laws, guidebooks, operating manuals, and handbooks of various kinds.

It is easy to see that a formal, functional definition of bureaucracy does not describe how most organizations really operate. Simply reading the rules and looking at an organizational chart does not allow us to understand all the dynamics of an organization. Informal practices outside of the "normal channels" evolve between people to facilitate their work (Blau 1955). The sheer complexity of organizations makes it impossible to specify every action that individuals or offices might be called upon to undertake. People take on tasks not in their formal job descriptions, bypass people or offices which serve as roadblocks, and bend the rules if necessary. These informal adaptations are necessary for organizations to function smoothly.

Schools as Modified Bureaucratic Organizations

Schools, like many organizations, possess some, but not all, of the characteristics of bureaucracies. For example, while teachers and other school staff are in fact hired for their professional training and skill, and while they do have job descriptions which encompass most of their required duties, they generally are rewarded for longevity rather than for merit. In addition, their written job description may not include many of the duties required for the performance of their work, like hours of grading papers after school and sponsoring extra-curricular student activities (see Chapter Four for a detailed description of teachers' work)

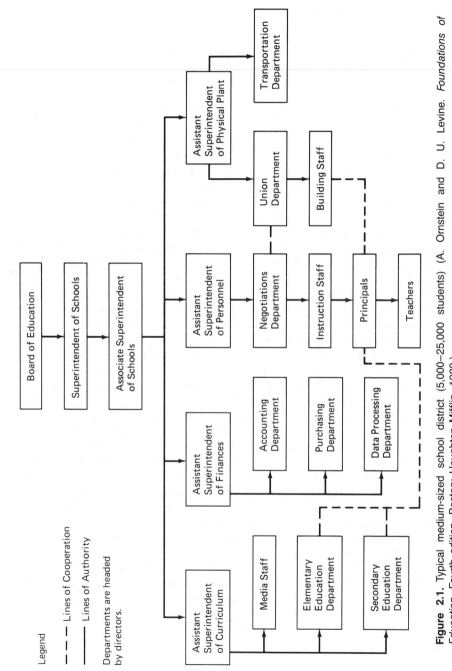

Figure 2.1. Typical medium-sized school district (5,000–25,000 students) (A. Ornstein and D. U. Levine. *Foundations of Education*, Fourth edition. Boston: Houghton Mifflin, 1989.)

Multiple Constituencies and Multiple Goals

In the ideal case, bureaucracies have clear and unambiguous goals, and their leaders possess more or less complete control over the means for realizing those goals. School bureaucracies clearly do not fit this model. Schools actually have many organizational goals; some are ambiguous or diffuse and others are contradictory.

Schools have multiple goals because they have multiple constituencies and clienteles, each of which has ideas about the purposes of schooling. Each group has its own agenda and pushes its own goals for the educational system. This is heightened by the unique mix of national, state and local finance and control which governs American public schools. While both educational systems in other countries and social service agencies in the United States are subject to interest group pressures, few are so potentially open or transparent to external influence as are the public schools in America, where the local electorate controls the purse strings. Most school districts cannot raise their own money. They must depend upon revenue from locally generated property taxes, much of which comes from people who have no school-aged children. Further, schools do not select their own governing boards; the public elects them. By law, meetings must be public. Parents can visit and parent groups often provide powerful pressure regarding the ideological direction of materials taught, the textbooks and instructional techniques used by teachers, and the extra-curricular activities supported by the schools.

Local control encourages diversity in schools as communities strive to make their schools reflect community values. It also makes them vulnerable to ideological fads, reforms, social movements or powerful lobbies. Tension is produced when the professional or personal ideologies of the community are at odds with those of the school staff, or state and national educational agencies. School officials cannot operate independently of their community because they do not entirely control their enterprise. Most important, they do not control the flow of revenue. If they cannot compromise, they must go to court. Conflicts over school goals have been generated by provisions for bilingual education (*Lau et al.* v. *Nichols et al.*, 1974) and ethnic studies, prayer in school (*Engel* v. *Vitale*, 1962; *Abington School District* v. *Schempp*, 1963), racial integration (*Brown* v. *Board of Education*, 1954), free speech for students (*Tinker* v. *Des Moines*, 1969) and the teaching of creationism and secular humanism in schools (*Smith* v. *School Commissioners*, 1987).

Under the onslaught of so many constituencies, each seeking control over some portion of school activities, it becomes difficult to determine what schools really can, or should do. Under these conditions, goal displacement may take place.

Goal Displacement

Organizations have many needs, only one of which is to attain their stated goals. As important are other goals, such as organizational survival, adaptation and accommodation to the realities of the environment, integrating, motivating, and maintaining the loyalties of participants, promoting consensus among participants and in the public eye that the activities of the organization are legitimate, and coordinating their operations (Boyd and Crowson 1981). Goal displacement (Sills 1970) is a common malady in bureaucratic organizations. It occurs when procedural activities—the how-tos, dos and don'ts of organizational life—become more important than the reasons for which the organization was created or when the resources intended for accomplishment of some original task are diverted to another purpose.

One of the most common forms of goal displacement occurs when ends become means in themselves; that is, when some practice which was adopted to help solve a problem becomes more disruptive of the original goals than the original problem. An example can be found in the proliferation of programs for assessing student and teacher competency. These programs were initiated as reforms, to ensure that teachers were teaching what was required and that students actually had mastered the subject matter. However, in many districts, tests which were designed to facilitate instruction have come to guide and often to supplant it. Almost as much time is spent in testing students as is spent in instructing them in the subject matter covered on the tests!

Another common form of goal displacement occurs when the survival of the organization becomes more important than the purpose for which the organization was originally created. For example, teachers' organizations and systems of tenure have been accused of fostering goal displacement when maintenance of teacher jobs assumes precedence over the quality of instruction. Schools, for example, continue to employ teachers, who are incompetent in their own subject areas or who are racists, who do not like children, and/or who have come to detest teaching, because too many legal and institutional obstacles must be overcome in order to fire them (see Dworkin 1985b). In addition, to fire one teacher for incompetence might call into question the competence of many. In these cases, people and practices which actually contradict the original objectives of the organization are preserved even while they may sabotage its goals. More energy is spent avoiding change than in carrying out the original mission.

We feel that schools are particularly vulnerable to goal displacement; many of the issues we discuss at length later in this chapter are illustrations. As we discuss the social organization of schools and the extent to which they resemble other kinds of bureaucracies in modern society, you may find it helpful to think about who controls the schools and the extent to which patterns of control affect what schools ultimately can and should do. You also may wish to examine how the original intentions of innovative educational practices came to be subverted.

THE BUREAUCRATIZATION OF SCHOOLS

The widespread existence of bureaucracy as a social organization is a relatively modern phenomenon. Small organizations with limited purposes do not need many employees; often their rules of operation can be informal and unwritten. However, as organizations come to handle more and more people and to carry out more and more activities, additional levels of management and coordination become necessary. Specialized individuals are needed to carry out complex, technical tasks. The process by which organizations increase in size and complexity, add levels of hierarchy and professionalization, and begin systematically to subdivide their work is called bureaucratization.

Four historical processes coincided with the development of bureaucratic organizations: the rise of a capitalistic economic system, the political development of nation states, industrialization, and the demographic shifts which led to urbanization. As a social process, bureaucratization is not limited to schooling. It has penetrated virtually every modern social institution.

Historical Background

Schools have not always been structured as bureaucracies. The "little red school house" was no complex urban bureaucracy; it was too small. Frequently it had no more than a few classrooms, a coat room, a shed for firewood or coal, and a field outside for recess. Its services were limited to book learning; in elementary school, teachers instructed children in the basic cognitive skills of reading, writing and computation. While there were no classes in science or social studies as such, textbooks like Noah Webster's *Blue-Backed Speller* and the *McGuffey's Readers* included heavy doses of instruction in these subjects, as well as in literature, morals, social values such as thrift, hard work, cleanliness, patience, abstinence, and correct social behavior.

Until the 1880s, secondary schools were only for those who intended to go to college. Most secondary schooling was provided in private "academies" and limited to those who could afford the tuition. Because educators were concerned primarily with book learning, or transmitting cognitive skills and cultural knowledge, the number of nonteaching staff required by schools was minimal. Administrators were "head teachers" and had no particular training in administration or supervision; teachers swept their own classrooms and lit the fires that kept them warm.

These practices, called "keeping school," had changed dramatically by the 1880s. By that time, a relatively coherent system of elementary, or "common," schools had been established in every state. One of the most important factors contributing to bureaucratization of schools was an increase in the number of school functions. Growth came most dramatically in what we call the "service sector" of the educational enterprise.

Addition of the Service Sector

A service sector began to develop in the late 1800s as civic leaders, educators, industrialists, and the churches saw in the elementary schools an opportunity to upgrade the social and moral levels of children of immigrants and the working class. This was defined as a monumental task. Between 1865 and 1900, 14 million immigrants were known to have entered the United States. Between 1876 and 1926 over 27 million immigrants entered the United States, a number which exceeded half the original population of 1875. While the original migrants to the United States have been from England and Northern Europe, most of the newcomers during this period were rural dwellers from central, southern and eastern Europe, whose languages, skills, habits and ethnicity differed drastically from the established residents (Butts 1978, p. 229). Migration continues to affect schools, especially as the characteristics of the migrants change. Immigrants have continued to arrive at a rate of about one million per year (Callahan 1962). Since the 1970s, the greatest pressure for entrance to the United States has been from so-called "Pacific Rim" people—those from Latin America, Asia and Southeast Asia.

The service sector of schooling includes a wide variety of noninstructional activities such as medical inspections (1894), health and nutritional services (beginning in the early 1900s), rehabilitation for the handicapped (the 1920s) and school lunches (as an emergency measure during the Depression and made permanent in 1946). During the 1960s, legislation included in the War on Poverty added programs to reduce racial prejudice and added a variety of support services, including dental care, clothing banks, free and reduced cost breakfasts, after-school care, sex education and drug abuse advice, programs for pregnant girls, and counseling for mental and physical health. Provision of these services has contributed substantially to the transformation of schools into large, complex bureaucratic institutions.

Several themes provided impetus for the provision of social services. One was custodial and derived from the belief that poor families were unable or unwilling to provide proper care for their children (Gumbert and Spring 1974). Another was the humanitarian acknowledgment that sick, hungry, and poorly clad children were too preoccupied with their physical needs to study. For families living in one-room apartments and amidst grinding poverty, schools and settlement houses often were the only places where immigrant children could be fed, bathed, provided warm clothing and given minimal medical care (*The Massachusetts Teacher* 1851; Butts and Cremin 1953; Albjerg 1974).

A final factor derived from the growth of class conflict during the late 1800s. It was exacerbated by an almost rabid fear which dominant groups had of immigrants and the lower classes. Concerns for law and order fueled the desire of policy makers to "Americanize" immigrant children as quickly as possible and to indoctrinate the children of the working classes with middle-class values (Higham 1969).

The School as Custodian for Children

The school gradually has come to be viewed as an all-purpose child care institution and ombudsman for children. As the custodial functions of schools grew, it became more acceptable for teachers and administrators to share with families responsibility for the health, well-being, and good behavior of young people. The responsibilities of schools—actual or hoped-for—have continued to grow beyond simple training in the "three Rs," in some cases supplanting those responsibilities once considered the exclusive province of families and the private sector.

Some of these services, like drug, pregnancy and prenatal counseling, day care for children, and drivers education, are attempts to alleviate difficult social problems such as the large number of students who drop out of school and the rising incidence of automobile-related fatalities. Other services, like training in the performing arts, are designed to provide for less affluent children privileges and opportunities once available only to the wealthy. Still other services, such as free lunches and free medical exams, attest to our society's recognition that sick and hungry children cannot learn. Finally, some, like classes and support services for the physically and emotionally handicapped, are congruent with contemporary belief that all children, regardless of their motivation, occupational aspirations or intellectual and physical shortcomings, are entitled to a free, public education until age 21 or graduation from high school. Adding social service functions, along with the resources and staff to carry them out, has hastened bureaucratization by adding to the size and complexity of school organizations. It also has added controversy, because the many constituencies who participate in and finance the schools have seldom arrived at a consensus as to whether the added programs are legitimate school functions.

Urbanization, Consolidation, and Scientific Management

After World War II, global changes in the distribution of population, natural resources, trade, as well as changes in the labor market, and in technology contributed to the bureaucratization of schools. These included urbanization, industrialization, and changes in the types of individuals available in the labor market (Chafetz and Dworkin 1986). These changes affected every facet of human existence and gave birth to modern society. In every corner of the globe, industrialization during the past two centuries has caused migration of the poor and landless to the cities. Urbanization of the poor has increased the percentage of economically disadvantaged in the labor force (Chafetz and Dworkin 1986).

The locally controlled "little red school house" could provide adequate educational services for rural and small town communities, but today, more than 75 percent of the United States' population lives in cities. Concentration of the population into cities accompanied widespread pressure for universal and compulsory education, in part because American cultural ideology promoted education as a means to improve the social and economic condition of the individual. Education was no longer viewed as appropriate only for the affluent; it was needed both for nation-building and to provide the skills requisite for an industrial nation. As other countries, even those in the less-developed world, also experienced urbanization and industrialization, similar pressures for educational expansion arose. As we shall indicate, these pressures often were conservative. While educational opportunities were, in fact, provided for children of the working classes and the poor, public education was to be different—more practical, oriented to civic training, and job preparation—from the classical liberal arts training traditionally sought by the wealthy. Educational reform was equated with creating social and economic stability; it was a way to avoid taking more radical steps to solve problems such as the incidence of poverty and social disorder in cities (Katz 1971).

Establishment of a Public System of Secondary Schools

Among these problems was the flood of people who immigrated to the United States between 1865 and 1900. It is difficult to imagine the fear which immigrants and the working class struck in the hearts of the affluent. Whether they were the Irish of the early part of the 19th century, the southern and Eastern Europeans of the middle and late 19th century, or the Jews who came even later, unassimilated immigrants were viewed with the same suspicion that card-carrying Communists were held during the "Red Scares" of the 1930s and 1950s in America. The immigrants were portrayed as vicious, immoral, mentally deficient, lazy, unhygienic and an imminent threat to the social and moral fiber of the nation.

Part of the fear came from culture shock. The immigrants differed from the established residents in language, religion, standard of living and customs, and they were accused of taking jobs from the native-born. They also had little power and few influential advocates in government (Higham 1969; *The Massachusetts Teacher* 1851). Established residents viewed education as a way to tame the threat that immigrants posed to the social order. The type of education advocated was, however, a departure from prevailing practice.

In the early years of the Republic, the demand for education was fueled primarily by an educated elite desirous of passing their status on to their children by means of college-oriented liberal arts instruction. Beginning in the 1830s, the middle and upper classes advocated public instruction to provide basic literacy and moral training for the children of the disadvantaged poor. The implicit purpose of this instruction was social control—to assure the continuance of a productive labor force and to forestall the civil unrest, drunkenness and immoral behavior to which it was felt an illiterate and unindoctrinated working class would be prone (Mann 1842; Resnick and Resnick 1985).

Many industrialists, civic leaders and educators believed that education of this kind could be effective only if it were provided for all children. Thus, regardless of the motivation, the number of children viewed as eligible for education increased dramatically. Strongly supported by the business community, which saw little difference between running factories and keeping school, mass schooling slowly became reality. Compulsory attendance laws became common between 1880 and 1920. Labor unions applauded the removal of competitive and inexpensive youthful workers from the labor market, and schools grew larger and larger. With the passage of the Smith-Hughes Act in 1917, secondary schools added vocational and non-college preparatory, or "general education," streams to accommodate advocates of "democratization" in public education. The comprehensive, nonselective public high school became known as a "poor man's college", and provided all the education most people needed.

By the end of the nineteenth century, the general structure of the American public educational system had been established and gradual bureaucratization was taking place. The public sector provided free or nearly free instruction from elementary school through land-grant colleges and universities, although it was clear that only a minority of the population would avail themselves of postsecondary schooling (Katz 1971).

In the absence of explicit constitutional provisions for schooling, control of public education was reserved to local municipal boards, rather than centralized in national offices as is the case in most other countries. Placing school finance and control under the control of local boards laid the groundwork for later racial and economic inequality, because rich communities had far more resources for the support of schools than poor ones. The public school system was paralleled by a loose system of independent private schools which generally served special interests, such as religious groups, people with alternative educational philosophies, and the wealthy.

During the first three decades of the twentieth century, schools began to assume the organization we know today. They did so because of pressure from supporters of a powerful industrial ideology to reshape schools along the lines of the most efficient of America's factories. In the next few pages, we draw heavily on the work of historians like Michael B. Katz, Joel Spring, Clarence Karier, Raymond E. Callahan, and Marvin Lazerson, who have questioned some of our conventional interpretations of historical data. Rather than assuming that institutional and industrial development in America was shaped by beneficent and inevitable forces, these researchers have examined how schools acted to reinforce social and economic inequality and benefitted members of the dominant culture.

THE SCIENTIFIC MANAGEMENT OF SCHOOLS

At the turn of the century, America's cultural heroes were industrialists—Andrew Carnegie, John D. Rockefeller, J. P. Morgan, and others. Belief in the efficacy and virtue of big business and industrial practices saturated American life. It was a logical extension of the "can-do" spirit of the legendary pioneers. Americans firmly believed that success—defined in terms of material acquisition—was the result of honesty and hard work. In keeping with another cultural myth—that America was an egalitarian, classless society—they also believed that success had very little to do with social background or education. Since businessmen and their activities had made America great, Americans tended to believe that the best way to solve problems of any kind was to subject them to good business practice. Similarly, marketability, or its tangible contribution to sale value or the ability of someone to get ahead, established the value of any commodity or enterprise.

Scientific Management

These ideas were expressed in a philosophy called **"Scientific Management,"** whose chief exponent was Frederick W. Taylor. Taylor was an industrial engineer who first came to prominence in 1910 when his theories of management were used as evidence in a widely publicized hearing before the Interstate Commerce Commission. The railroads had asked for an increase in freight rates to compensate them for higher wages granted to railroad workers. The government's lawyer, Louis Brandeis, argued in opposition that the railroads were being operated inefficiently, and that if they introduced Taylor's new techniques of scientific management, they would not only be able to increase wages, but also to reduce costs. Taylor went even further, suggesting that if his principles were implemented, more productivity could be elicited from fewer workers. His ideas took the industrialized world by storm and were applied to everything from baking cakes and sewing trousers to carrying ingots of pig iron and getting students to study harder. Taylor prescribed the following "scientific" operating principles:

1. Management must be responsible for analyzing, planning, and controlling every detail of the entire manufacturing process. In so doing, management must use scientific methods to isolate the very best methods for performing each aspect of every task carried out in the plant.
2. Each step in each task must be standardized, and tools must be developed for them which are appropriate both to the task and to the workers who were to carry them out.
3. Planning departments must be established to develop the science of each job, including the rules, laws and formulae for its execution. These rules would replace the judgment of individual workers.
4. Detailed records must be kept of every activity and transaction so that accountability could be established and traced.
5. Managers must carefully train workers in the exact execution of their tasks, and closely supervise them to make sure that they are following directions.
6. Assessment procedures must be established so that performance could be measured, and exemplary performance be rewarded.

Taylor's system effectively placed all power in the hands of managers and planners, introduced a rationale for meticulous observation, testing, and record-keeping, and wrested from workers any control over the execution of their tasks. While it was criticized by individuals in industry and universities, the voices of protest were drowned by the chorus of enthusiasm for a process which appeared to increase productivity while reducing costs. The outcry coincided exactly with a wave of dissatisfaction over the public schools (Callahan 1962).

Waste, Inefficiency, and "Laggards" in Our Schools

If businessmen were the most capable individuals in America, then it stood to reason that they should be intimately involved in public institutions like schools. The political reform movement of the early 1900s involved a distrust of political machines, and encouraged a shift away from political appointment of administrators in both municipal and educational administration. Council-manager forms of municipal government, in which an elected council appointed a city manager, became popular because they were congruent with the desire for management by scientifically trained professionals rather than amateurs.

School districts soon followed suit, hiring as administrators graduates from colleges of education providing what purported to be professional training for school administrators. Communities increasingly elected to school boards businessmen who evaluated school performance and operation by the same criteria which they used for factories. Educators became vulnerable to the same kinds of criticism as factory workers and managers: why couldn't the product be manufactured more efficiently and at less cost?

Scrutiny of their operations showed that educators were sadly lacking in both business acumen and accounting skills. Many could neither account for nor justify their expenditure of the taxpayers money to the satisfaction of their boards and communities. Schools also were criticized for retaining large numbers of "laggards," or children who were overage for their grade level, in classrooms. No one examined whether or not the so-called "retarded" children were immigrants who had entered late or had insufficient mastery of English to cope with material appropriate for their age, or children who had been held back because they had failed courses. School efficiency came to be defined in terms of how fast children could be pushed through the grades: an "efficient" school had every child on grade level for his or her age, regardless of extenuating circumstances. Double-promotion or skipping grades was considered a particularly good practice. School administrators were criticized for the amount of time their buildings stood unused—in the summers, during holidays, and at night. Course offerings were judged by their cost per pupil unit and their utility in moving students immediately into jobs, notwithstanding any measure of intrinsic worth or external cost.

The perceived solution to these problems was the application of more business-like practices, which, in effect, accelerated the process of routinization, specialization, and bureaucratization in schools. With pressure from taxpayers and school boards in mind, superintendents had to learn new ways and go back to school. When they attended the university, superintendents were steeped in the doctrine of scientific management, which the universities training school administrators for the most part had wholeheartedly embraced. Curricula, supervisory techniques, and instruction were altered accordingly (Callahan 1962).

The Legacy of Scientific Management

Most of the changes introduced from 1915 to 1930, the heyday of the efficiency expert, were major departures from the tradition of "school-keeping." These changes have been permanent, and have welded the educational establishment ever closer to the image of corporate and bureaucratic America. Perhaps the most obvious change created a management level in education, which added layers of administrative hierarchy to school districts. No longer could teachers rise into administration with no special training. While administrators still come through the ranks—most programs in educational administration require three years of successful teaching as a prerequisite for entrance—the requirement of a "professional" credential is here to stay. It is nearly impossible to be hired as a principal or other administrator without first receiving certification from an approved graduate program.

Other changes were made in school recordkeeping. Many of the changes were needed to introduce system and rationalization into an enterprise that had become increasingly large and chaotic (Butts 1978). Uniform rules were created for codifying attendance, financial records, curricula, and time allocations for instruction. However, the rules also were harbingers of the paperwork avalanche which often overwhelms today's school staffs.

The impact of Taylorism also was felt in equipment and design. Time-and-motion study experts were greatly concerned with developing tools suitable to both the job and the worker. Their efforts meant, for example, that children now sit in chairs which fit their bodies and are an appropriate size, that lighting is adequate for reading, that left-handed scissors are available and that small children have big crayons which are easier for them to hold. The efficiency bureaus established in some districts have evolved into departments of research, testing and evaluation.

Other survivors of the efficiency movement left more mixed blessings. They include the continued interest in split-sessions and the year-round school as a solution to overcrowded buildings, and the "platoon school" or "Gary Plan"—named after Gary, Indiana, where the experiment first was implemented—which was developed as a means to use school buildings efficiently. The Gary Plan was based on the idea schools would be more efficient if no room were ever empty. Space could be saved if one group—or platoon—of students were outside on the playground at all times so their classroom could be used by another group. Implementing such a plan required subdividing the students, careful scheduling, and constant movement of people among the available rooms. It subordinated instruction to the dictates of a time clock, interrupting instruction regardless of student interest or the difficulty of the subject matter. Teachers no longer could decide how to allocate their instructional time, and students were evermore rigidly divided into batches by age, rather than ability or intellectual interest. The Gary Plan lives on in the hallways of today's middle and high schools, as students move every fifty minutes to a different classroom.

Taylor's human cost-accounting survives in practices such as treating teachers as "FTE's" (full-time-equivalents, or the number of workers multiplied by the number of hours worked each day), and the practice of demanding that course offerings justify their existence not on the merit of the material or the rigor of the course, but on the basis of per-unit cost calculated in "credit hour generation," or the number of students enrolled per course. Other accounting survivors include counting "Carnegie units" (a course or class defined by a specified number of hours taught in a given subject area) to determine graduation requirements, and the per-pupil-expenditure figures which appear each time a school election is held.

The practices which probably have had the most impact upon the daily life of students and teachers include "Taylorizing" the curriculum into easily taught, measurable objectives and the massive systems of testing for academic competency and achievement which have evolved for students, teachers and even administrators. These practices, often instituted as part of educational reform measures, act systematically to "de-skill" teachers, removing from their control decisions over how and what to teach, as well as their prerogative to evaluate student progress. We discuss the impact of these practices in detail in Chapter Six.

The Impact of Scientific Management on Teacher Autonomy

Perhaps the most ominous legacy of scientific management is the authoritarianism built into Frederick Taylor's insistence on three factors: (1) granting managers absolute control over the definition, assignment, and assessment of tasks; (2) breaking down tasks into discrete, measurable sub-units, and (3) requiring the complete and unthinking acquiescence of laborers in everything employers asked them to do. As incorporated into schools, these principles of scientific management ultimately changed the pattern of control and decision-making in schools, removing jurisdiction over instruction from teachers.

Some shifts of control already had occurred by the 1920s, when Taylorism hit the schools. Many of the most important curricular decisions were made outside the classroom. School boards, administrators and textbook committees decided what courses should be taught and which books would be used. How to teach the material and how to manage the children were all that remained to the teacher. However, proponents of scientific management proposed that even these decisions be made centrally and imposed upon teachers, on the grounds that teachers worked inefficiently at best, and could not be trusted to cover material adequately and objectively. While not specifically born out of the cult of efficiency, the move to "teacherproof" the curriculum was a logical outcome.

"Professional educators" or experts—usually university professors and administrators, not classroom teachers—broke down instructional tasks into measurable "behavioral objectives" and then prescribed how they should be taught to children. This had the effect of organizing and standardizing instruction, and of facilitating assessment and comparison of results. These practices, however, also robbed teachers of the opportunity to decide what, in their professional judgment, was most valuable to teach and how to teach it. Teachers no longer could rely exclusively on their own judgment for assessment of student ability; children were grouped for instruction on the basis of external tests. Teachers were assigned textbooks which might or might not match the ability levels of their students. They were given lessons with scripts to follow and prescribed answers for children to emit as well as tests with which to assess their progress. Good instructional objectives were those accompanied by specified reading materials to reinforce their acquisition. Usually these also required a great deal of recordkeeping on the part of the teacher. While these records ostensibly were used to chart the progress of children, they also could be used by administrators to monitor the teacher's conformity with the prescribed curriculum. They had the effect of enforcing progress; teachers had to move their students through a certain number of curricular units per semester whether or not they felt the material had been covered adequately.

Schooling and the Hegemony of Corporate America

Schools now are criticized for mirroring corporate America and for too closely resembling factories. We need, however, to remember that the forces which led to bureaucratization were unleashed because people believed they led to highly desirable outcomes. The tenets of scientific management were introduced—some would say forced upon—the schools under the banner of the best-intentioned democratic reform. The alacrity with which scientific management was embraced is an illustration of the power of external control or "hegemonic domination" over education, as we discussed in Chapter One.

Because they had so completely accepted the legitimacy of business ideology, educators did not usually have to be forced to adopt the latest business practices. In fact, they could not move quickly enough to justify their activities in the language of business and to restructure their institutions, as much as they could, to resemble the latest in industrial practice. They did not foresee that scientific management had many other consequences, some of which they might not have thought so desirable. While it was marketed on the basis of fostering efficiency, industriousness, hard work, and entrepreneurship, the "factory school" did not, in fact, train entrepreneurs. On the contrary, factory-like conditions fostered obedience for everyone but supervisors, rather than the risk-taking and nonconformity of industrial capitalism's early heroes. For this reason, the factory schools were most popular in the central cities. In more affluent areas, the rigidities and excesses of Taylorism were blunted, and extras which efficiency experts deemed wasteful, like foreign languages, Greek, and smaller classes, survived to differentiate the education of the rich from that of the poor. But in cities, where the majority of the industrial poor and working class lived, where financial shortages mandated money-saving practices and where hardworking obedient workers were needed by industry, schools which mirrored life in the factories flourished.

Schools continue to resemble factories. In fact, school reform legislation in the 1980s, which concentrated on standards for entrance and graduation from academic programs and the content and structure of instruction, accelerated the process. However, pressures for de-bureaucratization are present. Teachers, principals, parents, and others at the bottom of the school hierarchy are exhibiting growing disenchantment with centralization of control and their concurrent disenfranchisement in the educational enterprise. Practices such as schoolbased management (which gives the principal and teachers of a school primary control over the curriculum, budget, and personnel decisions of a school), collaborative writing projects, and even the growing power of teachers unions demonstrate the recognition by many educators of the power of human agency to transform seemingly intransigent social institutions. In the forefront are some school-university collaborative projects initiated by critical theorists as a way to train teachers to be change agents, "critical pedagogues" and "transformative intellectuals" (Giroux 1988). Whether or not these programs will have a major effect on the power structure of schools remains to be seen.

THE INTERNAL ORGANIZATION OF SCHOOL DISTRICTS

We now turn from our discussion of the historical development of school organization to a more detailed look at the actual structure of schools. This is a very difficult thing to do dispassionately, because both you, the readers, and we, the authors, already have spent most of our lives going to school. We are all far too familiar with them to be objective! To facilitate the task, we will use a device often employed by anthropologists—"making what is familiar strange" (Geertz 1973). This means treating something that we know very well as if we have never seen it before.

Let us begin by imagining that we are scientists from another galaxy. We have been sent to study the social institutions of Earthlings. Not knowing the language, we begin by describing the things we see, knowing that the physical setting of a social system often determines to a great extent the behavior and attitudes of the people who live in them. We probably would use some Martian form of structural functional categories to organize our description.

We alien scientists at first would be struck by the sheer size of the educational enterprise. We would note that school buildings are among the largest edifices in most communities, and that except for the very smallest of communities, most school buildings house at least 250–300 people. From this, we would infer that whatever happens in these buildings must be of great importance to the communities which support them, since so many resources are devoted to them. In fact, in many communities, the educational system is the biggest industry and the largest employer in town.

Differentiation as an Organizing Principle in Schools

In our first day of field work, we aliens would note that everything in the building is divided into clearly defined chunks or categories; every chunk has a place and each place has a distinct function. From the clearly framed (Bernstein 1970) social and physical environment, we would infer that there are strict rules governing the use of such a place and the activities which can and cannot take place in its various sectors. The setting seems to abhor ambiguity; where it exists, as in open-space classrooms, people try to impose a framework. Where they cannot, they have difficulty clarifying which kind of interaction is appropriate there or the tasks they must accomplish.

Differentiation of Space. Analysis of the use of space would indicate that work predominates in schools and that teachers control and direct it. Work space for children is subdivided into two types: classrooms for academic work, workshops and laboratories for vocational and other subjects which need to be taught, but require more equipment than simply books, papers, and audiovisual materials.

From the predominance of classrooms over other kinds of work space, it would be clear that whoever runs the schools gives primary importance to book learning. A look inside the classroom also would verify the existence of hierarchial authority relationships. While desks and chairs might be moved around from time to time, in most cases, the children face front, listening to the teacher, who is in charge. Although each school has some sort of recreational space or playground for the children, purely recreational activities, both for teachers and students, clearly are not given high priority, since they often are preempted for other activities. Playgrounds become parking lots, and teachers lounges become offices when space is tight. A problem in classification would be the large amount of space devoted to athletic playing fields and gymnasia, especially in schools for older children. Later analysis would confirm that these reflect cultural preferences for community entertainment. High school athletics are a major source of civic pride in many communities, especially in suburbs and smaller towns. The games are widely attended and well-supported by local businesses and other donors.

We aliens would notice that schools are pivotal community organizations in other ways; often the school auditorium or gymnasium is the only space in the community adequate for concerts, theatre and other cultural events. Rooms in the school are used for public meetings and by civic organizations and at every election, the polling places are located in the school lobby, halls or cafeteria.

Some service space is used by both children and adults. It includes assembly halls, a lunchroom (often these are combined, and include a stage for dramatic productions), parking lots, and the nurse's office. Others are presided over by adults for service to children, such as rooms for counseling and testing, the cafeteria kitchen, the boiler room, and maintenance shop. Still others, like lounges and bathrooms, are segregated by age and status—one for adults and one for children.

The location of administrative spaces, or offices, reinforces the authority hierarchy noticed in the classroom. Even if administrative offices are not located right in the entryway of the building, visitors must locate them and obtain permission before gaining admission to the school. As alien scientists, we would note that this geographical arrangement helps control what goes on in the school, and often is used to keep out people who are viewed as hostile to its enterprise. This process sometimes is facilitated by making the offices difficult to find. They may be located far from where visitors are allowed to park; front doors may be locked, and imposing entryways may make many schools seem forbidding.

Differentiation of Time. We would then make a key observation concerning the episodic nature of activity in schools: time is segmented and encapsulated, and no activity lasts more than about 50 minutes. Of that, a good portion is devoted to getting organized for activities to begin and end (LeCompte 1974, 1978b, 1980). Use of the buildings is governed by bells or buzzers. Bells continue to ring at regular intervals throughout the day, and in response, people move from room to room and activity to activity. For younger people, movement is controlled by having them line up by gender and size; this is monitored by an adult. Early morning is very busy as hordes of children and adults arrive; in general, adults enter the building any time, but children must wait for the buzzer. The process is more or less repeated in midafternoon. Though some people stay later to participate in school activities or projects, most children and many adults are gone within 15 minutes of the closing bell. Following observations of the physical and temporal layout of the school, we would begin to examine the differences among human inhabitants. Trying to use human rather than Martian canons for distinction, we would note initially that the people in schools are differentiated by age, training, their purposes for being there, and their ability. Only later would we begin to notice more subtle forms of differentiation and segregation by gender, ethnicity, and social class.

Differentiation of People. In Chapter Three, we will discuss in detail the characteristics of student participants in schooling. Our purpose here is to analyze the structural differences between the way children and adults participate in the educational process.

"Making things strange" means taking care to notice and not take for granted the simplest and most obvious things. As we continue to "make school strange," we would carefully document that students and other people in schools differ most obviously by age. Students are younger than teachers and staff. Age alone, rather than intellectual ability, determines when children enter school and the grade level into which they are placed; hence, children are divided into classes or grade levels by date of birth. While this is done for administrative convenience in processing the masses of people involved, it creates many problems for instruction, because intellectual development and chronological age may be only vaguely related in individual children.

A second and less obvious pattern of differentiation among children is that they are grouped by ability. While the initial admission by age criteria reduces differences among children, ability grouping restratifies them (Dreeben 1968). In some ways this permits school staff to overcome the initial instructional difficulty imposed by age-grading. As we shall see, however, ability grouping creates semipermanent cliques of differing social status and self-esteem which often predict the future occupational and social chances of their members (Borko and Eisenhart 1986; Bennett 1986; Powell et al. 1985; Oakes, 1985).

Children as well as teachers are differentiated by gender and ethnicity. Certain activities are participated in only by girls, others by boys. Some activities, such as physical education, are not only differentiated by type, so that what boys do is different from girls, but segregated, so that the two sexes do not engage in the activities together. Some activities, like teaching math and science, coaching football, and being an administrator, are more likely to be done by male rather than female staff members. We also would notice certain kinds of concentration based upon what appears to be differentiation by ethnicity or race. Asians would be concentrated in high level academic courses, but not in sports. Black students would be more prevalent in remedial and vocational classes; they also would predominate on the football, basketball, and track teams, but not in golf, swimming, or tennis (see Chapter Seven).

While we will address these kinds of differentiation in later chapters on inequality and equity in education, it is important to notice them here as components of the organization of schools. The organization of instruction and the availability of subjects is predicated in large part upon characteristics of the student population (Oakes 1985). Minority dominated schools often provide fewer advanced courses, fewer electives and are more oriented to vocational training than schools whose students are expected to attend college. Teachers in these schools complain that they frequently have to teach many sections of remedial classes rather than advanced courses in their area of specialization. In addition, such schools often provide more support services and feel the need for ancillary staff such as security officers.

Differentiation by Employment. Adult participants in school are differentiated by those who work there for pay and those who don't, as well as by the type of training they possess. Those who work in the school but are not paid include volunteers, parents, observers and student teachers. Some of the adults in schools work part-time, and include consultants and teachers who "float" among several schools, teaching subjects such as music, art, physical education. Special services instructors, such as those who give aid to handicapped or limited English proficient students, also often serve several schools. The marginal presence of these staff members, whose part-time status is a function of the inability of each school they serve to support a full-time employee in their field, means that they and their activities seldom have much impact upon the day-to-day operation of the school. This situation exacerbates the resistance of schools to change, especially when consultants whose purpose is to induce change in instructional or management practices are brought into the schools. They often find their influence wanes as soon as they are out of sight.

In Chapter Four, we will discuss in more detail the characteristics of adults who make up the work force in schools—teachers, administrators, and service personnel. Here, it is important to discuss the differences which distinguish children from adult participants in schools: the way in which they enter or are recruited to schools; their training; the ancillary organizations which support their participation; and the rewards they hope to reap.

Differentiation in Recruitment. Perhaps the biggest difference between children and other participants in schooling is the way they enter. Children come to school because they have to; they are recruited universally and according to their chronological age. Every child, regardless of his or her mental or physical condition, must attend some sort of school from about age 6 to age 16. Everybody else—with the possible exception of parents, who come because their children have to—comes to school voluntarily, either because they have a job or because they have some special interest in education (Nadel 1957; Bidwell 1965).

Differentiation in Rewards. Because people come to school for different reasons, they expect to reap different kinds of rewards. Children really are somewhat short-changed in the rewards category. The best they can hope for is that their experience will not be dismally boring and that they will acquire skills which will equip them for a good job, sometime in the distant future. School staff try to reinforce the idea that learning is intrinsically worthwhile, and that the payoff to schooling has substantial material value. They do so primarily by dispensing symbols—grades, gold stars, praise and awards, and eligibility for extracurricular activities. Staff, on the other hand, garner both immediate extrinsic rewards in the form of regular paychecks and long vacations, but also intrinsic values such as those inherent in doing a job one has chosen, working with children, associating with professional colleagues, and performing a task they deem necessary and socially useful. These rewards may pale, however, as the working conditions for teachers change and grow more difficult (see Chapter Four).

Differentiation in Training. While children are grouped by ability in schools, adults are grouped by the type and length of their training. Children clearly are not specifically trained for the roles they hold in school. They are, in fact, in school because they are deemed to be *in need* of training. Professional staff like teachers, administrators and counselors, on the other hand, must undergo rather lengthy training which gives them claim to expertise and to a certain degree of autonomy in their activities vis-a-vis students. Their training and subsequent experience leads them to feel that other adults—even parents of their students—have little competence to direct instructional or administrative practices. It also creates tension and sometimes hostility between school professionals and other members of the outside community. Service personnel like custodians, secretaries and clerks also have some degree of training, but their training is not specific to schools. Unlike that of teachers, it fits them for similar jobs in many kinds of organizations.

Other adults in the community may claim expertise in the field of education on the basis of special knowledge—of children because they are parents; of school financial matters because they are taxpayers; of athletic programs because they are city boosters, school alumnae, or former athletes; of educational materials and issues because they are consultants, textbook vendors, lobbyists or members of special interest groups such as churches and political parties; of vocational training because they are businessmen and employers in the community. Despite the energy of their involvement in schools, none of these groups is trained specifically for their role in the educational enterprise. They do not have an automatic and compelling voice in school operations, but they do constitute the multiple constituencies whose interests penetrate the school. We will enumerate them and their impact later in this chapter.

THE GEOGRAPHY OF CONTROL

Having established the organizing principles which humans use to differentiate events and occupants of schools, we aliens next would examine the impact of spatial arrangements on how people work in schools. First, we would note that schools seem to come in two basic architectural types—multi-story rectangular brick buildings or sprawling campuses with many detached or semi-detached buildings. Inside, they possess remarkable similarity, resembling motels, with long strings of equally sized rooms, capable of accommodating about 30–40 children and an adult, placed on either side of long corridors. The rooms fall into four categories, depending upon the kind of tasks carried out in their space. There is *work* space and *recreational* space for the smaller inhabitants, or children, and *administrative* and *service* space for the adults.

Administrative space typically is arranged in clusters around a larger central waiting area. We aliens would notice that, as is the case back home on Mars, architecture often follows cultural fads. In support of this supposition, we would make note of some exceptions to the motel-like construction of school campuses. In some of the buildings, open space, loosely divided with bookshelves, replace the motel arrangement of classrooms. In most cases, however, this seems to be a vestige of the past, since temporary and semipermanent walls have appeared to re-divide much of the space into more conventional arrangements.

We also would notice that in most communities, school systems are geographically decentralized. Schools and central administrative headquarters usually are dispersed throughout the community. It often takes much time to travel from building to building or from one part of an individual campus to another. Telephones and intercommunications systems facilitate communication, but the physical decentralization of school systems leads to structural looseness, or what many social scientists have called *loose coupling* (Bidwell 1965; Metz 1978; Corwin 1970).

Loose Coupling and Its Impact on Control

Loose coupling refers to the fact that direct supervision and control is difficult in school systems. The geographic dispersion of supervisory staff contributes to structural looseness as does the "autonomy of the closed door" (Lortie 1969). Central administrators usually do not visit each school building daily. In large school systems they may visit individual schools only once a year. Similarly, principals and their assistants cannot be in every classroom each day; teachers need only close their classroom doors to avoid surveillance.

Dispersion and closed doors also affect collegiality of teachers and their ability to organize in opposition to administrative practices. In the motel-like configuration of most schools, teachers are socially and professionally isolated. They may interact only with the staff members whose classrooms are across the hall and on either side of their own. Departmental meetings are infrequent and devoted to business. In general, teachers spend all day in their own separate classrooms, cannot leave their students unsupervised, and have little free time to talk to each other. Elementary school teachers often must supervise their students during lunch hour and before school; if breaks or planning periods are provided, they must be devoted to preparing for instruction, rather than to developing solidarity with other teachers.

Loose Coupling and Teacher Autonomy

While the isolation of teachers makes collective action more difficult because it inhibits communication and interaction, some researchers feel that these conditions help individual teachers develop a sense of professional autonomy because they make direct monitoring and control of teachers by administrators more difficult (Lortie 1969). On one hand, teachers may use the "autonomy of the closed door" to engage in innovative practices not used or even approved of by their supervisors and colleagues. On the other, teachers can teach as they wish when the door is closed, avoiding conformity to administrative dictates regarding even salutary innovation.

THE MATRIX OF CONTROL AND POWER IN DECISION-MAKING

As alien social scientists we would find the most incomprehensible aspect of American schooling to be the ambiguity in patterns of control and decision-making. Schools operate within a matrix of competing constituencies, all of which have a legitimate interest in what goes on in schools. Some, like school boards, superintendents' offices and building level administrators, are directly charged with the day-to-day governance of school systems. Others, like local, state and national governmental agencies and national accrediting associations, exercise regulatory and watchdog power. Still others, like parent groups, teachers' unions and other professional education associations, youth organizations such as Scouts, and social service agencies, have an interest in the welfare of the adults and children who participate in school activities. More distantly related are community organizations such as churches, local employers, taxpayer organizations, cultural associations, political interest groups, and the media. While they can attract a great deal of attention, these organizations serve primarily as lobbies. They cannot regulate school activities directly. Who, then, does establish policy for and regulate the schools? We begin with an examination of control at the local level, including the school board and the superintendency. We then discuss how the influence of the state and national interests permeates local activities.

The School Board and the Activities of the Superintendent

At one level school districts are run by officials who are elected by the community and who hire a professionally trained administrator to be the chief executive officer of the school district. School boards establish overall policy, ratify the budget and overall curricular and instructional directions, and oversee the hiring of personnel.

The ideas of school boards tend to reflect prevailing business ideology. Business and professional people dominate school boards all over the country, constituting more than three-fifths of the members. Housewives, usually middle and upper class wives of professionals account for 7.2 percent, and skilled and unskilled workers for 9.4 percent. Boards in larger cities and appointed boards tend to have an even larger proportion of business and professional members (Fantini 1975). In 1987, women made up 26.5 percent and blacks 2.4 percent of all elected school board officials in the country (Cull 1989).

Board members tend to be more conservative in fiscal matters than their superintendents, but they are more open to change in other respects than the people who elected them. Many also tend to view election to the school board as a springboard to further political careers (Cull 1989).

While school boards are elected to represent the community and to set educational policy which will be implemented by the superintendent whom they hire, in reality, real power at the local level generally rests with the superintendent and the professional staff, primarily those in the central office. In the first place, superintendents are hired because they represent a particular educational philosophy or track record which appeals to the board. In addition, most board members lack expert knowledge about educational issues. Finally, as old board members socialize new ones, the board itself becomes allied with the superintendent and dependent upon his or her expert knowledge. The role of the school board members often becomes one of legitimizing the actions of the superintendent to the community (Kerr 1973). The whims of school board decision-making also are limited by state and national dictates regarding curricula, aid for special categories of children and requirements for graduation and testing. In recent years, some school boards actions have violated stipulations in the United States' Constitution regarding separation of church and state and equal protection of all races. Many of these conflicts have resulted in court litigation.

Limitations on the Power of the Superintendent

While superintendents in large districts find it easier to maintain administrative independence than those in small districts, their actions still are somewhat limited. In the first place, superintendents do not have absolute control over the ideological direction of education; that responsibility resides with the school board. However, since superintendents are appointed by the Board, boards and superintendents often share educational philosophies.

Second, regardless of the size of their districts, superintendents must maintain the support of the school board. Much depends upon the political ability of individual superintendents to muster and maintain a consensus. Longevity in office for superintendents depends partly upon the ability to manipulate the flow of information to school board members so as to justify expenditures and either make test scores appear within acceptable ranges or convince the board that academic progress is being made (Fantini, Gittell, and Magat 1974).

Third, decisions also are constrained because they are not made in the same way as they are in business and industry. Major decisions are not made on a day-to-day basis; many, like textbook or budget adoptions and curriculum changes, occur infrequently—once a year or biannually.

Fourth, lines of control and supervision in school districts, even within the superintendent's office, are blurred by distinctions between line and staff areas of responsibility. Line and staff offices create separate hierarchies, each of which reports to and is controlled by the superintendent, but which are not accountable to each other. Line offices generally are those involved with individual school campuses—teachers, students and principals—while staff offices provide noninstructional services. The superintendent's office exercises central control over many administrative functions affecting the whole district, including offices of finance, maintenance, personnel, security, transportation, records-maintenance, and procurement. The supervisory lines in these departments radiate directly from the superintendent's office and probably are the most unambiguous in the system.

The position of other service departments is less clear, and their relationship to the lines of authority and control in the organization more ambiguous. These departments are concerned with curriculum and instruction; they provide advisory assistance and monitoring to school level personnel. Staff departments are responsible for developing curricula and providing staff development and training in the various subject areas such as English, mathematics and social studies, as well as in specialized areas such as education for children who are handicapped or who do not speak adequate English. These offices have staff, rather than line, responsibilities; they can provide advise, develop materials and train teachers, but they do not supervise and cannot enforce the use of their products. The offices responsible for vocational, gifted, remedial, alternative and handicapped programs also may blur the lines of administrative control. While these offices may have staff functions, they also run programs. Some almost constitute districts-within-the-district, in that they often have responsibility for their own special schools, including hiring of teachers and administration of budgets.

Voluntary Organizations

A major source of pressure on school personnel comes from voluntary organizations whose members have an interest in the school, but are not affiliated with it directly. They have particular power over schools as voters in the local community and potential contenders for positions on the elected school board; they also make petitions to the school board, appear at public meetings, and campaign in the media for the support of their particular agenda. These groups include taxpayer coalitions, curricular "watchdog" groups who monitor instructional activities for a variety of ideological reasons, and groups which pressure the schools for the addition or deletion of a variety of subject areas, including drug and sex education, and school prayer. Their activities are episodic in that they usually are generated in reaction to some event initiated by the school system. They often represent conservative special interests critical of what educators view as good innovative professional practice. Because these groups are often unpredictable, they are most problematic for school systems; they often act as a strong deterrent to innovation and reform.

For example, the state educational agencies in many of the larger states, including Texas and California, periodically review textbooks, recommending for statewide adoption those which pass their scrutiny. Each time the textbook adoption committees convene, a number of controversies arise. Creationists lobby against the teaching of evolution. Right-wing religious groups protest against texts which they feel do not sufficiently promote traditional attitudes toward the family, sex roles, and social morality. At stake is millions of dollars in book purchases for publishers (Spring 1988a). Equally serious is the concern of educators that the textbooks they choose be up-to-date so that the students in their states will be competitive in the national arena.

At the local level, anything having to do with sexual behavior, religion or finance can stimulate citizen protest. This can include groups protesting institution of sex education classes or day-care programs for children of students, purchase for the school library of books which concern sexual behavior, even if they are of recognized literary merit, display of a Nativity scene at Christmas or the need for school bond issues and tax increases. These and many other particularistic issues pit school people against segments in the community and threaten the control of school personnel over educational matters.

Patterns of Control beyond the Local Level

The American educational system operates within a system of direct and indirect controls. The direct controls tend to operate at the local level. As one moves farther from the home community of the school district, controls tend to be regulatory and indirect. They consists of "strings" and guidelines attached to funds beyond those raised by the local community for day to day operation of the system. Functionalists view the control and support of all nonlocal agencies simply as part of the system. Critical theorists, by contrast, have a bias toward democratic localism. They believe that current school systems are oppressive to the extent that local individuals are unable to determine their own destiny. Hence, they view the influence of state and national agencies, whether private or governmental, as evidence of further penetration into school affairs of the hegemony of dominant groups.

State Level Jurisdiction

Each state has an educational bureaucracy whose organization parallels that at the local level. At the top is a chief state school officer or superintendent, an elected or appointed state board of education, and an executive branch or agency which carries out the activities of the department. The focus of state regulation is different from that of the national government and has a greater impact on the day to day operation of schools. It specifies the scope of state supported education, establishes the content of the curriculum and minimum time allocations for each subject, sets minimum standards for promotion and graduation of students, describes the rights and competencies of teachers, defines the characteristics of administrative structure, and creates rules for the physical safety of school inhabitants (Wirt and Kirst 1974; Benson 1982). Some state departments of education adopt curricular guidelines which teachers must follow, and many states govern the adoption of specific sets of approved textbooks. State involvement in education was relatively limited until the mid-1960s.

Two factors served to increase activity at the state level. The first was the passage in 1965 of Title V of the Elementary and Secondary Education Act, which provided federal funds to bolster the professional staffs of state education agencies. Among the activities these funds supported were increased research, media, and consulting services to local school districts and the administration of federal funds for compensatory education. These activities had two effects. First, they increased the level of bureaucratization at the state level, and second, they permitted the influence of the federal educational policies to penetrate closer to the local level. This brought an important shift in the locus of power and control in school systems. While national educational agencies still had little influence over day to day behavior in the classroom, districts which accepted federal funds found that they were constrained to use them in specific ways and to carry out systematic evaluation of their actions.

In the 1980s, state departments of education became heavily involved in testing the competency of students and teachers and with mandating the establishment of "career ladders" for teachers. We have described these activities earlier in this chapter as a legacy from Taylorism and the actions of the efficiency experts during the 1930s. The programs are now linked to the national educational reform movement of the 1980s. The programs have required the establishment of test development offices as well as staff for assessment and enforcement of the laws. Like the administration of compensatory programs did in the 1960s, these programs also have greatly increased the complexity and bureaucratization of state level agencies and further reduced the control of local districts over recruitment and promotion of staff and students.

Regulation at the Regional and National Level

While the primary activites of educational systems are subject to levels of governance no higher than the state or local level, the influence of regional and national agencies in both the public and private sector is exercised by means of financial incentives, certification standards, court enforcement of national laws and provisions of the United States Constitution as well as federally funded research activities.

The Public Sector: The Role of the Federal Government

Despite the fact that primary responsibility for establishing and operating systems of education in America is reserved to the individual states, there has long been concern that decentralization might lead to great inequalities both in the capability and willingness of the states to provide educational services. In 1867, educators overcame legislative distrust of federal influence in educational matters and established the first federal Department of Education. Its charge was limited to providing statistics and information about educational matters and promoting the establishment of an efficient educational system (Butts 1978).

Since that time, federal influence has grown, especially as the federal government began to take responsibility for enforcing the provision of equal opportunity in education for all segments of the American population. The courts have been used to ensure that equal protection provisions of the United States Constitution were applied to educational matters and enforced on local school districts. Though its power, influence, and reporting structure have varied and it has gone through a number of title changes, the federally established Office of Education has provided financial aid to states and local districts for specific programs and sponsored research on topics felt to be in the national interest. These have included vocational educational programs and the teaching of science, bilingual education, English as a second language, and foreign languages. Federal funds also have provided sponsorship of basic research for improvement in instruction in critical subject areas such as math and science as well as for the improvement in techniques for teaching the disadvantaged. In addition, the federal government has financed research and evaluation staff to assure that federal funds are being used as they were intended. Since the 1960s, each federally funded project has had to include an evaluation component, even if its tasks are carried out by staff members from local school districts.

The federal government also has provided scholarships and loans to special classes of individuals. These have included people returning from military service under the Servicemen's Readjustment Act of 1944 (the "GI Bill"); people who would study certain subjects such as foreign languages and science under the National Defense Education Act; and ethnic minority students under the provisions of the War on Poverty legislation during the 1960s. Individual undergraduates were helped with Pell grants, while graduate study was encouraged under the Smith–Mundt and Fulbright legislation, the National Science Foundation, and other scholarship and loan programs.

The national government also provides regulation to protect the educational rights and welfare of certain groups of students, including the poor, the handicapped and those with limited proficiency in English. Members of these populations have been provided with school nurses, lunches, certain medical examinations, clothing, remedial instruction, and other compensatory services. The national government has enforced laws and regulations regarding discrimination on the basis of race, gender, religion, and national origin, and has placed constraints on communities which wish to use the schools for religious purposes. Affirmative action and laws outlawing discrimination in public agencies meant that schools, in particular, came under close scrutiny by the Office of Civil Rights and the courts.

The Private Sector

Regional Accreditation Agencies and Research Foundations. State education agencies exercise surveillance over the quality of instruction in local districts and make sure that students who graduate have received the proper amount of instruction. Their efforts are reinforced, however, by the activities of regional

accrediting agencies. During the nineteenth century, course offerings in secondary schools were so diverse that universities had no way of knowing how much
their incoming students knew or what they had studied. Since universities could
not cater to each student, they established the practice of certifying the curricula
of given schools and accepting students from those schools without entrance
examinations. The institutionalization of these certification practices resulted in
agencies which made visits to high schools and approved their curricula, certifying their students and "accrediting" their programs. While the effect of these
agencies has been to make the course offerings in secondary schools more
uniform, at least for college preparatory programs, it also has created an external watchdog function which again reduces the autonomy of individual schools
and districts.

*Private   Research   Institutes,   Local   Businesses   and   Philanthropic
Foundations.* While private institutions have far less money to dispense than
does the federal government, many such institutions are far more accessible to
local school districts. Many are operated by local corporations or derive from
the legacies of local philanthropists and are enthusiastic about sponsoring programs in the schools, especially small grants for teachers, which are congruent
with the purposes of their charters. A few very large private research foundations, such as the Rockefeller, Ford, and Spencer Foundations, have a pervasive
effect not only on the topics of investigation and methods by which they are
carried out, but upon the use of research data. In addition, recipients of awards
from these agencies form an elite network of intellectual opinion leaders and
referees whose judgment is sought on educational matters in both the public and
private sector (LeCompte 1972).

The influence of local businesses and industries are particularly powerful.
School-business partnerships have been promoted heavily as ways to help minority youth make the transition to the workforce and reduce their drop out rate
(*see*, for example, Hargroves 1987). Corporations also have loaned executives to
school districts as teachers in speciality areas such as math, science, and computer technology. Vocational curricula in high schools often reflect the dominant
industries in the community; the schools do initial training and students then are
preferentially hired by local businesses.

EXTERNAL OR ANCILLARY ORGANIZATIONS
IN SCHOOL CONTROL

School officials tend to view with caution anyone who comes into their buildings. Whether or not one is defined as a trespasser or invader who could
undermine the authority of administrators or threaten their independence of
action depends upon what visitors want and how supportive the organization
they represent is seen to be (Van Galen 1987). The many constituencies which
educational systems serve have interests which are articulated through a variety
of organizations which generally fall into two categories: The first consists of

those ongoing organizations which are organized directly for the benefit of the school and which are sanctioned by it—such as parent-teacher organizations, athletic booster organizations, school-business partnerships which provide employment and training for students, contribute supplies and equipment for educational programs, or donate the time of business people to teach classes or tutor students. The second category includes on-going organizations which are made up of individuals directly involved in the school but which are not necessarily sanctioned by the school, including teachers' unions and other professional associations.

Parent and Booster Organizations

The outsiders with perhaps the most legitimate interest in the schools are the parents of children enrolled in a school. In the first place, their activities can make a big difference in the workload of teachers. Volunteer parents serve as aides, room or grade parents, and as librarians, and occasionally provide transportation for field trips, sponsor extracurricular activities, and raise money for computers and other materials which the school budget cannot cover. In the second place, teachers, researchers and administrators believe strongly that parent activity makes a difference in pupil achievement. For example, in Houston, Texas, schools whose students had the highest achievement scores had five times as many parent volunteers as those with the lowest achievement (Tedford 1988). A strong correlation has been demonstrated between achievement scores of children in reading and whether or not their parents read stories to them (Boehnlein 1985). The War on Poverty of the 1960s and 1970s heavily stressed teaching parents how to help their children study; success of the educational reform movement of the 1980s is believed to rest on getting parents involved in the schooling of their children.

However, the involvement of parents and others who are not directly and professionally linked to the school is viewed with ambivalence by teachers and principals. They are truly comfortable only with volunteer effort which they can control and which does not question their authority. They do not look favorably upon upstart student groups or underground community newspapers, unfavorable newspaper publicity, or organized groups of reform minded parents who are dissatisfied with their children's academic progress or the educational activities provided for them.

On one hand, parent groups can be perceived as a serious threat to the school because their children provide parents legitimate access to school affairs. On the other hand, the tenure of children in a school is relatively short, and if parents cannot be discouraged, coopted, intimidated or ignored, school personnel can always resist their pressure by waiting until the children move, drop out, or graduate. Stern (1987), for example documented how public schools train black parents to accept unquestioningly the low evaluations given to their children, "cooling out" those who resist by locking the doors, canceling meetings, and retaliating against their children. Deyhle (1987) has described how cultural differences in childrearing lead white administrators to define Navajo and Ute parents as uninterested in the education of their children, despite ample evidence and participation to the contrary. Parent participation also has grown more problematic in recent years as the structure of the family changes and more and more parents work full-time (see Chapter Three).

Teachers' Unions and Professional Organizations

The tension over whether teachers are workers or professionals with power and control over their work is echoed in arguments over status discrepancies: should teachers be represented by professional associations or unions? (See Chapter Four.) Here, we wish to examine the origin of teacher efforts to act collectively and their impact upon control of schools. Symbolic of the difficulty which the profession has is that there has been a consistent press to create an umbrella professional organization to serve groups whose interests are as disparate as classroom teachers, administrators, and professors from teachers colleges. The result, as we shall see, is not one big happy family, but a collection of warlike tribes who fail to serve well the interests of any of the participants. The alternative, a teachers' *union*, has suffered identity problems as well, because although the members of teachers' unions are not blue collar workers, the orientation of the organization, like that of unions for steelworkers and truck-drivers, is adversarial.

The first teacher organization was the National Teacher Association, founded in 1857. Its merger in 1870 with the National Association of School Superintendents and the American Normal School Association created the National Education Association. It also set the precedent for dominance of the NEA by supervisory personnel and college professors, rather than teachers. The NEA sees itself as a professional association. It has primarily been interested in development and evaluation of curricula in elementary and secondary schools and teachers colleges, as well as credentializing and certification of teachers. It historically has avoided controversy; only when forced by the militancy and success of teacher unions in the late 1960s did it begin to accept the concept of collective bargaining for teachers and sanctions against districts which violate teachers' rights (Scimecca 1980). It also was out of touch with the problems of teachers. Until recently, the NEA record on civil rights, and the rights of women—who numerically dominated it—and minorities was weak. Not until the late 1960s did the NEA establish a task force on urban problems. Despite heavy recruiting, the association never has attracted the allegiance of a majority of teachers (Brenton 1974, p. 82).

By contrast, teachers unions are more militant and have primarily been concerned with teacher welfare, civil rights, and academic freedom. The first teachers' union, the relatively short-lived Chicago Teachers Federation, was organized at the turn of the century by two women, Margaret Haley and Catherine Goggin. Haley forced the election of Ella Flagg Young as the first woman president of the NEA in 1910, and for a short time, the NEA was more responsive to demands for equal pay for equal work, women's suffrage, and more teacher control of school affairs.

The American Federation of Teachers was founded in 1916 and affiliated with the American Federation of Labor that year. Over the years, school districts, courts, and local, state and national government initiated draconian union-busting efforts. Union organizers and sympathizers were harassed and fired, striking teachers lost their jobs, and courts tried to declare that union practices and teacher participation in them were illegal. The AFT survived all of these efforts to obliterate it and remains the most powerful teachers union in America today.

It would be a mistake, however, to think that today's teacher organizations are immensely powerful. They are hedged by laws limiting their right to bargain and strike, plagued with teacher apathy and open resistance to participation, and riddled with infighting. Although the number of teacher strikes has increased dramatically, from three in 1960–1961 to 180 in 1970–71, for example, teachers still express ambivalence as to whether they should be permitted to strike (Ginsburg 1988). Participants in strikes generally account for less than a quarter of all teachers (Brookover and Erickson 1975, p. 206). Militant teachers are very much a minority and are atypical of the portrait of a teacher contained in Chapter 4. However, despite the fact that conventional wisdom supports the notion that teachers who belong to unions are less professional than those who do not, there is evidence that teachers who join unions are, in fact, more career oriented and committed to their profession. Falk, Grimes and Lord (1982), for example, state that teachers whose attitudes are more cosmopolitan, who are less likely to say that they want to leave the profession, and who have advanced degrees are those most likely to support union activity.

Shifts in Power: The Impact of Unions

Two watershed events, both in New York City, changed the pattern of relationships between unions and school managers. The first was the 1962 strike of the United Federation of Teachers, the largest teachers' local. It not only won raises for teachers, but successfully kept the district from retaliating against those participating in the strike. The second event was the Ocean-Hill/Brownsville strike in 1968, wherein an alliance of the UFT and the very conservative school administrators of the Council of Supervisory Associations fought off attempts to give control over hiring and firing of teachers to decentralized local community school boards (Scimecca 1980).

Since these events, there is evidence that teacher militance has initiated some important changes in patterns of control and power in education. While these changes are not universal, and while their full effect still is unknown, they point the way to future shifts in the governance of education. First, the changes have tended to radicalize the NEA and other more conservative organizations. Second, they have reduced the arbitrary decision making power of school boards and administrators with regard to teachers. Third, the changes have made clearer the dichotomy between teacher and administrators interests. Fourth, they have greatly reduced the power of building level principals. Because teachers in moderate to large districts can use their union representatives to negotiate directly with higher district officials, the principal can be circumvented (Scimecca 1980). Finally, because the teachers' unions have affiliation with national organizations, the growth in militancy may produce a more cosmopolitan outlook among teachers. It shifts teacher concerns from purely local problems and local initiatives for solving them to state and national arenas (Brookover and Erickson 1975).

SUMMARY

In this chapter, we have described the organization and control of school systems in America. Our goal has been to provide a context for the rest of the book, in which we describe the process of schooling and its impact upon participants. We hope that you have begun to understand that schools and educational programs are not neutral. In fact, they exist in a highly politically charged arena. Because schools have more contact with children than any other social institution (excluding the family), and because they are the single agency most amenable to public manipulation, the groups who control the schools also have a profound impact on indoctrination and training of future generations. We believe that the sociologist, Max Weber, was correct in stating that it was possible to tell a great deal about the power structure and patterns of social differentiation in a society if you could determine how the schools were organized, the content of instruction offered, and who benefitted from attendance. In the pages which follow, we will explore these issues.

KEY CONCEPTS

Rationalization in the sociological sense does not refer to the making of excuses. Rather, it means the application of principles of reason to a task or course of action. In practice, it means the application of modern methods of efficiency to the methods of work and organization of industrial and service institutions.

A Formal Organization is one which is organized for some specific long-term purpose and which has a legally established identity. Formal organizations are distinguished from informal friendship groups, associations and families in that they are governed by specific charters, by-laws or rules and regulations. They exist independently of the identities of individual participants, and their life span exceeds the tenure of individual members.

Bureaucracy is a term sociologists use to refer to a specific kind of social organization. Bureaucracies are large, hierarchially structured formal organizations whose purpose is to carry out some complex task. Both work and administration in bureaucracies is rationally subdivided and supervised by career professionals specifically trained for their jobs.

Scientific Management was invented by an industrial engineer, Frederick W. Taylor. It is a way to improve the operation of industrial organizations by analyzing how workers use time, machinery and resources. It pioneered the use of "time and motion" studies to improve the efficiency with which work practices were organized and carried out.

Line Offices are those positions in an organization located in the vertical supervisory structure. People in lower line offices report to and are supervised by those directly above them in rank, who in turn report to and are supervised by those above them. They carry out the actual tasks for which the organization exists. In schools, teachers, principals and superintendents hold line offices.

Staff Offices are located in a horizontal position in the reporting structure; their tasks are ancillary or consultative to the overall work of the organization. In schools, counselors, secretaries, curriculum staff, and media specialists are examples of staff. While their own departments may have an internal linear supervisory structure, they can only assemble information and give advice to line personnel; they have no direct power to enforce their suggestions.

Professional Organizations and Unions are organizations established to further the status and power of a particular occupational or professional group. They are distinguished mostly by the characteristics of their members and the degree to which they see the interests of their members as philosophically opposed to the interests of management. Professional organizations are white collar associations, while unions were established for the blue collar workers. Unions traditionally have viewed political activity and collective action—especially strikes—as legitimate ways to secure benefits for their members. Professional organizations have been more conservative and reluctant to engage in conflict with dominant groups in society.

EXERCISES

1. Obtain a copy of the school organization chart from the central office of your local school district. How does this compare with what you have learned in this chapter about the way schools are organized?

2. Interview a school administrator who has been involved in your local school district for a long time about the changes in the school organization over the past decade or more. What are some of these changes? What does the administrator think of the ways the bureaucracy has changed?

3. Interview a veteran teacher about changes in the school organization since she began teaching. What were some of these changes and what does she think about them?

4. Think about the organization of the high school you attended. How was it organized? Who controlled the school? Who were the people in power positions? How did they maintain this power? Do you think this organization was effective? Why or why not?

5. If you had the power to change the organization of schooling within a school district, how would you do it? Why?

6. Attend a school board meeting. Find out about the background of the members. Notice the interactions in the meeting. Who speaks, who introduces new measures and which positions do the members take on different issues? What special interest groups are in attendance? What role does the superintendent play? What types of actions are on the agenda? Who determined the agenda?

7. Identify community groups in your area that desire to influence education. What constituency do they represent? What changes would they like to see? What tactics and strategies do they use?

8. What examples of goal displacement can you describe in your own experiences with school organizations?

9. How are you affected in your daily life in schools by practices grounded in scientific management?

SUGGESTED READINGS

Classic Works

Blau, Peter. M. (1955). *The dynamics of bureaucracy*. Chicago: University of Chicago Press.

Blau, Peter M., and Scott, Richard W. (1962). *Formal organizations*. San Francisco: Chandler.

Durkheim, E. (1973). *Moral education: A study in the theory and application of the sociology of education*. New York: The Free Press.

Katz, M. B. (1971). *Class, bureaucracy and the schools*. New York, Praeger Publishers.

Rogers, David. (1968). *110 Livingston Street: Politics and bureaucracy in the New York City schools*. New York: Random House.

Sills, D. L. (1970). Preserving organizational goals. In Oscar Grusky and George A. Miller, *The sociology of organizations*. New York: The Free Press.

Useem, Elizabeth L., and Useem, Michael, eds. (1974). *The educational establishment*. Englewood Cliffs, NJ: Prentice-Hall.

Modern Works

Borman, Kathryn M., and Spring, Joel. (1984). *Schools in central cities: Structure and process*. White Plains: Longman, Inc.

Chafetz, J. S., and Dworkin, A. G. (1986). *Female revolt: Women's movements in world and historical perspective*. Totowa, N.J.: Rowan and Allanheld.

Holmes Group. (1986). *Tomorrow's teachers*. A Report of the Holmes Group, East Lansing, Mich: Holmes Group, Inc.

Resnick, D. P., and Resnick, L. B. (1985). Standards, curriculum and performance: A historical and comparative perspective. *Educational Researcher*, *14*(4).

Spring, J. H. (1988). *American education* (4th ed.). White Plains: Longman.

Spring, J. H. (1988). *Conflict of interests: The politics of American education*. White Plains: Longman.

CHAPTER 3

Youth Culture and the Student Peer Group

INTRODUCTION

Most texts carefully look at all but one aspect of schooling. They analyze the curriculum, instruction, teachers, administrators, buildings and their organizations, unions, and standardized testing—everything but the clients for whom schools are intended—the students. Despite this, most studies of young people are carried out while they are in school, because schools are where children can most easily be found in large, accessible quantities. Researchers seem to assume that schools are the only places children spend time. Perhaps this convenient fiction exists because schools are the aspect of the collective life of children most firmly controlled by adults.

Because researchers primarily study children while they are in school, they have attributed far more prominence in the lives of children to school-related activities than may be valid. Because we believe that out-of-school events in students' lives are at least as important as are those which occur in school, we look closely at both.

Until recently, the voices of students simply have not been heard, even to describe what schools really mean to them. As we shall see, how many students feel about school is widely divergent from what educators would prefer. Furthermore, the attitudes which students have toward school are at least as important to their tenure there as patterns of instruction and school organization. An increasing number of children have become convinced that schools have little to offer them; in response, many students have become mentally, if not physically, absent from school more than they are present. Schools have lost a great deal of centrality in the latitudes and values of students. For many students, what goes on outside school is far more salient. Teachers no longer can assume that they and their pupils share similar views about the value of education and its pay off. How long students stay in school, how committed they feel, and the quality of their performance often depend upon their social class, race, and gender, as well as characteristics of the community, pressures from outside the school, and attributes of the school itself.

The term student refers to a social role and depends upon enrollment in an educational institution, whereas being a child has no such institutional correlate. Successfully enacting the role of student means mastering certain institutional requirements; being a child does not. In this chapter, we distinguish between children *as children* and children *as students*, in order to highlight the importance of out-of-school events and activities to children and to their lives as students.

The first part of this chapter is devoted to the process of growing up and how that process has changed for all children. We define **peer group** and **youth**

culture and trace their historical development. We suggest that the specific cultural content of any given youth group is context specific, and that while there may be common developmental, economic, social and cultural variables faced by all young people, how they respond varies according to the special and particular circumstances in which they live.

It is clear that some special kind of energy exists between and among young people. In the minds of many social scientists, this energy possesses enough force and longevity to generate a culture of its own. In modern society, this culture conforms to its own internal norms, but can be, and usually is, directed in opposition to the culture of school, parents, and adult institutions in general. On one hand, this opposition, however mild or intense, constitutes a way for young people to establish an identity separate from their parents and elders. However, as a collective entity, the "student peer group" can be a major problem in schools.

Parents want their children to "hang out" with friends whose behavior and values are acceptable. Teachers speak of the powerful influence which friends have upon each other, and teachers split up children who habitually get into trouble when they work together. Social scientists cite studies which demonstrate that one of the strongest predictors of children's futures is what their friends do. Police, probation officers, therapists and social workers try to keep juvenile offenders away from the deleterious influence of their old friends.

In the second part of the chapter, we specifically look at schools and how they affect the lives of students and the impact of peer groups. We are particularly interested in the overt and covert resistance of young people to the inflexibility of their educational experiences, especially in regard to the social definitions and standards for success which going to school impose on them. Ours is a perspective applicable most directly to western European culture and subordinate groups under its influence. Hence, some of our assertions about youth and what they like to do may not apply for some minorities, such as Navajo teenagers. While these cultural biases should be kept in mind, the analysis provides a valuable perspective on the western European definitions and cultural forms which dominate school life in the United States.

WHAT IS YOUTH CULTURE?

The two terms, peer group and youth culture, often are used interchangeably. However, they refer to quite different phenomena and have their origin in different social science disciplines. The term peer group derives from sociology. A peer group refers to relationships which people have because of special characteristics such as age, race, gender, professional or social status, and means a group composed of people who are similar or equal to each other in their possession of those characteristics. Peer groups are not synonymous with friendship groups, although friendship groups often consist wholly of people who are peers.

Often, the equality of peers is defined rather loosely. The phrase, "a jury of one's peers," has generated many court battles over the degree to which the composition of a given jury really did equate with the social standing, race, gender, or ideology of the defendant. The same might be said of student peer groups. While the student peer group most commonly is defined as an age or grade-level cohort—a group of students who are the same age and in the same grade in school—that definition is too narrow. Many other factors, including differences in place of residence, social philosophy, dress, academic prowess, social status, race, religion, and interests cross-cut similarities of age and grade level, such that it probably is more correct to speak of multiple student peer groups, rather than just one (Epstein 1983).

The term youth culture derives from anthropology, and is a broader term than peer group. Anthropologists have defined culture as the way of life of a people (Linton, 1945); that which anthropologists have observed about the behavior of a group of people (Harris, 1981). Tylor (1958) defined culture as all the learned behavior acquired by people as members of a society including their arts, customs, knowledge, law, morals, and any other of their capabilities and habits. In general, anthropologists agree that culture includes the entire body of attitudes, values, beliefs, and behavior patterns of a group of people (Spradley and McCurdy 1972). This includes language, kinship patterns, rituals and beliefs, economic and political structures, patterns of reproduction and childrearing, life stages, the arts, crafts and manufacturing, and technology (Goetz and LeCompte 1984).

Cultural development is profoundly affected by the physical environment in which people live. The environment strongly influences the possessions they make or buy, their family structure, beliefs about religion, morals and sexuality, attitudes and behavior toward work and government, and patterns of dress, personal adornment, and recreation. The concept of culture also includes an historical dimension, in that the past activities of a group affect its current behavior, as do its beliefs about what will happen in the future.

Can Youth Have a Culture?

Many scholars have argued that youth cannot have a culture, since individuals grow up and become nonyouth. In the inevitable loss of their youth, people lose the primary characteristic defining them as a part of the culture. Still other scholars argue that one can move into and out of cultures as one gains and loses the statuses which earned one entry in the first place. For example many professions, such as teaching, medicine, and the arts, and many institutions, such as prisons and religious organizations, develop sufficiently distinctive sets of attitudes, values, beliefs and behavior patterns—even distinctive patterns of dress, personal adornment and language—as to constitute cultures (Sykes 1958; Goffman 1959; Becker and Geer et al. 1961; Ebaugh, 1977). In this view, individuals who cease to practice the given profession or who leave the institution are no longer a part of a professional culture, in the same way that youth grows up and leaves the youth culture.

We do not feel that youth culture necessarily requires that individuals remain children all of their lives, because in fact, youth culture can be perpetuated as practices are passed from one generation of children to another. Bennett (1988b), for example, describes the way succeeding generations of Yup'ik Eskimo girls learned cultural norms and folk tales through "story-knifing," a way of telling and illustrating folk tales and stories by cutting pictures in soft sand or mud with a dull knife. Similarly, Lever (1976) discusses how gender differences in patterns of play teach children the social roles they will enact as adults.

We view youth culture as defined by those distinctive behavior patterns which children and adolescents develop, often in opposition to the power of adults and their institutions. These patterns differentiate young people first of all from adults, and then from other cliques and subgroups within their age cohort (for example, "punkers" are differentiated from "preppies" in American high schools). The two terms, peer group and youth culture, are linked and must be used together. Culture is the set of distinctive practices and beliefs, while the peer group is the social entity which develops and carries it out. To the extent that the youthful peer group is defined by its relationship to school, we can speak of a student peer group. While peer group influence is important in the lower grades, it becomes more profoundly problematic for schools during adolescence.

Developmental Factors in the Generation of Peer Groups

Conformity. One of the characteristics of growing up is not wanting to be different. Children are fad-followers. On one hand, they want to have the most up-to-date fashions, toys, and equipment; on the other hand, they don't want to be too different from their friends, or to be caught liking or possessing something which others think is outrageous, outmoded, or stupid. Part of the "herd instinct" which afflicts young people involves role-modeling and trying on different identities, as exemplified in the behavior of their friends or significant adult figures. Part also involves practice in learning the norms and values of a group by trying to stay within them. It is important to note that the conformity of young people is *internal* to the norms of their chosen peer group. Some types of youthful solidarity actually facilitate conformity to the norms of teachers and other adults, as was the case with the "'earholes" described by Willis (1977). In other cases, such as Willis's "lads" and Marotto's (1986) "Boulevard Brothers," peer group norms lead to the formation of groups which oppose the rules and dictates of adults.

Rebellion. While most children abhor being different from others in their own clique, they find equally distasteful being similar to their parents. Rebellion against adult symbols of authority is an important component of growing up in modern urban societies, whether it consists of the cranky independence of a two year old or the outlandish dress and behavior of adolescents. The actual content and direction of student rebellion is hard to characterize, other than that it is in opposition to whatever strong adult presence, whether parental or institutional, is salient in the lives of young people. Rebellion against authority may make these groups a mirror image of adult society; what is "bad" to adults becomes "good" to kids.

You hafta make a name for yourself, to be bad . . . [to] be with the 'in' crowd . . . It's just all part of growing up around here . . . (McLeod 1987, p. 26)

He's the baddest, He shot a fucking cop . . . That's the best thing you can do . . . (McLeod 1987, p. 27)

Thus, the rebellion of students of the eighties may be seen in part as a conservative reaction to the radicalism of their parents in the 1960s, just as the worldwide student uprisings of the 1960s might be viewed as a reaction to the conservatism, alienation, and repression of 1950s (Keniston 1968; 1971; Miles 1977).

Idealism. A third characteristic of young people which affects the formation of the student peer group and its culture is idealism and a sense of immortality. We define *idealism* as a desire to transform the world and make it a better place. It is a tendency to simplify problems and to look for unambiguous or black and white solutions. Doing so is a necessary stage in the development of a young person's personal philosophy (Belenky et al. 1986). While it frees young people, making them daring, brave, and capable of action on issues which adults, with their more sophisticated understanding of complexities, would sooner abandon, it also makes them prey to outrage and despair when solutions are delayed. Idealism also makes many young people indifferent to the dangers of practices such as truancy, drug use, reckless driving, and unprotected sex.

Their belief in invincibility, immortality and high ideals permit young people to feel that they cannot be harmed by actions which would endanger most people. This permits them to grow and to change in response to a changing culture by challenging existing definitions and ways of doing things. It also facilitates growth because it encourages risk-taking behavior. In western societies, this is important, because individuation and personal development are valued. Developing these attributes also involves some danger; they are not engendered in people who have no capacity for experiencing risk.

These characteristics of youth—conformity with peers, rebellion against adults, and youthful idealism—facilitate the growth of contemporary children away from their families of origin into separate lives as mature adults. The desire for conformity leads to formation of strong friendship groups among young people, groups composed of individuals who share similar likes and dislikes, similar attitudes toward work, family, school, and the opposite sex; similar aspirations and expectations for the future, patterns of language, dress, and recreation. Cultural differences may cause variation in the specific content of these attitudes and preferences, but the formation of peer groups as a major socializing force for young people remains constant in modern life. The relative indifference of young people to physical and emotional danger complicates their relationships with school, however, if the cultural patterns and attitudes shared by the peer group are antithetical or indifferent to behavior required for success in school.

Social and Historical Factors in the Development of Youth Culture

Certain structural characteristics of societies, such as age grades, clans, and schools with patterns of academic tracking, facilitate formation of youthful peer groups. In most cultures, people go through life identified as a member of a generation or age-grade. In some traditional cultures, these have ritual significance and are recognized as one of the primary organizational structures in the society. Where each age grade performs specific tasks or functions which are integral to the support and sustenance of the culture, as they are in certain East African and American Indian societies, the social structure of youthful groups does not promote opposition to the "mainstream" (Evans-Pritchard 1940; Bernardi 1952; Wilson 1963; Bowers 1965; Bernardi 1985).

In contrast, however, contemporary society is characterized by the opposition of youth groups to adult values and to traditional ways of growing up. We believe that this opposition has occurred because the widespread advent of schooling has changed the way young people grow up and has made them susceptible to developing their personalities and ways of operating in the world with only limited or minimal contact with adult culture. In fact, among the families of immigrants, adult-child relationships often are switched. Children become teachers to their parents, serving as interpreters and intermediaries between the culture of origin and that of the new country. Young people maintain stronger contacts with each other, the media, and their own youthful culture than they do with that of their families. In the pages which follow, we will discuss how this has come about.

Socialization in Traditional Societies

Unlike animals, children must be socialized; they are born without the knowledge or instincts to survive. Either by formal instruction or by watching others, they must be taught social, cognitive, and technical or mechanical skills. They also must learn the history and acquire the knowledge base of the people to whom they belong. In many preindustrial, or traditional, cultures, where formal schooling is not the primary agent of **socialization** children learn how to be adults initially by watching and modeling the behavior of parents and family members. Later they may acquire more technical skills or sophisticated knowledge of the culture from indigenous specialists. Learning takes place within and is controlled by the community and reflects its structure and values. Young people may "sow their wild oats," but they do not, as a **cohort** or a peer group, develop values and behavior patterns which are wildly at variance with those of their parents. Puberty rites, whose specific purpose is to create a dramatic break in the developmental stream, signify a change in status from biological childhood to physical maturity, but there is no clear distinction between youth and adult culture. Whatever culture young people have is a fairly close approximation of that of their parents; they marry and/or go to work on or even before physical maturity.

In cultures where this is an expected behavior pattern, parents do not always tell children directly what to do and how to behave. It is assumed that they will learn by watching adults. When children feel that they can perform appropriately, they will model their behavior after what they have seen adults do. Such learning is not limited to learning how to herd sheep, make clothing, care for children, hunt seals, or farm. It also includes learning how to interact appropriately with others, participate in social life, and adhere to the moral precepts of the community. Only when children misbehave are they punished, and often then only indirectly, through the telling of stories, or gentle reminders (Basso 1984).

Historically, children spent very little time in school. School learning was not necessary for most people; economic necessity meant that other than the very wealthy, few families could afford the luxury of permitting male children to be in school and out of the work force. Females, too, were needed at home for help in child rearing and household chores, as well as adjuncts to the economic endeavors of adult women. For example, young Moslem girls in Africa, who are permitted to move freely in the community until puberty, facilitate the trading activities of their mothers, who are restricted by *purdah* to their family compounds (Schildkrout 1984).

To some extent these patterns still prevail. Until the twentieth century, American educators believed education to be wasted upon girls. Even if they were intellectually capable of acquiring the necessary skills, jobs where they could use the skills were not open to females. Considerable doubt also was cast both upon the suitability of education for girls and their ability to absorb it. As recently as the late 1880s, the study of geography for girls was opposed because it might make them disatisfied with their homes and inclined to travel (Curti 1971). Some educators—and even medical experts—believed subjects like math, science, and physical education to be so taxing as to cause mental and emotional deterioration and even damage to the reproductive organs of girls who undertook to study them (Smith, 1905; Hall 1904; Kaestle 1983). These beliefs, rather than patterns of discrimination or intractable conflict between family life, childrearing duties and careers in an era predating birth control and affirmative action, were used to explain why most of the few women who did become highly educated and had careers remained childless and unmarried. Women were relegated to the home, despite the fact that "careers" as sheltered-wife-and-mother-with-a-spouse-who-supported-her always were more myth than reality. Social beliefs ignored the fact that wars, the distant or intermittent employment of spouses, poverty, death and abandonment left many women fully or at least partly responsible for taking care of themselves and for raising families alone.

With the exception of a small elite whose male children did spend long years being educated, childhood for most children in all cultures remained a brief prelude to adult responsibilities (Aries 1962). In fact, until the 1920s, and then only in industrialized societies, adolescence for most young people, if it existed at all, was very short and included no more than a few years of schooling.

The Development of Adolescence as a Life Stage

Adolescence is a fairly recent phenomenon produced, as we shall see, primarily in modern industrialized societies. In traditional societies adolescence usually begins at the onset of puberty or the achievement of a certain age—as in a *bar* or *bat mitzvah* for Jewish children—and is celebrated with special celebrations or rituals. It lasts only until marriage, the birth of the first child, or the point when the young person demonstrates economic self-sufficiency, mileposts which are achieved shortly after biological maturity or puberty. In these societies, youths are closely supervised by adults, and concentrations of young people are diluted by the presence of and association with many adults. The period of youthful irresponsibility is short and leisure time is limited or taken up by the need to work or to train for it, so young people have no opportunity to develop a distinctive cultural style separate from adults.

Adolescence as a Liminal State. Anthropologists (Gennep 1960; Turner 1969, 1974) define *liminal* points as social or developmental transitions—periods after leaving one clearly identified social status state and before entering the next or another. Liminal people exist in a state which is "ambiguous, neither here nor there, betwixt and between all fixed points of classification." (Turner 1974, p. 232) Initiates in clubs and fraternal orders exist in liminal states; so do brides on the day of their wedding—after they wake up and before they are married. They are, in a sense, neither married nor single; their in-between state is a state of **liminality**. We consider adolescence to be a liminal state because adolescents are neither children nor grown up.

Attitudes about liminal people are somewhat ambivalent. As novices, they are newly grown and fresh; they are "structurally if not physically invisible in terms of [their] culture's standard definitions and classifications (Turner, ibid.). As such, certain kinds of liminal people are thought to be vulnerable and in need of protection because they have not yet learned how to behave in their new roles. They are innocents, who might do something which would harm them. However, they also are perceived as unfettered by the rules of society because they do not as yet hold any clearly defined social role. Because they do not know the rules, they could violate them with impunity; hence, like witches, they pose a potential danger to others.

In most cultures, special precautions are taken to protect liminal people from actions which would endanger them or their future status; other members of society also are protected from potentially asocial actions which liminal people might take. That societies have ambivalent feelings about liminal people is not necessarily a commentary on their character; it is simply that, having left one state and not yet properly entered the new one, a liminal person is innocent of the proper way to behave, and as such, must be resocialized in order to learn the rules of his or her new status in life.

In traditional societies, rites of passage or transition from one social status to another are characterized by rituals which include a period of liminality. During this period, the initiates, or liminal persons, often are subject to avoidance taboos, caused to wear special and distinctive adornments, placed in a kind of protective custody, isolated from other people, and made subject to special kinds of ceremonies or training. Turner suggests that this segregation emphasizes the equality and comradeship of people who are in a liminal state; it promotes development of group norms, cultural values and a sense of community.

We believe that in western societies, schools, especially high schools, act as the institutions where the rite of passage from early childhood to adulthood takes place. Borman and Spring (1984, p. 238) suggest that adolescence in modern society is a period of transition in which adult status is incrementally achieved. During adolescence, youth occupy "multiple and conflicting statuses;" they go to school full time . . . but they also work. They can drive a car and join the army, but they cannot vote or buy and drink alcoholic beverages. They are biologically old enough to procreate, but considered too young by many parents to be told the "facts of life." Schools segregate adolescents in much the same way as formal rituals of passage do in traditional societies. In this manner, schools act as an incubator for youth culture.

Schooling and Adolescence

Aries (1962) suggests that the recognition of adolescence as a lifestage is directly related to the lengthening of the period of schooling considered mandatory or desirable. In modern urban societies growing up is a more complex process than in traditional, usually rural, societies, and going to school becomes a more and more important part of a child's life. While recent growth in the "home schooling" movement (see Pitman, 1987, for a description of home schooling and its supporters) and increases in the incidence of private schooling are evidence of groups which oppose the publicly controlled institutionalization of learning, for the vast majority, childhood instruction takes place in public schools. For example, by 1981, only 3.1 percent of the total elementary and secondary school enrollment in the United States was in Catholic schools, and only 3.3 percent was in nonCatholic private schools (O'Neill and Sepielli, 1985, p.23); see Table 3.1.

Further, the more technologically advanced a society is, the more years children spend in school. We believe that the number of years spent in school is associated with the development of strong peer relationships among people in the same age group. As a consequence, the longer a society schools its children, the greater will be the tendency for young children and adolescents to develop a youth culture which is in opposition to adults, even where students change schools frequently. This is because it is only in age-graded schools that so many people of the same age and sex are forced by law to remain in close proximity for so long a time.

Compulsory Schooling. By the end of the nineteenth century, universal primary school attendance had been mandated in most of the western world. By the middle of the twentieth century, serious efforts had been made worldwide to institutionalize primary schooling for all. The expansion of day-care, preschool, secondary and postsecondary school which followed, especially in urbanized and industrialized countries, reflected a changing labor market, especially for women, as well as changing attitudes toward children and childrearing. As the knowledge base deemed necessary for survival became more complex, and as custody of the young increasingly came to be supervised by the state, instruction more and more was separated from what parents know and can teach. Parents came to be viewed as incompetent to teach children the cognitive and technical skills they needed as workers and citizens, and the family came to be viewed as an inappropriate place for this kind of instruction (Durkheim 1961; Coleman and Hoffer 1987). Children began to spend relatively less time exclusively in their family, neighborhood and close community and correspondingly greater proportions of their developing years in institutions whose purpose was formal instruction. Compulsory attendance laws in the United States mandate schooling until students reach 15 or 16 years of age. In many countries, children whose parents

TABLE 3.1. ENROLLMENT IN EDUCATIONAL INSTITUTIONS BY LEVEL OF INSTRUCTION AND TYPE OF CONTROL, FOR SELECTED SCHOOL YEARS: 1939–83 (FIGURES IN THOUSANDS)

Beginning of school year	Elementary school grades 1–8 and kindergarten			High school grades 9–12		
	Public	*Private*	*Percent private*	*Public*	*Private*	*Percent private*
1939	18,832	2,153	10.3	6,601	457	6.5
1949	19,387	2,708	12.3	5,725	672	10.5
1959	27,602	4,640	14.4	8,485	1,035	10.9
1969	32,597	4,200	11.4	13,022	1,300	9.1
1970	32,577	[1]4,100	11.2	13,332	[1]1,300	8.9
1971	32,265	3,800	10.5	13,816	1,300	8.6
1972	31,836	3,700	10.4	13,906	1,300	8.5
1973	31,353	3,600	10.3	14,076	1,300	8.6
1974	30,921	3,600	10.4	14,132	1,400	9.0
1975	30,487	3,600	10.6	14,304	1,400	8.9
1976	30,006	3,600	10.7	14,310	1,400	8.9
1977	29,336	3,600	10.9	14,240	1,400	8.9
1978	28,455	3,600	11.2	15,156	1,400	9.0
1979*	27,884	3,700	11.7	13,694	1,400	9.3
	(27,349)	(3,541)	(11.5)	(13,994)	(1,122)	(7.4)
1981	27,374	3,582	11.6	13,523	1,119	7.6
1982	27,128	3,585	11.6	13,004	1,118	7.9
1983	26,909	3,650	11.9	12,792	1,218	8.7

*For 1979, the figures in parentheses are from the Current Population Survey.
[1]For 1970 through 1979, the figures for private school enrollment (from NCES) are estimated.
(Source: D. M. O'Neill and P. Sepielli. Education in the United States: 1940–1983 [CDS-85-1]. Washington, D.C.: U.S. Department of Commerce, Bureau of the Census, 1985.)

work often begin "school" in infancy and continue into university, more than twenty years later.

Age Grade Segregation. In schools, young people are concentrated by age groups where they effectively are segregated from contact with all adults but the teachers and other school staff who control and organize their activities.

Compulsory schooling isolates youth in a way which, as Turner suggests, facilitates the development of group solidarity. Youth culture, especially one which is more or less in opposition to that of adults, developed hand in hand with the expansion of compulsory schooling and the concomitant creation of adolescence (Aries 1962). Schools created ample opportunity for the development of idiosyncratic youth-oriented culture by giving students something to do in the long interval between childhood and adulthood. (See Table 3.2.) They also provided a way for society to maintain custody over large groups of people deemed too old to be children and too young for the responsibilities of adulthood.

Separation of Biological from Social Maturity. In contemporary westernized and industrialized societies marriage or pairing off and the ability to support oneself does not coincide with or closely follow puberty. During the gap between biological and social maturity which constitutes adolescence, children are kept in an extended period of liminality, which coincides with a legally enforced emotional and socio-economic dependence. The institutions—like schools—which have arisen to occupy adolescents thus rendered liminal substitute for the ceremonies, taboos and rituals of the traditional society. These institutions serve the same purpose—to protect liminal persons from themselves and society from them.

Protective Custody and Economic Dependence. Part of the custodial function of schools has been to protect adult laborers from the cheaper, and hence "unfair," competition of youthful workers. In the Third World, young urban shoeshine boys, apprentices, "tour guides," beggars and car-watchers, rural shepherds, gardeners and child care providers perform critical economic functions for their families. However, in the industrialized west, young people are denied substantial access to the labor market and often are paid lower wages than adults when they do work. They cannot support themselves well even if they want to. While Groce (1981) states that rural children differ from urban dwellers in that the former must perform many tasks of gardening, animal care and housework, even they usually are not left to fend for themselves. Tradition requires of children in the urban western world few responsibilities for their own and their families' maintenance; upper and middle class children in the urban western world enjoy a prolonged childhood enforced by economic dependence upon their families.

A second aspect to custody involves inhibiting sexual maturity and premature adulthood. Aries (1962) suggests that the prolonged period of immaturity common in western society fostered ideas of childhood as a time of youthful

TABLE 3.2. SCHOOL ENROLLMENT AND RATE, BY AGE: 1970 TO 1985 [IN THOUSANDS, EXCEPT RATE. AS OF OCTOBER. COVERS CIVILIAN NONINSTITUTIONAL PERSONS. BASED ON CURRENT POPULATION SURVEY.]

Age	Population			Enrollment[1]			Rate		
	1970	1980	1985	1970	1980	1985	1970	1980	1985
Total 3 to 34 years old	106,996	115,434	120,000	60,357	57,348	58,013	56.4	49.7	48.3
3 and 4 years old	7,135	6,215	7,192	1,461	2,280	2,801	20.5	36.7	38.9
5 and 6 years old	7,820	6,116	6,967	7,000	5,853	6,697	89.5	95.7	96.1
7 to 13 years old	29,168	23,928	23,024	28,943	23,751	22,849	99.2	99.3	99.2
14 and 15 years old	8,019	7,414	7,505	7,869	7,282	7,362	98.1	98.2	98.1
16 and 17 years old	7,699	8,013	7,260	6,927	7,129	6,654	90.0	89.0	91.7
18 and 19 years old	6,958	8,160	7,204	3,322	3,788	3,716	47.7	46.4	51.6
20 and 21 years old	6,118	8,112	7,679	1,949	2,515	2,708	31.9	31.0	35.3
22 to 24 years old	9,476	11,858	12,239	1,410	1,931	2,068	14.9	16.3	16.9
25 to 29 years old	13,415	18,487	21,046	1,011	1,714	1,942	7.5	9.3	9.2
30 to 34 years old	11,188	17,131	19,885	466	1,105	1,218	4.2	6.4	6.1
35 years old and over	82,950	93,118	103,458	(NA)	1,293	1,766	(X)	1.4	1.7

*NA Not available.   X Not applicable.   [1] Enrollment in nursery school and above.

(Source: U.S. Bureau of the Census, Current Population Reports, series P–20, No. 404 and earlier reports; and unpublished data.)

innocence, a period when children should be protected and given time for play and irresponsibility. It is associated with the romanticized or idealized Victorian notion that children are sexually naive, gentle and nonviolent, that parents should perserve their innocence, chaperone and supervise their passage through adolescence, and prohibit them from entering into early marriage. In western societies, children spend this stage of their lives segregated together in schools and the military, where they acquire a protective veneer of intellectual, social and vocational skills in preparation for the work force. Protective custody reinforces prohibitions against early marriage, parenthood, and exploitation in the work force, activities which are considered appropriate in traditional societies, but an impediment to one's chances for economic well-being in modern western societies.

In the first half of the twentieth century, graduation from high school came to be regarded as a significant rite of passage, symbolizing achievement of adulthood in modern society. However, this is changing, as we shall see. Global demographic and economic shifts have increased the number of young people who have had to find ways to feed, clothe and house themselves. Increasing poverty has transformed many children into *de facto* adults. Decreasing economic opportunity and a glut of diplomas has substantially weakened the impact of high school graduation.

YOUTH CULTURE AND MODERN LIFE

Growing up has become more complex for several reasons. As we have discussed, it is harder to know when one has achieved being adult. Second, there are many obstacles along the way. Third, even though it takes longer and involves more training, being an adult may not appear to signify rewards commensurate with the effort. In the following pages, we shall discuss how children have responded.

Material Culture

Patterns of Consumption. Children growing up in America, most of the western world, and in the urbanized portions of the nonWestern world grow up in a world in which the monetary value of commodities is paramount. Children have become prime targets of advertising. They are a market for fashionable clothes, up-to-date cars, electronic toys, and other consumer goods. The global village has spawned global patterns of consumption for children; kids in Tokyo, Lagos and Los Angeles look remarkably alike. Sometimes these patterns, or fads, are adopted specifically because they represent a collective departure from the ways of parents. When fads go to school in the form of behavior deemed antisocial or antischool, they often constitute visible manifestations of an oppositional culture.

Youth Employment. While children under the age of 18 in the United States still are legally and economically regarded as minors, their relationship to the

work world has changed. Most students, from junior high school through graduate school, are employed. Prior to 1970, being a full-time student from the
middle classes seldom meant combining school with substantial committments to
the work force. Working and lower class students often did, and still may have
to work to help support their families during their teenage years. However,
many students, often those from middle and upper class families, now become
parents while still in school, and must get jobs to support their own children.
Still other more affluent students now work not so much to help themselves or
their families survive or to save for college, but in order to live more luxuri-
ously, providing themselves with clothes, cars and consumer goods their parents
are unwilling or unable to provide (McNeil 1983; Powell, Farrar and Cohen
1985). Regardless of their reason for working, more than 70 percent of all 16-
year-olds who are in school now work, and they are spending much more time
on the job. In 1970, 56 percent of the employed in-school male high school
students worked more than 14 hours per week (Steinberg et al. 1982, p. 363).
This has had a profound effect upon the centrality of school in their lives;
students now devote to working, time they used to spend on homework and
extra-curricular activities (Powell et al. 1985).

Jobs may provide an alternative source of self-esteem and gratification for
students who do not do well academically, or who cannot excel in athletics,
school government, clubs and other activities of the school controlled extra-
curriculum. Perhaps because of this, some studies have indicated that working a
few hours a week may enhance a student's performance. However, for the
majority, jobs tend to interfere with school, especially when the immediate
financial gratification of wages and what they will purchase supercedes the
deferred gratification promised for successful performance in school.

While the jobs students hold are not usually full-time ones, they may
consume as many as 30 hours a week, often in the evening hours. Despite the
fact that many students do not devote long hours to homework, and many more
cannot, even if they wanted to, schools still are structured as if students were
able to devote all of their time to school-related activities. Teachers are faced
with students who have little time out of class to read books, do projects, or
work math problems; who fall asleep in class because they worked late at their
jobs the night before, and who refuse to let school work interfere with their
jobs. In response, teachers reduce the number and complexity of assignments,
lower their aspirations for students, and teach less (McNeil 1983, 1988; Powell,
Farrar, and Cohen 1985).

Technology. Technological factors differ somewhat from other cultural factors in
that they have habituated children to patterns of interaction, transmission of
information, and communication radically different from those once common in
schools. This has forced teachers and curriculum developers to change their
expectations of how and what children will learn.

While television, video games, the telephone, calculators and computers,
portable radios and audio equipment are, indeed, cultural artifacts, their impact
is more complex and powerful than the mere fact that some people have them

and others do not. In fact, their presence has altered irrevocably patterns of human interaction and communication, and perhaps even patterns of perception and cognition. In the first place, use of these artifacts absorb a great deal—in some cases, the vast majority—of the leisure time of young people. The teenager on the telephone, the urban adolescents with "ghetto-blasters" or miniature tape recorders perpetually glued to their ears, the toddlers who view the television set as their primary caretaker; the adolescents who cannot do homework without the television or radio blaring—all are stereotypes which have developed because they represent reality for a very large percentage of children. The impact of these technological innovations is profound, controversial, and still being studied, but we wish to mention a few of the results of the impact.

First, these innovations eliminate face-to-face interaction. Telephone conversations lose the immediacy of visual, tactile, and olfactory contact with communicants. Answering machines leave messages for someone who isn't even present. In the classroom, computers and interactive video sometimes substitute for direct instruction by teachers, leaving children to work in isolation, each with his or her own keyboard.

Second, technological devices like calculators and videogames shorten the period of attention needed to solve problems. Third, they have most commonly and widely been adapted for the simplest of cognitive tasks. Instead of enhancing more complex cognitive skills, computer assisted instruction most often is used for drills—simple memorization and recall. Simplifying knowledge to the presentation of single datum "factoids" and presenting them in the form of "sound bites" has penetrated many other aspects of life—entertainment, the media, and even religion. As a consequence, educators are left to assume that they must accommodate instruction to limited attention spans and simple solutions. No message or lesson can be longer or more complex than is considered manageable and appropriate for the assumed attention span of a mesmerized child.

Economics and Demography

Size and Urbanization. Because they must deal with people and distance on a scale far larger than any other generation, today's children face a paradox. As the external world becomes more familiar and intimate, their immediate surroundings become larger and more impersonal. On one hand, they live in a shrinking world where areas once remote and inaccessible now can be viewed nightly on television and visited by tourists. On the other, urbanization has made the once familiar strange. Most people now live in urban areas. Even the ostensibly bucolic suburbs have become urbanized. Children live in apartment complexes and high rises, not houses; their families are renters rather than owners as the cost of home-owning prices most families out of the market (Cohen and Rogers 1983; Reeves 1988). Especially as the supply of moderately priced rental housing decreases, many are faced with the spector of homelessness (Joint Center for Housing Studies 1988). The situation is so serious that, in the late 1980s, the majority of homeless are families with children, and the prototypical homeless person in New York City in early 1988 was a four-year-old boy.

Adventure has become too perilous to be challenging; international travel is too familiar to be an adventure; adventure closer to home is too dangerous to be permitted. Parks are dangerous and there are few fields or open spaces where children can run and explore unsupervised. The attendance zones of schools are so large that walking to school is impossible. Friends from school may live so far away that they can only be visited with great difficulty. As a consequence, children either see only those children in their apartment complex or immediate neighborhood, or spend a lot of time driving or being driven to activities and the homes of friends. Young people may be quite familiar with the customs of people on the other side of the globe but not know anybody on their block or corridor. In the inner city, children may be even more isolated. There, in the housing projects, shelters for the homeless or the blighted neighborhoods where many urban children live, a visit to friends next door or even down the hall may lead to an encounter with drug-related violence.

Children may find it difficult to participate in any school-related activities before or after school, since most live far from school and must come and go according to the whims of a parent's schedule, the timing of the bus route, or the car-pool. This further reduces the capacity of the school to be of central importance in their lives and leaves children subject to the same social isolation afflicting contemporary urban adults. Under these conditions, the peer group develops its attitudes and behaviors even less influenced by parents and teachers; the primary influence becomes street life and the media.

Poverty. As school loses its centrality, family structure also has changed so that it is less able to provide support and guidance. The increase in divorce and single-parenthood means that the *normal childhood experience* will become life with one parent. The majority of children—59 percent of all children born in 1983, for example (O'Neill and Sepielli 1985, p. 3)—at some time in their lives, will live in single-parent homes (Brown 1986). The percentage is even greater among many minority groups; 90 percent of all black teenaged mothers are unmarried.

More children than ever also are growing up in families that are very poor. In 1987, 25 percent of all children under the age of six lived in families below the poverty line; one in six had no health insurance coverage, and fewer and fewer were receiving public assistance or food stamps (Children's Defense Fund 1988). Although at least three million children were eligible in 1985 for Head Start, funds were available to enroll only 400,000 (Hodgkinson 1985). The rising incidence of divorce and unwed childbirth aggravates the number of children living below the poverty line because female headed homes are more likely to be poor. Of all the children living in poverty in 1985, fifty percent lived in female headed homes, but only 12 percent in homes where a male was present. The situation is worse for minorities; forty percent of all minority children live in impoverished homes, and the situation is far worse in those headed by a female (O'Neill and Sepielli 1985).

Family Structure. Even children in intact and "blended" nuclear families cannot rely upon the presence of a homebound parent, because most homes with children require two incomes to maintain themselves. What this means is that children are caught between the expectations of schools and the reality of their family life. Schools still operate as if most children have two parents, one of whom is a full-time parent available for helping with homework, parental consulations with teachers, making cookies for the homeroom, and other school-related tasks. However, 51.9 percent of the mothers of children one year old and younger are in the workforce (Collins 1987). Up to 33 percent—over four million—of all elementary school children are "latch-key" children (O'Neill and Sepielli 1985) who take care of themselves after school, get help with homework from a telephone hotline if available, and cope with overworked parents in the evening. They are expected to be emotionally mature and to demonstrate adultlike independence even in pre-school, because their parents have few economic or emotional reserves left after the pressures of daily survival (Woodhouse 1987).

Children are also deluged with invitations to engage in illegal activities, use drugs and alcohol and to become sexually active. They find it easy to do as drugs permeate all echelons of society. Children see drug related behavior where they work, on the streets, in their schools, and among their family members, and their parents often are too busy working to supervise them during their leisure time.

The Labor Market. Regardless of where they live, the economic context of growing up for most young people in the latter part of the twentieth century is one of frustrated aspirations and limited expectations. As the lower paying service sector of the labor market grows, opportunities for more lucrative professional positions shrink. Consequently, room at the top of the economic ladder is increasingly less available (Bluestone and Harrison 1982). Young people must reduce their aspirations in accordance with the reality of the more humdrum, less lucrative jobs which remain available (Littwin 1987). Status competition for more desirable professional positions is keen, and feeds both a ferocious battle for those willing to join the fray, and hopelessness among those who deem the costs of competing to be too high. It also feeds racism and bigotry, as members of the dominant white culture feel themselves to be unfairly disadvantaged by affirmative action programs which assist some members of minority groups. The lower income white young men whom McLeod (1987) studied typify these feelings:

> SHORTY: "He got laid off because they hired all Puerto Ricans, blacks and Portegis (Portuguese)"

> SMITTY: "All the fuckin' niggers are getting the jobs. Two of them
> motherfuckers got hired yesterday [at a construction site]; I didn't
> get shit. They probably don't even know how to hold a fuckin'
> shovel, either".
>
> FRANKIE: "Fuckin' right. That's why we're hanging here now with
> empty pockets . . . . hey, they're coming on our fucking land
> . . . They don't like us, man, and I sure as hell don't like
> them".
>
> SHORTY: " . . . *Listen*. When they first moved in here [into the housing
> project], they were really cool and everything. We didn't bother
> them. But once more and more black families moved in, they
> said, 'Wow, we can overrun these people. We can overpower
> them.' That's what their attitude was." (pp. 39–40)

Violence, Environmental Degredation and Potential Annihilation. Children
have immediate personal and global survival on their minds as well. James
Gleick has suggested that

> the explosion of the first atomic bomb stands . . . as the central moment in
> the history of our time, the threshold event of an age . . . Its prelude was [a
> belief in] an irreversible mastery of science over nature; its sequel was
> violence and death on a horrible scale. (1989, p. 1)

Growing up in the shadow of atomic, chemical, and biological war clouds,
children wonder how growing up can be considered a viable proposition. The
whole world might be blown up before they have any say in the matter whatsoever. They know that the activism in the 1960s neither solved the social and
economic problems against which young people protested, nor caused a revolution. In addition to the interpersonal violence they witness daily in the media,
children see themselves or people they know being abused by parents. Their
own parents abuse each other. Students in their schools use drugs and carry
guns and knives; children worry about how to get through the school hallways
or back home after school safely.

These conditions spawn apathy and egocentrism among young people. All
of these conditions have made growing up in the past few decades a far more
difficult process, one which requires young people to set out upon virtually
uncharted waters. One response has been to simply avoid growing up for as
long as possible.

THE POSTPONED GENERATION

Joan Littwin (1987) suggests that middle class young people in America have
responded to the factors enumerated above by postponing adulthood. We feel
that her phrase, the "postponed generation," fits more than just middle class
youth.

Being grown-up in western culture means economic self-sufficiency rather than biological maturity; self-sufficiency means the ability to pay for one's own home, to support oneself, to acquire and support a family. Until the late 1960s, it more or less corresponded with completion of high school or military service—somewhere between 18 and 22 years. At this point, individuals were old enough to work full-time and most could make a decent living. Increments of success were predicated upon obtaining skills not widely held by others, or which were in demand. Schooling gave a competitive edge, whether or not it corresponded to increments of skill, because years of schooling, in our society, served as a proxy for ability. Unfortunately, this is no longer always the case.

Inflation of Educational Credentials

As more and more people possessed the basic complement of schooling, how-ever, the increment needed to stand out and be competitive increased. As more and more people need more and more education to compete for jobs, a real labor market dilemma arises: people are over-educated for the work they do; the levels of schooling required to obtain many jobs are higher than the skill levels needed to do the work. Littwin (1987) calls this a "job gap," or the degree to which individuals must work at jobs which are below the level they expected to acquire, given their education and training. The job gap forces poorly educated or less skilled individuals out of the job slots to which they reasonably aspired because of competition by more highly educated people who also have had to revise their job expectations downward. Especially for graduates in the liberal arts, social sciences, and humanities—fields which historically held the most promise for creative individuals—interesting and desirable white collar jobs are becoming increasingly scarce.

The job gap is aggravated by two factors. First, "our economy is very good at generating new jobs—but most of them are low-paying service jobs which require little education" (Hodgkinson 1985, p. 8). Since the number of young people who have done well in school exceeds the supply of entry-level jobs which fit their qualifications, many of the most talented of young people must wait a long time to get a job at all, let alone one in or near their chosen field (Borman 1987; Littwin 1987). In 1983, one out of every five college graduates worked in jobs which required no college education at all (O'Neill and Sepielli 1985).

The second factor exacerbating the job gap is current population trends (see Figure 3.1). High birth rates between 1946 and 1964 produced the generation known as the "Baby Boomers." These individuals now are in their prime working years; their presence in the labor market increases the number of individuals competing for the best jobs.

All of these factors prolong adolescence, or at least the period of time young people must wait before they can begin what they thought was to be their life work. They also must adjust to the reality of a lower standard of living than they expected, one perhaps lower than that of their parents, not only because the initial jobs at which they must work earn a low rate of pay, but also because the jobs they ultimately get are less prestigious and lucrative than their aspirations indicated.

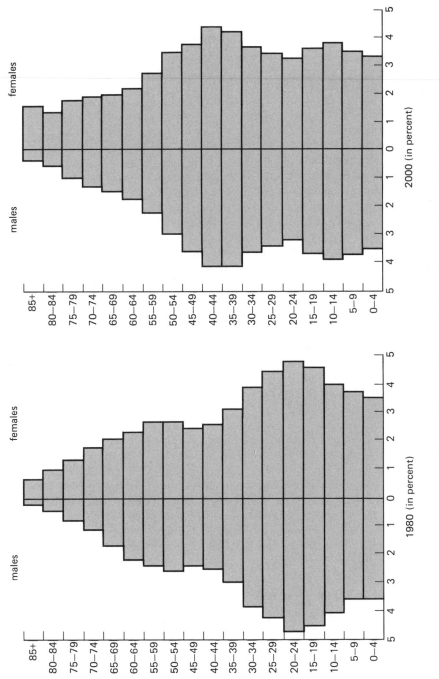

Figure 3.1. The Baby Boom Ages (H.L. Hodgkinson. *All One System: Demographics of Education, Kindergarten through Graduate School.* Washington, D.C.: Institute for Educational Leadership, 1985.)

Postponed Maturation. The consequence is a "postponed generation." Its members start to grow up later than previous generations, and the process of attaining economic independence takes longer. They may spend several years moving from one low-paying entry level job to another (Borman 1987). They often are unemployable for long periods of time and have difficulty in making a commitment to work which does not coincide with their aspirations. Both academically successful students and those who were less successful and had lower aspirations to begin with suffer similar feelings of *ennui*, or bordeom, because they find it difficult to find gainful employment and to settle into family life.

Many also are unrealistic about what it takes to get and hold a job. Fine suggests that this is because the schools do not provide them with information unless it is legally mandated to do so. As a consequence, students do not learn what it takes to get into college, the military, or pass the GED. Fine's respondents, all dropouts, believed that "the GED is no sweat, a piece of cake" . . . "you can get jobs, they promise, after goin' to Sutton or ABI" [trade schools and business colleges, most of which currently have dropout rates of close to 70 percent (Fine 1986; Berger, 1989). . . . "in the Army I can get me a GED, skills, travel, benefits . . . " (Fine 1987, pp. 169–170). Hess (1988), Powell et al. (1985), and others suggest that this situation is not unique to dropouts. An example:

> [To become a pediatrician] you have to go to community college for two years. Then you go to medical school for four years. After that you are an intern for two years. Then you are a regular nurse for two years. Then you do a residency, and after that you can be a doctor and start at $65,000 a year. (Firestone and Rosenblum 1988, p. 291)

Only the most motivated of students obtain realistic and adequate advice from school personnel (Cicourel and Kitsuse 1963; Sarason 1971; Powell et al. 1985).

A small decline in the job cohort in the 1990s may alleviate the situation somewhat; however, there is evidence that although the Baby Boomers postponed childbirth for a while, their children will now create another population bulge. In addition, changes in the population will not affect decline in professional level jobs. The consequence for youth is that most will end up hitting a job ceiling at least for a while, and all will cope with extended periods of liminality.

Postponed Minority Youth. Most middle class children eventually get back on track. However old they may be, they have a "safety net" of family connections and cultural knowledge which eventually helps most to work the system. Tobier (1984, quoted in Fine 1987) states that white high school dropouts living in affluent sections of New York are far more likely than black high school graduates from Harlem to be employed. (See Table 3.3.) Thus, the consequences of postponement for minority or disadvantaged youth are far more severe; they may never even get started. Minority youth often find themselves out of school lacking the diploma or the skills necessary to get a job.

TABLE 3.3. CIVILIAN LABOR FORCE—EMPLOYMENT STATUS, BY SEX, RACE, AND AGE: 1985 [FOR CIVILIAN NONINSTITUTIONAL POPULATION 16 YEARS OLD AND OVER. ANNUAL AVERAGES OF MONTHLY FIGURES. BASED ON CURRENT POPULATION SURVEY.]

Age and Race	Civilian Labor Force			Male (1,000)			Female (1,000)			Percent Of Labor Force			
	Total (1,000)	Percent by age		Total	Em- ployed	Unem- ployed	Total	Em- ployed	Unem- ployed	Employed		Unemployed	
		Male	Female							Male	Female	Male	Female
All workers[1]	115,461	100.0	100.0	64,411	59,891	4,521	51,050	47,259	3,791	93.0	92.6	7.0	7.4
16–19 yr	7,901	6.4	7.4	4,134	3,328	806	3,767	3,105	661	80.5	82.4	19.5	17.5
20–24 yr	15,718	12.9	14.6	8,283	7,339	944	7,434	6,640	794	88.6	89.3	11.4	10.7
25–34 yr	33,550	29.2	28.9	18,808	17,564	1,244	14,742	13,644	1,098	93.4	92.6	6.6	7.4
White	99,926	100.0	100.0	56,472	53,046	3,426	43,455	40,690	2,765	93.9	93.6	6.1	6.4
16–19 yr	6,841	6.3	7.5	3,576	2,985	592	3,265	2,783	482	83.5	85.2	16.6	14.8
20–24 yr	13,469	12.6	14.6	7,122	6,428	694	6,348	5,807	541	90.3	91.5	9.7	8.5
25–34 yr	28,640	28.9	28.4	16,306	15,374	931	12,334	11,571	763	94.3	93.8	5.7	6.2
Black	12,364	100.0	100.0	6,220	5,270	951	6,144	5,231	913	84.7	85.1	15.3	14.9
16–19 yr	889	7.6	6.8	471	278	193	417	254	164	59.0	60.9	41.0	39.2
20–24 yr	1,854	15.3	14.7	950	726	224	904	673	231	76.4	74.4	23.6	25.6
25–34 yr	3,888	31.1	31.8	1,937	1,669	268	1,951	1,656	295	86.2	84.9	13.8	15.1

[1]Includes other races not shown separately.

(*Source: U.S. Bureau of Labor Statistics, Employment and Earnings, monthly.*)

Even those who do graduate and are literate often find that no jobs exist in their community (Wilson 1987). Minority youth in the inner city suffer from a flight of industry to the beltways and suburbs outside the city. Transportation networks often do not make it possible to travel easily to new work places, even if they were willing to hire poorly trained adolescents. Some girls from minority groups can become mothers, which is a culturally acceptable alternative, but boys find themselves in a particularly desperate situation. In a society which values gainful employment above all other means of demonstrating self-worth, they find no jobs and nothing else to do, except drink, use drugs, and often to die before the age of thirty, in ill-disguised forms of suicide like substance abuse, fights, or motor vehicle accidents (see, for example, Conant 1988).

When they can find them, young minority men drift from one deadend job to another. They often are unable to support themselves or a family except through illicit means—robbery, pimping for prostitutes, and the drug trade. These activities can land them in prison, if not in a morgue, before the age of thirty (Mclaren 1989). The situation is worse on Indian reservations and in rural areas, especially those areas where subsistence has been the traditional mode of life (Conant 1988; Deyhle 1988). These areas have no agricultural or industrial base and little hope for building one outside of the tourist industry, and most young people do not wish to follow traditional subsistence practices.

While many middle class youth postpone growing up by hanging out at home and working at make-do jobs they see as temporary; poor, working class, and minority youth may feel that they have no opportunity to grow up. Bennett's work in rural Alaska indicates that young Yu´pik Eskimo men continue their peripheral involvement in school, hanging around the school yard playing basketball because the only opportunity in their community that can give them something to do and a source of self-esteem is being a local basketball star. Fine documents how minority youth know that "there ain't no jobs waitin' for me" (1986, p. 399). They pass their time hanging around street corners or other gathering places, talking, smoking, and drinking until they find some sort of work or get arrested (Marotto 1986). The hopelessness of their situation is illustrated by McLeod's description of reactions by the "Hallway Hangers" to a question about what they would be doing in twenty years:

STONEY: ". . . I could be dead tomorrow. Around here, you gotta take life day by day . . . " (p. 61)

FRANKIE: ". . . I live a day at a time. I'll probably be in the fucking pen . . . I can work with my brother, but that's under the table. Besides, he's in [state prison] now". (Ibid.)

SLICK: "Most of the kids around here, they're not gonna be more than janitors . . . I'd say the success rate of this place is, of these people . . . about twenty percent, maybe fifteen". (p. 68)

JINKS: "I think most of them, when and if a war comes, they're all gone. Everyone's going. But for jobs—odds and ends jobs. Here and there. No good high-class jobs". (Ibid.)

The problem is that even those young men who try to join the military as a last resort often find that they cannot qualify. Theirs is a youth culture of hopelessness:

> FRANKIE: "We were all brought up, all we seen is our older brothers and that gettin' into trouble and goin' to jail and all that shit. Y'know, seeing people—brothers and friends . . . dying right in front of your face. You seen all the drugs . . . We grew up, it was all our older brothers doing this . . . the drugs, all the drinking. They fucking go; that group's gone. The next group came, our brothers that are twenty-something years old. They started doing crime. And when you're young, you look up to people . . . And he's doing this, he's drinking, doing drugs, ripping off people. Y'know, he's making good fucking money; it looks like he's doing good. So bang. Now it's our turn. What we gonna do when all we seen is fuckin' drugs, alcohol, fighting, this and that, no one going to school?" (McLeod 1987, pp. 117–118)

What becomes clear is that the system is less and less responsive to the varied and sometimes desparate needs of young people. It also has room only for a few people from disadvantaged families. The remaining disadvantaged young people are pushed systematically out of schools which promise a good job in return for solid effort. For them, equality of opportunity is a myth. The system operates to reinforce and widen the gap between rich and poor. Most, like Fine's dropouts, internalize the reasons given by the dominant culture for their failure. The system and its values is legitimate; the failure their own.

THE LESSONS OF SCHOOLING

Going to school represents a sharp break from being at home. First, going to school introduces a new role: children become students—one of the first insitutional roles they acquire. Second, schools are structured differently (Durkheim 1961; Dreeben 1968). Functional theorists have suggested that families and schools are structured differently because they have different purposes and represent different values. They believe that the discontinuity schools create between the past and present experience of children is both necessary and proper. They base their argument on the differentiation of function which modernization brings to social institutions.

In complex industrialized societies, no one institution such as the family can hope to impart all of the skills children need for adult life. Therefore, a division of labor evolves whereby the tasks of socializing the young can be divided. Each institution in which young people participate carries out the task for which its structure is most uniquely appropriate. The family, which is smaller, more intimate, and idiosyncratic, is responsible for the development of individual personality, close relationships, and specific moral values. The larger, more impersonal, diverse and universalistic school is responsible for technical training, including cognitive skills, and preparing children to be responsible citizens and workers. Coleman and Hoffer (1987) summarize the functional position, arguing that schools explicitly were an

> instrument that alienated the child from the family, an instrument that bene-fited the child by bringing it into the mainstream of American society, but at a cost to the continuity and strength of the family. The cost was not great when a school served [an ethnically and religiously homogenous] local com-munity, for then the culture of the local community pervaded the school and made it consistent with the functional community of adults whose children it served. The cost was great, however, for cultural minorities in [heterogenous communities]. (p. 140)

Critical theorists do not argue that there are differences between school and family life, but they believe what schools actually do is mobilize and prepare a work force stratified by class, race and gender, maintain the existing power structure, and reproduce the system of social classes in society. They do not train citizens to govern themselves and work in a meritocratic, egalitarian soci-ety. As one dropout put it:

> In school we learned Columbus Avenue stuff and *I* had to translate it into Harlem. They think livin' up here is unsafe and our lives are so bad. That we should want to move out and get away. That's what you're supposed to learn. (Fine 1987, p. 164)

In the pages which follow, we discuss the structural and organizational differences between school and family and indicate how they help to prepare the ground for development of youth culture and its opposition to adult forms of life. We also describe how children resist the power of teachers and school staff, as well as how educators have created institutions within the school to coopt their oppositional behavior. We begin with a discussion of what children encoun-ter when they first go to elementary school and what it teaches them. Many scholars refer to this as the "hidden curriculum" (Jackson 1968), or the "tacit teaching to students of norms, values and dispositions that goes on simply by their living in and coping with the institutional expectations and routines of schools, day in and day out for a number of years" (Apple 1979, p. 14). We then move to an analysis of high schools and their relationship to students.

Becoming a Student: Elementary School

Schools are not organized to coincide with the natural impulses of children, and they seldom involve a child's most favorite activities. Because we are so famil-iar with them, we tend to forget that the way schools are organized is not inevitable, but has evolved under the impact of social and political pressures. In Chapter Nine, we describe alternative models for organizing schools.

We also forget that children are conscripts. While staff are voluntarily recruited because of their skills and professional credentials, children are recruited involuntarily because of their age status as minors (Nadel 1957; Bidwell 1965). Nowhere else is such a large group of noncriminal individuals forced to remain in an institution for so long, a fact which makes the attitudes which children possess about the ways they participate diverge markedly from that of adults.

Crowds and Noise. The organization of schools is very different from that of the family. In the first place, schools are much bigger. Most people remember going back to their elementary school and being shocked to discover how small it really was. But to children, the school building, no matter how tiny, still is much larger than their house or apartment. Physical size is not the only difference. There also are many more people, and they are apportioned differently. Where a family in western society usually contains no more than between 3 and 7 members, classrooms usually contain at least 28–30. The adult-to-child ratio changes as well; there usually is at least one adult for every 2 or 3 children in a family, but in the classroom, the ratio is closer to 30:1. This means that children in school receive significantly less adult attention than is possible in the family (Dreeben 1968). In fact, schools are crowded noisy places where adults are badly outnumbered by children (Jackson 1968).

Coping With Diversity. Schools also are marked by considerably more heterogeneity than families. Families usually are relatively homogenous; most parents belong to the same racial, socioeconomic and religious group. However, in schools, children begin to learn about people who are quite different from themselves. Elementary schools, which are tied to neighborhoods, usually are more homogenous with regard to the student clientele than are junior and senior high schools, but as children grow older, they find that the schools they attend bring them into contact with more and more challenging social situations (Dreeben 1968). Homogeneity is becoming less and less possible in public schools as minority populations grow in the western world. Desegregation programs also have made inroads into patterns of educational and residential racial segregation.

However, even where the students form a homogenous group, teachers and their students may have very little in common, ethnically, socially, or economically. They probably do not even live anywhere near each other, and may be totally unfamiliar with the lives each leads outside of the classroom.

Losing Individuality. While most people remember the size differential, they probably do not remember how it felt to lose the sense of demographic uniqueness that the family provides. Unless they contain adopted children, twins or triplets, families seldom contain more than one child of each age and sex. Treatment of individual children within the family is predicated upon these age and sex categories; behavior is deemed appropriate or inappropriate based upon whether one is old enough to carry out an activity, young enough to justify specific actions, and of the correct gender to participate.

Labels and Categories. In school, however, children learn to be treated as members of social categories. First is age; children initially are grouped in school exclusively by their birth date. When the children arrive, they discover that there are many boys and girls of the same age, all of whom are in the same boat. While physical attractiveness and general deportment do affect the reactions of teachers to individual children, fewer allowances based upon their special characteristics are made than in the family, and all are expected to conform to rather standardized patterns of acceptable behavior. In fact, it is treatment and grouping upon the basis of similarity of category, rather than upon individual differences, that constitutes one of the hallmarks of life in school.

Separating Roles from Persons. School is the place that children begin to learn the difference between parents and all other adults as well as to distinguish between social roles and the people who occupy them. They learn, for example, that the social role—its expectations and obligations—of teachers remains constant from year to year, even if the occupants change. They also learn that their teachers do not respond as their parents do, and that the staff are not present to nurture their individual idiosyncracies. Instead, they have jobs, which are to control them and to impart knowledge (Dreeben 1968). In fact, some researchers suggest that the differences between students and staff eventually diverge into "fighting groups" whose interests in school and goals for life in them differ widely (Waller 1932; Connell 1985).

Learning to Achieve

The second measure by which children are categorized is achievement. It is almost as powerful an influence on development as age, sex, and race (Dreeben 1968). One's relationship to this category begins to be constructed before the child's arrival at the schoolhouse door. It remains, almost immutable, until school life ends, structuring the school experience and, to a large extent, determining one's future occupational status. Children usually arrive at school having taken "readiness" tests or with records of pre-school teachers and daycare workers. On the basis of these, but sometimes with the addition of tests and evaluations made by their classroom teacher, the children are grouped or stratified for instruction based upon their perceived ability to learn. The word "perceived" is an important one, because how able a child is often is subjectively defined, and may have less to do with native intelligence than with way children behave, what their ethnicity and social class background is, and how much affinity the teacher feels with them (Rist 1970, 1973; Rosenfeld 1971; Ortiz 1988).

However they happen to be placed into ability groups, children find that they are "tracked", "streamed" or "grouped" from the day they enter school. These groups are obvious to children, despite heroic efforts of teachers to disguise them. Tracks or ability groups engender characteristic patterns of behavior and belief in children, and they play an important role in defining for students the kind of individual they believe themselves to be. An insidious characteristic of ability groups is that they construct failure. No matter how high the achievement of the lowest group is, children in it feel like "dummies" "retards" or "basics." Page (1988) for example, studied a "dream high school," where none of the students really were disadvantaged. Yet even in this setting, the lowest students—who might well have been the most advanced pupils in an inner city school—thought of themselves as "dregs" and a "circus," adopting the antischool, rebellious attitudes usually attributed to lower and working class students.

Ability groups are critical in the formation of student peer groups because ability groups determine friendship groups. Study after study shows that friendship groups form almost exclusively within the groups with which one studies and learns, and with which one shares a common academic track record (Gordon 1957; Coleman 1961; 1965; Borko and Eisenhart 1986; Bennett 1986; Gamoran and Berends 1987). Students in the academic groups also tend to be the most popular students (Gamoran and Berends 1987, p. 427).

Evaluation and Gratification. Schools and families also differ in the relative emphasis they place on different modes of evaluation (Dreeben 1968). Whereas families evaluate children on the basis of what they are as individual personalities, schools evaluate children primarily on the basis of how well they achieve in their school work. The way impulse gratification is handled also differs. While parents are warned to recognize that young people are oriented to rewards in the immediate present, and not to promise rewards which cannot be given, or which must be delayed, schools operate on the premise of deferred gratification. Teachers encourage children to believe that hard work now will receive tangible rewards in the future; grades only symbolically represent the material rewards to which success in school eventually will lead. This is, of course, not particularly congenial to teenagers, for whom the future is far away indeed.

Cognitive knowledge is not the only kind of knowledge children acquire in school. In elementary schools, children learn about the separation of student and teacher roles and something about appropriate sex-role behavior (Goetz 1981). They have internalized the rules of the organization and constructed their own definition not only of how to survive, but of how well they can be expected to do. They have some idea of the degree to which their efforts will pay off in terms of grades, and they may have learned how to "make deals" with teachers as to how much they will be taught (Powell et al. 1985; Borko and Eisenhart 1986). Most of them have acquired some rudiments of the cognitive skills, and they have fairly well formed personalities and sets of social relationships. By the time they reach high school, they are interested in other matters.

Becoming Pre-Adult: High School

The Opposite Sex. In high school, students become deeply interested in working out their own gender identity and relationships with the opposite sex. Especially for girls, sex complicates the development of attitudes and aspirations about work, careers, and their future. Weis (1988) and Holland and Eisenhart (1988b) studied the "ideology of romance" (McRobbie 1978) which suffuses the lives of young women. Although Holland and Eisenhart (1988b) studied college students, we feel that their analysis also applies to students in high school, who are only a year or two younger. Holland and Eisenhart stress the importance of the "world of peers" in the determining gender identity. Students

> spend most of their time around age mates, are constantly exposed to peer-organized activities, learn age-mates' interpretations and evaluations of all aspects of . . . life . . . have most of their close, intimate relationships with age mates on campus, and learn ways to understand and evaluate themselves from those peers . . . (pp. 17–18)

Holland and Eisenhart (1988b) suggest that the peer culture competes with schoolwork, derails some students, and affects even those who don't participate in it directly. This is because it provides a system or cultural context with which students must cope. Whether they are identified as punks and badasses, greasers or jocks, preppies, nerds or dropouts, young people cannot totally dismiss what the other kids say and feel about them, no matter how far they might try to distance themselves.

Getting Ahead. Adolescents recognize that there are many kinds of achievement. One is oriented around success in personal, social, or familial arenas. Another involves demonstrated athletic prowess. A third derives from the status which conspicuous consumption bestows; the guy with the fancy clothes, expensive watch and brand-new car smells of success, regardless of how the means were gained. A fourth, and the only one which schools are designed to facilitate, is organized around success in academic and professional arenas.

Children go to elementary school to learn cognitive skills of reading, writing, and computation, and to high school to acquire both the knowledge base and the social skills and values which will fit them for various roles in the occupational structure. Their success is measured in terms of how well they do in these tasks, as measured by grades, teacher assessments, and standardized test scores.

Adolescents, however, know that success in school is different from getting good grades, because the criteria for success are more diffuse and complex. Two classic studies (Gordon 1957; Coleman 1961) demonstrated that grade point averages are of little importance; in high school, extra-curricular position or one's place in the juvenile social status system supercedes attention to academic endeavors. For boys, the primary criterion was athletic prowess, followed by conformity to norms regarding in-school behavior, dating, dress, and recreation. For girls, the highest positions went to the prom and yearbook queens; such status was gained by means of adhering to particular patterns of dress, service to the school, having a "good" personality and being friendly, being a leader in activities, and maintaining Puritan standards of morality. While the students in these studies were primarily from the white middle class, we feel that the dynamics today are similar for minorities and the underclass as well. Grades still are relatively unimportant, and while yesterday's teen wore bobby-sox and pleated skirts, and today's might "punk up" their hair, adherence to the prevailing "dress code" and standards for social behavior and recreation make all the difference in the status hierarchy.

Thus, high grades alone are not sufficient to ensure a successful career in school, even from the perspective of teachers, just as low grades will not always preclude students from feeling good about their life in school, being envied by their peers, and being defined as "successful" students. Students consider social, personal, and familial achievement to be as important, if not more important, than academic achievement; they also want very much to be accepted by their friends. This means adopting the same youth cultural values that their friends have; if their friends do not value academic achievement, neither will they.

In point of fact, many can see little, if any, immediate or future benefit from the boring studies they slog through (Sizer 1984; Powell, Farrar, and Cohen 1985; McLaren 1980; McLeod 1987). Young people want to be in school, but less to study than because their friends are there. All they can do outside of school during the day is read, watch television, hang around the streetcorners and shopping malls, and generally get into trouble. If their friends are antischool, they may drop out, especially if they feel that conformity to school will alienate them from their peers. This is especially problematic for successful members of minority groups who are pressured to view conformity to school as selling out or "acting white" (Fordham and Ogbu, 1986):

> People are afraid to show that they can speak grammatically correct English. When I do, my friends in my neighborhood will say, "you nerd!" or "Talk English! Talk to us like we talk to you."
>
> I've been *per se* called an oreo because black as I am and bright, everybody thinks I'm too proper and talk white . . . and people tend to *tease* me. (Fordham and Ogbu, quoted in Erickson, 1987)

Alienation from school is exacerbated when students respect very few of their teachers, either because they feel that teachers don't like or respect them, or that the teachers are incompetent to teach their subjects. Students form their opinions from the way teachers talk to them and treat them.

> Some teachers talk down to you like you're stupid when you ask questions.
> Some teachers embarass you in front of the class. They make jokes about failed tests, poor grades, and things. (Firestone and Rosenblum 1988, p. 289)
> My teacher would put me on her knees in the corner and whip me with

wet newspapers and the rest of the class would laugh. (Dixon, quoted by
Greene 1989)

The teacher laughed and said, "well, here's a student who can't see how
to get to class." [the student speaking is a Navajo whose name is Cantsee.]
(Deyhle 1987)

Examples like these clearly indicate that the students' perceptions are correct.

The Extra-curriculum

To channel the energy of young people and to seduce them into school-related
activities, educators have created an "extra-curriculum" of sports, clubs, and
entertaining activities to accompany the formal academic curriculum. These
nonacademic functions of school help to contain the influence of the student
peer group. They also absorb the vacant time which children are believed to
have before and after schools and on weekends with activities sanctioned by the
school. They reinforce academic performance standards because adequate performance in academic work and conduct is required for participation in these
activities. They also reinforce traditional gender roles. Activities for males emphasize what are considered appropriate male qualities of achievement, competi-
tiveness, toughness, goal fulfillment in the face of pain and discomfort, and
aggression. Activities for girls reinforce the fact that females are rewarded for
having a pleasant, bubbly personality, maintaining neat, clean hair, a trim figure,
and a calm, agreeable facade—even under adverse circumstances—and playing
a supportive role to male activities (Eder and Parker 1987). Extra-curricular
activities also accustom students to the legitimacy of an unequal distribution of
status and rewards in society, just as the academic curriculum does (Ibid.,
p. 205).

Winners. The existence of the extra-curriculum has fostered the caricature of a
white, successful, middle-class American adolescent, whose life is filled with
proms, athletics and cheerleading. However, regardless of class or ethnicity,
many students "major" in the extra-curriculum, finding the academic side of
life too difficult or too meaningless. They often are encouraged to do this by
peers, as well as by teachers and parents who believe that success in the extra-
curriculum is therapeutic to students who otherwise do not do so well. It is
considered a boost to the self-esteem of those who cannot succeed in the
academic side of life. The extra-curriculum can supplant academics where athletes and other special students are given passing grades to maintain eligibility
for outside class activities despite lack of demonstrated performance. Controversy over this kind of pressure has led to the passing of "no-pass, no-play"
legislation in many states, and to subsequent public outrage by coaches, alumni
associations, students, beleaguered parents and teachers on both sides of the
controversy.

Until recently, only the lighter side of the caricature got attention. Studies
conducted before the 1970s were concerned with suburban middle class students

or the white working class (Coleman 1961; Kahl 1953; Hollingshead 1949; Stinchcombe 1964). Parents and educators registered dismay at finding that the majority of students found academic work to have little intrinsic value, and that for most, the "gentleman's C" was the highest standard to which they aspired.

> Yeah if you're a straight A student you get razzed . . . (McLeod ibid.)
> [you have to] hang out at _____'s. Don't be too smart. Flirt with boys. Be cooperative on dates (Coleman 1961, p. 371).

The dark side of extra-curricular activities consists of outgroups—wimps, nerds, losers, greasers, "badasses," and punks or delinquents—who cannot or will not participate.

Losers. Middle- and working-class white parents in the 1950s and 1960s assumed that teenage hijinks and aversion to work would dissipate with age and that students would settle down and become productive members of the community. Nobody examined what happened to the high school underclass—minorities, dropouts, the unpopular, and the poor. This group now is garnering a great deal of attention, since it has become much larger than previously believed. No longer does the disaffected and dropout population constitute a minuscule proportion of the school-aged cohort. In most large cities, it makes up nearly the majority of the population (Powell et al. 1985; Hess et al. 1987; LeCompte and Goebel 1987). It also is much louder and more expressively violent in its opposition to school than the mild underachievement believed characteristic of the middle class. Further, its members *do not* eventually assimilate into a semblance of middle class life. Rather, they remain a disaffected, under-and-unemployed underclass as adults, just as they were an underachieving and alienated underclass in high school. This raises some important questions:

- Why are students in general and resident minority groups in particular beginning to believe that going to school will not help them to succeed?
- Why do they sense that the American Dream does not apply to them?

To understand this it is necessary to recognize that schools do not exist in isolation from the world community, and that not all of the problems schools have can be resolved by instructional programs offered in the classroom. Rather, it is necessary to look beyond the confines of any given school and its community into the larger world society. As we have seen, the failure of the disadvantaged actually acts to preserve existing patterns of domination.

SURVIVING SCHOOL

In the preceding pages we have tried to described what life is like for teenagers and how they spend their days in contemporary society. We have defined peer culture and how it has developed. We also have discussed some of the societal issues which we feel complicate the process of growing up. We have suggested that a critical aspect in the maturation of comtemporary children is their long period of schooling, where they learn from each other and establish collective ideas about the world and how to live in it. We also have suggested that at this stage of their development, adolescents find the ideas of their friends and the media a much more powerful influence over their actions than those of most adults.

However, not all young people are alike. They differ according to sex, academic achievement, socioeconomic status, ethnicity, whether they live in large cities, suburbs, small towns or rural areas, and by neighborhood. They also respond differently to school, both individually and in groups. While factors such as economic status and whether or not young people become parents in high school contribute to the alienation of young people from school, the impact of these factors is heightened by the extent to which their friends are similarly alienated. Even very bright and highly motivated students with helpful pushy parents find it difficult to study when none of their friends do. If students already are in trouble because of family divorce, pregnancy, low grades, difficulty in finding jobs, or knowledge of the shrinking opportunity structure, their potential for disaffection with school depends upon how many of their friends are in similar trouble.

Valli (1983), who studied young women planning to become clerical and office workers, suggests that there are three different forms of response to cultural institutions: acceptance, negotiation, and resistance. Which of these shapes the reaction which young people have to school depends upon how much hope they have for the future, and how much going to school will contribute to realization of their aspirations.

Acceptance

Acceptance involves internalization of the school's promise that academic success and educational longevity will pay off in terms of material success and social status. Students who accept the premise of schooling struggle to believe the American cultural myth of the linkage between education and occupational status (LeCompte 1987b; LeCompte and Dworkin 1988). Many students work hard to maintain the status inherited from their family of origin—their putative place in the top echelons of society—or, like Horatio Alger, they struggle to do better than their parents did.

Children who adopt this response generally come from several kinds of families. Most obvious are those from middle-class or affluent Anglo and dominant culture families or immigrants who, like many Southeast Asians, are well-educated and once were wealthy, but lost their status when they became refugees (Dworkin 1985b; Perillo 1980). Most of these parents have benefited themselves from education and they push their children. Even if they are not immigrants or the beneficiaries of education, most know how to exert pressure on the school system when their children have problems, to negotiate placement so that their children get into classes which will prepare them for college, and to help them with their homework. They also obtain tutoring, psychological counseling, and other kinds of help when it is deemed necessary (Ziegler, Hardwick and Mc-Greath 1989). Other children who tend to do well in school are children of immigrants whose parents—and, indeed, they themselves—find that their present situation, however bleak it may seem, is infinitely more promising than the opportunities they might have had in their old homes (Ogbu 1987; Gibson 1987b; Valverde 1987; Suarez-Orozco 1987).

The "immigrant psychology" of hope (Ogbu 1987) helps to explain not only the hard work and academic success of refugee children from Southeast Asia, but also the fact that fewer children born in Mexico whose parents recently migrated to the United States seem to drop out of school than do Mexican-American children born in the United States (Valverde 1987). The issue is not limited to migration across national boundaries. McLeod (1987) points out that while both groups of high school young men whom he studied were from similar extremely impoverished and crime-prone backgrounds, the "Brothers," who were black, experienced relatively greater academic success, and expressed greater belief in the efficacy of school learning than did the "Hallway Hangers," who were white. McLeod suggests that the difference may be because the families of the Brothers had moved fairly recently to the mostly white public housing project in which both groups lived. They saw the project as an improvement over life in the ghetto. By contrast, to the Hallway Hangers, whose families had lived in the projects all their lives, the project symbolized their incapacity to escape from a hopeless, dead-end existence.

Negotiation

Negotiation is not whole-hearted acceptance of the premises of schooling. Rather, it is recognition that while the pay-offs for completing school may not be monumental, the consequences of not doing so are worse. The reasons for staying are unimportant; students might be motivated simply by the wrath of their parents. The important point is that schooling has extrinsic, rather than intrinsic value; hence, negotiators seek to make a deal. They aspire to achieve completion of their schooling with minimum effort. Fuller's study (1980) of young black Caribbean women students in England demonstrates how these students consciously or unconsciously negotiate an exchange of reasonable work for reasonable demands from their teachers. Negotiators neither buy into the premises of school wholeheartedly nor think that it is exciting and worthwhile. In fact, they may feel that most schoolwork is boring beyond belief (Sizer 1984; Holland and Eisenhart 1988b; Powell, Farrar, and Cohen 1985). However, they believe that the acquisition of a high school diploma or college degree is necessary, and as a consequence, will work hard enough and conform sufficiently to the rules to assure that it can be obtained. They may seek to minimize work by "scoping out" their teachers to find out what is expected and how to get around them; they may take less advanced courses which still meet graduation requirements; they may even "make deals" with teachers, so that they will be required to do miminal work. In exchange, the students will guarantee to teachers an orderly classroom and a respite from harrassment. In Chapter Four, we describe how McNeil (1988b) feels this affects teacher morale.

While the most active and overt negotiators are older students, some researchers have described the process in elementary school. Borko and Eisenhart (1986) demonstrated how second graders in the lower reading groups induce teachers to simplify their lessons. When asked questions they thought were too hard, the children would respond with difficulty, or very slowly. Their teachers then assumed the work was too difficult. Subsequently, they would "dumb down" their teaching, revising lessons to include less material. This achieved the student's objective to make school less taxing. McNeil (1983, 1988b) has suggested that an unforeseen consequence of this interaction is, however, that students are progressively more handicapped in school; as they learn less, they fall farther and farther behind their classmates.

Though we have described it as such, much of the negotiation we describe actually is not seen as a bargain struck consciously, like a union contract. In fact, most students are swept along by the inevitability of adult expectations and institutional constraints, and the rules and practices for negotiating survival in school evolve as cultural knowledge within the student peer groups, which pass them on to each succeeding generation of kids. Insofar as the rules for negotiation still require conformity to minimal academic standards, teachers may complain about the loss of student proficiency and energy, but they do not define their students as engaging in active resistance to school. Accepters and negotiators cause less concern to school staff because their conformity gives the impression that they have bought into the premises of schooling. They follow most of the rules and are likely to graduate. There are, however, students who do not wish to negotiate on the school's terms. These are the students we define as resisters.

Resistance: Its Definition, Purpose, and Types

Resisters are a problem for schools because they cause trouble and are likely to drop out. Resistance to institutional constraints is more than simple misbehavior. Resistance is principled, conscious and ideological. The nonconformity of resistors has its basis in philosophical differences between the individual and the institution. It involves "witholding assent" (Erickson 1987, p. 237) from school authorities; students who resist may disagree with the way they are treated in school on the basis of their gender, ethnicity or social class; they may disagree with the academic track or category to which they are assigned; or they may disagree with the esteem in which their gender, ethnicity, academic or social category is held. They become resistors when their disagreement is actively expressed.

Resistance can serve to salvage the self-esteem or reputation of the individual engaging in it. In some cases, the acts of resistance do not entirely sabotage the careers of students.

Assertiveness. Schools consistently try to avoid, simplify or deny the existence of controversy (McNeil 1983; Powell et al. 1985; Page 1987). Some students, however, refuse to be silenced and demand the right to hold complex opinions or to maintain contradictory consciousness (Gramsci 1971). Fine describes how Deirdre, a bright black senior, refused to accede to a teacher's demands that she decide whether the actions of Bernard Goetz, the "subway vigilante" who shot four young men he thought were about to rob him, were right or wrong. From the supposedly silenced middle of the room, she declared:

> It's not that I have no opinions. I don't like Goetz shootin' up people who look like my brother, but I don't like feelin' unsafe in the projects or my neighborhood either. I got lots of opinions. I ain't being quiet 'cause I can't decide if he's right or wrong. I'm talking. (1987, p. 164)

In another example, Rose (1988) was puzzled to find that black students in her college persisted in their use of Black English, even in written composition, despite the fact that they knew the Standard English alternatives and realized that the practice would lower their grades. At first she thought it was a way to reinforce a black identity. The explanation the students gave, however, was that for their purposes, Standard English just did not sound right. Not using Black English was like not using inflection and punctuation; Standard English simply did not convey the meaning they wanted.

Hyper-Achievement: Beating Them at Their Own Game. A few students chose to repudiate the negative labels assigned to them by the school. A dramatic example is that of Carrie Mae Dixon, of Yates High School in Houston, Texas. She is black and economically disadvantaged; she has been an orphan with no legal guardian since kindergarten. She is pregnant, unmarried, and the mother of a two-year-old child. In third grade, the teacher called her dumb for getting in trouble every day in school. She also has been at the top of her class in every grade since the end of elementary school and graduated as valedictorian of her high school class. She has been accepted to university and awarded two scholarships for the fall; she now wants to be a chemical engineer. The turning point was a classmate's insult. "After that, I decided I would show her who was dumb and who wasn't . . . In tenth grade is when I found out what the valedictorian is. They explained to me that this is the person with the highest grade point average and I said, 'OK, that's what I want to be.' "

Plans for her valedictory address almost went awry when a principal of her school decided that a pregnant valedictorian set a poor example for other students and indicated that she would not be able to participate in the graduation ceremony. It took national media attention to change the minds of the school officials (Greene 1989).

The kinds of resistance we have just described are used by students who are more or less successful in school. They may win peer approval, or, like some of the students who "act white," not encounter so much adverse response from peers that they drop out. Other forms of resistance, however, lead to further and further alienation from school. Students may define the academic part of school as meaningless. Some students may disavow schooling altogether, insofar as they not only do not identify with the academic part of school, but also fail to find its extra-curricular aspects alluring. These students choose alternative avenues for achieving status, since they cannot acquire it altogether through avenues like the extra-curricular activities as defined by the school. Some of them are sanctioned or at least accepted by the establishment; others are not.

In the paragraphs which follow, we will discuss a number of ways students express their alienation from and lack of engagement with school. It is important to realize that most students engage in at least some of these expressions at some point in their careers. These acts do not constitute resistance, however, unless they involve active, conscious, and principled opposition to a specific way in which the school has chosen to define a student.

Resistance may begin with simple nonconforming behavior, and then be transformed into resistance by the negative responses of school staff. Under these conditions, students who are dropout risks become "push-outs"—forced out of school by an establishment which will not or cannot accommodate them. This occurs when student behavior diverges farther and farther from the pattern which school staff find acceptable and bearable. As teachers, counselors, and administrators mobilize to neutralize, isolate, or otherwise eliminate the behavior, (and often, the student engaging in it), students may find themselves in a less and less congenial environment—detention, suspension, remedial classes, and repeated confrontations with parents and school staff. They also may find that nobody cares to rescue them and stop the process.

Boredom and Alienation: The Initial Phase of Resistance. Resistance usually begins when students stop studying or begin to engage in mild forms of smart-aleck behavior and vandalism. In an attempt to be considered more mature, they may begin to adopt what Stinchcombe (1964) calls symbolic adult behavior—use of drugs and alcohol, smoking, early dating and sex (Ekstrom et al. 1986). They get jobs, which make them feel good both because they may involve some responsibility, and because they provide funds to buy clothing, cars, and other material goods with which to impress their friends. Girls may have a baby, feeling sorry because motherhood interferes with school and seeing friends, but happy to have a baby (Greene 1989, Sege 1989). Both jobs and babies can take so much time and energy that they seriously compromise a student's ability to cope with schoolwork. Students who cannot get licit jobs or who find that licit jobs pay very little may engage in illicit ones—selling drugs, burglary, pimping and prostitution. Alienated students often form gangs of similarly inclined peers, and may go beyond simple vandalism and harrassment of school staff to adopt real terrorist tactics to intimidate both the students and staff of a school.

Tuning Out: Dropping Out in School. The ultimate form of resistance is to stop coming to school. There are many ways to accomplish this; some students simply start by sleeping in their classes. Those who have jobs after school may do so as a logical response to lack of sleep. Others begin to cut classes. They don't leave the school building, they simply ditch the classes they find most distasteful. Selective class cutting is increasingly wide-spread; Hess et al. (1987) has documented what he calls a "culture of cutting," wherein students spend more time in the hallways and hiding places of the school than in class. These students are in-school dropouts, or "tune-outs." They are more likely to be average middle-class students—and those whom we have called the "negotiators." While they have not yet actually cut their ties with school, they are bored with or disaffected from school, and they receive little more instruction than students who actually have dropped out. They are, however, increasing in numbers, and they are at great risk of becoming droputs.

Dropping Out: Giving Up on School. Statistics on dropouts are notoriously unreliable. Even figures on the absolute number of students who fail to graduate are questionable; a few of the procedures used for counting students overestimate the numbers who drop out, but most probably underestimate the numbers significantly (Morrow 1986; LeCompte and Goebel 1987; Rumberger 1987). However, since the 1960s, at least 25 percent of any given age cohort in the United States failed to finish high school (Steinberg, Blinde, and Chan 1984; McDill, Pallas, and Natriello 1985). It probably also is correct that in most cities, and among what Ogbu (1978) calls "caste-like minorities"—blacks, Hispanics, Native Americans—dropout rates exceed 40 percent and may be as high as 80 percent (Orum 1984).

It is even more difficult to determine why students drop out than it is to count their numbers. Most students who drop out do not appear at the school door to say goodbye. They simply stop coming and eventually are placed in a "whereabouts unknown" category, then dropped from the records. Those who do announce their departure often lie about their plans. It is more socially acceptable to state that one has a job, is transferring to another school, or will join the military than to admit that one is simply giving up on school (Hammack 1986; LeCompte and Goebel 1987).

Most data on the reasons for dropping out consist of demographic correlations: students, it is said, drop out because they are poor, from minority or single-parent families, or because they are girls who have had babies. This descriptive data neither does very much to address the real motivations for leaving school, nor, because of its focus upon "victim characteristics" over which the school has little control, does it provide much assistance in remedying the problems. It is true that some young people must leave school for legitimate reasons, such as the need to support their family or take care of siblings or their own children. However, the evidence suggests that the majority of students who leave school before graduating do so because of school-related factors. Many of these students already were part of the culture of opposition to school, a culture which acts to exacerbate their difficulties by inducing them to violate norms for appropriate behavior in school or to engage in activities which interfere with schoolwork. For others who had serious personal problems, school requirements became the final straw. In contemporary schools whose major task is the batch-processing and crowd-control of huge numbers of children, little individual time and few resources exist for students with difficult problems, such as finding day-care for their babies or psychiatric care for emotional disturbance, drug addiction or physical abuse. Many of these students—or their problems—are defined as either intractable or just not the business of the school. For some, that indeed may be true. Schools cannot, for example, be expected to treat acting-out, psychotic students or those who are on drugs.

Most students, however, do not fall into such extreme categories. They are bored; they hate school; the work is too difficult or too easy. Their degree won't amount to anything when they get out. The staff told them they were failures or unwanted; teachers didn't care, were incompetent, or didn't understand. They were pregnant and embarrassed to "show." They couldn't find a babysitter; their guardian was dying and they were needed for nursing care; they had no car and couldn't get across town to the dropout center. In all cases, the school was too inflexible to accommodate to their needs (Holley and Doss 1983; LeCompte 1985; Fine 1986; Valverde 1987; Williams 1987; Wehlage 1986; Delgado-Gaitan 1988; Deyhle 1987, 1988). Thus, we believe that most students who drop out are those who were already at risk and who were pushed out of school altogether by an unresponsive institution. It wasn't that they didn't learn how schools work; it is just that following the rules didn't work for them.

SUMMARY

In this chapter, we have discussed the formation of youth culture and the student peer group in the context of global patterns of consumption, technological change, the labor market, family structure, and cultural survival. We suggest that the advent of compulsory schooling and the prolongation of adolescence are linked and facilitate the development of oppositional youth culture. We also describe how curricular and extra-curricular experiences in school socialize children for participation in a society stratified by achievement, but biased by race, class and gender. Finally, we suggest that students respond differentially to the realization that the rewards of schooling are mirrored in the rewards of society. Some accommodate to school and survive, but others resist and drop out.

KEY CONCEPTS

Peer Group refers to relationships which people have because of special characteristics such as age, race, gender, professional or social status.

Youth Culture is a broader term than peer group and refers to the total way of life, the distinctive behavior patterns and beliefs of, in this case, young people.

Socialization refers to the process of teaching and learning behaviors, values, roles, customs, etc. considered appropriate in a society.

Adolescence refers to the transition stage in a person's life which usually begins at puberty and ends when one participates in activities normally associated with adulthood—economic independence from parents, marriage or the birth of a child.

Liminality refers to the time after leaving one clearly identified social identity and before entering another. Adolescence is a liminal state between childhood and adulthood.

Cohort is a demographic term identifying a category of people who share a single common characteristic such as age or the date at which they entered an institution. Sociologists frequently refer to an "educational" or an "age" cohort, meaning people who are of the same generation or who entered the educational system or other social institutions at the same time.

EXERCISES

1. Think back to your high school experiences. What were the student groups in your high school. Describe how these groups distinguished themselves from others. What did they call themselves? How did teachers and school administrators relate to each of these groups? Was there a relationship between social class background and peer group membership?

2. Interview several high school students about the peer groups within their schools today. With the help of these students, make a chart to illustrate the status hierarchy of the peer groups within the schools. Which groups hold more power? How does this power get translated into privileges within the school and outside the school? How do these peer groups compare with the groups you had when you were in high school?

3. Interview several high school teachers about the peer groups in their schools. Find out how they perceive the relationship of these peer groups to their academic performance in school. What kinds of student do they think are more able?

4. Visit a high school during its lunch period. What student groups can you identify? What distinguishes them from other peer groups? Discuss your findings in class.

5. Talk to a group of elementary school students, and then a group of high school students. Ask each of them what strategies they use to "get back" at teachers, what kinds of tricks they play on teachers, and how they get around assignments. Would you define any of these activities as kinds of resistance?

SUGGESTED READINGS

Classic Works

Aries, Phillipe. (1962). *Centuries of childhood.: A social history of family life.* New York: Vintage Books.

Coleman, J. (1961). *The adolescent society.* Glencoe, Ill.: The Free Press.

Dreeben, R. (1968). *On what is learned in school*. Reading, Mass.: Addison Wesley.

Hollingshead, A. B. (1949). *Elmtown's youth*. New York: John Wiley.

Jackson, Phillip (1968). *Life in classrooms*. Chicago: University of Chicago Press.

Kahl, J. A. (1953). Educational and occupational aspirations of "common man" boys. *Harvard Educational Review*, 23(3).

Keniston, K. (1971). The agony of the counterculture. *Educational Record*, *52*, 205–211.

Liebow, E. (1969). *Tally's corner: A study of negro streetcorner men*. Boston: Little, Brown and Co.

Rosenfeld, G. (1971). *Shut those thick lips*. New York: Holt, Rinehart and Winston.

Stinchcome, A. (1964). *Rebellion in a high school*. Chicago: Quadrangle Press.

Waller, W. (1965). *The sociology of teaching*. New York: John Wiley.

Willis, Paul. (1977). *Learning to labour: How working class kids get working class jobs*. London: Saxon House.

Modern Works

Children's Defense Fund (1988). *A call for action to make our nation safe for children: A briefing book on the status of american children in 1988*. Washington, D.C.

Cohen, J., and Rogers, J. (1983). *On democracy: Toward a transformation of American society*. Middlesex, England and New York: Penquin Books.

Delgado-Gaitan, C. (1988). The value of conformity: Learning to stay in school. *Anthropology and Education Quarterly*, *19*(4), 354–382.

Eder, Donna, and Parker, Stephen. (1987). The cultural production of gender: The effect of extracurricular activities on peer-group culture. *Sociology of Education* vol. 60 (July), 200–213.

Fine, M. (1986). Why urban adolescents drop into and out of public high school. *Teachers College Record* 87(3), 393–410.

Gibson, M. A. (1988). *Accommodation without assimilation: Punjabi Sikh immigrants in an American high school and community*. Ithaca: Cornell University.

Littwin Joan, (1987). *The postponed generation: Why America's grown-up kids are growing up later*. New York: Morrow.

Powell, Arthur G. Farrar, Eleanor, and Cohen, David K. (1985). *The shopping mall high school: Winners and losers in the educational marketplace*. Boston: Houghton Mifflin.

Weis, Lois. (1988). *Class, race and gender in American education*. Albany, N.Y.: State University of New York Press.

CHAPTER 4

The Labor Force in Education: Teachers, Counselors, Administrators, and Ancillary Staff

OVERVIEW (cont'd)

INTRODUCTION

In Chapter Three we suggested that children are placed in school in large part to work at tasks set for them by adults. In this chapter, we are concerned with teachers, counselors, administrators and ancillary school staff, whose qualifications for being in schools rest upon specific professional training. These adults relate to the school differently from students because they *are* adults, because their participation in school work is voluntary, and because they are paid for their labor and, at least in theory, can be fired for poor job performance. Students, on the other hand, "qualify" for attendance in schools simply by virtue of their age status as minors; because they are required by law to attend, they are "involuntary recruits" who are not paid for the work they perform and cannot be fired for malfeasance (Nadel 1957).

We will be limiting our consideration of adults in schools to "educators," that is, professionals whose primary tasks are defined by their direct relationship to the teaching of children. Security personnel, maintenance engineers, dieticians, cooks, janitors, bookkeepers and clerks, personnel specialists, bus-drivers and gardeners also work in schools, and are critical to their smooth operation. In many cases, the relationships these workers form with educators and students are of profound importance to the teaching and learning process. For example, in his classic book, *The Sociology of Teaching* (1932), Willard Waller posits that janitors (who in his book are males) are among the most powerful people in schools and often serve as role models for male students. However, the work of all of such staff members is structured by tasks other than teaching children, such as preparing food, cleaning buildings, and hiring workers. Such tasks can be and are performed in many different kinds of institutions. The work of educators, however, is structured by and dependent upon schools and schoollike settings. While it may seem all too obvious, the practice of their profession also requires the presence of students—the too-often forgotten recipients of educators' labor.

How Do Sociologists View Educators?

Sociologists view teachers—and other educators—in the context of their work. The questions they ask parallel those which researchers in the sociology of work and occupations ask about other professions. This chapter is organized around those questions. We first discuss the definition of a profession, asking how closely teaching approximates professional status. We then examine the characteristics of educators, addressing the following issues:

- How has the historical evolution of the profession affected its current development? What are the demographic characteristics—such as age, sex, socioeconomic background and race—of educators? How distinct are educators as a group from people in other professions? What relationships exist between these demographic characteristics and the specific tasks to which various groups of educators are assigned, the way they carry out their tasks, and how they feel about them? Is the profession stratified by race, class, gender, and other demographic characteristics?

We then move to a discussion of teachers' work. The questions we examine are:

- What is the nature of the kind of work educators do? How do the characteristics of that work affect how teachers behave and how they feel about their jobs? What kinds of power and control do teachers have over their work and how is power differentially distributed among various kinds of educators? How does the work of educators and their relationship to the labor market in general compare with the experience of other kinds of workers?

Throughout the chapter, we call attention to the tensions and ambiguities of power and status which constitute the political context of those who work in schools.

ISSUES OF POWER AND STATUS: PROFESSIONAL ESTEEM AND PUBLIC DISREGARD

Educational professionals have an image problem, and whether they are university level or elementary school teachers, counselors or principals, coaches or superintendents, they suffer from disjunctures between the status they would like to enjoy in society and the power they actually wield. Neither social analysts, policymakers, the public, nor educators themselves can decide whether educational practitioners are scholarly professionals like doctors and university professors, or members of the laboring workforce, like clerks, salespeople, or skilled laborers. In part this is because of the discrepancy between the salaries teachers actually earn and what they "ought" to get, given the supposed value of the work they perform. Though the case of ministers, artists, and bartenders makes it clear that income does not necessarily correlate with social standing, teachers are considered to render community services so crucial that their right to withhold those services often is abrogated by laws forbidding them to strike. However, public unwillingness to pay for these services is demonstrated repeatedly by low salary scales and repeated failure of school tax levees. Table 4.1 depicts teacher salaries compared with salaries in other occupations. The question becomes: Is the critical service teachers render an instructional one? or is it that they warehouse children, keeping them occupied, off the streets and out of the labor market?

Even though they are considered to be professionals, public school teachers are ranked only slightly above electricians and musicians in indices of social status, and far below doctors, lawyers, dentists, college professors, and airline pilots. Their ranking in scales of occupational prestige has fallen steadily (Hodge, et. al., 1966, p. 325). Figure 4.1 depicts the status of teachers compared to other occupations.

While teachers insist that their professional training and expertise justifies community esteem, they despise those very teacher education courses as the least rigorous part of their education (Lortie 1969, p. 24). By the same token, there is widespread public deprecation of teacher education; people believe that "anyone can teach."

Careers in teaching have different status levels for different people. They are considered socially desirable and appropriate for women, and the highest attainable occupation for blacks, Hispanics, and Native Americans, but mere entry level positions or low-status dead ends for white men (Lortie 1969, p. 20). While parents would be proud of a daughter who chose to be a teacher, they would be distressed if she married one.

Differential status based on age of students, subject matter and gender divide the profession. Highest status is accorded to those who teach the oldest students. The top of the status hierarchy includes university professors; secondary school teachers and instructors in technical and vocational schools occupy the middle, and elementary school teachers and day-care workers rank at the bottom. There is differentiation even within these levels. Administrative rank counts, as does subject area specialization and the age and sex of the students taught. Thus, supervisors and administrators rank higher than instructors. Teachers of the "hard sciences" out-rank philosophers and English teachers; teachers of graduate students and fifth graders outrank those who deal, respectively, with undergraduates and kindergartners. Sex and ethnicity in general count; men's athletic programs are funded at a much higher level than any programs for women. In general, women and minorities enjoy less status than men and dominant culture individuals in the same positions or programs. Finally, differential status is accorded to specific philosphical outlooks; school bureaucracies

TABLE 4.1. AVERAGE STARTING SALARIES OF PUBLIC SCHOOL TEACHERS COMPARED WITH SALARIES IN PRIVATE INDUSTRY, BY POSITION: 1975 to 1986

(Except as noted, salaries represent what corporations plan to offer graduates graduating in the year shown. Based on a survey of approximately 200 companies)

Position	1975	1978	1979	1980	1981	1982	1983	1984	1985	1986
Teachers[1]	$8,233	$9,739	$10,138	$10,754	$11,758	$12,769	$13,360	$14,500	$15,400	(NA)
College graduates:										
Engineering	12,744	16,880	18,288	20,136	22,368	25,428	25,800	26,644	26,880	28,512
Accounting	11,880	13,464	14,748	15,720	16,980	18,648	19,478	20,172	20,628	21,216
Sales—marketing	10,344	12,635	13,092	15,938	17,220	18,372	18,648	19,620	20,616	20,088
Business administration	9,768	12,048	13,464	14,100	16,200	17,448	18,554	19,416	19,896	21,324
Liberal arts	9,312	11,400	12,744	13,298	15,444	15,924	18,264	19,344	18,828	21,060
Chemistry	11,804	14,700	15,816	17,124	19,536	21,492	22,344	24,192	24,216	24,264
Mathematics—statistics	10,980	13,632	15,000	17,604	18,600	21,516	21,696	22,416	22,704	23,976
Economics—finance	10,212	12,072	13,068	14,472	10,884	17,532	19,740	20,484	20,964	22,284
Computer sciences	(NA)	14,150	15,432	17,712	20,304	22,250	23,208	24,664	24,150	26,172
Other fields	10,464	13,848	14,556	17,544	20,028	22,716	21,158	23,136	21,972	28,724
INDEX (1975=100)										
Teachers[1]	100	118	123	131	143	155	162	176	187	(NA)
College graduates:										
Engineering	100	131	144	158	176	200	202	211	211	224
Accounting	100	113	124	132	143	157	164	170	174	179
Sales—marketing	100	122	127	164	166	178	180	190	199	200
Business administration	100	123	138	144	166	179	190	198	204	218
Liberal arts	100	122	137	143	166	171	196	208	202	226
Chemistry	100	123	133	144	164	181	188	203	203	204
Mathematics—statistics	100	124	137	160	169	196	198	204	207	218
Economics—finance	100	118	128	142	165	172	183	201	205	218
Computer sciences[2]	(NA)	100	109	125	144	157	184	178	171	185
Other fields	100	132	139	188	191	217	202	221	210	255

NA Not available.   [1]Estimate. Minimum mean salary for those with bachelor's degree. (Source: National Education Association, Washington, DC, Estimates of School Statistics, annual (copyright).)
[2]Computer science index (1978=100). (Source: Except as noted, Northwestern University, Evanston, IL. The Northwestern Endicott Report, by Dean Victor Lindquist (copyright).)
(Source: U.S. Bureau of the Census. Statistical Abstract of the United States: 1987 (107th Edition). Washington, D.C., 1986.)

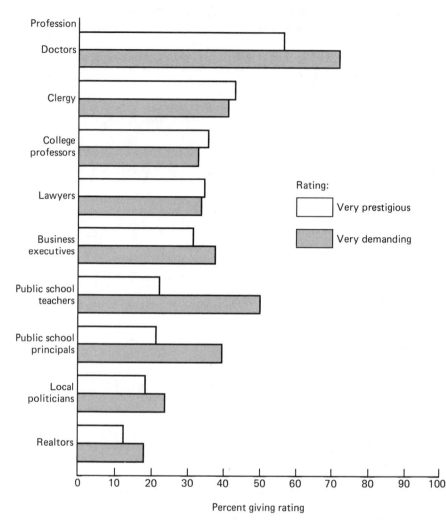

Figure 4.1. Public Ratings of the Professions (Source: *Survey of NEA K–12 Teacher Members 1985* (Washington, D.C.: National Educational Association), p. 12.)

are conservative and slow to change, so that the most prestige is accorded to those who deviate least from the norm (Aronowitz and Giroux 1985).

We believe that the source of these ambiguities and disjunctures can be found in the structural and historical evolution of the profession, the age, racial, and gender characteristics of educators, the nature of teacher's work, patterns of control and status in the profession, the nature of career paths and the reward structure of education. In the pages which follow we will discuss each of these from a traditional functionalist perspective as well as the critical perspective which informs our own thinking.

CONTRADICTIONS IN THE STRUCTURE OF THE PROFESSION

The traditional functionalist view is concerned with comparing the structure and organization of teaching with other professions. It describes how differences in structure lead to ambiguities and disjunctures between how teachers ideally want to be regarded by the public and their peers, and the reality of the level of status they actually enjoy. Defined this way, structural ambiguities have to do with the nature and organization of tasks, how people are trained to execute them, and how much control they have over their performance.

Definition of a Profession: The Traditional View

Professions can be differentiated in terms of the complexity of tasks performed; the type, rigor, and duration of training; the nature of control, power and autonomy in the profession, and the relationship between the actual work done and the physical context in which it is performed. Max Weber first delineated the characteristics of the "ideal typical" professional, taking as his models occupations like doctors, priests and lawyers. Weber wrote that professionals shared the following characteristics: they were self-employed providers of services, who entered their profession because they were "called" to it out of some deep personal commitment, and their qualifications were based upon their possession of "expert" and esoteric knowledge.

This knowledge was possessed only by a few and attainable only by means of long and rigorous study. Professional services dealt with serious, often life-or-death matters, and professionals were remunerated by fees from clients for them. Communication between these professionals and their clients was legally privileged; courts of law could not require its disclosure. Most important, entrance to these professions was controlled by professional peers, who set requirements for entry, training and certification, and who engaged in peer review to ensure maintenance of standards and competence (Weber 1947).

In establishing this set of characteristics, Weber did not intend to make value judgments about the relative merit of occupations. Rather, his purpose was to provide a uniform set of descriptors against which all occupations could be compared. Today, the profession which most closely approximates this model is medicine; however Weber's model continues to provide a standard, one from which education deviates in substantial degree.

Initial discussions of teaching as an occupation were preoccupied with the most important ways in which teaching deviated from the Weberian model (Etzioni 1969; Lortie 1969; Simpson and Simpson 1969). These included the nature of the knowledge base in the field of education and the training required to attain it, the degree of control which teachers have over entry to the profession, maintenance of standards, and the depth of commitment which teachers, as a group, have to their calling.

Training. One of the most obvious differences involves training. All of the traditional professions require at least five years of training, including several years of rigorous study beyond college. Many also require a supervised apprenticeship or internship. Elementary and secondary school teachers, however, typically spend two undergraduate years in liberal arts courses and two more undergraduate years in pedagogical studies (learning how to teach the subjects they have just been taught). Actual teacher training still resembles the normal school tradition, where teachers taught those just below their own academic attainment. Only one-and-a-half years of actual coursework in pedagogy is required; the remainder is student teaching, which is quintessentially experiential learning, located off-campus, and only lightly supervised by university personnel.

Many perceive teaching as based not upon technical knowledge requiring intellectually rigorous study, but rather upon experiential knowledge acquired primarily in apprenticeship, either in the very short period of student teaching or in the unsupervised apprenticeship of the first year of teaching. Increased expertise in teaching is a matter more of adding to a "bag of tricks" than of achieving increasingly complex levels of skill and expertise. Moreover, though the cumulative knowledge we acquired from teachers is critical to our functioning in everyday modern adult life, lack of any single chunk of it is not a life or death matter. Medical and legal workers may hold the lives of their clients in balance, but nobody ever died of a split infinitive.

There really is no "science" of education, any more than there is a "science" of medicine; both are applied fields which make use of information and techniques developed in the natural and social sciences (Turner 1985, quoted in Ginsburg 1988, p. 28). The difference seems to be the seriousness with which medicine and other more traditional professions address the need for these courses. Extensive study, beyond introductory courses, of biology, chemistry, physics, and other background courses is required *prior* to learning the techniques of medical practice. By constrast, the four years of teacher training are so crowded that there is little time, for example, for studies of the social and psychological anatomy of learning or the logical structure of mathematics and social studies. Students generally regard these courses as "too theoretical" and deem them far less important than learning "how-to" methods for teaching discrete "factoids" (Morgenstern 1989) of reading, mathematics, and foreign languages.

Recent national studies, including those by the National Commission on Excellence in Education (1983), the Rand Corporation (Darling-Hammond 1984), the Holmes Group (1986) and the Carnegie Task Force of Teaching as a Profession (1986) have questioned the quality of this training. Some have suggested requiring a fifth year of study in the "content areas" for teacher education degrees (The Holmes Group 1986). However, these suggestions, as well as others designed to make teacher education more rigorous, meet resistance from sources as disparate as University departments of curriculum and instruction, who see their control of teacher education eroded by student course requirements outside their departments, and students, who see that additional years of study produce no comensurate raise in pay.

Teacher education programs are frequently moneymakers for their universities because they are cheap to operate. Their students pay the same tuition as others but their per-student cost is less because the teacher education faculty generally has the lowest pay scale in most Universities, and because students do not use university facilities during their student teaching. Profits from teacher education programs finance other, less-cost effective programs, and university fiscal officers are reluctant to reduce those profits by adding a year to the degree requirement.

Standards for graduation from teacher education also are set by legislatures more at the whim of current educational fads and political exigencies than they are based upon pedagogical or social scientific findings. For example, courses in multicultural education became popular requirements in the 1970s and have virtually vanished in the 1980s. As a consequence, many such courses often are not treated seriously by the faculty and administrators of teacher preparation colleges, who know that courses can change radically with each administration.

Certification. Control of the profession is another critical issue. Market factors and legislative fiat govern teacher certification and entrance to the profession, rather than panels of professionals. While teachers are supposed to have special training for each subject they teach, individual school districts can waive requirements if qualified personnel are not available. They can assign people to teach courses in their minor area of study, or in areas for which they have had no preparation at all. Certain subject areas, such as mathematics and science, bilingual education and education for the handicapped, experience chronic teacher shortages. Cities with very large populations of children who are not native speakers of English and a tremendous shortage of certified bilingual or ESL teachers, routinely hire English monolingual teachers for bilingual classrooms on temporary certificates, pairing them, where possible, with bilingual aides or colleagues (LeCompte 1985). Where aides are used, often the aides provide the bulk of instruction to the poorest and most disadvantaged students (Ortiz 1988; Bennett 1986).

A recent national survey demonstrated how widespread are these practices. In some states, the "percentages of high school classes taught by teachers who did not have a major, minor, or 20 quarter hours of preparation included Geography, 92 percent; Physics, 43 percent; Chemistry, 43 percent; Math, 36 percent; History, 32 percent, and English, 30 percent." The percentages in middle schools and junior high schools were even worse. This means that the areas most typically mis-assigned are in the core curricular areas of math, science, language arts and history. Specialized offerings, such as fine arts and vocational education, are not so profoundly affected. Middle schools have the worst record of all for assigning teachers outside of their areas of specialization (Robinson and Pierce 1985, p. 33). Table 4.2, which presents data from 1983, indicates that the shortage of qualified teachers will persist.

TABLE 4.2. TEACHER CANDIDATE SHORTAGES AND UNCERTIFIED TEACHERS IN ELEMENTARY AND SECONDARY SCHOOLS, BY FIELD: 1983 [As of November]

| Field | Candidate Shortages[1] | | | | Uncertified Teachers[3] | | | | | |
| | Number | | Ratio[2] | | Number | | | Percent of all teachers[4] | | |
	Total	Public	Total	Public	Total	Public	Private	Total	Public	Private
Total	3,970	3,410	1.6	1.5	88,260	35,690	52,560	3.4	1.6	15.6
Preprimary education	80	80	.9	1.4	12,370	760	11,610	13.7	1.3	37.6
General elementary education	740	640	.8	.9	21,230	6,390	14,840	2.4	.9	10.1
Art	180	120	3.6	2.8	1,590	340	1,250	3.1	.8	18.8
Basic skills and remedial education	120	110	2.9	2.7	840	560	280	2.0	1.5	7.2
Bilingual education	260	260	8.8	9.1	3,590	3,470	5 110	12.0	12.0	5 13.0
Biological and physical sciences	230	180	1.7	1.5	5,360	2,820	2,540	4.1	2.5	15.5
Biology	50	50	1.7	2.0	1,090	500	590	3.7	2.0	14.7
Chemistry	30	20	1.9	1.5	590	200	400	4.0	1.6	15.8
Physics	40	5 30	4.5	5 4.3	490	200	290	5.6	2.8	18.3
General and all other sciences	110	80	1.4	1.1	3,190	1,930	1,260	4.0	2.7	15.2
Business (non-vocational)	20	20	.4	.4	990	260	730	1.8	.5	14.8
Computer science	30	5 20	3.7	5 3.6	790	270	530	8.6	3.9	21.8
English language arts	170	130	.9	.8	4,560	1,900	2,650	2.5	1.2	12.8
Foreign languages	80	70	1.5	1.8	2,830	790	2,040	5.5	2.0	18.6
Health, physical education	100	100	.8	.8	2,920	920	2,000	2.2	.8	14.0

Table 4.2. (cont.)

Home economics	30	20	.7	.4	360	200	160	.9	.6	10.4
Industrial arts	80	50	1.9	1.2	620	380	240	1.4	.9	18.0
Mathematics	260	250	1.8	2.0	6,080	3,160	2,930	4.1	2.4	16.1
Music	240	150	3.1	2.2	2,390	640	1,750	3.0	.9	19.1
Reading	20	20	.4	.5	1,560	650	910	3.2	1.5	20.8
Social studies/social sciences	70	60	.5	.5	3,380	1,360	2,020	2.3	1.1	13.1
Special education	1,030	910	3.9	3.6	9,340	7,820	2,520	3.5	3.1	10.9
Mentally retarded	150	110	2.8	2.0	1,800	1,440	[5] 370	3.3	2.7	17.7
Seriously emotionally disturbed	100	100	3.7	4.3	1,250	870	[5] 380	4.7	3.8	[5] 9.9
Specific learning disabled	190	190	2.6	2.7	3,050	2,560	490	4.2	3.6	17.7
Speech impaired	180	160	6.3	6.1	400	280	[5] 120	1.4	1.1	[5] 13.9
Other special education	410	350	5.0	4.5	2,840	2,670	[5] 170	3.5	3.4	[5] 3.7
Vocational education	70	70	1.1	1.1	2,350	2,260	90	3.6	3.5	14.4
Other elementary education	30	30	1.1	1.2	900	280	[5] 620	3.0	1.0	[5] 23.6
Other secondary education	120	120	2.2	2.7	4,220	450	3,770	7.8	1.1	34.1

[1] In full-time equivalents. Positions for which a teacher was sought and could not be found during recruiting (spring to fall 1983) and for which the opening was vacant or was withdrawn, abolished, or transferred to another field. Includes positions for which a temporary substitute was found.
[2] Rates per 1,000 full-time equivalent current teachers.
[3] In full-time equivalent. Teachers who do not hold a regular or standard State certification in field of assignment. Includes continuing teachers who have only an emergency, temporary or provisional certification.
[4] Estimated full-time equivalent.
[5] Due to large standard errors and small number of cases, caution should be used when drawing conclusions. (Source: U.S. Department of Education, Center for Statistics, Condition of Education, 1985.)

Hospitals would never be permitted to hire a dermatologist to do brain surgery, no matter how severe the shortage of brain surgeons. However, such practices are routine and acceptable in education.

Finally, a profession is considered to be a lifelong calling. However, as we shall indicate later in this chapter, teaching is considered to be an interim career, practiced at the convenience of marriage and children for family-oriented women, and used as an entry-level occupation for men and women who aspire to administrative jobs or other, more lucrative and less stressful careers. While many people do make teaching their life-work, and while the rate of quitting decreases the longer a teacher remains in the profession, the average number of years committed to teaching is no more than about five years (Charters 1970; Anderson and Mark 1977; Mark and Anderson 1978). In fact, teachers on average have among the shortest career trajectories of all the professions.

Semi-Professions

Initial analyses of teaching tried hard to equate it to the standards of practice in the traditional "autonomous" professions. However, later functionalists developed other ways of looking at teaching. In a comparative analysis, Etzioni (1969) grouped teaching with two other occupations, nursing and social work, describing them as "semi-professions". Semi-professions share some, but not all, of the characteristics of the classic professions. Like the traditional professions, they are white collar occupations which provide services, rather than produce goods. The training which they require, however, is considerably less intellectually rigorous and time consuming; their status is less legitimated; their right to privileged communication less well established, and the body of knowledge applicable to the field is less esoteric and uniquely their own.

The semi-professions also have less freedom from supervision or societal control than the traditional professions. Practitioners of the semi-professions are not typically self-employed; rather, they are "bureaucratized" existing within the confines of service bureaucracies and paid by means of salaries instead of client fees. Thus, they are "more" than clerks and secretaries, but "less" than doctors and lawyers (Ibid. pp. i–v).

There is little agreement over standards for excellence in the semi-professions; both establishment and enforcement of standards is affected by the needs of the bureaucracies which employ most of the practitioners. In addition, the knowledge base with which semi-professionals deal is communicated, rather than created. While both professionals and semi-professionals apply knowledge, semi-professionals have less discretion over what they apply and they are supervised in how they apply it. They also are supervised by people who have had the same training. Since school administrators all have had to serve as teachers, teachers may question the legitimacy of their supervisory decisions as based on no greater level of training than they have had. Typically, the similarity in training bases serves as a constant source of tension and conflict because teachers view administrators as bosses or management, not as colleagues or a respected reference group (Etzioni 1969, pp. v–xvi).

A Critical Note

While functionalists have focused upon the nature of training and qualifications in teaching, comparing teaching *up* to doctors, lawyers, and priests, critical theorists have focused on the character of the work itself. They have compared *down,* finding teachers to be more comparable to factory workers than free professionals. Both critical theorists and functionalists have examined the nature of control and power in the profession, and both dwell upon the fact that teaching is primarily a profession for women. They both use this to explain many of the profession's unique characteristics. However, functionalists treat the asymmetrical patterns of control and power in teaching, as well as the lower status of women, as understandable and immutable. By contrast, critical theorists view both as a function of institutionalized patterns of oppression and subordination in contemporary capitalist society, conditions which not only serve to perpetuate the weaknesses of today's educational systems, but which could and should be changed. In the pages which follow, we will examine the themes of feminization, control, and work from both perspectives.

WHO ARE TEACHERS?

A Brief History of a "Feminized" Profession

While teaching has seldom been a field chosen by those in search of great fortunes, and its status as a career has often mutually reflected the social esteem of those individuals who choose it, it has not always been considered women's work. Until the middle of the nineteenth century, all formal education was directed primarily at male students, especially at the secondary level. For the most part, girls who were educated came from well-to-do families and were tutored in their homes. All teachers and administrators, whether their students were male or female, were men.

Education Up to the Reformation. During the Hellenic and Roman eras, military leaders, town governments, and royal courts encouraged the establishment of public schools for the teaching of arts, rhetoric, music, literature and grammar. After the fall of the Roman Empire, the thriving municipal schools for grammar and rhetoric collapsed. By the year 400 A.D., literacy survived primarily within the ranks of the priesthood and among a very few aristocrats (Boyd 1966; Marrou 1956). Monastic orders preserved the remaining libraries, produced teachers, and copied books. The very few universities were governed by canon, or church law; most professors were priests and both teachers and students were treated as if they were members of the clergy. Some families of the nobility employed tutors and established schools at their court for their own children and those of their entourage; these teachers often were priests who were basically high level servants, as were the dance-master and troubadours. In addition, the use of Latin as a *lingua franca* began to be replaced by the ancestors of modern European languages; songs and oral literature were developed in these, not ancient classic languages.

The Protestant Reformation served as a catalyst for a broader based literacy. At the time of Martin Luther, Latin had been transformed into an esoteric language used only by priests and scholars. Literacy in Latin, however, was key to the power of the Catholic church hierarchy since the Bible was written only in Latin, and since only priests were permitted to read and interpret it. One of the tenets of the Reformation was to reduce the power of priests by translating the Bible from Latin to the languages the common people spoke, making it accessible to all who could read.

The Reformation drew its power from the gradually rising power of the middle and lower classes, groups which hitherto had relied upon family socialization and apprenticeship to prepare young people for adulthood. Schooling for the children of these groups was deemed essential by church and political leaders alike to inculcate in them the virtues of religion and laws of society. As we pointed out in Chapter Two, education then and later was widely viewed as a cure for social disorder, especially among the working classes. However, the existing educational provisions were inappropriate for mass education. They were designed for an aristocracy and linked to university level training for boys; they included tutoring in the traditional curriculum of Latin, Greek, grammar, rhetoric and mathematics, followed by university-level training in law, medicine or theology.

As an alternative, religious and civic leaders wanted schools with which to indoctrinate and enlighten the children of the poor. In response, towns and religious orders set up elementary level catechetical schools teaching the rudiments of literacy, the catechism, and sometimes a little arithmetic. The result was the beginning of a dual system of education, one which was oriented to the classics and university training for the rich, and another conducted in vernacular languages and linked to vocational training for the poor (Resnick and Resnick 1985). Each required teachers with a different kind and amount of training.

The Entry of Women. By the end of the 1600s, women were beginning to enter the teaching profession, although not as teachers in formal educational institutions. Dame schools, taught by a woman in her home for children in the neighborhood, became a common way for children to learn the ABC's and the catechism. The English Poor Laws, whose objective was to insure that the children of the poor would not become public charges, facilitated the education of orphans and girls from poor but respectable families to learn to be governesses and tutors in the homes of well-to-do families, since, if unmarried, they would have no other respectable means of support.

Proponents of elementary school education, like Comenius and Froebel in Europe and Horace Mann in America, also encouraged the use of women as teachers of young children. In the first place, women were considered to be good influences on children; their supposed motherly instincts, virtue, and less violent nature better suited them for work with young children, and served as a curb to the passionate, war-like nature of the young men they taught (Boyd 1966; Curti 1971; Binder 1974, p. 124). Perhaps more important, they were cheaper to hire than men (Curti 1971; Boyd 1966).

We need to remember that education still was differentiated by social class. The young children of the rich were taught at home, in an education dominated by study of the classics, Latin and Greek. Older boys attended college preparatory academies, taught by men; they alone were eligible to attend university. If girls received any kind of secondary training, it was primarily in the arts of homemaking and in those ornamental social skills deemed appropriate for upper class women: French, fine needlework, music, dancing, and writing. Female teachers were restricted to teaching at home—in their own, in the dame schools, or in the homes of the wealthy. Children of the poor received an education oriented to social control—sufficient literacy to understand the laws and contracts which governed their public life and labor and the doctrines of the Church.

The great influx of women into teaching really began after the American Civil War. The expansion of provisions for universal elementary schooling and the complete lack of schools for Blacks in the South coupled with northerners' distrust of native southern teachers during Reconstruction, created a great demand for teachers which could not be filled by the available pool of willing males. The "Yankee Schoolmarm" became a prototypical model for the female schoolteacher—single, dedicated, and often adventurous, willing to leave home and travel to hardship towns and frontier areas in search of the only jobs widely available for educated women (Kaufman 1984).

Teaching as Women's Work. The events of the nineteenth century established many of the patterns which characterize teaching today, the most important of which was the feminization of teaching. While the teaching profession entered the twentieth century with a work force dominated by women, it was governed by men, who held virtually all of the administrative positions available. This situation still prevails; it is used as an explanation for the lack of autonomy, weak career commitment, and low professional status characteristic of teachers (Simpson and Simpson 1969, p. 196).

From early times in America, teachers earned low wages. In areas dominated by subsistence farming, teachers earned hardly more than common laborers; only those lucky enough to teach in cities or in secondary level academies catering to the sons of wealthy families could eke out a fairly comfortable living. A college graduate could make more money in almost any other profession; as a consequence, most male schoolmasters avoided making a career of teaching (Main 1966). The entry of women into teaching exacerbated the practice of paying teachers poorly; women were hired because they were, in fact, willing to work for less than men.

Teaching also acquired low status because, in an era which valued hard manual labor, teaching was defined as "easy"; it did not require the full physical efforts of an adult man. Nor was teaching judged mentally taxing, since teachers qualified for their profession by attaining only the level of education immediately higher than their own. Thus, elementary teachers typically became women, who had attended, or even graduated, from a high school or normal school (Lortie 1969).

High levels of turnover, also a familiar problem in teaching, were institutionalized in the nineteenth century by a profession which failed to pay men a living wage, and which, though designed to attract women, required them to leave their jobs upon marriage (Lortie 1973, p. 488).

While writers like Simpson and Simpson (1969) and Pavalko (1970) addressed the prevalence of women in the teaching force, they did so in a context which accepted existing patterns of restrictions upon and discrimination against women and failed to examine the larger patterns of opppression and subordination which generated them. In fact, Simpson and Simpson dismiss these patterns on the grounds that "when discrimination does occur, there may be valid grounds for it from the organization's point of view" (1969, p. 222). They ignore the long history of male resistance to permitting women access to higher education, or to giving university status to programs like normal schools which were designed for the training of women (Ginsburg 1988).

Such resistance was justified on both gender and class bases. Higher education was described as unsuitable to the nature of women and a threat to male hegemony. Teacher education programs, which recruited both women, who had low status, and people from the lower socio-economic classes, were perceived as diminishing the status of universities with which they were associated (ibid.).

Critical theorists, by contrast, view the feminized nature of teaching as crucial to understanding the political, economic and ideological modes of control in the profession. It is not so much the nature of the work itself which is problematic, but that it is performed by subordinated, *woman* workers; it can best be understood in terms of analyses of the labor process and patterns of class domination (Apple 1986).

All during the early part of the twentieth century, women poured into the teaching profession. Their presence, plus a unique set of historical and economic circumstances, made the decades of the 1950s and 1960s appear to be a "Golden Age" of excellence in teaching in America. First, as the barriers prohibiting their enrollment fell, an unprecedented number of middle- and upper-class women begin to graduate from colleges and universities. For example, female enrollment in higher education rose from 29 percent of the total enrollment in 1948 to 51 percent in 1980 (O'Neill and Sepielli 1985, p. 27). In addition, government scholarships and preferential loan programs encouraged men and women to pursue careers in teaching.

Finally, notwithstanding their high level of academic qualification, educated women in the 1950s and early 1960s found that patterns of sex discrimination in employment still precluded them from virtually all professional positions but teaching. Table 4.3 illustrates the male domination of school administration: in colleges and universities, the professors in colleges of education were over‍whelmingly male. The few women who do attain administrative rank do so by

TABLE 4.3. MALE AND FEMALE PUBLIC SCHOOL ADMINISTRATORS, UNITED STATES, 1972–82

Position	1972–73[a]		1976–77[b]		1981–82[c]	
	% male	% female	% male	% female	% male	% female
Superintendents and assistant superintendents	96.1	3.9	94.6	5.4	96.2	3.8

Position	1972–73[a]		1976–77[b]		1981–82[c]	
	% male	% female	% male	% female	% male	% female
Principals	92.2	7.8	87.1	12.9[d]	84.0	16.0
Other administrators supervisors, directors)	35.0	65.0	45.4	54.6[e]	Not Available	

Note: These data are from four different sources, and categories of administrators change in each data collection. There are no data available from national data collection sources on sex of administrators in the 1980s.
[a] *Source*: Adapted from National Education Association Research Division, *26th Biennial Salary and Staff Survey of Public School Professional Personnel*, 1972–73 (Washington, D.C., 1973), pp. 9–10. [b] *Source*: Adapted from B. Foster and J. Carpenter, *Statistics of Public Elementary and Secondary Day Shcools* (Washington, D.C.: Department of Health, Education and Welfare, 1976), p. 20. [c] *Source*: Adapted from Effie Jones and Xenia Montenegro, *Recent Trends in the Representation of Women and Minorities in School Administration and Problems in Documentation* (Arlington, Va.: American Association of School Administrators, 1982), pp. 4, 9, 12. [d] Includes principals and assistant principals. [e] *Source*: Adapted from Equal Employment Opportunity Commission, *Elementary-Secondary Staff Information* (EEO–5) *Annual Surveys* (1976), unpublished; reported in Elizabeth Havens, "Women in Educational Administration: The Principalship" (Washington, D.C.: National Institute of Education, Contract 400-79-0698, 1980), p. 2. *(Source: U.S. Bureau of the Census. Statistical Abstract of the United States: 1987 (107th Edition). Washington, D.C., 1986.)*

means of career paths markedly different from those of men (Grow [Maienza] 1981; Ortiz 1981).

Not only are the type of tasks performed by educators highly differentiated by level, but routes to these levels as well as the incumbents themselves also are highly differentiated by gender. In the pages which follow, we will examine demographic characteristics of the people who choose to become educators, the nature of tasks done in the "gendered" profession as teaching, as well as the structures in which they are carried out.

Demographic Characteristics of Teachers

The most salient factor about teaching is its stereotypically female work force. Table 4.4 summarizes selected characteristics of public school teachers over the past two decades: In 1983, the average teacher was a white, married woman in her midthirties with two children. She came from a middle to upper-middle class family, received her training at a public university, and was likely to teach

TABLE 4.4. SELECTED CHARACTERISTICS OF PUBLIC SCHOOL TEACHERS:
SPRING 1961 to SPRING 1986

Item	1961	1966	1971	1976	1981	1986
1	2	3	4	5	6	7
Sex (percent)						
Men	31.3	31.1	34.3	32.9	33.1	31.2
Women	68.7	69.0	65.7	67.0	66.9	68.8
Median age (years)						
All teachers	41	36	35	33	37	41
Men	34	33	33	33	38	42
Women	46	40	37	33	36	41
Race (percent)						
White	—	—	88.3	90.8	91.6	89.6
Black	—	—	8.1	8.0	7.8	6.9
Other	—	—	3.6	1.2	0.7	3.4
Marital status (percent)						
Single	22.3	22.0	19.5	20.1	18.5	12.9
Married	68.0	69.1	71.9	71.3	73.0	75.7
Widowed, Divorced or separated	9.7	9.0	8.6	8.6	8.5	11.4
Highest degree held (percent)						
Less than bachelor's	14.6	7.0	2.9	0.9	0.4	0.3
Bachelor's	61.9	69.6	69.6	61.6	50.1	48.3
Master's or specialist degree	23.1	23.2	27.1	37.1	49.3	50.7
Doctor's	0.4	0.1	0.4	0.4	0.3	0.7
Average annual salary as classroom teacher	$5,264	$6,253	$9,261	$12,005	$17,209	$24,504

(Source: National Education Association, Status of the American Public School Teacher, 1985–86. (Copyright 1987 by the National Education Association.) (This table was prepared July 1987).

in a suburban elementary school. She would not be politically active and though she put in a slightly longer work week than the average blue collar worker, she would bring home a slightly smaller pay check. She also would be comfortable in her rather traditional gender role. She was older than her male counterparts by almost eight years, was somewhat less likely than he to have acquired a master's degree, and probably came from a family with somewhat higher socio-economic status (NEA 1963, 1972; Feistritzer 1983; Spencer 1986).

Career Commitment: Teaching as a Second Choice Job

Whether they are male or female, teachers are likely to have selected teaching as a second choice. The decision to teach is often made relatively late in the college program, as students find that they lack the ability or financial and familial support to pursue a preferred career of choice (Simpson and Simpson 1969; Pavalko 1970; Eisenhart and Holland 1988); more college students transfer their majors *into* education than out of it (Davis 1965). Most of those who enter teaching do not plan to make it their life-work. One-third of those who are trained to teach never enter a classroom (Simpson and Simpson 1969); 65 percent of beginning female teachers expect to leave within five years; and 70 percent of new female teachers eventually want to become homemakers. Although five out of six plan to return to teaching when their children are in school (Pavalko 1970), many do not. As much as 60 percent of the total number of people trained to be teachers are not teaching at any given time (Corwin 1965). In general, teacher turnover stands at about 17 percent of the cohort annually (Charters 1970; Anderson and Mark 1977; Mark and Anderson 1978). Increasing rates of divorce and single parenthood may be changing this situation, however; by 1971, the number of female teachers with breaks in service had declined by 13 percent. In addition, attrition rates for both men and women tend to decline if they survive the first year or two of teaching (Charters 1970; Mark and Anderson 1978).

Committment patterns for male teachers are similar, though for different reasons. Most men who enter teaching plan to move into administrative roles within five years. Most do not want to spend their lives as teachers; if they remain in the classroom, they express great unhappiness with their jobs by age 40 (Lortie 1973, p. 489). Another difference is in the percentage of male teachers with breaks in teaching service. Lortie found that the percentage of male teachers who had interrupted their service increased by 6.6 percent, while the percentage of women who interrupted their teaching careers declined. This indicates that men who remain in the profession try to leave it more often than women do, even taking into consideration women's breaks for childrearing.

Intellect and Ideology

Although some studies indicate that those who are initially recruited to teaching are of higher measured intelligence than the average college student (Pavalko 1970), many studies indicate that the standardized test scores and grade-point averages of students who graduate from teacher education are among the lowest of all college programs. This may be because the more able students drop out of teacher training; the more able also are less likely to remain in the profession. Pavalko indicates that of the women who did graduate and become teachers, those with higher measured intelligence were more likely to drop out of the profession (ibid.). In any case, the appeal of teaching is not in its intellectual rigor; rather it appeals to the heart—to those who like working with people rather than ideas (Simpson and Simpson 1969)—or, to the critical theorist, to those who have no more desirable alternative.

Teachers tend to be politically conservative; 16.9 percent describe themselves as conservative, while 43.6 percent describe themselves as tending to be conservative (NEA 1972). They tend to be ambivalent about collective action in their behalf (Ginsburg 1988); when asked, "Do you believe public school teachers should ever strike," only 10 percent felt that teachers should be permitted the same right to strike as other employees. While 21 percent felt that teachers should never strike, and 64 percent believed that teachers should strike only in the most extreme cases, when all other means had failed (NEA 1970).

Social Class Status

Data on the socioeconomic origins of teachers is mixed. Teaching traditionally has been thought of as an avenue for upward mobility; in 1911, 52 percent of all teachers came from farm families, and 26 percent had parents who were blue-collar workers However, that percentage has dropped steadily. By 1960, only 26.5 percent came from farm families, and 30 percent from blue collar families (Betz and Garland 1974). This probably reflects a drop in the overall number of farm families and growth in the industrial sector, but it also reflects a substantial increase in the number of individuals from middle-and upper-middle class backgrounds who chose to become teachers.

These figures, taken from Mason's (1961) often-quoted study, combined both rural and urban districts. They may somewhat underestimate the contribution of the urban middle class, in that teachers with rural origins are more likely to be recruited to teaching, to remain in the profession, and to remain in rural areas (Pavalko 1970; Hare 1988). When figures from urban areas are examined, the contribution of the middle class to teaching is even higher, especially when figures for men and women are examined separately. The conventional wisdom that teaching is a career for those with blue collar origins tends to be true for men as well as for the five percent of the teaching force which is Mexican-American; but white teachers, especially women, come disproportionately from professional, technical, managerial and business backgrounds. Since the 1940s, black teachers increasingly have had similar backgrounds (Dworkin 1980). Thus, while women from high socioeconomic status backgrounds are initially over-represented in teaching, women from less-advantaged backgrounds are much more likely to continue working as teachers than those from middle and upper class backgrounds (Betz and Garland 1974). This may be a function of the latter group having alternatives to teaching (Dworkin 1986). It also may be that women from the working classes, like men, see teaching as an avenue to higher status, or, as Maienza suggests, base their persistence in the job on the role-model provided by their own working mothers (Maienza [Grow] 1981).

In any case, blue collar children of both sexes seem to be encountering increasing difficulty in gaining access to teaching careers, perhaps because of both the rising cost of higher education and the curtailment of financial aid for disadvantaged and middle-income families. Given the salary they can expect as teachers, few young people may want to encumber themselves with the degree of debt a college education now requires. The consequences for the profession are that it will increasingly become a profession with white-collar and service-sector origins, and that it will remain predominately white and female.

Minority Teachers

While there are substantially fewer minority than white teachers, Gottlieb (1964) and Dworkin (1980) reported that turnover among minority teachers is much lower than for whites, perhaps because of their greater job satisfaction. Fewer desirable occupations are open to minorities, and members of minority groups are more likely to experience upward mobility by becoming teachers. While minority teachers were few and usually relegated to racially segregated schools prior to 1964, more black, Hispanic, and other minority teachers entered the profession during the period of educational expansion in the 1960s and early 1970s. Males, too, became teachers in increasing numbers to avoid being drafted. These changes, however, were temporary. When the draft was eliminated, the incentive for men to become teachers ended; curtailment of scholarships and aid programs for the disadvantaged in the 1980s produced a drop in the number of minorities able to attend college at all, much less become teachers.

In addition, as discriminatory barriers to their employment in more prestigious fields attentuated, educated members of minority groups no longer were forced to choose teaching as the highest level occupation to which they could aspire. As a consequence, the teaching force remains primarily white and middle-class at the same time that the school population, especially in urban areas, becomes increasingly minority dominated (Hodgkinson 1985). More and more teachers are working with children whose background and ethnicity is radically different from their own. These conditions have important consequences for the amount of culture shock and stress teachers encounter on the job (LeCompte 1978a, 1985; Dworkin 1987; Dworkin, Haney and Telschow 1988).

WHAT TEACHERS DO: CONTRADICTIONS IN THE NATURE OF TEACHERS' WORK

Teaching in the United States has inherited a "divided legacy": the ideal that education is essential for democratic citizenship and at the same time an organization for schooling that subordinates learning to routine degree provision or "credentialling." Ironically, both notions are born of the same democratic imperative: the mandate for universal education, which has created public schools so large that they require management by complex, impersonal and bureaucratic organizations which obviate and are at cross-purposes with their educational intentions (McNeil 1988a, p. 337).

Teaching also has an ambiguous place in the occupational structure because it is neither an autonomous profession, like medicine, nor a bureaucratized occupation, like automotive assembly (Dreeben 1973, p. 453). This gives teachers what has been called a "contradictory class location" (Wright 1978). They are not blue collar workers, and cannot be expected to act in the same way as factory employees or clerks in large corporations. While many of them (especially men) have blue-collar origins, most do not adhere to working class ideologies.

At the same time, their status does not equate with that of "real" professionals. In the next sections of this chapter, we will discuss the nature of these complexities and contradictions. Their source lies to some extent in the type of work teachers do and how it is organized; it also is partly attributable to the differentiated sex-ratio in the profession. We begin with a functionalist analysis of the teaching profession. Then we examine what teachers do and the purposes these activities serve. We then discuss some of the ways analysts have begun to view teachers and their work in a critical perspective.

The Conditions of Labor

The Workload. Forty-five percent of the teachers in America teach in school districts with from 3000 to 25,000 students enrolled. The average teacher works for a white, male principal. Teacher's jobs require them to be in their classrooms 37 hours per week. In addition they perform eight additional hours of uncompensated, but required duty. They teach an average of 181 days each year, and most do so without help; only 5.5 percent had teacher aides of their own, while an additional 24.7 percent shared aides with one or more other teachers (NEA 1972). These figures, compiled in the 1970s, have remained more or less unchanged.

Teachers have little respite from their classrooms; few have free periods, and the number who do has declined. Teachers enjoy a daily lunch break of less than forty minutes, which often is shared with supervisory duties in the children's cafeteria and which has declined by as much as five minutes since 1950.

Teachers also are badly outnumbered. While pupil-teacher ratios have been declining to some extent in the past decades, most classroom teachers face some 27 to 35 students every time they enter their rooms. Jackson states that nowhere, except in schools, are humans required to spend so much time so physically close to one another and the physical design of classrooms seems highly conducive to frequent disruption, particularly in the lower grades. Thus, a teacher's primary task is to design and engage pupils in learning activities sufficiently engrossing that they find those activities substantially more attractive than outlawed alternatives (Jackson 1968, pp. 85–90). However, they spend only about half the school day in actual instruction (Adams and Biddle 1970, pp. 41–45); elementary school teachers may divide their time equally between instruction and classroom management (LeCompte 1978b).

Classrooms are "three ring circuses" in which the competent teacher serves as ringmaster (Smith and Geoffrey 1968). The school day is characterized by high rates of interaction and frequent changes in activities—as often as every five seconds in an active classroom and every 18 seconds in a quiet one. Changes in who talks can occur more than 174 times each lesson, totalling between 650 and 1000 interchanges daily between teachers and students. Teachers themselves initiate as many as 80 interchanges per hour with students

(Dreeben 1973, p. 464). Under some circumstances, the teacher can feel like a stand-up comedian with an audience full of hecklers; at best, the teacher ends the day with sensory overload.

Fragmentation. Sensory overload is exacerbated by fragmentation and interruptions. Teachers' work is fragmented by the way the curriculum is organized, by bureaucratic time schedules, and by exigencies of school life which interrupt the flow of teaching. As we have indicated, the curriculum divides school knowledge into subjects, the subjects into courses, the courses into chapters and units, and these, in turn, are divided into sets of objectives (McNeil 1988a).

Most subjects are treated as if they have little, if any relationship with each other; reading in math has nothing to do with reading in social studies. In fact, there is fragmentation even within subject areas, such that students study European history and art without ever considering the relationship that there might be between European events and American history and art. The school schedule divides actual teaching activities into discrete time allottments, taught at specific times of the day. Teachers have little lattitude to teach longer to make a point, combine areas which seem related or to omit things which are unimportant. Thus, it is difficult to be carried away into a "grand sweep of history", or general theory of mathematics.

Finally, teaching is fragmented by everyday life in schools. The flow of instruction regularly is interrupted by announcements over the intercom, lunch count, children asking to leave the room, others coming in with notes or requests from other teachers, fire drills, assemblies, athletic activities, fights, and other contingencies.

Isolation. Teachers, alone among virtually all other professions, work in almost total isolation from other adults. In the motel-like structure of most schools, teachers only get to see their colleagues between classes or at lunchtime, periods when they often are engaged in supervisory tasks as well. If they have a free period, it is occupied with school tasks and shared by only a few of their colleagues. Under these conditions, there is little opportunity for collegiality, sharing of ideas, or collective organization. Teacher knowledge of their job and feelings of competence are, then, deepened by means of introspection over their own daily experiences with students, rather than broadened by encounters with colleagues sharing similar or different experiences or ideas. They are left very much on their own to determine what they are doing right or wrong; in a sense, teachers are taught by their own students (Lortie 1969, p. 469).

Control of Students. Knowing one's subject is not sufficient. Teaching also is contingent upon the good will of students (Connell 1985). Teachers cannot just enter a classroom and begin to teach; there first must exist a minimum level of order and attentiveness, as well as an agreement on the part of students to assimilate what the teacher presents. Learning the rules for this agreement constitutes a "hidden curriculum" the importance of which is that competence in teaching is judged more on how orderly the classroom is than on how much students learn, perhaps because quiet is easier to assess than achievement. Lack of quiet also disrupts the smooth routine of bureaucratic order.

School policies require that teachers be "fair," exhibit affective neutrality around their students and judge students by uniform and universalistic standards. Students expect this, demanding that their teachers keep order, explain things carefully, not be boring, and not play favorites (Nash 1976). Violation of these expectations or too much rigidity precipitates student retaliation and loss of control, which is only maintained by creating a balance between personal force-fulness and intimacy in teacher-pupil relationships. In order to accomplish this, Bidwell (1965, p. 1011) suggests that teachers allocate rewards in classrooms so as to disrupt and weaken the power of student peer affiliations and establish their own power base.

Lack of Tangible Results. Both the quality and quantity of what teachers do is difficult to assess. Connell (1985) succinctly describes the lack of tangibility:

> "Teaching is a labor process without an object. At best, it has an object so intangible—the minds of the kids, or their capacity to learn—that it cannot be specified in any but vague and metaphorical ways . . . [it] does not produce any *things,* nor, like other white collar work, does it produce visible and quantifiable effects—so many pensions paid, so many dollars turned over, so many patients cured . . ." (p. 70)

In the elusive nature of its product, teaching differs from both the factory work and the professional service sector to which it often is compared. Teachers can, indeed, count the number of their students who pass certain tests or courses, graduate from high school, or attain degrees. However, even these measures are deceptive, because most teaching is cumulative and subjective; it is difficult to attribute to any one teacher all the credit for the performance of any given individual or group of students.

Multi-Dimensionality. While the work of teachers ostensibly is teaching, they do many other things besides teach: they develop instructional materials, coach athletic teams, sponsor extracurricular activities, serve on committees related to the academic and administrative operation of schools, engage in tutoring and counseling of students and perform social work duties for their families, and do police work in school corridors, lunchrooms, playgrounds, toilets, and buses.

The multi-dimensionality of teaching is one of the things contributing to its appeal as a career; it keeps the job from being boring and may be regarded as one of its intrinsic rewards. However, sometimes these activities become so time consuming that when they are added to the actual time spent in the classroom, time spent in preparing lessons and grading homework assignments and tests, teaching becomes much more than an eight-hour-a-day job.

Stress, Burnout, and Victimization

Teaching has grown more and more stressful over the years. We attribute this to several factors. School consolidation has increased the size of schools and districts; urbanization and growth in minority populations has increased the heterogeneity of students; and finally the whole social, economic and cultural context of schools has changed radically during the professional lifetime of most contemporary teachers (LeCompte and Dworkin 1988). While teachers virtually always have counted discipline and crowd control among their primary professional concerns, more of today's teachers are subject to extreme social and psychological job stress than ever before.

Stress for teachers has several sources. One is the sense that one is inadequate to carry out assigned tasks. Another comes from the discrepancies between what teachers expect to find when they enter the profession and what they actually encounter. Stress also develops when the rewards earned do not seem commensurate with the effort expended. Finally, stress is generated by alienation, or a sense that one's work has become meaningless—that one has lost the power to make the changes necessary to bring meaning back into the job; that one can neither understand nor control the circumstances of life; and that one is without allies to improve the situation (Needle et al. 1980; Dworkin 1987, p.7). All of these conditions characterize the working situation of an increasing number of teachers. The result often is what we call "wear out" or "burnout" (Dworkin 1987).

Teachers burn out for a variety of reasons. Some burnout occurs naturally as a consequence of the sensory overload which we described earlier in this chapter; teachers usually cannot take a restorative sabbatical from their jobs. Isolation also increases the likelihood of burnout in two ways: first, as we have indicated, the physical layout and scheduling constraints of schools give teachers few opportunities to blow off steam with other teachers; and second, because teachers tend to find most of their friends among other teachers, they get less input from people with other viewpoints (Ginsburg 1979).

Expectations also play a role. People are attracted to teaching because they perceive teachers as catalysts for student learning. When they find that they are unable to make children learn, whether because of institutional or time pressures, student misbehavior, or interpersonal conflicts, they become subject to stress and burnout (Needle et al. 1980).

In addition, many teachers feel physically unsafe in their schools. Each year, twelve percent of all teachers report that they have been robbed at school; twelve percent also say that they avoid confronting students because they are afraid of them. One percent per month are physically attacked at school. Student attacks on teachers totalled over 110,000 in 1978 (NIE 1978) and seventy-two percent of all teachers report being concerned about the amount of vandalism and destruction of property in school (Phillips and Lee 1980). The majority of violence reported takes place in secondary schools but elementary teachers are not immune. While many reports have minimized the amount of actual danger in schools, perhaps more important is the dismaying feeling that "you might be next": 75 percent of teachers knew someone who had been verbally abused, and 35 percent knew someone who had been physically attacked. The installation of metal detectors by several of the largest urban school districts in the late 1980s and the rising indices of drug use and crime among preteen children give these feelings of victimization and vulnerability additional credence. The result is a widespread disaffection with the profession.

In a major study of teachers, nearly one-third indicated that they felt their work to be meaningless and that they were powerless to do anything about it (Dworkin 1987). These feelings were more common among those teachers most numerous in the profession—female, white, middle-class, less than thirty years old, and with less than five years of teaching experience. Elementary teachers also were more likely to feel stressed than secondary teachers. Significantly, feelings of discrimination, victimization and burnout also were more likely to occur when teachers were "racially isolated", or teaching in a school where the predominant race of the student body was different from their own. (Dworkin 1987). As we have indicated, demographic change in the coming decades is likely to assure that this kind of isolation will become increasingly common (Hodgkinson 1985) and that culture shock will become more and more common among teachers.

WHAT IS THE REWARD STRUCTURE OF TEACHING?

Teaching is a profession which traditionally has produced few extrinsic rewards for excellent performance. Most of its benefits, as we have described earlier, are intangible and derive from direct classroom activity and interaction with children. Financially, standardized salary schedules prevent giving bonuses or raises for exemplary work. Typically the only tangible rewards which administrators can give to teachers concern working conditions—a desirable classroom, assignment to gifted students, a free period, permission to teach a speciality course or time off to go to a conference. Teaching also has a "flat" career trajectory; teachers cannot be promoted for good teaching except by moving into administration, which means leaving the classroom.

Critical Area Pay

Recently, incentive systems of various kinds have been initiated. "Combat pay" has been offered to teachers who would teach in inner-city or especially tough schools. "Critical area pay" was offered for teachers certified in subjects in short supply, such as math, science, and bilingual education. It adds substantially to the remuneration of some teachers, but as Dworkin (1987) indicates, increases in pay cannot compensate teachers for adverse working conditions.

Merit Pay

Many districts have tried, and discarded, merit pay plans. The major complaint about them was that the criteria for establishing merit was vague, subjective, and too prone to administrative manipulation; teachers do not trust their administrators to be fair. These plans are continually aired, however, and just as continually rejected by teacher organizations, who have consistently struggled to equalize pay for teachers across disciplines and grade levels.

Career Ladders

As a consequence of the reform movements of the late 1980s, many states have mandated "Career Ladder" programs which attempt to eliminate the "flat trajectory" of the profession. These plans create levels in teaching based upon seniority, advanced preparation, and excellence in teaching performance. Career ladders are a variation of merit pay; they attempt to avoid the charge of subjectivity which plagued earlier plans by making the steps for acquiring merit very explicit. This very systematization of the career ladder steps has been criticized, however, for turning teaching performance and its assessment into a rigidly prescribed and routinized activity. Current research indicates that where career ladder programs have been instituted, they have not resulted in fundamental changes in the work roles, responsibilities and reward structures for teachers. In fact, existing distinctions in rank among teachers became the basis for levels in the career ladder. The result has been that those who always had been favored continue to be (Malen et al. 1987).

DE-SKILLING, ROUTINIZATION, AND THE ENFORCEMENT OF BUREAUCRATIC CONTROL

Teachers control only certain aspects of their classrooms. Lortie describes the "variable zoning" (1969, pp. 13–15) involved in teachers' decision-making, by which he means that teachers have "hard" jurisdiction in some areas where their judgements will not be questioned and "soft" jurisdiction in others. Lortie and other functionalists have suggested that the privacy of the closed classroom door ensured that instructional decisions were "hard" ones for teachers, while they had less discretion over such things as record keeping and administrative matters. "Hard" decisions in instructional matters were seen as the teacher's area of discretion or autonomy, one which strengthened their sense of professionalism. However, this also meant that "that which is most central and unique to schools—instruction—is least controlled by specific and literally enforced rules and regulations (Ibid., p. 14).

As schools have become increasingly bureaucratized in recent years, critical researchers have noted erosion in the "harder" areas of teacher discretion. Apple describes the degree to which decision-making about curriculum and instructional matters has passed out of the hands of teachers, leaving as their exclusive province only the behavioral control of those students in their own classroom (Apple 1982, 1988). He calls this "**de-skilling**", because it strips from teachers the ability to utilize their special training and expertise, and attributes it in part to technological innovation in curricular delivery—the use of computer assisted instruction and other preprogrammed forms of instruction—as well as behaviorally-based curricula with prespecified teaching programs and lessons "bits". He also suggests that work typically performed by women—secretaries, clerks, nurses—is among that most prone to de-skilling.

Cuban (1984) suggests that teachers have direct influence over only five areas of classroom decision-making, all of which are related to the groupings and spatial arrangements used in dominant modes of instruction:

1. arrangement of classroom space
2. the ratio of teacher to student talk
3. whether most instruction occurs individually, in small groups, or with the entire class.
4. whether or not learning or interest centers are used by students as a normal part of the school day
5. the degree of movement students are permitted without asking the teacher (p. 5)

These are all basically management concerns; they deal with matters of crowd control and traffic patterns, the degree to which instruction is individualized, and the amount of student talking and teacher-pupil interaction in the classroom, rather than the content of instruction.

Teacher decision-making begins to attenuate at this point. Decisions about curricula are made by local and state educational agencies which mandate which subjects will be taught and how much time will be allocated to each of them; state textbook committees also generally provide a list of approved textbooks to be used. Individual school districts may use teacher committees to help choose which books from the approved list they will purchase, but individual teachers may not select alternatives. Teachers even may be restricted in the supplementary books they assign by community watchdog committees and district regulations.

Teachers also are written out of decision-making about curriculum by the use of standardized, subject-area criterion-and norm-referenced testing programs. In response to calls for improved standards of performance in education such programs have been instituted in almost every state. To the extent that school districts base instructional content on the items in externally developed and administered tests, teachers lose control of daily classroom instruction. This is especially true when promotion, retention and graduation of students is tied to performance on the tests.

Loss of control over content is a serious matter, because it prevents teachers from using the skills in the content area of their specialized training. However, de-skilling can take even more insidious forms: teachers may even lose control over *how* they teach. "Teacher-proof" curricula come not only with instructional objectives, but with lesson plans, mandated readings and exercises, pre-and post tests, and supplementary activities. Such curricula routinize and bureaucratize the teaching process, hedging it with rules and regulations, and making it difficult for teachers to improvise, create, or follow up on what they might think important.

McNeil's (1988c) recent case study comparing the attitudes and behavior of teachers before and after institution of educational reform programs amply documents the effect that de-skilling has upon enthusiastic and dedicated teachers. She describes how, in the name of improving student performance, the content of courses in one large school district was "taken apart, sequenced, numbered, and sub-numbered", not by teachers, but by central office test producers in a manner "perhaps unwittingly modelled on the activity analysis which efficiency experts used for pacing activities on an assembly line." Their purpose was to create measurable behavioral objectives for each component of the curriculum, then develop tests which assessed student mastery. Ultimately, uniformity of instruction and assessment of students was to be assured for each student in the district. The result was to transform the tasks of the teacher into a set of "generic behaviors."

McNeil states that the curriculum reforms generated an immense amount of new work for teachers. Not only were teachers required to teach what they perceived to be much more material (the value of some of which they questioned), but both the new instructional management systems and the preoccupation with administration and grading of tests generated a massive volume of paperwork. Teachers felt they had become little more than assembly line workers or clerks, whose job only was to organize, disseminate, and process pre-developed student tasks.

Many of the teachers in McNeil's study engaged in principled resistance to the formalization and enforcement of bureaucratic control. Some quit teaching. Faced with an overwhelming volume of content to cover so their students could pass the tests, some gave up on good teaching. They engaged in "mystification", ommission of controversial issues, and compression or "defensive simplification" of complex topics. This involved teaching "concept recognition," rather than understanding, and presenting outlines and lists of important facts to be memorized rather than analysis and synthesis of material. Written composition was eliminated altogether. While these strategies undoubtedly made instruction less onerous, they also caused teachers to lose credibility in the eyes of students, who no longer found their serious questions answered, and who found teachers no longer seemed to have any demonstrated expertise. (McNeil 1988b)

Re-skilling and Alienation

The educational reforms of the 1980s not only greatly increased the work load for teachers, they have also changed the content and focus of tasks. Teachers are "de-skilled" as control over instructional matters pass out of their hands, but "re-skilled" to be managers of complex technological and behavioral management systems for students. Many respond, at least initially, with feelings of enthusiasm and competence rather than alienation. Apple (1986) attributes this to the fact that they *are* learning new skills, even though it shifts them away from their areas of competence. The process of learning new things, as well as the fact that they are in fact working very long, hard hours, makes them feel as though they are doing a good job. Because most teachers also believe that American education is in need of reform, they also believe they are participating in exciting educational innovation. Under these conditions, teachers feel that they share a definition of the problem with external reformers—district administrators and state agencies—and jointly are working toward a mutually satisfactory way to solve it. Their efforts may be illusory, however, because the ultimate effect of centralized curriculum management is to remove control from the jurisdiction of teachers.

In McNeil's study, by contrast, meaning was constructed in a different way. Teachers in the school she studied already had been defined, by themselves and the district, as excellent teachers in an exemplary magnet school. They interpreted the district's imposition of a curricular reform program and testing as an indication that they were no longer considered experts and resented the loss of status and control which the innovations created. We feel that the situation McNeil describes is more common; however, Dworkin's research (1985b, 1987) on teacher burnout indicates that principals and other administrators can ameliorate alienation in these circumstances. Regardless of the level of stress they encounter, teachers who view their principals as supportive are less likely to engage in resistance activities or to experience burnout.

Having outlined the general conditions under which teachers work, we now move to a discussion of the work of administrators and ancillary staff.

ADMINISTRATORS AND ANCILLARY STAFF

We already have described in detail the characteristics of teachers. We introduce administrators and counselors at this juncture, because initial experience as a teacher is the common denominator for all professional level staff in public schools.

Administrators

Virtually all administrators in school districts, whether they supervise teachers, counselors, bus drivers, evaluators, or record-keepers, are required to have teacher certification. Entrance to university level programs for administrator training, which is required for most public school administrative positions as well as for faculty positions in colleges of education, typically requires at least three years of teaching in elementary or secondary schools. This requirement guarantees a certain uniformity of outlook in the educational profession; it also assures a large proportion of professional level staff will be drawn from the same initial pool of recruits.

Administrators do not constitute a representative sample of teachers, however. While they resemble teachers in their socioeconomic status and religious affiliations, administrators differ radically by sex. For example, 93 percent of all high school principals in the United States in the mid-1970s were male (Boocock 1980). While searching for respondents for a survey of female United States school superintendents, Frasher et al. (quoted in Maienza-Grow 1981) were able to locate only 131; of the 82 who responded to the survey, over 70 percent served in small school districts with enrollments of less than 3,000 students.

Male and Female Career Patterns. In addition to the dramatic differences in numbers, male and female school administrators appear to follow different career patterns once they make the initial move from the classroom. While there have been few comparative studies of male and female administrators, Maienza [Grow]'s study (1981) indicated that men who enter administrative careers appear to have decided to do so early in their years as teachers. Male administrators typically taught for a little more than six years, started and completed graduate school in their thirties, and had had about eight years of administrative experience, usually as secondary school principals or upper-level central office staff, before attaining their first superintendency. By contrast, women did not decide to become administrators until after finishing the master's degree. They entered and completed graduate school in their forties or fifties and attained their first superintendency after almost 13 years of lower-level administrative experience. Only five years of the delay in career advancement seems attributable to breaks in service for child-rearing. (In fact, while most male administrators are married, women, especially at the superintendent level, tend to be single—never married, widowed, or divorced [Maienza [Grow] op. cit.]). Women do have a career pattern in educational administration, but it differs from men, leading through lower level central office positions to elementary principalships, not from secondary principalships and upper level central office positions to the superintendency (Gaertner 1978). As Ortiz (1981) puts it:

> Men are more likely than women to occupy those positions with greater potential for power and opportunity as well as those at the upper levels of the hierarchy. Male mobility tends to be vertical through a series of line positions entailing the administration of adults . . . Women tend to move through positions involving instruction and interaction with children from which vertical movement is rare. (p. 81)

Minorities. Ortiz also points out that members of minority groups tend to be limited to instructional duties and containing other minorities. Because they are viewed as specialists in minority problems, when they are appointed to the principalship, they tend to be assigned to schools defined as "problem schools" because of their large minority enrollments. Reyes and Halcon (1988) call this "type-casting" and the "Brown-on-Brown" taboo; they suggest that the very fact that minorities are considered experts in the problems of their own people is seen to disqualify them as experts on the problems of others. This causes them to be regarded primarily as crisis managers, rather than administrators capable of handling the broad range of responsibilities required in higher positions (Ortiz 1981); it acts to limit the appointment of minorities to "one per pot" (Reyes and Halcon 1988) or department and to reduce their chances for promotion.

Counselors and Ancillary Staff

Like teachers and administrators, counselors also must first be certified as teachers. Like administrators, counselors are not a representative sample of the teaching population. They tend more often to be older, male, and white. While we tend to think of schools primarily in terms of the activities of teachers, both the number of counselors and other ancillary staff in schools and their importance in educational functioning have grown dramatically in the past decades. In 1980, there were over 32,000 counselors in the United States (Boocock 1980). Their presence "bears witness to at least two things: there are problems in the school, and the usual personnel cannot, or have not been able to, resolve them" (Sarason 1971, p. 127). They are an indication of the growth in what in Chapter Two we called the "service sector" in education.

Since counselors often are counted as instructional personnel, their numbers tend to deflate statistics on pupil:teacher ratios; classroom teachers actually instruct a greater number of students. However, counselors do not teach, and their career paths are different. Such paths generally include a bachelor's degree in teaching and experience in the classroom, followed by a master's degree or doctorate, usually in guidance and counseling or school psychology. The relationship of counselors to the overall system of administrative control in schools is more ambiguous than that of teachers, as is their status. While they have more education, it has not been acquired in instructional areas; they have substantial power over students (Cicourel and Kitsuse 1963; Sarason 1971); but they are peripheral to the predominantly instructional life of the school.

The Contradictory Role of Counselors. The discrepancy between expectations and actual accomplishments probably is greater for counselors than for any other school professionals. Originally, counseling was designed for academic purposes only. It was instituted in secondary schools as curricular offerings differentiated into more than one academic stream. Counselors customarily were assigned to a given grade level, usually from 200–300 students, and made responsible for carrying out the clerical function of assuring that students were placed in appropriate classes and fulfilled the necessary requirements for graduation. They also assisted those interested in finding and applying to the appropriate colleges and universities. However, both the training that counselors now receive and the expectations which parents, students, administrators and the public now have for their activities has broadened considerably.

As educators became aware of the importance to cognitive learning of social, emotional and psychological factors, counselors were expected to engage in "social work," attempting to solve the psychological problems which kept students from learning. Their graduate training came to reflect a more clinical or therapeutic orientation. However, their work loads did not lighten; student-to-counselor ratios of 420:1 and 350:1 are commonplace. Powell et al. (1985, p. 49) report that a school with a 200:1 ratio felt that its situation approached the national ideal.

Under these conditions, the burden for seeking help falls primarily on students, who may not even know that they need advice. Even when students do get an appointment with a counselor, their average visit is less than ten minutes; often the counselor has not had time to review student records before seeing them. The paper work is overwhelming. Counselors must see to it that eligible children receive appropriate special-needs programs and that the multitudinous standardized test scores are recorded. Fully 75 percent of counselors' time can be consumed with these clerical duties, leaving little for the therapeutic interactions which they prefer and are trained to do. The result is that only those students with problems—pushy parents, personal persistence, serious discrepancies in their records, or visibly flamboyant misbehavior will receive attention. Finally, students do not get placed in programs appropriate to their capabilities and minority children fail to get the encouragement and guidance they need to stay in school and aspire realistically to college. Even many normally achieving students reach their senior year without realizing that they have serious deficits in their transcripts which will prevent them from graduating.

Functionalists view the activities of counselors as part of the status allocation function in society. That is, counselors help the school to function as a mechanism for social differentiation, sorting students by perceived abilities into academic, vocational or remedial curricula comensurate with what is believed to be their ultimate occupational role (Cicourel and Kitsuse 1963). While the decisions are supposed to be made on fair and objective grounds, using incontrovertible data such as test scores, Cicourel and Kitsuse demonstrated how other, more subjective measures played a role in student placement. These include counselor judgments of student social class, whether or not the student was perceived to be popular, a good athlete, a trouble-maker, or an underachiever. These judgments are critical, because they can bar students deemed unable to perform—for whatever reason—conclusively from the courses of study they wish to follow or which would help them to achieve their potential. While counselors are gaining increasing power over a student's academic—and occupational-destiny, there is evidence that their services are not distributed equitably. Those who counselors see most often are those who need it least—students with high levels of academic achievement and extra-curricular participation from the middle and upper classes who seldom have been in trouble (Armor 1969). Shultz and Erickson describe how this process takes place, suggesting further that the differentiation is facilitated by language patterns; counselors can avoid spending much time with students by setting them up to give inadequate answers to questions, answers which fail to elicit the needed help. Fine (1987) calls this a "policy of enforced silencing" (p. 167) by which information about the consequences of dropping out was systematically withheld from students. We submit that enforced silencing also acts to preclude disadvantaged students and women from getting adequate information about appropriate courses to take, requirements for jobs, and ways to get into colleges and other forms of higher education. We will talk in more detail about the relationship of social class, race, and gender to academic differentiation in Chapters Five, Seven and Eight. There, the impact and consequences of variable treatment of students by teachers, administrators and counselors will become apparent.

WHAT IS THE NATURE OF ADMINISTRATIVE WORK IN SCHOOLS?

The daily routine of school-level administrators is almost as multi-dimensional as that of teachers. As we have indicated, school administrators are recruited from the ranks of teachers; promotion is based upon further examination or experience as a school administrator. This closes off the system to outsiders and nonschool administrators (Fantini et al. 1974). Historically, administrators served as instructional leaders. Some still return occasionally to the classroom; many districts require that they do. Labor in the schools, however, has been increasingly subdivided both functionally and temporally; the resulting bureaucratization has created a rather wide split between instructional and administrative duties (Bidwell 1965). Those at the bottom of the chain of command—teachers and principals—find it difficult to make daily decisions without constantly looking upward for approval; but those in the central office are so removed from building level activities that actions constantly are delayed or postponed. Sometimes this is deliberate, as bureaucrats use the structure to avoid making decisions they would rather avoid (Rogers 1968). Increasing distance leads to mistrust; central office staff believe that building level personnel, especially teachers, lack objectivity and flexibility, while teachers and principals depict themselves as "on the firing line" far from the "ivory tower" of headquarters (ibid.).

A number of researchers have described the daily activities of typical school administrators (Wolcott 1973; Cuban 1984, Borman and Spring 1984). Because of the great diversity of schools as well as recent changes in how administrators are expected to do their work, we shall outline the categories of responsibility for which schoolbased and central office administrators are accountable. In so doing, we will illustrate the tensions and ambiguities inherent in these roles.

"Loose Coupling" and "Variable Zoning" in Administrative Control

The gradual change from instructional to administrative responsibility has created contradictions between the role educational managers play and what Lortie called "zoning" in their areas of legitimate authority. On one hand, having been on the firing line as teachers, administrators claim special understanding of teachers and instructional problems. On the other, they are viewed by teachers as management, not labor. They are also perceived as lacking expertise in the teachers' own subject areas. As a consequence, teachers accept the authority of principals as legitimate (or "hard") only in matters which do not deal directly with instruction—financial matters, parent relations, and contacts with agencies outside the school, for example (Becker 1953).

This division produces constant tension in matters of control and supervision and is exacerbated by the looseness in structure or "coupling" of schools (see Chapter Two). The closed classroom door and geographic disperal of buildings and personnel means that top administrators have little daily contact with teachers; their capacity for direct supervision of teachers on a daily basis is limited (Bidwell 1965; Dreeben 1973, p. 452).

Principals also have limited power over hiring and firing of teachers. They must choose from among those teachers screened by central office staff and sometimes must take teachers transferred from other schools; they can only fire teachers in the most extreme circumstances. In most cases, undesirable teachers only can be transferred to another school if a willing recipient can be found.

While schools resemble bureaucracies to some degree, the decision-making routine of top school administrators differs substantially from that of chief executive officers in corporations. In the first place, decision-making is scheduled, routinized and episodic. Budgets are established annually or biennially, and the remainder of the fiscal cycle consists of administering decisions which were made long ago. Hiring is done at the beginning of the school year. In the second place, school officials have little control—other than lobbying for tax increases or corporate beneficence—over fund raising. How much revenue schools receive is in the hands of taxpayers.

Some researchers have attributed to this periodicity and routinization the relative lack of crises and emergencies in school decision-making. However, it is our belief that neither the periodic nature of fiscal and personnel decisions, nor the absence of crises over such things as sales, marketing and procurement mean that schools operate peacefully, especially in urban areas. The crises which occur are of a different nature, and require different, largely human relational, skills from educators.

Maintenance of Fiscal and Professional Standards

One area of potential crisis for school administrators is fiduciary. School leaders are public officials. As such, they are caretakers of public funds and reponsible both to governmental agencies and their public constituencies for maintenance of appropriate standards for professional and even personal conduct among school staff. These are the touchiest areas for school people; instructional mismanagement is not dramatic and takes a long time to be noticed, but fiscal mismanagement or behavioral impropriety creates the kind of scandal which topples superintendencies and causes principals to be fired.

Batch Processing and Quality Control

In tension with their ever-increasing managerial and fiscal functions, school administrators find pressure to exercise more supervision over instruction. American schools do not educate individuals; they process age-level cohorts of students in batches. Batch-processing practices, the structural looseness of schools and the long period of time over which cohorts of students are trained provide many opportunities for exercise of autonomy in teaching as well as diversity and idiosyncracy in grading. Policy makers, however—whether from business, the government, or the educational establishment—demand some kind of standardization or uniformity of competence among high school graduates. This creates a press for rationalization and routinization of instructional and assessment activities (Bidwell 1965, pp. 976–977). It leads to further bureaucratization of schools. Responsibility for quality control, coordination and monitoring to assure that this happens falls to administrators, from building-level principals to the central office. Centralization at the top, however, removes control from the teachers at the bottom.

Administrators have been encouraged in the 1980s to exercise more and more control over instructional activities in their schools by the plethora of commission reports (for example, "A Nation at Risk", National Commission on Excellence in Education 1983) decrying the absence of standards in American education. Increased control by administrators has had two effects. First, administrators, like teachers, have experienced work overload; many feel that they cannot both adequately supervise instruction and effectively carry out their administrative duties. They, too, experience burnout. Second, the requirement that they engage in serious monitoring of instruction exacerbates de-skilling; it is resented by teachers, who see their "hard" area of jurisdiction over instruction further eroded. Principals are caught in the middle, like factory foremen who must enforce the dictates of reform upon an unenthusiastic work force (Borman and Spring 1984). Some districts have proposed dividing the duties of principals into two offices—an instructional principal and a business manager. While these proposals seem a sensible way to lighten the load for building level supervisors, it also promises to subject them to the same de-skilling and loss of control which afflict teachers.

Relationships with the School Board and Community

Blumberg (1985, p. xiii) suggests that conflict is the most appropriate and central orientation for understanding the nature of a superintendent's work life. Public relations is among the most important functions of school administrators. Principals must establish relationships with the parent-teacher organization at their schools and cope with those parents whose children are problems. Superintendents must maintain the uneasy balance between advice and control with their lay school boards. This is made more dificult by the fact that until recently, school boards exercised direct managerial control over district activities. Boards have been slow and reluctant to relinquish this power, and since they can fire superintendents who disatisfy them, it has become one of the primary responsibilities of superintendents to maintain good board relationships. This can be difficult in communities where racial and economic cleavages produce disagreement over educational goals and procedures.

Superintendents develop a range of strategies to maintain consensus and to prevent community cleavages from interfering with school operation. These include lobbying board members on important issues in advance of meetings; peppering them with so much information before meetings that they cannot possibly assimilate it all and thus must rely upon the judgment of the superintendent; and hiding important policy issues in meeting agendas laden with personnel, budgetary and other diversionary topics. A cardinal rule is to see that open conflict never erupts in public meetings; as a result, many decisions are made first in executive sessions (Fantini, Gittell, and Magat 1974; Kerr 1973; McGivney and Haught 1972).

Centralization and Decentralization

In his classic study of the New York City school system, David Rogers (1968) has argued that schools have become so overcentralized that they have turned into "pathological bureaucracies." Decisions take forever; services are difficult to obtain; incompetent personnel find it easy to hide behind patterns of avoidance, blind obedience, compulsive rule following and enforcement, and loyalty to internal cliques. More time is spent working out internal power struggles than delivering instruction. Since the publication of his study, the growth in sheer size and complexity of many urban school districts (See Borman and Spring 1984; Peterson 1976) has precipitated a cautious rethinking of school governance.

Decentralization. Some districts have experimented with decentralization of school districts as a way to reduce the size of individual units and make rigid bureaucracies more responsive to teachers and members of the community. Two avenues have been attempted. In the 1960s, large districts were carved into smaller sub-units, each with control over a wide but varying range of administrative functions including hiring and firing of teachers. Local community school boards were instituted which presumably were more representative of the immediate community around the school. In the 1980s, decentralization has focused on "schoolbased management," which gives considerable autonomy to individual principals to operate their schools in accordance with their own wishes. In both cases, decentralized districts and schoolbased principals received their fiscal allocation from the central office, but were given relatively more independence in how they allocated the funds. They have also generated considerable community controversy over handling of funds, competency of administrators, and what should be taught in the schools.

Business Managers. Schools also have experimented with dividing the duties of the principal. Principals would become "instructional leaders" or "headmasters" with reponsibility for supervising teachers and acting as guides for implementing the curriculum. A specialist would be hired to handle the business aspects of schooling—especially those dealing with finances. Such a person would be trained in business administration, not education. While this plan is congruent with the efficiency movement described in Chapter Two, it has been received with mixed acclaim. Although it would free principals for more contact with day-to-day instruction, they are uneasy about the loss of control over budgetary matters, especially if the business manager reported to the central office, not the principal. Teachers worry about the extent to which principals would increase control over their teaching. We can expect to see more of these innovations in the future, but their impact upon overall school governance still is unknown. They do, however, make teachers much more subject to direct supervision.

SUMMARY

In this chapter, we have outlined the contradictory nature of the teaching profession. We have suggested, with the functionalists, that the work of educators really does not equate with that of the traditional professions. We also have traced the development of forces which increasingly remove teachers and building level personnel from the center of control in schools.

We have shown how the patterns of control and training which prevail in teaching make it difficult for teachers to acquire the pay and prestige they desire. We have noted that the fact that teacher work has come to be defined as female work acts to reduce its status; feminization of the teaching force also has reinforced the patterns of teacher turnover and lack of commitment which characterize the profession.

Control of standards also is an issue; how teaching is carried out and who is permitted to teach is more a function of external political, ideological and economic pressures than of concerns over expertise and technical skill. It is work deemed critical to the operation of society, but often for reasons irrelevant to pedagogy. While critical theorists have argued that teachers must act to transform the conditions of their work, we suggest that the number of teachers actually engaging in such activity forms a miniscule proportion of the work force. Teacher militancy at the collective level seems limited. We do, however, see a hopeful sign in the fact that teachers who engage in union activity are more concerned with increasing the amount of control and autonomy which teachers exercise over curriculum and with respect to their administrators than they are with bargaining over wages (Falk, Grimes and Lord 1982). We believe that the crisis in urban education of the late 1980s bodes well for the possibility of change, and challenge you to examine each of these for their immediate, as well as long-term consequences for education.

KEY CONCEPTS

Loose Coupling refers to the degree to which units within a school system are not closely linked to one another in the authority structure. It is a consequence of geography and training. Supervision is difficult in school systems because the units are geographically isolated from one another and work—especially that of teachers—takes place out of the sight of supervisors. Supervisors also have little special claim to authority because the training they receive is similar to that undergone by teachers.

De-Skilling refers to a process by which the level of specialized, professional knowledge and skill needed to carry out a task progressively is reduced and the degree of autonomy and control which workers have over the execution of their work is constricted and shifted upward to supervisors.

EXERCISES

1. Divide your class into three groups and assign students to interview elementary, middle and high school teachers. Ask teachers from each of these groups to describe what they do each day. How much time do they spend teaching? How much is devoted to non-teaching duties? What do they perceive to be the rewards of their profession? What factors are most disagreeable? How many plan to stay in the profession? In your class discussions, compare your findings.
2. What are the demographic characteristics of teachers and administrators in your local school district? How many males, females and minority group members are represented in teaching and administration at each of the three levels: elementary, middle and high school? What are the demographics of your local school board? How does this compare to the information you have read in this chapter? Critically examine your findings and compare them with others in your class.
3. What is the ratio of male to female professors in your college of education? There are three professorial ranks: assistant, associate and full professor. How many males and females are in each category in your college? How many of your teachers are instructors without professorial rank? Why do you think you found what you did? Discuss your findings in class.
4. Interview a leader of your local teacher's organization or union. What kind of organization is it? What has been the history of teacher organization in your area? What obstacles have been overcome? How many teachers are active members?

SUGGESTED READINGS

Classic Works

Adams, R.S. and Biddle, B.J. (1970). *Realities of teaching*. New York: Holt, Rinehart and Winston.

Armor, David. (1969). *The American high school counselor*. New York: Russell Sage Foundation.

Becker, Howard S. (1953). The teacher in the authority system of the public school. *Journal of Educational Sociology*, Vol. 27, pp. 128–141.

Charters, W.W., Jr. (1970). Some factors affecting teacher survival in school districts. *American Educational Research Journal*, Vol. 7, pp. 1–27.

Cicourel, Aaron V., and Kitsuse, J. (1963). *The educational decision makers*. Indianapolis: Bobbs-Merrill.

Dreeben, Robert. (1973). The school as a workplace. In R.M.W. Travers, ed. *The second handbook of research on teaching*. Chicago: Rand McNally, pp. 450–473.

Lortie, Dan. (1969). The balance of control and autonomy in elementary school teaching. In Amitai Etzioni, ed., *The semi-professions and their organization: teachers, nurses, social workers*. New York: The Free Press, pp. 1–54.

Lortie, Dan. (1973). Observations on Teaching as Work. in R.M.W. Travers, ed. *The second handbook of research on teaching*. Chicago: Rand-McNally, pp. 474–496.

Rogers, David. (1968). *110 Livingston Street: Politics and bureaucracy in the New York City schools*. New York: Random House.

Sarason, Seymour B. (1971). *The culture of the school and the problem of change*. Boston: Allyn and Bacon.

Modern Works

Apple, Michael W. (1986). *Teachers and texts: A political economy of class and gender relations in education*. New York: Routledge and Kegan Paul.

——— (1982). *Education and power*. Boston: Routledge and Kegan Paul.

Aronowitz, Stanley, and Giroux, Henry (1985). *Education under siege*. South Hadley, Mass: Bergin and Garvey.

Connell, R.W. (1985). *Teachers' work*. North Sydney, Australia: George Allen and Unwin.

Cuban, Larry. (1984). *How teachers taught: Constancy and change in American classrooms, 1890–1980*. New York: Longman Inc.

Dworkin, Anthony Gary (1986). *Teacher burnout in the public schools: Structural causes and consequences for children*. Albany, N.Y.: State University of New York Press.

Ginsburg, Mark (1988). *Contradictions in teacher education and society: A critical analysis*. New York: The Falmer Press.

Holmes Group, The (1986). *Tomorrow's Teachers: A Report of the Holmes Group*. East Lansing, Mich: The Holmes Group, Inc.

National Commission on Excellence in Education. *A Nation at risk: The imperative for educational reform*. A Report to the Nation and the Secretary of Education, U.S. Department of Education, April 1983.

CHAPTER 5

Social Class and Its Relationship to Education

OVERVIEW

INTRODUCTION

In the previous chapters, we have discussed the characteristics of schools and the people who participate in them. We now turn to an examination of the impact which schools have on children. We begin this section of the book with a discussion of **social class** for several reasons.

First, the variable social class constitutes perhaps the single most powerful source of inequality in society. Second, social class was one of the first factors—other than intelligence—which modern sociologists examined as a possible source of the differences in achievement observed among children. Explicating the relationship between social class and education has been one of the most important contributions which sociologists have made to our understanding of education.

Notions of social class are so inextricably linked to our thinking about ethnicity or race and gender that it is difficult to discuss them separately. However, we have attempted to disentangle them in this chapter and Chapters Seven and Eight to clarify their individual impact, and to show the complexity of the interrelationships between and among education, **class**, ethnicity and gender.

In the first part of the chapter, we discuss the history of the concept of class and some of the most important thinkers who have contributed to its development. Next, we look at the way social class and education interact to stratify society into a class structure. Finally, we examine some of the mechanisms in systems of education which lead both to reproduction of the existing class structure and social class bias in what purports to be a meritocracy based upon achievement.

WHAT IS SOCIAL CLASS?

Before we can talk meaningfully about the relationship between social class and education, we must understand what the term social class means, its history, and how it has become one of the key concepts which shape how we think about our world.

A *class* of things is a category—a number of things grouped together because they share common characteristics. As defined by social scientists, social classes are groups of people who share certain characteristics of prestiges, patterns of taste and language, income, occupational status (though not necessarily the same jobs), educational levels, aspirations, behavior and beliefs. Social classes are "stratified," that is they are arranged in a pyramid-shaped hierarchy according to their prestige and power. Throughout history, thinkers have had different opinions as to why certain kinds of people have had more prestige and power in the stratification hierarchy than others. As we shall explain, the social scientific view based upon socioeconomic status is a relatively new way of thinking about class.

The Historical Perspective: A Hierarchy of Virtue

What we have termed an "aristocratic perspective" consists of the degree to which people confuse a hierarchy of social class with a hierarchy of moral virtue and intelligence. This confusion has had and still has a profound impact upon social and educational policy. It derives from the fact that the concept of social class is a very old one, predating by centuries social science disciplines like sociology, economics, political science and anthropology, which use it as an analytic concept. Until very recent times, philosophers, religious leaders and politicians, as well as the general population believed that class status was determined by how valued, wise and virtuous a person was. These ideas were reinforced by the idea of the "divine right" of kings to rule; because people from the highest social classes were considered to be the brightest and most virtuous, they also were considered to be those most capable of ruling. Virtue and wisdom were attributed to them because of their birth-rank and role, whether or not they were justified by actual behavior. For example, kings and queens were believed to be anointed by God. They ruled with God's permission and were held up as behavioral exemplars. The American Puritans also felt that wealth and prestige in this life were indications of God's favor and a guarantee of salvation in the hereafter. High levels of wealth and prestige, as well as of educational attainment, were taken to be rewards for or the natural outcome of hard work, great spirituality, or moral superiority, rather than the consequence of social inheritance and affluence.

In fact, many gentlemen were not very gentle; nor were all kings kingly, nor all ladies very lady-like. Unfortunately, characteristics which were treated as attributes of a superior intellect and morality often simply were functions of superior wealth. The illiteracy, social deviance, crime, moral depravity, lack of hygiene, brutish behavior, and general lack of culture attributed to members of the lower classes were believed to be a function of innate or hereditary tendencies rather than of environmental influences. This belief persisted despite the fact that it was a great deal easier to be cleaner, kinder, gentler, better educated, more cultured and generous if one were fortunate enough to be born into an affluent family.

This kind of thinking has had a powerful influence on popular thinking about class, status and caste. It argued against both social welfare programs and attempts to include the poor in decision-making in their own behalf; the poor were not thought to be capable of more elevated behavior. Social Darwinists even argued that it would be harmful if social policies were promulgated to help the poor, since relief would only encourage the propagation of people who were mentally or morally defective and waste resources which could better be used for more productive and deserving populations (Sumner 1883; Spencer 1851, 1898). Since poverty was considered a consequence of innate human characteristics, the only rational and humane response was to learn to live with it, rescuing from the dregs those few members of the "deserving poor" whose values could be shaped to resemble those of the middle and upper classes. This kind of thinking still exists today and impedes the institution of serious attempts to eliminate poverty and oppression.

Because class status was considered to be an hereditary characteristic, few philosophers or social theorists considered that their belief in the association between affluence and virtue, leadership ability, literacy and the like might be circular. However, these beliefs did not hinder attempts by policymakers and educators to use the schools as a means of social control. The curricula they developed were designed to teach children of the lower classes obedience to the law, temperance, sexual restraint, good hygiene, thrift and punctuality—values which were acceptable to the upper and middle classes. In fact, some of the earliest educational sociologists felt that schools were the only appropriate place for children to learn civic virtues. As we explained in Chapter Three, Durkheim believed that as societies modernized, parents no longer could prepare their children adequately for adult life. Families had to specialize in what they could do best: developing and nurturing the individual personality; to the schools fell the task of nation-building, or developing citizens capable adhering to the laws of the land and of carrying out their responsibilities to the state.

Durkheim developed his ideas in a treatise called *Moral Education* (1961), which was written in 1901 and based upon a series of lectures he delivered to preservice teachers. His ideas of moral education are echoed in contemporary theories of poverty which describe the incompetence of poor families to raise and educate their children; courses in citizenship, free enterprise and other virtues still are popular today, and clearly represent an effort to use the schools to create a consensus on patterns of authority and acceptable ways of relating to the political order.

The Genetic Perspective: Class and Intelligence

Traditionally, social class standing was associated with morality. A modern variation has been to equate class and intelligence, or IQ as measured on so-called intelligence tests. Conventional wisdom supported this notion; ordinary people observed that the poor usually were badly educated or illiterate; this led them to assume that poor people and minorities had low levels of educational attainment because they lacked intelligence. These beliefs, coupled with the racism of the nineteenth and early twentieth century, led to a considerable volume of "scientific" research supporting the existence of causal relationships between intelligence and social class. Evidence was provided by studies of brain size and shape, or "craniometry," which "proved" that lower class people, Africans, and other minorities had inferior brains with less cranial capacity than or different construction from those of Europeans. The connection between class and intelligence was bolstered by the advent of intelligence testing, since lower class people and minorities scored lower on IQ and other forms of intelligence tests.

The results of these studies since have been shown to be based upon misinterpretation or fraud (Gould 1981). Samuel George Morton, for example, attempted to show that Asians, Africans, and Native Americans were intellectually inferior to Northern Europeans because their brains were smaller. He used the comparative weights of birdshot poured into the cranial cavities of skulls from various ethnic groups to substantiate his claims. Unfortunately, whenever he obtained results which indicated that some group actually had a larger cranial capacity than Anglo-Saxons, he finagled the data to come up with a conclusion more favorable to his biases. Gould feels that Morton intended no fraud: "All I can discern is an *a priori* conviction about racial ranking so powerful that it directed his tabulations along preestablished lines." (Gould 1981, p. 69). The work of others, however, was not so innocent.

Sir Cyril Burt (1883–1971) was one of the most influential educational psychologists of his time. Burt was a pioneer in testing and mental measurement, and from the beginning of his career, believed that intelligence was an innate and immutable characteristic. Nature, not nurture, determined the destiny of individuals. Furthermore, people were poor because they—and their parents—were less intelligent; thus the observed differences in achievement and status between social classes were the consequence of hereditary differences in intelligence. Not till after his death did investigators determine that the vast majority of Burt's research was based upon data flawed by inadmissable carelessness, fakery, ommission, and outright fraud (Gould 1981, p. 235).

Notwithstanding the flimsiness of their work, these researchers have left a powerful legacy to educators and social policy-makers. As late as the 1970s, Arthur Jensen (1969), William Schockley, and Richard Herrnstein (1973) could publish articles in respectable scholarly journals advocating educational and social policies based upon the premise that the intellect of minorities, especially blacks, was genetically inferior to whites.

The Sociological Perspective: Class and Status

As sociologists, we reject the notion that class status and virtue are synonymous or that class is a function of innate intelligence. We also feel uncomfortable with attempts to use the schools to mask problems in society by teaching children to accept that the *status quo* is the only legitimate alternative to social chaos. While we do believe that class status and the behavioral and attitudinal characteristics associated with it are, to some degree, inherited, heritability does not consist so much in genetic factors as it does in the fact that the environment into which children are born has a profound effect upon their future development. Furthermore, because our work is informed by critical theory, we look behind the "givens" of class identity. Rather than treating class status and its attendant inequalities as a given, we believe that it and the identity it gives is "constructed." It develops as a sum total of the interactions people have. Thus, a child *becomes* an upper-class prep school graduate with medical school aspirations, or a lower-class teenaged-mother about to drop out of school, not just because they were born into a particular kind of family, but because family background sets up a set of expectations for present and future behavior, as well as influencing how other people will react to and interpret the consequences of that type of background. The net of mutual expectations is not totally inescapable, but it does, to a large degree, affect the direction of individual development.

Sociological Definitions of Class, Status, and Power. When sociologists look at the inequalities which rank order people in society, they distinguish among class, status and power. Power refers to the ability to realize one's will, even if others resist. Weber suggests that power which is legitimated by others constitutes *authority*, while power which is not legitimated is coercion or force.

The term *status* is descriptive; it refers to a state of being or position. In sociology it connotes the distribution of prestige (Gerth and Mills 1953) based upon what people have—including material goods, where they live, who their family and friends are, how much and what kind of education and training they possess, and what occupations they have. Status is associated with culture; status groups "subjectively . . . distinguish themselves from [one another] in terms of categories of *moral evaluation* such as 'honor,' 'taste,' 'breeding,' 'respectability,' 'propriety,' 'cultivation,' 'good fellows,' 'plain folks,' etc. Thus the exclusion of persons who lack the in-group culture is felt to be normatively legitimated." (Collins 1978, p. 125).

Sociologists believe that status and power are a function of social class. Class is defined by sociologists as groups of people who share similar economic life chances because they have similar opportunities in the labor market. For Weberians, class is positional, a function of one's occupation, income, and to some extent, one's educational level. For Marxists, class is relational, a function of one's interaction with others in the processes of production. Specifically, one's class is determined by the extent to which one both owns the means by which one's livelihood is obtained and one can hire, control, or supervise the labor of others.

Some sociologists divide the social hierarchy into six classes: upper-upper, lower-upper, upper-middle, lower- middle, upper-lower (or working class), and lower-lower (Bensman and Vidich 1971). Marxists divide it into three, whose importance and power are directly related to the kind of work their members do and how much control they have over the use of their own labor. At the bottom of the heap are the proletariat, workers, or manual laborers, who own no part of the factories or businesses in which they work, whose tasks are completely organized and controlled by their supervisors, and who have to sell their labor to others. The ruling classes consist of two groups: capitalists, who own the means of production, purchase the labor of others, and who do not sell their own; and petty bourgeoisie, who do not sell their labor or purchase that of others, but who own their own means of productions (Wright and Perrone 1977). Capitalists, who include landed aristocrats, profit from the "surplus capital", or profits generated by workers. In this formulation, teachers are considered to be workers, because they neither supervise labor nor own their means of making a living (Wright and Perrone 1977).

Marx wrote at a time when ownership of land as a source of power was diminishing; his description of society better fits the eighteenth century factory and industrial pattern than it does today's technologically oriented economy, where managers and professionals replace traditional capitalist owners, and manual labor and heavy industry have lost importance to service sectors in an "information: society. However, his ideas about social organization and the

TABLE 5.1. EXPANDED MARXIST CRITERIA FOR CLASS

	Criteria for Class Position			
	Ownership of the Means of Production	Purchase of the Labor Power of Others	Control of the Labor Power of Others	Sale of One's Own Labor Power
Capitalists	Yes	Yes	Yes	No
Managers	No	No	Yes	Yes
Workers	No	No	No	Yes
Petty Bourgeoisie	Yes	No	No	No

(Source: E.O. Wright and L. Perrone. "Marxist class categories and Income Inequality," American Sociological Review 42 (1977), p. 34.)

origins of power, inequality, and conflict in society still are salient. Table 5.1 summarizes, and to some degree, updates Marx's ideas of social class structure.

Regardless of their orientation, sociologists agree that people with the most wealth, power, and prestige are at the apex of the pyramid and are influential in controlling policies and practices which maintain their position. While power comes from various individual sources—the political structure, business, the media, and the military (Mills 1956; Domhoff 1967)—these sources tend to overlap. The degree of overlap, as well as the means of exercising control, often are not obvious to the majority of the population.

The Material Conditions of Life. Peter McLaren uses a Marxist definition of *class* which defines class as the "economic, social and political relationships that govern life in a given social order," and states that the source of inequality in society is based upon the concept of "surplus labor" and the unequal access which people have to it. Surplus labor is the work that workers do beyond what is necessary for their survival and the subsequent profits earned from their efforts. A Marxist or critical analysis makes clear how surplus labor, the genesis of social class variation, is produced. Social class relations "are those associated with surplus labor [or profit], who produces it, and who is a recipient of it." (McLaren 1989, p. 171). In capitalist systems, those who benefit from surplus labor are not the workers themselves. The amount of surplus labor is a measure of the degree of exploitation in a society, because it explains the extent to which those who benefit—or profit—from it are not those who produced it.

The critical perspective which informs this book stresses that social classes originate in the material, and specifically the economic, conditions of life. These are at the center of human activity; they involve using the forces of production—or levels of technology, land, labor, capital, and available energy and the social relations of production—or how human effort is organized—for productive activity (Persell 1977, p. 7). Membership in a social class is determined by the way people relate to the economic and material conditions of life, how much of them they control, and how much they are beneficiaries of the productive efforts. Those individuals who control more of, or who benefit more from, the economic order are those at the top of the pyramid; those who control less and benefit less are toward the bottom. Because stratification patterns also are patterns of social and cultural domination and subordination, it may be more accurate to use the term "structure of dominance" (Weber 1947, p. 426) than the common sociological term "social stratification" when referring to economic and social hierarchies. Thus, those who control more and benefit more also have more power, or ability to dominate others.

Social classes, or the structure of power and domination, are differentiated by the prestige and status ascribed to them within the hierarchy as well as by the actual power they wield. Members of a social class do not need to know one another, though they usually choose their friends and associates from the same class as their own. Neither do they have to be conscious that they are a member of a class to belong to one. Some theorists would argue that class cannot exist without class consciousness; that is, people have to know that they belong to it for a social class to exist. Critical theorists believe that as they become conscious of their class membership, people begin to develop opposition to the oppressive practices which have masked class differences and preserved the status quo. One of these practices is to foster social beliefs which deny that oppression and inequality exist.

The Mythical American Middle Class: Control through Ideology. Class consciousness is very low in America because our cultural **ideology** describes us as an egalitarian society. Americans generally refuse to assign each other to a hierarchical social ranking; traditionally, most describe themselves as "middle-class", regardless of their actual income level, occupational status, or educational attainment (Persell 1977).

The existence of a "myth of the middle class" constitutes a social ideology which also helps to maintain the existing class structure. Ideologies are "way[s] of viewing the world . . . that we tend to accept as natural and common-sense." They provide the categories, concepts, images and ideas through which people interpret their world and shape their behavior (McLaren 1989, p. 176); and as such, they are instruments of *hegemony.* Hegemony is a kind of domination without the use of force. Hegemonic domination maintains the domination of the existing status system through a consensus about what people say and do (or, in this case, the belief that everyone is middle class), and by means of "social forms and structures produced in specific sites such as churches, the state, schools, mass media, the political system, and the family" (McLaren 1989, p. 173). There is no need to institute more stringent means of social control—like exclusionary laws, imprisonment, and torture—when there is general agreement that the *status quo* is legitimate, even if not personally satisfactory.

The belief in "being middle-class" is one way in which actual social class differences are hidden in America. People believe that whatever differences do exist are only a matter of degree. This is a convenient fiction; it permits them to ignore extremes of wealth and poverty. This is facilitated because of the low visibility of the rich in America, who are segregated in private neighborhoods, schools, social clubs, and occupational circles (Persell 1977, p. 31) and the equal invisibility of the poor. Until recently, it cost middle- and upper-class Americans very little effort to avoid almost entirely an encounter with homelessness or abject poverty. However, during the 1980s the myth of a relatively "classless" or egalitarian society has been exploded by the growth and visibility of the poor—especially the "underclass" of the inner cities (Wilson 1987). That the poor do not revolt against their condition is a function of the power of ideology. They have internalized what schools have taught them—the tenets which dictate that people are rewarded for hard work. Even if they do not believe that they live in an egalitarian society, they tend to feel that they, not the system, are responsible for their plight. Either they weren't lucky enough, or they just didn't work hard enough.

That is why schools play such an important role in maintaining existing patterns of domination. They perpetuate a middle-class ideology which states that status and social mobility in American society are based upon merit, earned competitively, and facilitated by schooling. While these are the attitudes, values and behavior patterns of the dominant culture, or the so-called middle and upper classes, they achieve legitimacy because some individuals actually do benefit from the system. However, those for whom the system pays off most often are those who already were advantaged—white middle- and upper-class males (Wright and Perrone 1977; Rosenfeld 1980).

THEORETICAL BEGINNINGS: MARX, WEBER, AND BOURDIEU

Both Karl Marx and Max Weber were concerned with the relationship between class and education, though from different vantage points. Both felt that educational systems were a reflection of the societies in which they were embedded. They differed as to what they felt was the basis of society. For Marx, the structure of society and of domination and subordination was based upon the economy, or the production and distribution of goods and services. Weber, however, felt that domination was based upon more than economics; critical to his analyses were politics and government, or the organization of power and authority, and their relationship to educational systems in a variety of societies, including those which were not industrializing. While Bourdieu rejected the single-minded emphasis of Marxists on an economic basis for class structure, he clarified the existence of differences in the status people have. Bourdieu added to the economic correlates of class the power which derives from acquiring specialized forms of social and cultural knowledge.

The Contributions of Karl Marx

Marx never treated education extensively. He considered that educational systems, like systems of aesthetics and religion, were simply a part of the societal superstructure which derived from and corresponded with the economic base of a given society.

Class Analysis. However, Marx did make explicit the relationship between social class and economic power, or ownership of the means of production, and demonstrated how these stratify, or create a hierarchy of classes, within a society. His analysis was so powerful that social scientists have been "Marxists" ever since, at least insofar as class and stratification have been critical to their analysis of social structure. Marxist analysis initially focused on class and **caste** at the structural level and did not examine either the relationship of education to class or the functioning of schools as organizations. Later Marxist theorists posited a closer relationship, stating that the educational system provided a legitimizing function for capitalist economic systems (Bowles and Gintis 1976; Scimecca 1980). Schools acted to defuse class antagonisms—as we shall explain later—because they indoctrinated students to accept the belief that the economic and social position they attain is the best they can achieve (Scimecca 1980, pp. 9–10). In this way, the school system was critical in reproducing the social class structure from one generation to another. This position is one which has been adopted by critical theorists as well.

Marxists and neo-Marxists also believe that there is a very tight and causal link between and across subsystems in society, so that changes in one subsystem directly lead to changes in the others. The supposed existence of such links can be applied to education; it has bolstered the argument of people who believe that education is closely linked to generation of economic inequality. While most people who wish to use the schools to transform society, or to solve social problems, are reformers, not Marxist revolutionaries, the appeal to utilize such links to eliminate poverty has powerful appeal to educators, policy makers, and social scientists. Especially with regard to education, however, current research has shown the links to be indirect and weaker than reformers would hope (LeCompte and Dworkin 1988). We will talk more about this later in this chapter.

Dialectical Analysis. Perhaps most important is Marx's use of dialectical analysis. This is a method by which all assumptions are assumed to contain their own contradictions, or opposites. Propositions believed to be true are analyzed as if they were false. For example, dialectical analysis would permit us to question the truism, "All men are created equal" by asking what was meant by the terms "men," "created," and "equal," and then determining if all men—or women—were equal and under which, if any, circumstances.

Dialectical analysis provided a framework by which the legitimacy of all conventional assumptions about the relationship between wealth and power could be questioned. It questioned the validity of analyses which made moral virtue the basis by which people were arranged into a social class hierarchy. It also identified sources of inequality, exploitation and oppression, and helped to forge an understanding that wealth was not necessarily a sign of superior effort or morality. On the contrary, Marxists looked at possession of great wealth in a bourgeois society as a sign of ill-gotten gains, attainable only through the exploitation of others. Critical theorists have used the concept of dialectical analysis to raise questions such as the following:

- Why is it that working class children get working class jobs, while children of doctors and other professionals become professionals?
- Could it really be true that the reason why 40 to 70 percent of all minority children in many major cities drop out of school is because they lack sufficient intelligence or ambition to graduate?
- Do the rewards of the educational system really go to those with the most intellectual merit?
- What are the consequences of educational reform? Will it really improve the achievement of minorities and the poor?

Alienation. Another major contribution of Marx has been a socioeconomic, rather than a psychological, definition of alienation. It has been of great importance to our understanding of why teachers and students lose interest in school-work and "burn out" (Dworkin 1985a, 1987).

Marx felt that workers could only find meaning in work that they directly controlled and in work places whose ownership they shared. They were "alienated" to the extent that they had lost control over what they did and how it was done. However Utopian that notion may sound in a world of multinational corporations and accelerated buy-outs, consolidation and merger of companies, alienation remains a powerful concept to explain industrial sabotage, teacher burnout, and other forms of occupational disaffection. Alienation simply means that one's work station is so far removed from those who actually control the work, and so far removed from those who use the products, that the actual daily activities become meaningless. People then engage in self-sabotage, shoddy work or rudeness, and destruction of equipment, products and materials simply in order to cope with the boredom and meaninglessness of everyday existence. Marx's concept of alienation is reflected in the formulation by critical theorists of the process of de-skilling and its impact on teacher morale.

The Contributions of Max Weber

Weber, by contrast, discussed education at length. He was especially interested in the curriculum taught, and the type of students who were recruited. He felt that each society created educational systems uniquely suited and closely linked to indigenous systems of power and authority. They were used to select and train the rulers or leaders of the society. Thus, an analysis of characteristics of schools and their populations would tell you who got into school and how; an examination of what was taught would reveal what kinds of information was deemed important for different groups in the society.

Education and the Structure of Authority. Weber distinguished among three kinds of authority: traditional, charismatic, and rational–legal. They were found in different kinds of societies, but were not entirely predicated upon the existence of a particular economic structure. Each of these types of authority required different leadership styles. Traditional societies produced kings; charismatic authority was that of the hero or guru, and rational–legal forms required bureaucrats and civil servants. Each of these types of leadership mandated differences in modes of training and education for elites (Weber 1947, pp. 426–434; Persell 1977). Weber illustrated the differences in training for elites in three case studies—the Mandarin Chinese (traditional), Christianity (charismatic), and the industrial civil service of late nineteenth century European life (rational–legal). A key contribution of Weber's was his understanding of (1) the degree to which the educational system could facilitate the succession of elites based upon merit and rationally assessed competence, rather than inheritance of leadership based upon divine right or some other, nonrational means of selection; and (2) whether or not the curriculum could be standardized and graded. Only rational–legal forms of authority with their emphasis on competence and specialized expert training required this. If authority were based on charisma, leadership could not really be taught; it was based upon "discipleship", and one could only wait for leadership capabilities to be awakened and demonstrated in some sort of trials or magical rites. And traditional kings were not trained; they ruled, competent or not, by virtue of birth, "divine right," and their ability to survive attempts to remove them from the throne.

Merit and Achievement. Weber understood that societies based upon meritocracy (Young 1971) could recruit able individuals for positions of wealth and power regardless of their initial social standing. Where achieved merit was the basis for rewards, it was possible to use educational systems to facilitate social mobility and exchange of ruling groups. Even within these societies, however, those who benefitted most from the educational system were those who already were somewhat advantaged.

The Contributions of Pierre Bourdieu

Having determined the basis for the establishment of social classes, sociologists then turned to an examination of the dynamics and impact of class structure. Among the questions they asked were:

- What distinguishing characteristics do people in various classes have?
- Can people move from one class to another, especially to a higher class?
- What rigidities stand in the way of movement from one class to another?

In Chapter One, we discussed class differences in language and communication patterns. But the differences are more profound that these alone. To fully understand what differentiates people in one social class from those in another, we must examine the concept of cultural capital.

Distinctions Between Class and Culture. Class and culture are terms which often are confused. Class, for sociologists is a position in the hierarchy or status; culture is the way people express that status, or "the particular ways in which a social group lives out and makes sense of its given circumstances and conditions of life" (McLaren 1989, p. 171). Culture includes the distinctive language, ideologies, behavior patterns, attitudes and values, artifact and patterns of dress, and shared historical experiences of a group of people.

Cultural Capital. Taken together, these create the "cultural capital" of a group—or the ways of talking and acting, moving, dressing, socializing, tastes, likes and dislikes, competencies, and forms of knowledge which distinguish one group from another (Bourdieu and Paesseron, 1977). Cultural capital is a resource, and just like natural resources, not all are valued equally. The social value of cultural capital is a function of the prestige of the group which possesses it—or conversely, the prestige of individuals depends upon how much of what kind of cultural capital they own. Cultural capital is an important concept to critical theorists, because it constitutes the constellation of factors to which people react in social interaction, and which shape the construction of social realities among people. Insofar as members of subordinant groups refuse to conform to the norms and values or to value the cultural capital of dominant groups, it can be the starting point for the development of resistance and oppositional culture.

SOCIAL CLASS AND THE STRUCTURE OF SOCIETY

Marxian and Weberian analysis laid the foundation for our understanding of the complex relationships between schools and societies at both the macrolevel of societal organization and at the microlevel of the organization of teaching and learning. Educational sociologists have been concerned with class and education at the macrolevel in the following areas: social mobility; relationships between class, academic achievement and educational attainment; social stratification and patterns of inequality, and the occupational structure. Until the 1970s, sociologists were primarily concerned with effects: how "inputs" to education—such as parents' occupation, parents' level of education and income, and certain attitudinal factors like aspirations for college and occupational expectations—affected "outputs" of education—like test scores, high school completion, college entrance, and occupational attainment. What went on *inside* the schools was of little concern (Hargreaves and Woods 1984, p. 1). Since 1970, greater attention has been paid to the microlevel of schooling, or what actually happens in schools and classrooms to create the inequalities which school attendance seems to produce. We will discuss processes at the microlevel later in this chapter and in Chapters Six, Seven, and Eight.

Social Mobility

Social mobility refers to the movement of individuals and groups from the social class of their birth to others which are higher or lower. Mobility takes place by intermarriage or by acquisition of the cultural capital which is associated with the new status.

Up the Social Ladder. In a meritocratic society, education has been the key to upward mobility. It takes place in two stages. First, one acquires at least some of the characteristics of the upper class, most important of which is a level of educational attainment which will provide competence in higher status jobs and give a luster to social and intellectual interaction. Second, one must learn the social graces and habits of behavior of the class to which one aspires. Practicing for status is called "anticipatory socialization" (Srinivas 1965); it is reflected in the desire of parents to send their children to the "right" schools.

Americans tend to conceive only of upward mobility, and they have encouraged all their children to get as much schooling as possible so that they can do better than their parents. Poverty in the lower classes was attributed to an absence of the ambition or ability necessary to acquire an adequate education. However, upward mobility can exist only where there is room for expansion at the top of the socioeconomic ladder. Room at the top is created when the top stratum is removed or made smaller, either by reduced birthrates among the elite, social upheaval or geographic relocation of those hoping to move upward—such as by moving to the colonies or out on the frontier—or by the creation of new economic opportunities, like the modern computer industry. It has been possible for Americans to ignore the possibility of downward mobility both because the economy offered a wide range of opportunity and because status in the American social system has not been heavily based upon cultural standing which could only be inherited, but upon economic wealth, which could be earned. America was blessed with expanding economic and geographic frontiers which provided opportunity for some people to escape their original destinies. The prestigious cultural goods associated with upper-class life could, in large part, be purchased once wealth had been acquired.

This model is, however, deceptive, because it is based upon generalizations about the success of a limited number of "deviant cases." Strategies which worked for a few individuals who did "make it" were applied indiscriminately to everyone. Hence, the Horatio Alger stories, in which hard work and diligent study won wealth and the hand of the factory owner's daughter for a poor boy, became the model to which the general population aspired.

Down the Ladder. The fact is, however, that not everyone can move up. Most societies are fairly stable and there usually are as many individuals moving down as are moving up. Where room at the top constricts, the net mobility downward may exceed movement up, no matter how much education people can acquire. This appears to be happening in the United States, as the society decapitalizes, industry moves to Third World countries, and high-paying jobs in the industrial and professional sectors are reduced in number or replaced by lower-paying, less-skilled jobs in the service sector (Bluestone and Harrison 1986). This is a real problem for America for several reasons. First, it devalues education, exploding the myth of the pay-off to hard work in school. It creates educational inflation as increased levels of educational attainment by the population in the face of fewer jobs requiring high levels of training make diplomas less valuable than before. College degrees are now required for jobs which once needed only high school diplomas. The prospect of downward mobility weighs particlarly heavily on middle class and poor students for whom education represented their only hope to maintain status or escape proletarianization, or a descent into the working class (Miles 1977, p. 436).

It also affects patterns of reward and control in school. Teachers no longer can promise a "deal" to their students: if they work hard, learn their lessons and respect the teacher, they will be rewarded with a good job. Finally, the anticipation of downward mobility can lead to student alienation and unrest as the "good life" promised by schools and society seems farther and farther out of reach to an increasingly large group of young people (Keniston 1971; Miles 1977).

Caste and Class

Up to now, we have been talking only about social *class*. Membership in a social class is not fixed, even though in many societies movement from one class to another is limited and often takes place only by inter-class marriage. However, where *castes*, rather than classes, structure a society, movement may cease to exist altogether. Membership in a caste is rigidly hereditary and is defined by occupational status. Caste members inherit the occupations of their parents; they are forbidden by law and social custom from engaging in any other profession unless it has the same social status as has been assigned to their customary occupation. Social interaction between members of different castes is limited and intermarriage is forbidden; often caste differences are highlighted by differences in dress, patterns of food consumption, ethnicity, language patterns and religion. Low-status castes often are stigmatized; that is, anything associated with a low-status caste is considered to polluting to a member of a higher caste. As a consequence, people from different castes cannot eat together or live in the same neighborhoods. Caste-based societies provide little opportunity for individual mobility; however, using the case of India, Srinivas (1965) and Rudolph and Rudolph (1967) describe group mobility, wherein certain low-caste groups have begun to raise the status of their group by becoming educated, changing their occupation, becoming vegetarians and adopting the religious observances of Brahmins. The Rudolphs' research indicates that an increase in education is not sufficient; these groups had to change their *cultural capital* as well.

Caste-like Minorities. Castes usually have not been thought to exist in America. However, Ogbu (1978, 1986) points out that the status of native-born, stigmatized minorities, like Mexican-Americans, Native Americans and blacks, is "caste-like." Ogbu believes that the systematic patterns of discrimination which these groups have experienced over many generations has transformed these groups into a virtually hereditary underclass of impoverished people. They do poorly in school as a group regardless of the special programs set up for them and are able to obtain only those jobs at the lowest end of the labor market. They share a fatalistic perspective: since no amount of work will lead to a better job, why try?

Ogbu also makes the important point that the disabilities under which caste-like minorities labor are contextual rather than inherent; when members of caste-like groups escape to another society which does not discriminate against them, they can be as successful as any other migrant group. As Gibson's work with Punjabi students in California demonstrates, they often can do this without foreswearing many aspects of their traditional culture (Gibson 1988).

We will talk more in Chapter Seven about minorities, education, and inequality. Some scholars have criticized Ogbu's analysis for its overly simplistic and deterministic view of the impact of labor market structure (Erickson 1987); others state that his analysis fails to account for the fact that minority children often conform to, rather than behave antagonistically toward, the authority structure and norms of the school (D'Amato 1988). His discussion, however, points out that schools are among the primary locations where the process of social differentiation takes place. In schools, children who start out with ostensibly equal capabilities end up sorted into groups whose achievement is markedly different. Furthermore, these differences in achievement are explained, in large part, by differences in social class (or caste-like status). Regardless of their ethnicity, poor students tend to be grouped with poor students and rich students tend to study with other rich students. In the remaining pages of this chapter, we will discuss how this happens and its consequences.

Occupational Attainment

Functional theorists in the sociology of education felt that educational systems played three roles in the larger society. First, they attributed to schools the functions of socialization for citizenship and social control (Durkheim 1961). Second, they believed that schools were sites for the meritocratic selection and training of leadership cadres (Weber 1947). Finally, they were the means by which individual members of society were meritocratically selected and trained for specific occupational roles.

The last function is accomplished by means of two mechanisms: the differentiated curriculum, which prepares students either for vocational careers or for movement to colleges and universities and subsequent professional training, and the system of grading and ability grouping, which serves as a rational means for placing students into curricula appropriate not only to their intellectual ability and interests, but also to their ultimate career destinations. In America, sociologists and educators preferred to believe that status was based upon achievement. To do so, they had to demonstrate that social status was not inherited. This meant that children's education, not their family background, would have to be the most important predictor of educational and occupational attainment.

The Blau and Duncan Model. Blau and Duncan's (1967) landmark study of young men examined the relationship between family background variables, including father's occupation and education, and the level of education and occupational destination attained by their sons. Blau and Duncan tried to develop a model to predict mathematically how much education contributed to ultimate occupational attainment of individuals. Their model had a profound impact upon the way social scientists thought about the relationships among education, occupation, and socioeconomic status. They did find that the impact of all educational factors combined was the single largest contributor to one's life chances. However, there were some significant limitations to their work. First, the numbers were not overwhelming; they indicated that education contributed only about 30 percent of the total predictive power to the model. Other sociologists then attempted to improve the predictive power of the model by adding other factors. Perhaps best known of these attempts was the work of Sewell, Haller, and their associates.

The Status Attainment Model. The so-called "Wisconsin Model" (Sewall et al. 1969, 1970; Sewell, Hall, and Ohlendorf 1970; Haller, Sewell, and Shah 1977; Jencks, Crouse, and Mueser 1983) asked the following questions:

1. What are the relative impacts of family background and schooling on subsequent attainments?
2. What is the role of academic ability in the attainment process?
3. How do aspirations and motivations determine attainment and what is the role of family and school in providing support for aspirations? Do social psychological variables merely transmit the effects of family background and/or ability or do they have an impact of their own? (Campbell 1983, p. 47)

These sociologists suggested that attitudinal factors in family background and aspirational variables were important mediating links between ascribed (or family background) status, educational attainment, and subsequent occupational attainment. In other words, family influence was not just passive; it involved transmitting to children active desires toward certain occupational goals and the expectations of their acquisition. They also examined the influence of "significant others"—teachers and parents. Some sociologists even interviewed children and their parents to trace the impact of parents' aspirations for their children. (Kahl 1953). However, these studies still did not explain why families from different social classes left their children with different goals, nor did they examine the constraints on occupational attainment which both market conditions—supply and demand for given services—as well as patterns of discrimination–legal and customary—impose (Persell 1977, p. 157).

Correcting for Race, and Gender Bias: The Rosenfeld Model. Blau and Duncan's model only looked at white males. It failed to examine the impact of mothers on sons, and it did not discuss the destiny of daughters at all. A number of years later, other researchers re-examined both replicated Blau and Duncan's work and the status attainment models for women and blacks. (Ayella and Williamson 1976; Rosenfeld 1978, 1980). As suspected, the model was not nearly as good a predictor for women—or blacks—as it was for white men. In the early stages—the first six years after completing school—white men and women receive about the same wage and status returns to their investment in education. However, after six years, the picture changes dramatically.

> At their potential, white men recieve greater returns to their human capital
> [education and training] than white women. They receive higher returns in
> terms of both status and wages to their years of formal schooling, get
> greater returns in terms of status to their white collar training, suffer less of
> a status disadvantage from having some formal preparation for a blue collar
> job, and receive considerably greater wage returns from both kinds of train-
> ing. (Rosenfeld 1980, p. 604)

Only non-white males do worse than white women.

The most important factors in ultimate occupational attainment for women are related not to education but to the labor market; they include the kind of work experience women have had, the types of jobs available, and the degree of discrimination women encountered in searching for jobs.

Notwithstanding these limitations, Blau and Duncan's work clarified several important ways that the meritocratic model did not work as predicted. Blau and Duncan found that the impact of education on educational achievement and occupation could not be explained without taking social background into account. This was because the most powerful predictor of how much education individuals obtained was the social class background of their parents, as measured by their income level, occupation, and education.

Their work also called into question the American view of meritocracy which assumed that intelligence or ability was equally distributed throughout the population, not skewed by social class. If a meritocratic situation really existed in America, researchers should have found that children from each social class were represented in high track as well as low track classes in proportion to their numbers in the population. For example, if ten percent of the total number of students in a school were recipients of public assistance, then no more than ten percent of the enrollment in each of the ability groups in the school—remedial, vocational, and college prep—should be constituted of students from welfare families. The same should be true of the representation of children from wealthy families. However, what researchers found was that children from higher socio-economic status families were greatly over-represented in classes and tracks for high-achieving students, as well as in college preparatory schools, higher education, and professional jobs. Similarly, there was a significantly higher percentage of lower-class students in the remedial, vocational and noncollege preparatory classes than their percentage in the school population. This measure of over-and under-representation meant that something was impeding the smooth operation of meritocracy; it became an indicator of inegalitarianism and class bias.

The Marxist Model: Class and Income Inequality. Very few studies of the causes of social inequality have used Marxist categories of analysis. However, one important study (Wright and Perrone 1977) does examine three classes— workers, managers and employers—to see what impact social class, in Marxian terms, rather than educational achievement, occupational position and family background, has on economic inequality. This study demonstrated that the class model is more powerful than status attainment models in predicting where a person will end up in the class hierarchy. Class matters more than education, and even overrides the effects of education. Thus, even with high levels of education, working class children will not achieve as much prestige as children from the upper classes. This is because working class children are handicapped by their background; they cannot translate their education into as much occupational prestige and economic success as can upper and middle class children with the same or inferior levels of education. Studies like these provided a catalyst for identifying the mechanisms by which biases against the poor and working class impeded their performance.

THE MECHANISM OF CLASS BIAS IN EDUCATION

Discussions of the relationship between class and educational achievement are almost inextricably meshed with discussions of race, since caste-like minority status, poverty, and low rates of educational achievement are highly correlated. However, we will argue while patterns of discrimination create castelike conditions for some people, and certainly systematically disadvantage women, social class, or patterns of economic domination and subordination create far more important distinctions among people. Hence, rich people, of whatever race, religion, or gender are far more similar to one another than they are to poor people of their own race, religion or gender. These differences are created, supported, and enhanced by participation in educational institutions.

Test Scores

Initial studies of social class impact used student test scores on standardized tests as a data base. This research was quantitative; it looked at test scores as output measures, and tried to predict them by looking at a variety of independent measures, such as sex, type of curriculum, mother's education, father's education, income, and race. All of these studies indicated that test scores are stratified by social class, ethnicity notwithstanding.

Ability Grouping

Test scores however, proved to be insufficient to explain why the social class biased patterns of differential learning in school existed, because they could not uncover the processes by which children were differentially treated. In the 1970s, a strong interest in microlevel, observational studies of classroom interaction developed. This work began to demonstrate how profoundly social class affects the placement of children in ability groups, because the studies showed the extent to which teachers grouped students on the basis of their *perceptions* of how able students are, rather than entirely on the basis of assessed merit and competence. Because lower class children often lack the cultural capital congruent with school life, they are judged by teachers to be less able. Teachers classified as brighter children who were clean, quiet, and who acted in a respectful manner to the teacher. Teachers also tended to favor and to judge as more capable children who shared their own values, regardless of the student's measured ability. Sometimes they were notably poor judges of actual ability. Teachers also had a difficult time giving failing grades to students they liked. Unfortunately, since most teachers either were born into, or have acquired the cultural capital, habits and aspirations of the middle class, they now find many students in their classrooms who do not share their values (Brophy and Good 1970; Rosenfeld 1971; Rist 1973; Spindler 1987; Ortiz 1988).

It probably is fair to say that teacher *perceptions* of a student's ability are a far more accurate predictor of the group into which a child will be placed than measured intelligence, or even past standardized test scores (Cicourel and Kitsuse 1963). While all teachers take into account a child's past record—often too seriously so—they will not fail to disregard evidence they disagree with, citing their own professional skills in diagnosis as authoritative.

As we will point out in Chapter Six, tracking, or ability grouping, acts to further differentiate students because it profoundly affects the amount and type of learning made available to students. Tracking affects the kind of management and control teachers exercise over their pupils; the treatment students receive from teachers and schools staff also reflects the kind of cultural capital which they bring to school.

Teachers interact far more with high track students, for whom they hold higher expectations. These students are praised more when correct and are criticized less when they are wrong than are students for whom teachers have low expectations (Brophy and Good 1970; Allington 1983; Grant and Rothenberg 1986). They also are far more likely to be given considerable autonomy in the execution of their school work; they are expected to work independently and are given opportunities to engage in higher order thinking skills and access to innovative programs like computer programming. They will be punished less for infractions of the rules, and will be given more chances and greater encouragement if they do poorly, if only because teachers fear the adverse reaction of middle- and upper-class parents.

By contrast, teachers of lower-class students employ custodial forms of behavior management; while much money and effort may be poured into special programs to enhance the achievement of these students, the programs often are remedial and simply repeat previous material; where computers are used they are used simply for an additional form of drill-and-practice. Placed in the lower tracks, less capable students get fewer hours of actual instruction and less rigorous coursework; "pull-out" programs of special tutoring actually diminish the time spent in regular instruction (Bennett 1986; Delgado-Gaitan 1988). Teachers of the poor do not expect their students to do well, and, assuming that they will fail, interact with them less, give them less encouragement and worry less about the dropouts. These findings have been confirmed in studies of classroom interaction (Rist, 1970; Borko and Eisenhart, 1986), in interview studies with low-achieving students (Willis 1977; Fine 1986; Williams 1987; Valverde 1987; McLeod 1987), and in analyses of curriculum distribution and content (Bennett 1986)

All of these findings are complicated by race, but one can find the same patterns of neglect and custodialism in schools which serve poor white students as are found for poor Black and Hispanic students.

The Social Construction of Identity

Some very early studies pointed to the heritability of social class. In his study of "Elmtown," Hollingshead (1949) suggested that children who grew up on the "wrong side of the tracks" remained there, as did *their* children. In the late 1970s, critical analysts began to look even more closely at classroom interaction in an attempt to explain the processes by which social class is replicated from one generation to another. In doing so, they used the methods of symbolic interactionists. As we explained in Chapter One, this approach states that people do not simply react automatically and unconsciously to any "stimulus or pressure they are subjected to, but they make sense of these pressures in terms of frameworks of meaning they have built up through their lives" (Hargreaves and Woods 1984, p. 2). The symbolic interactionists have discovered what these frameworks of meanings are, how to get people to talk about them, and how they reciprocally affect the behavior and beliefs of people as they engage in social interaction. They have explained the *reflexive*, reciprocal nature of human behavior as people "work at" constructing reality around them.

Becker (1953) for example, described teachers' notions of the "ideal" student, and showed how teachers treated pupils differently in accordance with how closely students approximately that ideal. Poorer, more disadvantaged students were far from the ideal; for them, teachers lowered standards for performance, spent more time in discipline and less in instruction, and taught more slowly. (See also Powell et al. 1985; Firestone and Rosenblum, 1988; Page, 1987b). As a consequence, the students became even more academically disadvantaged as the school year progressed. Other researchers have demonstrated how students treated in this manner pay less attention in class (Eder 1982), come to define themselves as "poor students", or "slow learners," or simply as "not college material", and adjust their performance standards and aspirations accordingly (Willis 1977; McLeod 1987; McLaren 1986; Page 1987). Erickson (1987, p. 336) has described this as "school failure," a reflexive process by which "schools 'work at' failing their students and students 'work at' failing to achieve in school . . . [school failure, in this sense, is] something the school does as well as what the student does."

Resistance. Schools do not fail all students with whom they are mismatched, and some students actively "withhold assent" (Erickson 1987) to attempts by educators to "cool them out" of the system.

Early work by critical theorists blamed teachers for the failure of students, paying special attention to how the labels teachers assigned to students destroyed their self esteem and stunted their intellectual growth. Data elicited from students bolstered the attack on teachers, describing in detail patterns of conflict and hostility among pupils, teachers and school staff. More recent studies have examined the patterns of mutual interaction between the inhabitants of schools, like the process which Erickson describes above. Researchers have begun to describe how people "work at" school, looking at how both teachers and students come to the classroom with preconceived notions and sets of definitions which permit them mutually to construct the day-to-day reality of their life in schools. While much of the empirical research in this area has looked at negative effects—how negative self-concepts both for teachers and students are constructed and how students and teachers resist being defined in ways detrimental to a positive self-image (See our discussion in Chapters Three and Four)—a number of ethnographic researchers who have studied classroom processes from varying perspectives have begun to explore ways in which "working at" school can be turned from a negative to a positive process. One perspective which focuses on ameliorating the impact of cultural as well as class differences is typified by Erickson (1984, 1987) and scholars from the Kamehameha Early Education Project in Hawaii and the Center for Cross Cultural Studies at the University of Fairbanks, Alaska (Au 1979, 1980; Au and Jordan 1981; Barnhardt 1982; Jordan 1984, 1985; Moll and Diaz 1987).

Empowerment. Another approach which concentrates more on a social class perspective, is a recent branch of "critical pedagogy" (McLaren 1989, p. 162) which views the existence of mutual construction of meaning as an opportunity for manipulating interaction in classrooms and schools. It advocates using schools to promote **empowerment** of subordinated and marginalized groups within society, especially teachers, minorities, the poor, and women.

By empowerment, these researchers mean that schools can be used to help people become conscious of the forces which oppress them and to learn strategies to overcome them. They emphasize the importance of researcher collaboration as a means to raise the consciousness of teachers and students, and their efforts have been limited more or less to work within individual schools and classrooms. Translated into a curricular philosophy, this means believing in

> conceptions of learning as something that happens to an individual as an internal and subjective action, as a process of inquiry and discovery; knowlege as something that can only be personally acquired and not given; as truths in each of us rather than as fixed and finite truths 'out there'; of development as personal growth, as the transformation of powers already present; of classrooms as communities of learners helping each other . . . for the enhancement of all. (Ashcroft 1987, p. 155)

As we point out in Chapter Nine, this perspective also is limited. While it develops awareness of patterns of hegemonic domination, its efforts are limited by its focus on microlevel and psychological processes rather than larger political and structural correlates of oppression.

SUMMARY

In this chapter we have demonstrated how our ideas of social class have changed over time, and how even our scientific explanations of why people were rich or poor were affected by social and cultural traditions. We have described how social class status is inextricably linked to educational achievement and occupational attainment. We also have shown how the work of sociologists has exploded some of the most cherished beliefs of educators. We now know that what appears to be intellectual merit may actually be the product of special treatment in the schools, given because of one's social class status. Similarly, what appears to be a student's lack of ability may be a product of teacher perceptions, based on the student's lower class status, plus the student's response to negative assessments by the school system.

We also have learned that the process by which students fail—or achieve—in school is composed of a very complex set of factors. It is insufficient to say that:

- Kids are lazy—or poorly prepared.
- Teachers are incompetent—or hate kids.
- Parents don't care—or don't know how to help their kids.

All of these explanations may contain some truth. But the reality of inequality in education is a mixture of many things, all of which are played out reflexively in the arena of schools and classrooms.

In the chapters which follow, we will look more closely at how the curriculum acts to widen the differences between students from different social classes. We also will discuss the impact of race and gender on educational achievement.

KEY CONCEPTS

Class refers to a category of things grouped together because they share common characteristics.

Social Class refers to groups of people who share certain characteristics of income, occupational status, educational levels, aspirations, behavior and beliefs. Social classes are arranged in hierarchies based upon prestige, power and status, as well how their members obtain a livelihood.

Stratification refers differentiation into levels, which usually are arranged into a hierarchy. Stratification of social classes is based on the prestige or power possessed by each group.

Caste refers to a social class whose membership is fixed by hereditary rules and defined by occupational status. Caste usually exists in societies where hereditary occupations are the primary means by which society is stratified.

A Caste-Like Minority (Ogbu 1978) is a native born stigmatized group whose destiny is caste-like, because it has experienced so many generations of systematic economic discrimination that its poverty becomes virtually hereditary.

Ideology is a system of values and beliefs which provide the concepts, images and ideas by which people interpret their world and shape their behavior toward other people. It is accepted as the natural and common sense explanation of the way the world operates. Ideologies often act to reinforce the power of dominant groups in society.

Social Mobility refers to the movement of people and groups from one social class to another.

Empowerment refers to the ability to become conscious of oppression and learn to implement strategies to overcome it.

EXERCISES

1. To which social class do you think your family of origin belonged? What social class do you think you belong to now? What evidence do you use for giving yourself a particular social class assignment?
2. Examine your family's genealogy. Were there changes in social class status over the generations? To what do you attribute these changes?
3. Think back to your experiences in elementary and secondary schooling. Were you aware that children came from different social classes? How? How did differences in social class status effect children's school experiences? Give specific examples from your own experiences.
4. Observe two primary school classrooms—one in a poor urban area and one in a middle class suburb. Pay particular attention to factors which help to identify children according to social class backgrounds. Can you distinguish between differences attributable to class and those which are a consequence of minority status? Observe the children in both classroom and playground situations. Based on your observations, what role do you think social class plays in the school experience of the children? Compare the two settings. What do you think of the school experiences provided to each group of children?
5. Interview a teacher. What is the social class background of this teacher? What is the social class background of his or her students? Does this teacher believe that social class background plays a role in students schooling experiences? In what way? Write a personal reaction to this interview.

SUGGESTED READINGS

Classic Works

Bensman, Joseph, and Vidich, Arthur J. (1971). *The new American society: The revolution of the middle class*. Chicago: Quadrangle Books.

Blau, Peter, and Duncan, Otis Dudley (1967). *The American occupational structure*. New York: John Wiley.

Bourdieu, Pierre, and Passeron, Jean-Claude (1977). *Reproduction: In education, society and culture*. London: Sage Publications.

Bowles, Samuel, and Herbert Gintis (1976). *Schooling in capitalist America*. New York: Basic Books.

Marx, Karl (1959). *Basic writings on politics and philosophy*. Lewis Feuer, ed. Garden City, N.Y.: Anchor Books.

Mills, C. Wright (1956). *The power elite*. New York: Oxford University Press.

Persell, Caroline (1977). *Education and inequality*. New York: The Free Press.

Sennett, Richard, and Cobb, Jonathan (1973). *The hidden injuries of class*. New York: Vintage Books.

Weber, Max (1958). *From Max Weber: Essays in sociology*, ed. and trans. by H. Gerth and C. Wright Mills. New York: Oxford University Press.

Willis, Paul (1977). *Learning to labour: How working class kids get working class jobs*.

Modern Works

Campbell, Richard T. (1983). Status attainment research: End of the beginning or beginning of the end? *Sociology of Education*, Vol. 56 (January) pp. 47–62.

Gould, Stephen Jay (1981). *The mismeasure of man*. New York: W.W. Norton and Co.

McLaren, Peter (1989). *Life in schools*. New York: Longman Inc.

McLeod, Jay (1987). *Ain't no makin' it: Levelled aspirations in a low-income neighborhood*. Boulder, Colo. Westview Press.

Rosenfeld, Rachel A. (1980). Race and sex differences in career dynamics. *American Sociological Review*, Vol. 45, (August) pp. 583–609.

Weis, Lois (Ed.) (1988). *Race, class, and gender in American education*. New York: State University of New York Press.

CHAPTER 6

What Is Taught in Schools: Curriculum and the Stratification of Knowledge

INTRODUCTION

In this chapter we first consider traditional notions of curriculum theory which have dominated how educators viewed what is taught in schools. We then consider **curriculum** from a critical sociological perspective, briefly discussing both the **sociology of knowledge** and **sociology of curriculum**. The sociology of knowledge is a subdiscipline of sociology which is broadly concerned with notions of what counts for "knowledge" in a society (Berger and Luckmann 1967). The sociology of curriculum is a more recent subfield concerned specifically with school knowledge and relationships between the curriculum, schools and the dominant society (Giroux 1988). We contrast the sociological view of curriculum with that of traditional educational curriculum theorists. We then provide a discussion of formal and hidden curricula and the stratification of curricula for different groups of students. In so doing, we will address the following questions:

1. What is curriculum?
2. What types of curricula are used in American schooling?
3. What knowledge is included in these curricula?
4. What values and attitudes are taught through the curriculum?
5. How does the curriculum change over time in response to sociocultural needs and political interests?
6. Who determines what is taught in schools in the 1980s?

WHAT IS CURRICULUM?

A curriculum is a course of study or a plan for what is to be taught to students in an educational institution. It is composed of information concerning what is to be taught, to whom, when and how it should be taught. Consideration of the curriculum must include its purpose, content, method, organization and evaluation (McNeil 1985). A simpler, but more comprehensive way to think about curriculum is that it is *what happens to students in school*. It is more than the formal content of lessons taught in schools. It is also the method of presentation, the way in which students are grouped in classes, the manner in which time and tasks are organized and the interactional patterns within classrooms. The term "curriculum" refers to the total school experience provided to students, whether planned or unplanned by educators. By conceptualizing the curriculum this broadly, we are able to include its intended as well as unintended outcomes.

Traditional Curriculum Theory

Traditional curriculum theory derives not from sociology but from psychology and subject area studies in pedagogy. Traditional curriculum theorists assume that there is a given body of knowledge which is objective and free from values and biases. The assumptions of traditional curriculum are summarized by Giroux:

> (a) Theory in the curriculum field should operate in the interest of lawlike propositions that are empirically testable; (b) the natural sciences provide the "proper" model of explanation for the concepts and techniques of curriculum theory, design, and evaluation; (c) knowledge should be objective and capable of being investigated and described in a neutral fashion; and (d) statements of value are to be separated from "facts" and "modes of inquiry" that can and ought to be objective. (Giroux 1988, p. 13)

Traditional curriculum theorists try to determine the best ways to impart a given body of knowledge to people. They apply a linear concept of causality to learning by studying how a given body of facts, concepts and understandings can be transferred effectively and efficiently directly from a teacher to a learner. Colleges of education have curriculum specialists who train preservice teachers and graduate students in the "science" of curriculum design. The history of traditional curriculum theory is a history of the application of rational, scientific principles to the management of "objective" bodies of knowledge. Models for the development of curriculum are produced by these specialists. Knowledge is viewed as something to be managed by administrators and teachers and given to students, usually in the form of prepackaged designs, kits, formulas, approaches, materials, and lists of skills and objectives. Educators categorize and manage knowledge and students are required to master it.

Sociologists of knowledge, the "new" sociologists of curriculum (Giroux 1988), and **reconceptualist** curriculum theorists (Pinar 1989; Shaker and Kridel 1989) challenge the assumptions made by the traditional curriculum theorists. The central questions for critical theorists of curriculum is not *how* to manage knowledge, but what kinds of knowledge are included in the curriculum and whose interests are served.

Sociology of Knowledge and Sociology of Curriculum

The term "sociology of knowledge" was first used by the German philosopher Max Scheler in the 1920's (Berger and Luckmann 1967). The sociology of knowledge is concerned with definitions of knowledge and particularly with how knowledge is constructed through the social interactions of individuals. In their classic book *The Social Construction of Reality: A Treatise in the Sociology of Knowledge* (1967), Berger and Luckmann state that:

Common sense "knowledge" rather than "ideas" must be the central focus for the sociology of knowledge. It is precisely this knowledge that constitutes the fabric of meanings without which no society could exist. The sociology of knowledge, therefore, must concern itself with the social construction of reality. (p. 15)

Implicit in the sociology of knowledge is the assumption that knowledge is power and that different types of knowledge are provided or withheld according to one's place in the social structure of society. As we illustrate later in this and subsequent chapters, certain kinds of knowledge are provided to or withheld from certain groups of people based on gender, race, ethnicity and social class status. Because of their position in society, those in power are more able to use their influence to advocate inclusion of certain types of knowledge in the schooling process. A central concern in the sociology of knowledge, then, becomes the study of the social interactional process by which certain types of knowledge become reality in the everyday lives of individuals within the society.

Research on the sociology of curriculum began in the early 1970s. Berger and Luckman's definition of the sociology of knowledge provided a theoretical framework for subsequent studies examining the knowledge taught in schools. School knowledge became the focus of studies known as the *sociology of the curriculum*, or sometimes the "new sociology of education" (Giroux 1988). Michael F. D. Young (1971) announced a marked shift in the sociology of education when he proclaimed the emergence of a "new sociology of education" at the Institute of Education in London. His edited volume, *Knowledge and Control: New Directions for the Sociology of Education*, was instrumental in promoting the sociological study of the school curriculum; with its publication, the "importance of [this] area of sociological study came to be widely recognized" (Whitty 1985, p. 13).

The sociology of the curriculum looks at ways in which the curriculum is organized and stratified. In other words, it examines how different types of knowledge are provided for different groups of students. It views curriculum within the social context of schools and as a reflection of interest groups within the broader society. For example, in examining the curriculum, sociologists may ask:

1. How do schools group children for instruction?
2. How much and what kinds of knowledge is presented by the teachers in these groups?
3. How do teacher-student interactions differ from one level group to another?
4. How are different people in society presented in school texts?
5. Are there differences in the amount and content provided in the curriculum according to ethnicity, class and gender categories?

Sociological research on knowledge and curriculum has added much to our understanding about how schools work. We have learned that in addition to the formally stated, explicit curriculum, there is a **hidden** or implicit **curriculum** that works to impart beliefs and values to students in schools. The following sections of this chapter will explore both the formal and hidden curriculum of schools.

Ideological Interests in the Formal and Hidden Curriculum

A central concern of critical theorists is that of uncovering the ideological interests embedded in both formal and hidden school curricula. Giroux explains that there are two kinds of **ideology**:

> Theoretical ideologies refer to the beliefs and values embedded in the categories that teachers and students use to shape and interpret the pedagogical process, while practical ideologies refer to the messages and norms embedded in classroom social relations and practices. (Giroux 1983b, p. 67)

In order for us to understand the various and competing ideologies inherent in schooling in the 1980s, we need to look at the formal curriculum as it developed throughout the twentieth century. In the next sections of this chapter, we will look at what is taught in schools from the perspective of both formal and hidden curricula. The following questions asked by critical theorists guide our discussion:

1. What counts as curriculum knowledge?
2. How is such knowledge produced?
3. How is such knowledge transmitted in the classroom?
4. What kinds of classroom social relationships serve to parallel and reproduce the values and norms embodied in the accepted social relations of other dominant social sites?
5. Who has access to legitimate forms of knowledge?
6. Whose interests does this knowledge serve?
7. How are social and political contradictions and tensions mediated through acceptable forms of classroom knowledge and social relationships?
8. How do prevailing methods of evaluation serve to legitimize existing forms of knowledge? (Giroux 1983b, pp. 17–18).

WHAT IS TAUGHT: THE FORMAL CURRICULUM

The debate about what knowledge should be included in the curricula of American public schools is as old as the public schools themselves. Since schools are highly political institutions, the content and form of instruction depends, in large part, upon which socioeconomic interests wield power in society. Since different groups disagree both over the relative value which should be accorded to different kinds of knowledge and the appropriateness of varying kinds of knowledge for different classes or groups of people, there never has been a consensus over which body of knowledge was appropriate for all the children in all the schools.

Today, many interest groups compete to influence what knowledge is transmitted in schools and how this transmission should take place. Spring's (1988a) discussion of the textbook publishing industry provides an excellent examination of the conflicting interests groups and their effects on educational policy and practice. He describes how the particular textbooks chosen determine what curricula will dominate in a school system. These choices are powerfully influenced by negotiations among the textbook publishing industry, state and federal educational policy-makers, special interest groups (teachers unions, association of school administrators, parent teacher associations, religious organizations, etc.) and corporations. Each of these interest groups differ radically in their beliefs about the purpose of schooling, its role in transmitting ideas and values, and which ideas and values should be taught in schools. Many of them also have a deep financial interest in the lucrative textbook market.

Despite the lack of consensus about what should be taught in schools and how it should be delivered, identifiable trends in curricular knowledge appear throughout the history of American schooling. Kliebard (1986) has described these trends in his book *The Struggle for the American Curriculum: 1893–1958*. Kliebard illustrates how the formal curriculum has been and continues to be the result of varied and conflicting ways of interpreting the goals of schooling discussed in Chapter One. Kliebard argues that four major types of curricula have dominated twentieth century schooling: humanist, social efficiency, developmental and social meliorist.

The Humanist Curriculum

The humanist curriculum is the model for the so-called "traditional liberal arts" program. Humanists view schools as "guardians of ancient tradition tied to the power of reason and the finest elements of [Anglo] Western heritage" (Kliebard 1986, p. 27). They believe that the purpose of schooling is to develop the intellect by transmitting a core of the finest elements of this heritage to all members of society. This position was argued by Charles W. Eliot, president of Harvard University and chairman of the National Education Association's Committee of Ten, whose 1893 report emphasized a curriculum which would seek to increase the reasoning power of students through traditional academic subject areas (foreign languages, mathematics, literature, sciences, history and the arts) and would be offered to all students whether they intended to continue on to college or not. The Committee of Ten believed that being taught, in the best possible ways, a common core of subjects was the best possible way to prepare all students for life, whether or not they later sought a college education (Kleibard 1986).

This same humanist viewpoint was promoted as recently as 1988 by former Secretary of Education William Bennett in his pamphlet, "James Madison High School: A Curriculum for American Students," and in his guidelines for "James

Madison Elementary School" (1988). Bennett's curriculum proposals are designed for "mastery of a common core of worthwhile knowledge, important skills, and sound ideals" (E.W. Bennett 1988, p. 7). Bennett's plan prescribes a curriculum of seven core academic subjects. The core of subjects required for his high school students include four years of English, three years each of social studies, mathematics and science, two years each of foreign language and physical education/health and one year of fine arts (music history and art history). Bennett's plan for elementary students in grades kindergarten through eighth proposes a similar curriculum consisting of English, history, geography, civics, mathematics, science, foreign language and fine arts.

At both the secondary and elementary levels, Bennett's descriptions of these courses continue the traditional humanist emphasis through the study of a Anglo-American cultural heritage. This type of curriculum reflects the functionalist theory that there is consensus on what should be taught in schools and that the purpose of schooling is to transmit this knowledge from one generation to the next.

The Social Efficiency Curriculum

Among the most profound influences upon pedagogy has been social efficiency theory. As we described in Chapter Two, it was developed from principles of scientific management, a movement based upon studies of organizations and industrial psychology. Social efficiency theorists believe that schools should facilitate the smooth functioning of the nation's economy by sorting citizens into job slots according to their abilities. Advocates of social efficiency apply techniques of industry to the scientific management of schools. In this way, schools can become efficient, smooth running machines, which in turn produce citizens for a similar society. In Chapter Two we examined the political context by which educators came to link schooling with manpower planning and social engineering, as well as how scientific management affected the scheduling of the school day and the use of school buildings. Here, we examine the form and content of a "scientifically engineered" curriculum.

The tenets of the efficiency movement affected how knowledge was conceptualized and evaluated and how learning tasks were organized. It included the practice of breaking down cognitive skills and substantive knowledge into component parts and then organizing learning around the mastery of sets of behavioral objectives based upon those components. For example, in teaching children to read, curriculum specialists examined and organized phonetic skills into lists according to perceived levels of difficulty. Beginning consonant sounds are taught before short and long vowel sounds, which are taught before vowel diphthongs. These lists of skills were then written into behavioral objectives which teachers checked off as children mastered the skills.

Elimination of "waste" became a critical concern. Students were to be moved through school as quickly as possible, and to that end, the degree to which children could be kept "on-task" became a measure of effective teaching. "Waste" also was defined as spending time on the teaching of subjects deemed unnecessary. In his article "Elimination of Waste in Education" (1912), John

Franklin Bobbitt argued that students should be scientifically measured to predict their future role in the society so that they could be taught only what they would later need to fulfill the social and vocational roles they would perform as adults. A differentiated curriculum would solve that problem, since knowledge and skills which would not be used would not be taught. Useful knowledge was defined as that which could be used immediately in a job setting; hence subjects like Latin, history, and foreign languages were viewed with suspicion.

Gender, too, became a determinant in curriculum planning. Since males and females would fulfill different social and vocational roles, students would only need to be instructed in those things which were appropriate for their engendered adult roles. To that end, the training suggested for females generally was limited to general literacy and homemaking skills. (See Chapter 9 for more detail on the engendered curriculum.)

Development of the differentiated curriculum relied upon "scientific" and "objective" methods of testing, assessment and measurement. I.Q. testing was considered at that time to be an accurate, scientific mental measurement by which children's native capacities could be determined. Educators considered it to be an effective way to determine how to place students efficiently in school programs appropriate to both their abilities and their anticipated future occupations (Kleibard 1986, p. 109).

By the mid-1960s, testing had become a major part of the school curriculum. Both the heavy reliance on standardized testing and the curricular tracking procedures routinely used in schools provide evidence that the influence of the social efficiency experts is alive and well in American schools. The National Center for Fair and Open Testing, operated by a consumer group which refers to itself as "Fair Test," estimates that American elementary and high school students take more than 100 million standardized tests yearly. Approximately 44 million of these tests are intelligence and admissions tests; the rest are measurements of achievement and basic skills (Fiske 1988).

American educators and public officials continue to rely on the belief that standardized testing is an accurate method by which to monitor students as they move through schools. In the elementary schools, tests are used to place children in reading ability groups, special education classes and gifted and talented programs. In high schools, students are tested to determine their placement in the appropriate curricular track: general, college preparatory or vocational. We present a more complete discussion of testing and tracking in the section entitled "The Stratification of the Curriculum."

Rather than advocating the development of a core curriculum for all students as humanists do, the social efficiency curriculum prescribes different programs of study for students according to differences in their abilities as measured by standardized testing programs. Programs of study usually include a college preparatory program composed of the same academic core courses advocated by the humanists: literature, social science, natural science, mathematics and foreign languages. Separate programs are provided for students whom educators consider to lack the ability or interest to successfully master the academic college preparatory curriculum. These students, who are not "college material," are placed in programs to prepare them for jobs which do not require college educations; they include vocational, commercial and general courses of study. A general or basic course of study has many courses with the same names as academic subjects in the college preparatory program, but they are less rigorous and usually presented at a lower conceptual level.

The Developmentalist Curriculum

The developmental curriculum derives from clinical and developmental psychology, and is the only curriculum which is "student-centered." Its focus is the individual learner, rather than the needs of society or the importance of a particular body of knowledge. It also is concerned with helping people understand knowledge both experientially, in the context of the real world and intellectually, as abstracted from the real world (Reisler and Friedman 1978). Developmentalists believe that curriculum should be designed to meet the needs of individual students throughout their various stages of intellectual, social and emotional development. Central concerns are the motivation, interests and developmental stages of students. Students are taught when they are intellectually and emotionally ready to learn, rather than in accordance with their chronological age. Learning is structured so that children enjoy what they are doing while learning.

The developmentalists mandated a radically different role for teachers; they were to be partners with children in the learning enterprise rather than bosses. Some metaphors used for teachers provide clues to this shift in pedagogy; teachers are described as advisers, supporters, observers, learners, facilitators, and senior partners (Silberman 1973). The open classroom and open concept school building are legacies from the developmentalists.

John Dewey is one of the theorists most often associated with this type of curriculum because of his emphasis on child-centered activities. Both A. S. Neil's school, Summerhill, established in the 1920s, and the alternative or "free schools" of the 1960s were based upon these ideas. Spring (1989) notes that of Kliebard's four types of curriculum, the developmentalist has been the least influential on American public school curricula, even though colleges of education rely heavily on theories of developmentalists such as Rousseau, Dewey and Piaget in the training of preservice teachers. One sees little evidence of this approach persisting in the daily activities of public schooling.

Despite its limited impact on public schooling overall, developmentalism survives in private and alternative schools, and occasionally surfaces in special programs in the public sector. A contemporary example of a developmentalist curriculum is the "whole language" approach to the teaching of reading and written language skills in elementary schools. This approach relies on the children's own language. They learn to read by telling and writing their own stories rather than relying on basal reading textbooks. The whole language curriculum is rapidly gaining support by teachers and administrators as an instructional method which uses the developmental stages of children rather than standardized measures of ability to guide instruction.

The Social Meliorist Curriculum

Second in its impact on American education after the efficiency movement is Social Meliorism. Its tenets provide a constant tension with those of the efficiency advocates. According to social meliorists, schools should facilitate social change by producing students who will fight inequities and oppression and make the world a better place. The social meliorist curriculum came to the forefront of educational reform during the early 1930s as a reaction to scientific management, although it already had a long history among philosophers in Europe and America, from Martin Luther and Horace Mann to John Locke and John Dewey. Dewey was mentioned above as a developmentalist, but also was a strong advocate of schools as agencies of social reform.

George Counts and Harold Rugg are perhaps the best known educators representing this position. As early as the 1920s, Counts had advocated that educators act as agents of social change. The Great Depression, however, gave impetus to his stance. In his book, *Dare the School Build a New Social Order?* (1932), Counts encouraged teachers to organize in order to bring about social justice and reform through the educational process. Like John Dewey and others, he viewed the public school curriculum as a tool for correcting social and economic injustices of society.

Rugg's social studies curriculum in American History was first published in 1929 and became very popular throughout the 1930s. This program addressed issues of racism, class conflict, and the struggles of oppressed people. The curriculum came under attack by conservative political groups and was forced off the market in the 1940s (Spring 1988a).

Currently, the educators most closely allied with the kind of social meliorist curriculum described by Kliebard are those known as critical theorists or critical pedagogues (cf. Giroux 1983, 1988; McLaren 1989; Apple 1986; Weiler 1988). The core concern of critical theorist is an examination of patterns of subordination and domination in society: Who has access to power and why? As a consequence, stimulating the struggle against oppression based on race, ethnicity, class and gender is an essential element in such a curriculum.

At the center of this type of curriculum is the notion of conflict and struggle. Students are provided with differing perspectives on events and are encouraged to engage in critical examinations rather than merely reading texts and accepting the viewpoint of the author. A variety of texts in many forms are used in order to analyze all sides of an issue. For example, in a social studies discussion of the nineteenth century western expansion of white settlers into Indian lands, original documents, diaries, novels and treaties could serve as texts. Active student engagement is crucial in order to develop meaningful dialogue and critical thinking. The underlying assumption of critical theorists is that by actively grappling with issues of struggle, domination and oppression in the curriculum, students will work towards building a more democratic society for themselves.

The Formal Curriculum in Schools Today

The influence of all four of these curricula is likely to be visible in public schools, but social efficiency theorists have had the most obvious and continuing influence in American schooling. Their emphasis has been on efficiency, measurement and differentiated curricula. Administrators are taught to be scientific managers of their schools. Public schools in the United States today continue to organize knowledge and offer differentiated curricula to students based on standardized assessments of their academic abilities. Individual teachers or groups of teachers may be guided more by social meliorist or developmentalist theories, but there is little systematic evidence of this in the standard curricula of public schools.

WHAT IS TAUGHT: THE HIDDEN CURRICULUM

The term "hidden curriculum" first was used by Edgar Z. Friedenberg in a conference in the late 1960s. His invention of the term called attention to the fact that students learn more in school than is included in their formal instruction. Giroux defines the hidden curriculum as "those unstated norms, values, and beliefs embedded in and transmitted to students through the underlying rules that structure the routines and social relationships in school and classroom life" (Giroux 1983b, p. 47). The hidden curriculum consists of the implicit messages we give to students about differential power and social evaluation when students learn how schools actually work, what kinds of knowledge there are, which kind of knowledge is valued and how students are viewed in relation to school. These are the things that are learned informally and are sometimes, but not always, unintentional outcomes of the formal structure and curricular content of schooling. Giroux further suggests that in addition to information about the social relationships in school life, the hidden curriculum conveys in the messages to students through the "form and content of school knowledge" and the "silences"—or by what is left out.

For example, if you observed a typical American high school history class over the course of the school year, you would find that very little curricular content in the text or in classroom dialogue addresses the history of women and/or minority groups. You would, however, find much space devoted to the military history of the United States. These omissions and inclusions give to students a clear, but implicit message about what knowledge society considers to be valuable and what is not.

Further, the hidden curriculum is conveyed and observed in social interaction. For example, traditional sex roles are reinforced by the way the teachers assign different classroom tasks to females and males; girls may be asked to engage in cleaning up the room while boys may be asked to carry books or other heavy items out of the classroom. While most writers have viewed the hidden curriculum primarily as the unintended outcomes of the schooling process (McLaren 1989), we think it is important to understand that the hidden curriculum is often intended and considered desirable by school personnel. In fact, children can flunk out of school more readily by failing to behave appropriately as dictated by the hidden curriculum than they can by doing poor academic work. Teachers reward a hardworking slow student, but penalize a high achieving troublemaker.

The purpose of the hidden curriculum is to produce specific outcomes for later life, particularly in terms of preparing students to accept as legitimate specific patterns of social behavior, positions in the social class structure, attitudes toward gender roles, and occupational placement. Functionalists and some interpretive theorists who see these behaviors, attitudes and values as necessary for later life in the society view the hidden curriculum as a necessary part of schooling. On the other hand, reproduction and critical theorists are more likely to examine the hidden curriculum for the extent to which it serves to reinforce current gender, class and minority group inequalities.

The Hidden Curriculum and Work Roles

Jackson (1968) argued that the hidden curriculum prepares students for the world of work by emphasizing such skills as learning to wait, accepting authority, coping with evaluations and adhering to the demands of institutional conformity:

> Yet the habits of obedience and docility engendered in the classroom have a high pay-off value in other settings. So far as their power structure is concerned, classrooms are not too dissimilar from factories or offices, those ubiquitous organizations in which so much of our adult life is spent. Thus, school might really be called a preparation for life, but not in the usual sense in which educators employ that slogan. Power may be abused in school as elsewhere, but its existence is a fact of life to which we must adapt. The process of adaptation begins during the first few years of life but it is significantly accelerated, for most of us, on the day we enter kindergarten. (Jackson 1968, p. 3)

LeCompte (1978) has argued that these attitudes and values are embodied in a core of activities which teachers require of students as minimal behavior standards in the belief that without these behaviors, learning cannot take place. In the "ideal" classroom today, we would see students sitting quietly at individual desks placed in straight rows with the teacher's desk in the front of the room. Students are expected to work individually from textbooks or worksheets without talking to each other; they are supposed to raise their hands to answer or ask questions and wait to be called on by the teacher. In striving to achieve these ideals, teachers provide hidden messages to children which attempt to prepare them for appropriate behavior in later work roles. The model provided rather clearly resembles the hierarchical working of a factory or other large-scale industrial enterprise. While it may be an appropriate model for many kinds of occupations, it is incongruent with the kinds of working conditions and skill training required in most high status and professional jobs, those requiring creativity and cooperation.

The organizational structure of schools teaches children that the social world of adults is hierarchical. Administrators manage teachers, teachers manage children and children manage their assigned tasks. Teachers determine what children do in school, when and how. Children learn that school knowledge comes from the teacher and from the textbook. They learn that teachers evaluate how much they have learned by their performance on tests and classroom assignments. The evaluation process is external and performed by someone in a higher position. Anyon (1988) explains that daily life in this type of organizational structure

> provides practical ideological support for unequal distributions of power in society . . . . [T]he present unequal organization of authority in classrooms and schools not only indicates unequal power in society, but may reify and legitimate this in consciousness, thus fostering the impression that unequal power is natural, logical, or merely 'in the order of things' and inevitable. (Anyon 1988, pp. 178–179)

Children quickly discover that learning takes place individually and in quiet settings. It is "good" classroom behavior to sit quietly and "do your own work." Cooperative efforts are usually not acceptable and sometimes discouraged. "Keep your eyes on your own paper" helps to reinforce this message.

Schools require that students be punctual, clean, neat, make efficient use of their time, take care of their equipment, work individually, and learn how to wait if they need something. Absenteeism is frowned upon and generally noted on evaluations. Classroom interaction conveys the message that there are different roles and expectations according to social class, ethnicity and gender. (For more detail see Chapters 5, 8, and 9). Students who exhibit appropriate behavior in response to these school expectations are rewarded and displayed as role models to others. These rewards are both at the school and district level in the formal presentations at assembly programs and at the classroom level through teachers' evaluative comments. For example, here are several typical comments made by teachers:

- "I like the way Mary is waiting."
- "I like the way you wrote your name so neatly on the top of the page, Sally. Could you try to do that next time, John?"
- "You are really working hard on that math sheet, Sam."

The Hidden Curriculum and Perceptions of Knowledge

The schools imply that both the structure of knowledge and social relationships are hierarchical. Knowledge is organized according to its perceived difficulty and its social value. Students who are expected to learn more quickly are given lessons containing information which is more complex, higher on the cognitive scale and more culturally valuable than are children who are deemed less able. Thus, working class children are placed less often in classes of higher mathematics and foreign languages and more often placed in vocational and industrial training than are middle class children (Oakes 1985). The effect is to prepare the latter for college and professional careers, and the former for life in factories and blue-collar jobs of less status.

Despite the close interrelationship of many academic subjects, knowledge often is broken up into discrete and very different courses, compartmentalized, and given to students as pieces of knowledge to be assimilated within certain periods or time slots. For example, students may have 30 minutes for reading, 30 minutes for language arts and 15 minutes for handwriting; they are taught art divorced from history and mathematics devoid of science.

Children fail to become seekers of information. They learn that knowledge comes from an external source such as the teacher or the textbook; that there is usually one way to learn a skill, and that skills are taught by specialists. For example, in many classrooms reading is synonymous with phonics; learning to read means learning to sound out words. A good reader comes to be perceived by other children as one who can "sound out words," not necessarily one who understand what the sounds mean.

Students learn that information is structured around multiple choice and true-false answers. They learn to avoid ambiguity; responses are either right or wrong. The tasks children are assigned and the types of questions they are asked in classrooms reinforce this notion. Knowledge is seldom presented as complex, ambiguous, or something to be questioned; rather, it is presented as "objective" fact. This is reinforced by standardized testing programs which may drive the curriculum. Students are seldom encouraged to think that knowledge is to be questioned or that reality might be subjective, based on a particular historical context or social setting.

The Hidden Curriculum, Perceptions of Competency, and Self-Concept

Children who master the messages in the hidden curriculum learn how to "do school" successfully. Those who have difficulty understanding the instruction of the hidden curriculum, for whatever reason, often are perceived by teachers as less than competent students. In a study of reading in a first grade classroom, Bennett (1986) discovered a hidden curriculum for measuring reading performance in the reading groups. This curriculum had little to do with how well students actually understood what they read; rather, it addressed issues of *performance* in reading. It included learning to (1) use the correct reading posture by sitting straight, still and quiet; (2) watch and listen to the teacher when she spoke; (3) use a paper "marker" to keep the place in the reading book; and (4) demonstrate "comprehension" of the reading material by restating *verbatim* what was read in answer to questions the teacher took directly from the text. Children who could exhibit these skills consistently were considered "good readers" by their teacher and were included in the top reading groups. Those who had difficulty meeting these behavioral expectations or who refused to conform were considered to be less competent readers and placed in lower ability reading groups, often without reference to standardized test scores which indicated that the placements were inappropriate. Research by Eder and Felmlee (1984) and Grant and Rothenberg (1986) support these findings.

Social standing in the peer group also is affected by academic placement. Children tend to choose for friends classmates who are in the same ability group or track as their own, so that the social organization of schools comes to reflect the academic organization (Borko and Eisenhart 1986). This has a profound effect upon self-concept; children internalize the evaluations teachers make of them as well as their standing in the social organization of the classroom. Since they see the teacher as the authority figure and expert, they blame themselves for their lack of ability and low status. Anyon argues that the individualistic focus and evaluation structure of schools teach children that they are responsible for their own failures and academic shortcomings. Schools teach students that the reason for failure lies in their own "lack of motivation, low ability, disadvantage or inattention;" schools foster "blaming the victim" by shifting the terms of failure to the student, rather than to the "failure of the institution to meet the student's needs by providing successful pedagogy" (Anyon 1988, p. 179).

STRATIFICATION OF THE CURRICULUM

When sociologists talk about social stratification, they are referring to a hierarchical arrangement in a society in which people are arranged according to how much they have of value in that society. For example, in American culture, wealth, power and prestige are highly valued. People who have more of these things are considered to be more valuable and therefore occupy the upper levels in the hierarchy. Both the formal and the hidden curriculum are stratified. That is, today's schools are organized so that children are provided different levels of curricula according to the location and resources of the school, the age of the children, the number of children per classroom and the school's expectations of how well those children will perform both in school and in future occupations.

When we discuss the **stratification of the curriculum**, we are also talking about a hierarchy of power. Underlying the stratification of the curriculum is the notion that some types of knowledge and some types of instructional practices are considered superior to others. Similarly, some programs within a school curriculum are more valued than others. For example, a college preparatory program is generally considered superior to a vocational program. Differential valuation occurs both because collegiate programs are believed to articulate with more desirable occupational futures and because the children assigned to them tend to be more valued and tend to have more social power within the school. These placements are often based on perceived levels of ability, but, as we indicate in Chapters Seven and Eight, they also are based on the expectations teachers have for the academic performance of children, as mediated by the teacher's knowledge of their socioeconomic backgrounds, abilities to interact with teachers and other students effectively, appearance, and so forth.

In the next section, we will discuss how stratification of the curriculum affects the life of children in schools. Questions to be considered include:

1. Which kinds of knowledge have more prestige in the school curriculum and why?
2. Who is eligible for inclusion in these programs?
3. Who is eligible to teach in the more prestigious courses and programs?

Ability Grouping

Students at all levels of schooling from kindergarten through the high school are placed in different groups according to their abilities as perceived by school personnel. This type of organization at the elementary school level is called **ability grouping**. It begins at least as early as kindergarten, and existing studies of nursery schools and day care centers indicate that it may begin much earlier (Woodhouse 1987). Students are most commonly grouped for instruction in reading and math. Throughout the kindergarten year, classroom teachers and administrators assess their students' abilities, both formally and informally. Students begin to be identified as having different levels of ability or as being different kinds of learners. Some seem to "catch on" faster than others. Some need lots of extra individual help from the teacher. Ability grouping is continued through subsequent years in school. At the middle and high school levels, children may stay in or remain during all school subjects throughout the school day in ability groups which first were established in their first year of school. Ability grouping even has echoes in higher education, as institutions themselves are stratified. The most able students are recruited for elite private schools; the next echelon consists of a set of elite public state universities and private liberal arts colleges. Following those schools are a whole range of multipurpose state and private colleges and universities. At the bottom are two-year community and junior colleges (Karabel and Halsey 1977).

Tracking

High school course offerings are differentiated both horizontally and vertically (Powell et al. 1985). Horizontal differentiation refers to the diversity in content, or the number of disciplines in which courses are offered. The horizontal differentiation of high school increased dramatically, for example, when vocational programs were added to their offerings. Vertical differentiation refers to the number of levels at which individual courses are offered. Vertical differentiation increases, for example, when senior high school physics is offered at the advanced, general and remedial level, or when the requirement for English can be met either by remedial reading or advanced placement literature which includes Chaucer and Beowulf. A single high school can have as many as six or seven levels of basic academic courses. These courses share similar titles, but the students encounter different subject matter and different intellectual experiences in them (Cusick 1983; Oakes 1985).

Vertical differentiation actually creates a vertical curriculum (Powell et al. 1985) when entire programs for students are created of courses at given levels. The creation of a vertical curriculum constitutes tracking. Students are organized into tracks according to their perceived abilities. By perceived abilities we refer to the students' abilities as determined by school personnel on the basis of standardized and nonstandardized testing and classroom performance. An example of placement into a vertical curriculum has been examined in a high school involved in a current qualitative study (Allison and Bennett 1989). Its tracking system contains five different levels. Admittance into each of the levels is determined by the district's Language Arts supervisor and based on students' scores on the Stanford Test of Academic Skills administered in the eighth grade prior to entry into high school. Level One is called the Adaptive Program. Those who are read at a third grade level and below, including non-readers, are placed in this track. Level Two is called Fundamental and is designed for those students who read at 4th, 5th and 6th grade levels. Level Three is the Basic Program for students reading at 7th and 8th grade levels and Level Four is Standard or College Preparatory for those reading "on grade" level. Level Five is an Honors Program to which students are invited if they score at or above the 88th percentile on their achievement test. This is fairly typical of the way high schools are organized, although some may be more explicit about the tracking system than others. Students who perform well academically in elementary schools generally go on to the tracks which prepare them for college. Those who are not as academically talented are scheduled for classes in the basic or adaptive tracks. Although tracking is a common management strategy for organizing students in secondary schools, a growing body of literature as well as public concern raises questions about the practice (cf. Oakes 1985).

Research on Ability Grouping and Tracking

Much of the current research reports that ability grouping and tracking have detrimental effects on students. Studies about reading instruction report substantive differences in the content, delivery, and amount of instruction in reading in ability grouped classes. Higher level groups read more actual text than the lower ability groups. Higher groups receive more direct teacher instructional time. Higher level groups are provided with more opportunities for independent silent reading in contrast to the public oral reading required of the lower level groups, putting a ceiling on the amount of actual reading practice the children receive. Lower ability groups are provided with fewer opportunities to actually read text (Allington 1977, 1980 a & b, 1983, 1984; Barr 1974, 1975, 1982; Bennett 1986; Borman and Mueninghoff 1982, 1983; Dreeben 1984; Gambrell, Wilson, and Gantt 1981; Featherstone 1987; McDermott 1976, 1977; Shavelson and Stern 1981; Borko and Eisenhart 1986). According to the *Harvard Education Letter*, "there is, however, no persuasive evidence that ordinary elementary schoolers benefit from tracking" (July, 1987, p. 1).

Research findings are much the same for tracking at the high school level. Oakes' *Keeping Track* (1985) found that students' school experiences in higher, more academic tracks were far different from those in lower tracks. There were significant differences in teacher expectations, academic content and student achievement based on the level of the class. High track classes involved more complex concepts, critical thinking, and discussion than those in lower tracks. There were higher expectations placed on the students in these upper level classes because of the teachers' understanding that these were "college bound" students.

The "Catholic School Effect"

Recently, attention was focused on the impact of Catholic schools on disadvantaged students. Studies indicated that Catholic schooling seemed to "push" achievement in disadvantaged students, regardless of their social class standing (Greeley 1982; Coleman et al. 1982). Lee and Bryk (1988) have, however, demonstrated that the supposed "Catholic School Effect" is a consequence of the less differentiated curricula in Catholic schools. Because they usually are smaller and have fewer resources than public schools, Catholic schools have fewer tracks. As a consequence, all their students are forced to enroll in a greater number of academically oriented courses and receive a correspondingly more rigorous instructional program. Catholic school students were twice as likely to be assigned to an academic track, and a far greater proportion of Catholic school students than public school students who *wanted* to go to college actually were enrolled in the requisite academically oriented program. Even general track students in Catholic schools took more academic courses than similar students in the public schools.

Lee and Bryk repeat the findings that disadvantaged students in public schools are more often found in non-academic tracks (Bowles and Gintis 1976; Cicourel and Kitsuse 1963; Oakes 1985). They also point out that the differentiated curriculum initially developed as an equitable means to serve the presumed needs of a highly diverse public school enrollment (Cicourel and Kitsuse 1963; Heyns 1974; Powell, Farrar, and Cohen 1985). However, because the public schools offer so many nuances in courses, they act to amplify the initial differences in socioeconomic status and achievement that students bring with them to school. The reverse seems to be true for Catholic schools. The more constrained the curriculum, the greater was the academic rigor for all students. Hence, the higher the achievement and the more likely it was for the effects of poor background to wash out. We believe that these findings demonstrate that activities initiated under the aegis of an ideology of democracy and egalitarianism actually can act to reduce equality. We will discuss these implications in Chapter Nine.

SUMMARY

In this chapter we have looked at the ideologies underlying the formal and hidden curricula of public schooling. We have also looked at the ways in which schools stratify this curriculum. We hope that you have begun to analyze and question your own beliefs and values regarding school knowledge. We also expect that you are now wondering what alternatives there may be to the way we "do school" now. In Chapter Nine we will explore some possibilities for alternative ways to organize school curriculum from a critical perspective.

KEY CONCEPTS

Curriculum is what is taught to children in schools, whether or not the instruction is intended.

Sociology of Knowledge is the study of knowledge and how we construct and organize knowledge through social relationships with others. Power and hierarchy of knowledge are central to this study.

Sociology of Curriculum is the study of the content and organization of school knowledge with emphasis on the relationships between school curriculum, students, educators and the political/economic structure of society.

Reconceptualist curriculum theory refers to the work of those who challenge and critique notions of traditional curricular theorists. Their work is informed by critical theory, phenomenology and feminist theory.

Hidden Curriculum refers to the unstated, implicit and sometimes unintentional messages transmitted to students through the content, routines and social relationships of schooling.

Ideology of Schooling refers to values and beliefs that educators and students hold that inform and determine how we "do school."

Stratification of the Curriculum refers to the organization of curriculum according to a hierarchy of levels in which different types of knowledge are considered more or less valuable than others.

Ability Grouping is the practice used in elementary schools in which students are organized into instructional groups based on their abilities as assessed by school personnel on the basis of classroom performance and standardized test scores. These groups are used primarily for math and reading instruction. In British literature, ability grouping is referred to as "streaming."

Tracking is the practice of categorizing students for classes at various levels of difficulty at the high school level. This is done by school personnel on the basis of assessment of their ability as measured by classroom performance and standardized test scores. The resulting organization usually differentiates high schools into college preparatory, general, remedial and vocational tracks.

EXERCISES

1. Observe a classroom of your choice. Take extensive notes on what is happening in the classroom. Try to write down verbatim as much classroom dialogue as possible. What activities are the students and teacher engaged in? Analyze your observations according to the notion of a hidden curriculum. What are the implicit messages given to students in this classroom?

2. Choose a textbook in your field of study. Analyze the content and format of the text for the implicit messages provided to students and teachers.
3. Think back to when you were in elementary school. What reading group were you in? Were you ever changed from one to another? Why? What do you remember about learning to read in these groups? What did you think about the students in other groups?
4. Analyze your high school experience in relation to the discussion on tracking systems. Which track were you in? How did this track differ from others? Did you have friends from other tracks? Were students from different tracks labelled with distinctive names? How many of the members of your track did the same things you did after high school?
5. Present a case for or against ability grouping and tracking. Support your arguments with evidence from scholarly journals.
6. Interview a teacher (supervisor, principal, school board member, parent, student) about ability grouping and tracking practices.

SUGGESTED READINGS

Classic Works

Apple, M. W. (1979). *Ideology and curriculum*. Boston: Routledge & Kegan Paul.

Berger, P. L., and Luckmann, T. (1967). *The social construction of reality: A treatise in the sociology of knowledge*. New York: Anchor Books.

Dreeben, Robert. (1968). *On what is learned in school*. Reading, Mass. Addison Wesley.

Jackson, Phillip. (1968). *Life in classrooms*. Chicago: University of Chicago Press.

Silberman, C. E. (1973). *The open classroom reader*. New York: Vintage Books.

Young, M. F. D. (1971). *Knowledge and control: New directions for the sociology of education*. London: Collier-Macmillan.

Modern Works

Apple, M. W. (1986). *Teachers and texts: A political economy of class & gender relations in education*. New York: Metheun.

Apple, M. W., and Weis, L. (eds.) (1983). *Ideology and practice in schooling*. Philadelphia: Temple University Press.

Gamoran, Adam, and Berends, Mark. (1987). The effects of stratification in secondary schools: A synthesis of survey and ethnographic research. *Review of Educational Research*, Vol. 57 (Winter), No. 4, pp. 415–437.

Kliebard, H. M. (1986). *The struggle for the American curriculum 1893–1958*. Boston: Routledge & Kegan Paul.

Lee, V. E., and Bryk, A. S. (1988). Curriculum tracking as mediating the social distribution of high school achievement. *Sociology of Education*, *61*, 78–94.

McNeil, Linda M. (1988). *Contradictions of control: School structure and school knowledge*. New York: Routledge.

Oakes, J. (1985). *Keeping track: How schools structure inequality*. New Haven: Yale University Press.

Pinar, W. F. (ed.). (1988). *Contemporary curriculum discourses*. Scottsdale, Arizona: Gorsuch Scarisbrick.

Whitty, G. (1985). *Sociology and school knowledge: Curriculum theory, research and politics*. London: Metheun.

CHAPTER 7

Ethnic Minorities: Equality of Educational Opportunity

OVERVIEW

OVERVIEW (cont'd)
KEY CONCEPTS
EXERCISES
SUGGESTED READINGS
  Classic Works
  Modern Works

INTRODUCTION

Minority status is another correlate of social and economic inequality. In America, the social status of minorities is largely a function of skin color and cultural background. You could think of a social status continuum arranged so that people with darker skin and more obviously different cultural backgrounds are at one end of the continuum occupying low status niches, while people who are more assimilated into mainstream American lifestyles and have lighter skin occupy positions of higher status at the other. For example, African Americans and Punjabi Indians occupy lower status niches than Jewish, Italian or Irish Americans. The more a group diverges from mainstream Anglo-Americans in skin color and cultural behavior, the lower their status is in American society. Members of lower status minority groups also are the victims of more racial prejudice than those in higher status groups.

Despite years of research, a multitude of educational policies and implementation of a range of programs aimed at improving school success, minority student populations are still overrepresented in dropout rates, lower academic tracks and special education programs—a fact that continues to be a source of concern and debate among professional educators, policymakers and parents. With the exception of Asian Americans whose school success in recent years has been extraordinary (Lee and Rong 1988), a significant gap in standardized achievement test scores for basic academic subjects exists between non-mainstream minority and white student populations (NAEP 1988; Sadker and Sadker 1988).

In this chapter we first define what constitutes a minority people. We then present a summary of the federal legislation related to equal educational opportunities for minorities. Next, we identify how social scientists have explained the question of school success and failure in minority student populations over the past two decades. Finally, we address a question we consider to be the core issue to our discussion of equality of educational opportunity for minorities: What is the purpose of schooling for minorities, anyway?

THE ORIGINS AND BASES OF MINORITY STATUS

Within American society, certain groups of people are perceived to be different from "mainstream" or the dominant Anglo-Americans because of their affiliation with a particular cultural group. In previous chapters we defined culture as a way of life shared by a group of people. In this chapter we are concerned with those cultural groups perceived in this society to be distinguishable from dominant Anglo culture—ethnic minorities. Although membership in ethnic minority groups cannot really be considered apart from social class status (See Chapter Five), for our purposes here, we direct our attention to definitions of terms of group membership based on racial and ethnic identification. However, we urge you to keep in mind as you read this chapter that an individual's identification is not solely related to membership in a particular ethnic group, but is complicated by gender and social class status positions. The experiences of a working class black female is profoundly different from those of an upper middle class black male.

What Is Race?

Race is the earliest term used by social scientists to address differences in group membership. Anthropologists and sociologists have used the term *race* to describe a group of people with common ancestry and genetically transmitted physical characteristics. Although there were many complicated classification systems developed in the nineteenth century to categorize different races, three racial groups traditionally have been recognized in anthropological writings: Caucasian, Mongoloid, and Negroid (Ember and Ember 1985). These classifications are based on traits such as amount and texture of hair, skin color and other physical attributes believed to characterize each group. People in the United States today tend to identify themselves as members of a racial group primarily on the basis of skin color, although many people do not fit easily into these rigid categories. The term race is too vague to have much meaning for contemporary scientists as a genetic category. However, while biologists have found few genetic or real differences between members of so-called racial groups, the term race has social meaning in that what people *believe* about race determines how they relate to other groups of people. Beliefs and misunderstandings about racial and ethnic identities serve as the basis for prejudice, discrimination and racist behavior.

What Is Ethnicity?

Ethnicity refers to "a group of people recognized as a class on the basis of certain distinctive characteristics such as religion, ancestry, national origin, language, culture" (American Heritage Dictionary 1983). In other words, ethnicity is comprised of shared values, cultural traits, behavior patterns, and a sense of peoplehood (Banks 1979; Spradley and McCurdy 1972). Irish Americans, Jewish Americans, Polish Americans, African Americans, Mexican Americans—all can be identified as distinct ethnic groups. Ethnic identity is a particularly useful term to facilitate our understanding of who we are as people. However, like race, the term ethnicity is insufficient for our purposes because it is too broad, too inclusive and does not address the question of the group's relative power position in the society, but simply refers to its common cultural ties. Each of us can claim ties to a particular ethnic group whether it is Irish, English, Native

American, black, Japanese, or Mexican and yet we do not all experience discrimination based on our ethnic identities.

What Is an Ethnic Minority?

The term ethnic minority is a more precise way to describe groups of people of concern in this chapter. What does the term mean? We already have defined what an ethnic group is, so we just need to look at the word **minority**. If our only concern is comparative numbers, all of us could be considered part of a minority group, given a particular set of circumstances. For example, a few Republicans at a national Democratic convention is a minority group. Because of their small numbers, women professors in engineering or women high school principals can be considered minority groups because of their smaller numbers. Male teachers in elementary schools could be considered a minority group for the same reason.

However, for our purposes, we use the terms *minority* or *ethnic minority* to denote groups which have more characteristics in common than mere numbers to unite them in group membership. Sociologists continue to struggle to find a definition for the term *minority* precise enough to be used by social scientists (Dworkin and Dworkin 1982). Dworkin and Dworkin offer four qualities which characterize a minority group: (1) identifiability, (2) differential power, (3) differential and pejorative treatment, and (4) group awareness (ibid. p. 16).

Identifiable characteristics of minority groups include distinctive patterns of language or dialect, religion, behavior or dress, as well as physical characteristics such as sex, skin color, or eye shape. In western societies, skin color seems to be the most crucial factor in group identification. The social and political power which ethnic minorities have depends upon how identifiably different they are from the dominant cultural groups in society. It determines where they are placed in the social class structure, how much prestige, power, and respect they are accorded, and how they are treated. For example, African Americans, Hispanics, and Native Americans are clearly identifiable on the basis of distinctive physical characteristics, language and cultural practices. As identifiable ethnic minority groups, they often are subjected to discriminatory treatment. They occupy less powerful positions than the white Americans who dominate institutions of political, economic and social control. The subordinate position of these groups is reflected by their relative lack of educational attainment, less prestigious occupational placement, and lower levels of participation in social and political life. Much of this is a product of discriminatory patterns of exclusion. Discriminatory treatment by others often acts as a catalyst for the development of increased awareness, a sense of group identification, and solidarity among members of ethnic minority groups.

Banks affirms these four qualities of minority groups. He defines ethnic minorities as those groups which often are a numerical minority in that they constitute a small part of the total population. They also are easily distinguished physically and/or culturally as distinct from Anglo-Americans, and they are treated by others in a discriminatory way (Banks 1979). Today, in the United States, the ethnic minority groups most likely to be defined in these social and political terms are Hispanics, African Americans, Asians and American Indian/ Alaskan Natives. These groups can be subdivided further into specific ethnic groups. For example, Japanese, Filipinos, Chinese, Asian-Indian Americans all are minority groups subsumed by the larger category of Asian Americans.

Identification of ethnic minorities is contextual; whether a group is labelled as an ethnic minority depends on the particular historical period and geographic location. For example, Irish immigrants in Boston in the nineteenth century were a distinct ethnic minority group, but today they have assimilated into mainstream Anglo culture. Although they can be considered an ethnic group, they cannot be considered an *ethnic minority*. Irish, Italians, Germans and other European immigrant minorities have adopted the culture of mainstream Americans and are able to blend into the majority population. (Dworkin and Dworkin 1982).

Ethnic minority status also depends upon where one lives. The impact of geographic location in the identification of ethnic minority groups is illustrated by the experience of approximately three million Appalachians from the mountains in West Virginia, Kentucky and Tennessee. These people moved to northern cities in the midwest between 1940 and 1970 in search of employment. Appalachians were clearly viewed socially as ethnic minorities by northerners, notwithstanding that the ancestors of most of them were from England, Scotland, and Wales. They were subjected to considerable discrimination and prejudice (Obermiller 1981), even though they lacked physical characteristics which distinguished them from other Anglo-Americans. This also precluded them from being categorized politically as an ethnic minority group; and consequently they were not declared eligible for federally funded programs for minorities. In the 1970s, Appalachians began a movement to identify themselves politically as a minority group. Their goal was to channel governmental funding to programs for Appalachians (Obermiller 1981; Zigli 1981).

Prejudice and Discrimination

A corollary to the human propensity to categorize people into racial, ethnic and minority groups is the tendency to evaluate others using one's own group as the norm or standard. This type of evaluation is known as **ethnocentrism** when it results in seeing other groups of people as inferior to one's own. Ethnocentric attitudes toward other groups of people are the basis for prejudice. Banks defines prejudice as

> a set of rigid and unfavorable attitudes toward a particular group or groups that is formed in disregard of facts. Prejudiced individuals respond to members of these groups on the basis of preconceptions, tending to disregard behavior or personal characteristics that are inconsistent with their biases. (Banks 1988, p. 223)

Prejudice usually results in two forms of behavior: stereotyping and the establishment of social distance.

Stereotyping. Stereotypes involve depicting people on the basis of preconceptions and limited information; it creates caricatures which are actually exaggerations of beliefs people have about the characteristics of a group. They then are applied unquestioningly to all members of that group. Hence, all Chinese women are described as shy, all Italians are expected to be excitable, and all Germans are expected to have bone-crushing handshakes.

Stereotypes can be both negative and positive (Dworkin and Dworkin 1982). They also become part of the dominant ideology, serving to justify patterns of oppression and social differentiation, as well as differences in treatment. They explain why some groups are greedier or lazier, more prone to irreligious or immoral behavior, more honest or sneakier, better lovers or more adept at mathematics than others. Stereotypes are the basis for and reinforce patterns of prejudices; they are difficult to dislodge by logic or new information.

Social Distance. Stereotypes help to define how people relate to others because they determine the amount of social distance groups require from each other. Social distancing involves the degree of intimate interaction people can maintain with one another without feelings of discomfort or repugnance. People will feel little need to avoid people whose stereotype is positive; in fact, such a stereotype encourages more social interactions. By contrast, a negative stereotype fosters social avoidance and even the desire for physical distance from group members. For example, if you agree with a stereotype which characterizes a particular group as intelligent, hardworking and interesting, you are likely to want to become socially involved with its members. In contrast, if you view a group of people as lazy, dirty, lacking in intelligence and untrustworthy, it is most likely that you would prefer to avoid them. You also are unlikely to be easily convinced that members of the groups could behave otherwise.

Racism

Race is the word root for the term "**racism.**" It is used to describe ethnocentric beliefs and behavior based on the notion that one race is superior to others. Racism in the United States primarily refers to the belief that whites or Anglos are superior to blacks, Jews, Asians, Hispanics and other ethnic minority groups. Categorization according to race and other ethnic group identification has provided a means for domination and exploitation of one group by another; it sets up a hierarchy in which some racial groups are relegated to social and economic positions dominated by others. Minorities in America, as in most other societies, are overrepresented in lower social classes (Banks 1979). The differences in socioeconomic status between Anglo-Americans and ethnic minority groups clearly are a consequence of racial discrimination.

THE FEDERAL GOVERNMENT AND EQUALITY OF EDUCATIONAL OPPORTUNITY

A primary concern among sociologists of education is the impact of individual and institutional patterns of prejudice and racism on the schooling experiences and achievement of ethnic minority students. At first, sociologists simply noted that minorities seemed to be less successful in school than other students. Then, they began to ask *why* minority students fared so poorly. Was it because, in a land of supposedly equal opportunity, these children somehow were treated unequally?

Equality of Educational Opportunity

Equality of educational opportunity involves giving everyone the same initial chance to receive an education (Spring 1989). The history of United States social reform is replete with attempts by Anglo policy makers to direct attention away from inequities in the economy by reforming the educational system, rather than by redistributing wealth and eliminating oppression. Rather than creating policies which ensured that everyone had an equal chance to compete for jobs, policymakers have concentrated their efforts on addressing the problems of equality of educational opportunity. This has proved to be very complicated. First, even if everyone had the chance to receive an equal education, societal patterns of discrimination on the basis of race preclude equality in the job market. Second, the roots of racism and unequal treatment in schools are so deep, and the practices so subtle, that it has been difficult to identify them, much less to change their course. In the next few pages, we will discuss how policy makers have tried to manipulate the educational system to ameliorate racial inequality and mask the deeper economic inequities in society. We present a short history of the major federal legislation and court cases concerned with equality of educational opportunity over the last century. This discussion sets the stage for our later examination of minority student failure in schools.

Equal Access

American schools foster a powerful ideology about the existence of individual freedom and opportunity. Young children are indoctrinated with the belief that anyone can be successful given enough ambition and hard work. These myths are belied, however, by reality. Equal opportunity requires and begins with equal access to the same facilities, and historically, ethnic minority groups have less access to economic and social opportunities (LeCompte and Dworkin 1988).

The Role of the Federal Courts

In 1895, the Supreme Court decision, *Plessy* v. *Ferguson*, involved a case in which Homer Plessy (one-eighth black and seven-eighths white) refused to ride in a separate "colored coach" of a train in Louisiana as required by law and was arrested. The Supreme Court decided that as long as the facilities were equal, they could be separate. This came to be known as the "separate but equal doctrine" and was used until 1954 to justify segregated facilities for blacks and whites. A landmark decision of the United States Supreme Court, *Brown* v. *Board of Education of Topeka, Kansas* (1954), overturned *Plessy* v. *Ferguson*, stating that separate facilities are inherently unequal and therefore, illegal, under the Fourteenth Amendment of the United States Constitution. The Brown ruling states in part:

> in the field of public education the doctrine of "separate but equal" has no place. Separate educational facilities are inherently unequal . . . We hold that the plaintiffs and others similarly situated . . . are, by reason of the segregation complained of, deprived of equal protection of the laws guaranteed by the Fourteenth Amendment.

In *Brown* v. *Board of Education*, sociological data was used by the Supreme Court for the first time as the basis for its decision. This research demonstrated to the satisfaction of the Supreme Court justices that separate treatment is inherently unequal treatment. The 1954 Supreme Court decision began the desegregation process of American schools and was justified on the basis of providing *access* to equality of educational opportunity. Minority students would have to attend the same schools as whites in order to have equal access. Despite the Enforcement Decree of 1955 which required that federal district courts be used to end segregation of public schools at the local level, the process was extremely slow.

After the 1950s, African Americans finally obtained legal access to equal schooling. Additional court cases, often on a district by district basis, began to ensure that a legal right became an educational reality. While African Americans no longer were provided with schools that were legally segregated from Anglo students, the fact of racial and economic residential segregation often meant that most children still attended racially isolated schools. The emphasis of subsequent legislation was on providing *equal access* for all children to obtain a high quality education in public schools. Soon, however, research results began to show that even after segregated schools were legally banned, equal access to education did not necessarily guarantee equal outcomes for minority children (Hess 1989; Metz 1978; Murnane 1975). Equal treatment for people who started out unequal did not permit disadvantaged people to "catch up." Subsequent legislation then began to provide *unequal* or **compensatory education** in order to offset the effects of economic and educational disadvantage. We will talk about these programs later.

This legislation has been part of a continuing struggle to insure the civil rights for all United States citizens, despite their ethnic affiliation. By **civil rights** we are referring to the rights belonging to individuals because of their status as citizens. These rights are guaranteed by the Fourteenth Amendment of the constitution, which provides "equal protection under law" for all citizens. This means that all citizens are to have equal access to opportunities for economic and social gain despite their racial or ethnic background, gender, age or handicapping condition. Civil rights are guaranteed by the constitution; the right to an education is not. Since the education of citizens was a responsibility left to state governments, schooling, particularly for ethnic minorities, varied from state to state.

In 1964, the Civil Rights Act was passed by Congress in order to speed up the desegregation of public schools by providing that school districts practicing racial discrimination would be denied federal funding. Title IV of the Civil Rights Act gave the U.S. Commissioner of Education the power to help desegregate schools and the U.S. Attorney General the power to initiate law suits to force school desegregation. This power was enforced by Title VI which prohibited the distribution of federal funds to schools with racially discriminatory programs. The threat of withholding federal funding to schools practicing racial discrimination served to hasten the desegregation of public schools.

School districts were given a clear message from the federal government that they must take steps to provide equal educational opportunities for minority students through the desegregation of American schools and through compensatory education programs. These were closely linked. In order to receive the federal funds provided in compensatory education programs, schools were required to desegregate.

Desegregation and the Coleman Report

The existence of unequal performance of minority students indirectly gave impetus to the desegregation of schools. Conventional wisdom argued that inqualities of performance must be a consequence of inequalities in the schools; schools with high achieving students must be spending more money on their students than those whose students did poorly. To test that theory, Section 402 of the 1964 Civil Rights Act authorized the Commissioner of Education to conduct a survey which would examine "the lack of availability of equal educational opportunities for individuals by reason of race, color, religion, or national origin in public educational institutions at all levels in the United States." The survey, conducted by James Coleman and his associates, was entitled *Equality of Educational Opportunity* (1966). It looked at material differences *between* districts, comparing such things as school and class size, the background and levels of training of teachers, provision of facilities like libraries and laboratories, and per-pupil expenditure. These data were aggregated at the district level; Coleman did not look at differences among schools *within* districts.

Coleman expected to find that poor schools produced poor students. What he found out was surprising. First of all, the differences between school districts were not large enough to explain the differences in student performance among the six racial groups in the study. Second, he found that the differences between minority and majority students' test scores grew increasingly large from the first to the twelfth grade. Third, he learned that minority and majority children did not differ in the value which they attached to school and academic achievement (Borman and Spring 1984, p. 204). What he did find was that minority students who attended school with white students seemed to have higher levels of academic achievement than those who attended all-minority schools. This research finding catalyzed a move to mix students racially in schools to improve the performance of minorities. And, while the impetus to desegregation certainly was congruent with American social ideology, it unfortunately was based upon a misinterpretation of Coleman's research: subsequent re-analyses showed that the real effect was not racial, but socioeconomic. What really seemed to have an effect on students was the peer group with whom they attended school; students who went to school with children from a higher socioeconomic group than their own did better in school, Since minority students usually were poorer than their majority classmates, it appeared that going to white schools made the difference.

Different methods have been used to desegregate American schools in response both to the 1954 Supreme Court decision, the 1964 Civil Rights Act, and the Coleman Report. American schools have tried to comply in a variety of ways, some more effective than others. A few complied only under court order; a few refused to disband systems of racially segregated schools and closed down the public schools until ordered to re-open by the courts. Many schools postponed compliance. As late as 1989, many districts still are fighting court battles over desegregation. However, they have been encouraged to desegregate by threats from the government to cut off federal funding and institute law suits (Rogers 1968; Kirby, Harris, and Crain 1973; Petersen 1976; Hughes et al. 1980; Borman and Spring 1984; Tatel et al. 1986).

Voluntary desegregation plans use programs such as magnet schools, minority to majority transfers, metropolitan redistricting and school pairing to achieve better ethnic balance in school districts. Magnet schools, usually inner city schools which have historically been predominantly for black students, are transformed into centers which offer specific programs designed to attract a variety of students from all over the district. In many cities, systems of magnet schools have been developed in response to desegregation orders of the federal courts as an alternative to busing. Schools specializing in arts, languages, computer science, applied arts, medicine, math and sciences, physical education and programs for the gifted, etc. have replaced inner city segregated schools. Students voluntarily apply to attend these schools and may even be required to audition as part of the entry procedures, such as in the inner city high schools in Cincinnati and Houston which were transformed into schools for the creative and performing arts or programs for the gifted and talented. The assumption is that if the school, despite its location, can offer an excellent district-wide program, students from outside the immediate neighborhood will be attracted to attend and thus reduce the effects of de facto or residential segregation (Borman and Spring 1984; Ferrell and Compton 1986). However, magnet schools have been criticized for drawing away the best students and resources from other schools in the district.

One of the most widely used and controversial plans implemented by school districts used busing procedures to achieve racial balance within schools. Under these plans, students from one neighborhood school—usually minority dominated—would be bussed to another, usually in white neighborhoods. Where enforced by law, this method is referred to as involuntary desegregation and has been met with resistance and hostility by both black and white parents. It has been argued that forced busing encourages whites to flee from the districts which practice it, that it destroys neighborhoods and disrupts the involvement of parents with the schooling of their children. Parents objected to the long bus rides to which their children were subjected, especially since the majority of the children bussed in most districts were minority children (Rist 1979; Crain 1983; Pettigrew and Green 1976; Borman and Spring 1984; Reynolds 1986).

The impact of social life in desegregated schools on children also has been disputed. Some kinds of school organization in desegregated schools facilitates the development of cross-racial friendships (Damico, Bell-Nathaniel, and Green 1980; Schofield 1982); and all of them have made the development of such friendships more possible. This has had a long-term effect on the persistence of racial prejudice (Braddock et al. 1984). However, desegregation has not always meant social integration, especially since minority children usually come to and leave from school in intact groups on a scheduled bus, and have little time available to socialize with classmates. Sometimes the bus children have even remained segregated in distinct classrooms. Especially where academic practices like ability grouping and tracking reinforce racial differences, students tend to remain in racially segregated groups in the lunchroom, on the playground, in classes, and on the bus. Differences in cultural styles also impede the formation of friendships; white children tend to be intimidated by blacks and to feel endangered by the noise and movement natural to interaction among blacks (Clement, Harding, and Eisenhart 1976; Wax 1980; Schofield 1982; St. John 1975; Hanna 1987).

Despite the Supreme Court rulings requiring the desegregation of schools and federal legislation mandating the withdrawal of funding to racially discriminatory school districts, the majority of American schools today continue to be relatively racially segregated, in large part because of persisting patterns of racial and economic residential segregation. Enforcement also is a problem; federal funding has not been withheld despite serious, continuing violations of the Civil Rights Act. Giving control over federal funds to state and local authorities, as happened in the early 1980s with the "block grant" program, also has affected the dispersion of funds; Fred Hess, executive director of the Chicago Panel on Public School Policy and Finance, stated that "more than 80 percent of all minority students in Chicago continue to attend segregated schools and receive no significant compensatory education to offset the effects of this segregation" (Hess 1989). In fact, the neediest schools and students in Chicago often actually get fewer funds than those in more affluent neighborhoods. (See also Knapp and Cooperstein 1986; Lecompte and Dworkin 1989). Hess and his associates called for shifting more resources from wealthier schools to deal with this problem. In large part these inequities exist because the ethnic composition of schools parallels the ethnic composition of neighborhoods. Most of the major cities in the United States have racially and economically segregated patterns of residence which have been enforced by custom and legal statute, a situation which is becoming worse rather than better despite Civil Rights legislation (Wilson 1987).

Compensatory Legislation

As we have described, the Coleman Report findings were contrary to the policymakers' expectations. Rather than school district characteristics, differential student achievement was strongly related to family background of students and aspirations of peers. Coleman's work led to an interpretation alleging the "cultural deprivation" of poor families. It gave scientific credence to the popular belief that children from ghetto families live in a "culture of poverty" (Valentine 1968) which puts them at a disadvantage in school. Federal policymakers used this argument to implement programs in schools which would compensate for the home environment and help schools to facilitate equality of results of schooling, rather than just equality of access (Karabel and Halsey 1977; Baratz and Baratz 1970). Initiated in the 1960s as part of the federally funded War on Poverty, these programs became known as "compensatory education". Justification for these programs was that poor and minority students needed more than an equal opportunity to make up for disadvantages resulting from their family backgrounds. The Elementary and Secondary Education Act, passed in 1965 as part of President Lyndon B. Johnson's "War on Poverty," provided approximately one billion dollars in federal funding for the improvement of schooling for these children through compensatory education programs (Ballantine, 1983). These funds were earmarked for instruction and services above and beyond those offered in the regular school program. Because they were predicated upon the assumption that early intervention was needed to compensate for and counteract the environmental effects of poverty, they were targeted for preschool and elementary school children from poor and minority families. While the various titles of the ESEA provided funds for a wide variety of programs, the most important for instructional programs was Title I. It provided programs such as Headstart for preschoolers and remedial reading and math programs for school-aged children considered to be educationally deprived.

The importance of the Elementary and Secondary Education Act of 1965 to the issue of equality of educational opportunity was that it improved opportunities for children by improving the kind of education they received. It also reinforced the Civil Rights Act by providing large amounts of federal funding to school districts in compliance with desegregation requirements. If a district wanted funding for Title I programs, it had to comply with the Civil Rights Act.

These programs still exist under the 1981 Education and Consolidation and Improvement Act (ECIA); however, lumping federal funds into state-disseminated "block grants" gives control of the program design and funding to local districts. As Hess (1989) pointed out, this often weakens their impact because local districts often structure programs so as to divert funds from those children most in need.

Special Needs Legislation

In the late 1960s and early 1970s there was continued concern with providing federal funding for programs targeted to specific student populations which had not as yet received special educational services. The 1966 Education of Handi-capped Children (Title VI) and the 1967 Bilingual Education Programs (Title VII) were added to the Elementary and Secondary Act. The Education of Handicapped Children Act provided for free, public education for all handicapped children. It provided at public expense services previously only available in the private sector and too costly for poor families. The purpose of the Bilingual Act was to meet "the special educational needs of the large number of children of limited English speaking ability in the United States." An Indian Education Act of 1972 provided funds for health and nutrition programs for Native American Indians as well as innovative and bilingual education programs. The Ethnic Heritage Act was passed in 1972 to assist in the planning and establishment of ethnic studies programs. All of these program were targeted to the needs of poor and minority students in an effort to provide them with the same type of educational opportunities in public schools that middle-class Anglo students had.

Underlying these programs was the assumption that if minority students could acquire the same cultural capital possessed by mainstream whites, they would have the same opportunities for economic success as whites. In other words, if you could teach them to "act white" (Fordham and Ogbu 1986), they would be equal. This is, however, an individualistic solution to what really is a problem generated by structural inequities in society. It ignores the reality of the how unequally distributed economic resources are in this country and how difficult it is for minority groups in this country to gain access to them.

RESEARCH ON SCHOOLING FOR MINORITY STUDENTS

The research on the performance of minority students over the last three decades has attempted to explain why these children do not succeed in school in the same way that Anglo children do. Three distinct theories have been developed to explain minority student school failure: unequal resources and treatment; cultural background, and access to the labor market.

A Theory of Unequal Resources and Treatment

This approach to school failure examines the imbalance of financial resources available to minority students and the differential treatment they receive in school. Jencks, in his work *Inequality* (1972), examined this theory, testing it at the macro-level in a further analysis of Coleman's data from the mid-1960s. Since it had been determined that school districts were not unequal enough to produce the observed differences in achievement, Jencks introduced what essentially was a class conflict explanation: poverty and poor performance were a function of social class rather than race (Scimecca 1980). He argued that family background was the most important determining factor in students' educational achievement. Students from families with higher incomes are more likely to acquire more education than those from lower income families. According to

Jencks, equalizing the resources for schools and the time people spent in school would not be enough to reduce economic inequality. He stated:

> There is no evidence that school reform can substantially reduce the extent of cognitive inequality, as measured by tests of verbal fluency, reading comprehension or mathematical skill. Neither school resources nor segregation has an appreciable effect on either test scores or educational attainment. (1972, p. 8)

He argued that large-scale redistribution of wealth, not school reform, was the key to a more equitable society. He criticized the legislation of the 1960s for concentrating on children, rather than directly attacking adult inequality. Unfortunately, though economic reform is certainly a necessary strategy in reducing inequality in the society, this argument was interpreted to mean that because of the determining power of family background, schools made no difference and could be ignored as sites for social change.

Rist, by contrast, examined inequality in the treatment of children at the micro level—inside schools and classrooms. Rist (1970) studied the school experiences of black primary-aged children from a poor, urban neighborhood. He found that the perceptions teachers had of the home lives of their students made a significant difference in the way teachers treated students. Students perceived to come from poor homes—as determined by their appearance as well as informal knowledge of family background—were placed in lower ability reading groups and provided with less direct instruction. Rist also observed that students in the top groups came from middle class homes. Kindergarten teachers spent two to three times more actual time instructing these children as they did children in the slower, lower class groups. Consequently, the "fast" group was able to complete the kindergarten curriculum, while the "slower" groups did not. The slow group entered first grade already far behind their peers academically.

Theories of Cultural Background

Cultural Deprivation. From an emphasis on schools, the pendulum now swung to an examination of the impact of families. In the 1960s researchers began to look at the impact of the home environment on school performance to explain why minority and poor children failed in schools. Cultural deprivation theory was in large part responsible for the development of the compensatory education program discussed previously. It posited that the existence of a "culture of poverty" (Valentine 1968) explained the poor performance of minority children. The core to this explanation of school failure was the alleged "cultural disadvantage" which their home environment created for children.

Children thought to be culturally deprived were described by policymakers and educators as those who lived in ghetto neighborhoods where they were not provided with proper nutrition and did not have adequate health care. They attended poor schools, were not adequately prepared for jobs and if and when they finished school, repeated this "cycle of poverty" in their family's next generation. The homes in which these children grew up did not provide them with the tools they needed to succeed in school. It was believed that parents in these environments did not read to their children; did not encourage the kinds of learning activities at home that were used by middle class parents and generally did not provide an intellectually stimulating home environment. Minority children often came to school with a home language or dialect that was not middle class or standard English (Berstein 1977). The common phrase for minority and poor children during the 1960s was "culturally deprived" or "socially disadvantaged"; they were believed to be deprived of the cultural or social advantages necessary to succeed in school (Baratz and Baratz 1970, Erickson 1987). Occasionally teachers today refer to students as "culturally deprived" when they believe that the home is not providing the appropriate experiences for children to succeed in school.

Schools were called upon to break this "cycle of poverty" through compensatory education programs such as Headstart and other preschool programs, Title I Remedial Reading and Math Programs, bilingual education and health and nutrition programs in schools. Politicians and educators believed that if schools could intervene with minority students prior to their entry into kindergarten, some of the effects of the home environment could be alleviated and the students would have a better chance to succeed in school.

The use of the term "culture" in this theory is misused in the anthropological sense. What was documented was not so much a culture, *per se*, but a response to oppressive conditions of racial isolation, powerlessness, and poverty. Anthropologists argue that growing up in one culture does not involve being deprived of another and that the children described as "culturally deprived" actually functioned quite well in their own milieu. Similarly, Anglo kids in a barrio setting would be "culturally deprived." The core to this explanation of minority school failure was the "cultural disadvantage" of the home environment.

The cultural deprivation theory was strongly criticized by scholars in the mid-1960s as ethnocentric. Rather than looking to the structure of schools or societal forces for explanations of the failure to achieve, blame was placed on the victims—individual children or minority groups (Ryan 1976). Educators, "frustrated by their difficulties in working with minority children, [were able] to place the responsibility for school failure outside the school" (Erickson 1987, p. 336).

Cultural Differences. To counter the cultural deprivation theory, social scientists began to look at differences or discontinuities between the culture of the school and the home, particularly as they existed in communication or interactional patterns. Researchers working with Appalachian, black, Hawaiian and Native American students found that interactional difficulty in schools can be related to cultural differences in communication styles (Au and Mason 1981; Cazden et al. 1974; D'Amato 1988; Erickson and Mohatt 1982; Jordan 1984; Labov 1972; Phillips 1972; Rist 1973; Heath 1983; Piestrup 1973). According to the cultural difference explanation, school failure is a result of differences between the culturally-derived white middle class communication patterns of the school and those of the home culture of students. Dissonance can be reduced if teachers have knowledge of the verbal and nonverbal communication patterns of both the school and home culture. If educators can increase the smoothness of classroom interaction and the effectiveness of communication through an adaptation to and respect for the culture of students, they may be able to increase feelings of comfort and communicative competence in minority students. As suggested by Erickson,

> it may be that culturally congruent instruction depoliticizes cultural differ-
> ence in the classroom, and that such depoliticization has important positive
> influences on the teacher-student relationship. Such a situation in the class-
> room might prevent the emergence of student resistance. (1984, p. 543)

These researchers believe that if classroom settings were structured so that cultural differences in communication patterns were reduced, achievement of minority students might be improved (Au and Mason 1981). Several examples of this type of research are presented here.

The work at the Kamehameha Early Education Program (KEEP) in Hawaii is a primary example of research which emphasized the need for cultural congruency in classrooms for minority students. Based on research in the local community, the team of teachers and researchers working at KEEP developed a way of teaching reading based on the communication style of the Hawaiian "talk story," where there is a rapid exchange of overlapping conversation and a cooperative building of the story. The basal reading program was reorganized so the everyday pattern of communication used by Hawaiian children replaced the Anglo structure in which children wait to be called on and speak one at a time. Researchers at the KEEP center documented increased academic achievement in reading using this more culturally congruent style (Au and Mason 1981).

The culturally congruent participation structures used in the KEEP program were then transplanted to a school with a Navajo population. Vogt (1985) reports that although in both the Hawaiian and Navajo populations the increased cultural congruency between students and teachers in the classroom interaction led to increased effectiveness in the reading programs, the original KEEP program had to be rather dramatically changed because participation structures were different for each group. What was culturally congruent for Hawaiians students didn't fit the cultural patterns of the Navajo students.

Van Ness (1981), in a study of Native Alaskan schools, found that the interactional smoothness of lessons taught by a native teacher could be attributed to cultural knowledge of the social situation. He argued that since social behavior is culturally organized, cultural congruency between the teacher and students allowed for smooth interactions even at the kindergarten level.

In a study of black children in two first grade reading programs, Piestrup (1973) reported differences in reading achievement which she attributed to the way in which each teacher responded to the use of Black English Vernacular (BEV). The children whose use of dialect was often corrected during lessons obtained lower scores on reading tests and acutally used more BEV than children who were permitted to use BEV in reading groups without correction. The uncorrected children actually scored higher in standardized reading tests, many above the national norms. Piestrup argued that when the dialect was treated as a barrier to communication, more time was spent working to repair and correct the dialect than time spent in actual reading.

Cultural difference theory calls for educators to understand the differences of minority students so as to establish a more culturally congruent classroom situation. However, critical theorists argue that it might be viewed as cooptation. Under the guise of cultural appropriateness, teachers can use a culturally congruent curriculum taught in culturally sensitive way to gradually lead students into adopting the ideology of the dominant class. This is a less painful or coercive way to colonize the minds of students (McLaren 1989), and for this reason, may be even more effective than force.

It is important to realize that its developers did not intend the cultural differences explanation for minority school failure to be seen as the only way to view the problem or as a means to coopt minority students. This explanation is restricted to the microlevel: a classroom view of factors in schooling which lead to minority student failure. It does not address the political and economic societal forces at the macrolevel which influence these students outside the structure of schools.

Labor Market Theory

A macrolevel or societal view of minority student failure is central to the work of John Ogbu. A core element in his theory is student perception of their chances in the labor market. The connections which minority students see between schooling and how successful they will be in the job market is reflected in their school performance. If they see school as a means to become economically mobile, they are more likely to cooperate with teachers and participate in the schooling process. If students do not consider school as a viable avenue to obtaining employment, they resist the experience.

Ogbu argues that students from minority groups vary in their reactions to their school experiences. Ogbu (1987) categorizes minority students into three groups: (1) autonomous, (2) immigrant, and (3) castelike minorities. *Autonomous minority groups* are those which possess a cultural identity distinct from Anglo Americans. While they may not be exempt from discriminatory practices, still they are not in subordinate positions in society. He notes that Jews and Mormons are examples of autonomous minority groups.

Immigrant minority groups are those who have voluntarily moved to the United States for economic, political or religious opportunities. Despite difficulties with the dominant culture which their language or ethnic identity cause, they view schooling as a way to advance socially and economically in this society. The recent influx of Asian immigrants are examples of this second group. Ogbu argues that newly immigrant minorities came to this country with distinct cultural patterns and reinforce their social identity to the group by maintaining these beliefs, behaviors, and sense of peoplehood.

The third group described by Ogbu is *castelike minorities*. These are involuntary minorities; they either were originally brought to the United States through slavery or experienced colonization or conquest at the hands of European invaders. Both have a history of subordination. Rather than maintain their primary identity to their ethnic group as in the case of immigrant minorities, castelike minorities

> appear to develop a new sense of social identity in opposition to the social identity of the dominant group after they have become subordinated, and they do so in reaction to the way that dominant-group members treat them in social, political, economic, and psychological domains. (Ogbu 1987, p. 323)

VARIABLE RESPONSES OF MINORITY STUDENTS TO SCHOOLING

The way in which Ogbu categorizes minorities is useful because it helps to explain why some groups succeed in schools despite vast differences in language patterns and cultural understandings and why others with language and culture closer to Anglo-Americans fail. Consider these recent statistics on minority student school success and failure:

- National dropout rates by group (Kunisawa 1988):
American Indians/Alaska Natives	42.0%
Hispanics	39.9%
Blacks	24.7%
Whites	14.3%
Asians/Pacific Islanders	9.6%

  Kunisawa notes that in some areas, the dropout rate is as high as 90 percent for Native Americans and 78 percent for Hispanics.
- According to the National Assessment of Educational Progress (NAEP), Blacks and Hispanics have made steady gains in mathematics achievement—more than the gains of White students; however, there continue to be "significant differences between the performance of White students and performance of black and Hispanic students" in math achievement (*Education Week* June 15, 1988, p. 29).
- 13 percent of Mexican immigrants (estimated to be largest single group of new immigrants) and 81 percent of Filipinos graduate from high school.
- Asians make up 2.1 percent of total United States population, but in fall, 1987 made up 14 percent of Harvard's freshman class, 20 percent at MIT and 25 percent at University of California–Berkeley (*NEA Today*, March, 1988, p. 14).
- 70 percent of Asian American 18 year olds take the SAT as compared to 28 percent of all 18-year olds. Asian students average math SAT score is 43 points above national average—518 out of 800 (*ibid. NEA Today*).

These figures demonstrate obvious differences in the school achievement of different minority groups. Asian Americans students are referred to in the media as "Whiz Kids" (*NEA Today* 1987). Asian Americans, including Chinese, Filipino, Japanese, Vietnamese, Korean, Asian-Indians, Laotian, Kampuchean students, have astonished educators in their abilities to overcome language barriers and surpass Anglo-American students in school achievement (Hirschman and Wong 1986; Lee and Rong 1988). At the same time, African Americans and Hispanics lag far behind white students in measures of academic achievement although with longer exposure to the culture and perhaps a common language. What accounts for the variability in school achievement for groups of minority students?

Ogbu argues that the primary reason for the school failure or success with minority students has its roots in the perceived relationship of schooling to the structure of economic opportunity. Immigrant minority students maintain a belief in the educational system as a way of succeeding later in the job market. It is bolstered by the fact that most immigrants can favorably compare their present status in America with their past; no matter how bad their situation is here at the present, it offers significantly more hope than life in their country of origin. This belief in the educational system is encouraged and reinforced by their families and communities.

Castelike minorities, on the other hand, have no such basis for comparison. Already at the bottom of the ladder, they can only compare up, to the unattainable status of more favored ethnic groups. They may pay lip service to the notion that success in school will lead to success in later economic life, but in actuality their experience of racism and oppression in this country prevents them from buying into the myth that ascending the socioeconomic ladder of success first requires succeeding in the educational system. They know that a racist American society puts a ceiling on their economic opportunities, even if they succeed in school.

School Success through Accommodation

Some minority students succeed in school through accommodation, a process by which they maintain their ethnic identity and cultural patterns but at the same time adopt behaviors of the mainstream society which they see as appropriate. This process is illustrated in Gibson's (1988) study of Punjabi Sikh immigrants in a California high school where the Punjabi students were more serious about school and attained higher rates of academic achievement than their Anglo classmates. Gibson attributes this success to parental expectations for their children's school success as well as intact cultural values which placed respect for family and authority at a premium. Punjabi parents urged their children to do well in school to obtain the credentials they need to compete in American society, but at the same time insisted that the home cultural values be maintained. Doing so permitted Punjabi students to be accepted in their home milieu, while retaining a belief that school was a way to succeed in the society. Punjabi students were able to accommodate to school life, even though maintaining Punjabi cultural traditions earned them ridicule and harassment from non-Punjabi school peers. Family life provided a meaningful haven for Punjabi students which not only buffered them from the prejudice they experienced at school but offered a viable cultural alternative to mainstream American life.

Student Resistance to School

In Chapter Three we discussed resistance as a way for students to oppose the culture of the school. Resistance, in the form of acting out, tuning out or dropping out of school, can be a way for minority students to reject degrading and racist experiences in schools. Kunisawa (1988, pp. 62–63) found that the ten states with the highest dropout rates were also all states whose minority enrollment exceeded 25 percent. Six of those states have minority enrollments greater than 35 percent. A labor market explanation of these figures would be that these are students from castelike minority groups who do not see school as a viable avenue to economic success.

Resistance is also a way in which minority youth establish their own cultural identities while rejecting dominant class ideologies embedded in schooling. Social scientists have documented resistance to school through the establishment of peer group cultures in working class Carribean, Anglo and Black communities (cf. McLaren 1980; McLeod 1987; Willis 1977). Dehyle's (1986) work with Navajo youth illustrates one way in which minority youth resist the imposition of the school's dominant culture on their lives by forming a peer group centered on break dancing. This group became successful break dancers in an:

> indifferent or negative school and community environment. As one young breaker explained with a smile, "It used to be cowboys and Indians. Now it is breakers and cowboys." With break dancing they had the motivation to assert themselves and prove to themselves and their peers that they were successful individuals. They worked hard, performed to the delight of many peers, and created a "space," even though it placed them on the fringe. (Deyhle 1986, p. 11)

Through this clique, Navajo youth were able to build self-confidence, achieve success through dancing, and establish identities which challenged those encouraged by school personnel.

Critical theorists view this active refusal by minority students to adopt the dominant group's beliefs as culture, class and race resistance to a school-imposed culture which is contrary to their lives (McLaren 1989). They explain school failure of minority students, then, not from the standpoint of individual student incompetencies, but from the perspective of a school system whose structure attempts to impose a dominant class culture on youth who do not accept that culture as a viable alternative to their own way of life. McLaren argues:

Teachers must be aware of how school failure is structurally located and culturally mediated, so they can work both inside and outside of schools in the struggle for social and economic justice. Teachers must engage unyieldingly in their attempt to empower students both as individuals and as potential agents of social change by establishing a critical pedagogy that students can use in the classroom and in the streets (1989, p. 221).

CONFLICTING PURPOSES OF SCHOOLING FOR MINORITY STUDENTS: CULTURAL ASSIMILATION OR CULTURAL PLURALISM?

Throughout the history of American schooling there has been a constant tension between those who believe in schooling for assimilation and those who believe in *cultural pluralism*. Assimilationists believe the purpose of schools for minority students is to teach all groups a common language, cultural heritage and set of values that are distinctly American. In most cases, the notion of the 'melting pot" means following a white middle-class and upper class model. As different cultural groups relinquish their ethnic identity, they are assimilated into American culture. The Americanization programs at the turn of the century tried to teach new immigrants to this country the language, customs and skills needed to fit into the mainstream society. That notion is still popular as evidenced recently in the "English Only" legislation passed in Arizona, Florida, and Colorado during 1987 elections. Now a total of seventeen states consider English to be the official state language. Thirteen of these state resolutions were passed in the last five years, an indication of the prevailing political conservativism in the United States.

Those who value cultural pluralism believe that minority groups can maintain their cultural identity at the same time they develop an allegiance to the nation. For example, a cultural pluralist believes that blacks, Vietnamese, Irish, and Mexicans can retain the supporting benefits of their cultural groups while considering themselves part of a larger American culture at the same time. Rather than a "melting pot," you could envision this process as a "stew pot" or a "salad bowl" in which each different ingredient maintains its own distinctive characteristics, but enriches the final product. Cultural pluralists believe in celebrating diverse cultures in school practices and embedded within the curriculum.

These tensions between assimilationist and cultural pluralists purposes of schooling are crucial to understanding minority student failure. Those who espouse assimilationist views explain minority students' failure in terms of individual incompetency or a failure to take advantages of the educational system in order to "get ahead" economically in society. They fail to recognize the limitations of schooling for minority students and end up "blaming the victim" for school failure. Consequently, the structure and practices of schooling are not questioned. Cultural pluralists, on the other hand, are more likely to attempt to understand minority student culture and alter school practices to better meet the needs of all students. Equality of educational opportunity as well as equality of economic opportunity are their goals. At the extreme are those who believe in neither cultural pluralism or assimilation. These groups believe that there is no accommodation or compromise possible between their beliefs and those of other groups. They remain a challenge to societies which, however poorly, retain an ideology of tolerance (Burtonwood 1986)

SUMMARY

In this chapter we discussed key terms: race, ethnicity and ethnic minority group. We then traced the historical development of the role of the federal government in schooling for minority students. In a discussion of research on schooling for minority children, we examined a theory of unequal resources and treatment, a cultural deprivation theory, a cultural differences theory and a labor market explanation. We illustrated the ways minority students respond to their schooling experiences through assmilation, accommodation or resistance with examples from recent research.

KEY CONCEPTS

Race is a term with more social than scientific meaning. It is used to refer to a group of people with common ancestry and genetically transmitted physical characteristics.

Ethnicity refers to group of people bound by a sense of peoplehood based on shared cultural traits such as religion, ancestry, national origin or language.

Minority refers to group of people who comprise a small proportion of the total population who are easily distinguished by physical or cultural characteristics and suffer discrimination because of their differences.

Ethnocentricity is the tendency to evaluate others using your own group as the norm or standard.

Racism refers to ethnocentric beliefs and behaviors based on the notion that one race is superior to others.

Civil Rights refers to those rights belonging to individuals because of their status as citizens; all citizens are guaranteed equal protection under the law by the Fourteenth Amendment of the United States Constitution.

Compensatory Education refers to school programs funded by the federal government to provide additional individualized education to make up for disadvantages resulting from poor home environments.

EXERCISES

1. What experiences have you had with minority group members? What biases do you think you may bring to the classroom as a teacher?
2. Ask your local board of education for its most recent figures on minor-

ity student enrollment, achievement and dropout rates. Do some schools have higher proportions of minority students than others? Do some schools within the district have higher dropout rates than others? How do you account for differences? Compile your findings and present them to your class.

3. Examine a textbook in your subject area. Analyze the treatment of minority groups by examining the number of minority group members depicted in the text, the way in which they are described and the extent to which they are integrated into the text rather than "highlighted" in a special section.

4. Do an ethnic map of your neighborhood. First, define the neighborhood and list all institutions—churches, stores, schools, places of entertainment—and classify them according to their ethnic group of origin. You will have to visit some of them. Determine if the clients who use them live in the neighborhood or elsewhere. Second, try to determine the ethnic breakdown of the residences in your area.

SUGGESTED READINGS

Classic Works

Bernstein, B. (1975). *Class, codes and control*, Vol. 3. London: Routledge and Kegan Paul.

Cazden, C. B., John, V. P., and Hymes, D. (eds.). (1972). *Functions of language in the classroom*. New York: Teachers College Press.

Coleman, James S. (1966). *Equality of educational opportunity*. Washington: U.S. Government Printing Office.

Jencks, C. (1972). *Inequality: A reassessment of the effect of family and schooling in America*. New York: Basic Books.

Ogbu, John U. (1978). *Minority education and caste: The American system in cross-cultural perspective*. New York: Academic Press.

Persell, Caroline Hodges (1977). *Education and inequality: The roots and results of stratification in America's schools*. New York: The Free Press.

Ryan, William. (1976). *Blaming the victim*. New York: Random House.

Modern Works

Deyhle, Donna (1986). Break dancing and breaking out: Anglos, Utes and Navajos in a border reservation high school. *Anthropology and Education Quarterly*, Vol. 17, pp. 111–127.

Dworkin, A. G., and Dworkin, R. J. (1982). *The minority report: An introduction to racial, ethnic, and gender relations* (Second Edition). New York: Holt, Rinehart and Winston.

Fordham, Signithia, and Ogbu, John U. (1986). Black students school success: Coping with the 'burden' of 'acting white'. *The Urban Review*, Vol. 18 (3), pp. 176–206.

Furlong, V. J. (1985). *Deviant pupil: Sociological perspectives*. Philadelphia: Open University Press.

Jacob, Evelyn, and Jordan, Cathie, eds. (1987). Theme issue: Explaining the school performance of minority students, *Anthropology and Education Quarterly*, Vol. 18 (4), December.

McLeod, J. (1987). *Ain't no makin' it: Leveled aspirations in a low-income neighborhood*. Boulder, Col.: Westview Press.

Ogbu, John U. (1983). Minority status and schooling in plural societies. *Comparative Education Review* Vol. 27, No. 2, pp. 168–190.

Wilson, William J. (1987). *The truly disadvantaged*. Chicago: University of Chicago Press.

CHAPTER 8

Gender: Equality of Educational Opportunity

INTRODUCTION

Children's identities as well as their school experiences are shaped by their membership in socioeconomic and/or ethnic minority groups. In Chapters Five and Seven, we demonstrated that students from ethnic minority or low socioeconomic groups have less access to equal educational opportunities than whites and/or students from more privileged social classes. Professionals concerned with equity in education generally direct their attention to the ways in which categories of race, ethnicity and socioeconomic class affect equality of access and treatment for students in schools. However, gender also directly affects the experiences children have in schools. It has been common for researchers to investigate only the separate effects of race, class and gender on school experiences. More recently, researchers have called for examinations of the ways in which these three categories together affect children's experiences. While it is impossible to separate the effects of ethnicity, social class and gender from one another where real people in schools are concerned, we have organized this book in order to examine each category separately. It is essential to remember as you read that each student comes to school *both* as an engendered person *and* with membership in a particular ethnic group and social class.

What Is the Difference between Sex and Gender?

Sex, like ethnicity, is a visible and usually permanent identifying attribute which is acquired at birth. Sex refers to the physical characteristics associated with being male or female, while **gender** is a broader term which includes not only physiological characteristics, but also learned cultural behaviors and understandings. Warren's (1980) summary of the differences between sex and gender is quoted in *A Feminist Dictionary*:

> Gender is often used as a synonym for *sex*, i.e. biological male or female-ness. However, it is also used, particularly by contemporary writers, to refer to the socially imposed dichotomy of masculine and feminine roles and character traits. Sex is physiological, while gender, in the latter usage, is cultural. The distinction is a crucial one, and one which is ignored by unreflective supporters of the status quo who assume that cultural norms of masculinity and femininity are 'natural,' i.e. directly and preponderantly determined by biology. (Warren, p. 181 quoted in Kramarae and Treichler 1985, pp. 173–174)

Children's gender determines the ways in which they are socialized, first by their families and later by school personnel, to learn what are considered to be appropriate male and female roles. Different patterns of behavior are learned by boys and girls through interaction with their primary caretakers and peers. **Sex-role stereotyping** occurs when children are socialized to behave primarily in ways that are considered to be gender appropriate. For example, girls may be encouraged to be nurturing and cooperative, while boys may be encouraged to be aggressive and competitive. These socialization patterns lead to different and unequal expectations of males and females in this society.

The differential patterns of socialization and treatment which females receive in schools puts them in positions very similar to educationally and economically disadvantaged minority groups. Although they are not a minority in the numerical sense since females constitute 51 percent of the population in the United States, females do fit our definition of minority status. From the last chapter, you will recall that attributes of minority group status were: identifiability, differential power, differential treatment and group awareness (Dworkin and Dworkin 1982). Hacker (1951), one of the first sociologists to utilize an understandings of race relations to create a theoretical framework for examining gender relationships, argued for the inclusion of women in minority group studies. Similarities between women and ethnic minorities in terms of group visibility, discrimination in the labor market, stereotypes attributed to them by majority members, and their accommodation to such treatment suggest that knowledge derived from other minority groups could be helpful in understanding women (Dworkin and Dworkin 1982).

Research data clearly illustrate that the treatment females receive in schools is neither the same nor equal to males, just as other categories of students considered to be minorities—the socioeconomically disadvantaged, handicapped and culturally different—also receive unequal and different treatment from people who are members of the mainstream, able-bodied middle class. Despite a growing body of literature detailing sexist practices in schools, gender is a sorely neglected category in recent reform literature calling for equity and excellence in schooling. Tetreault and Schmuck (1985) report that gender is virtually ignored, as a category for concern in equity issues in schooling, by at least eight of the major commission reports. While the reports call for more attention to the needs of particular groups such as minorities, language minorities and handicapped students, they make no mention of gender. Tetreault and Schmuck (1985) argue:

> Gender is not a relevant category in the analysis of excellence in schools. When gender was considered, it appears to merely embellish the traditional—and male—portrait of the school. The proposed vision for excellence in the schools is of education for the male student in the public and productive sphere. Because gender, as a relevant concept, is absent, even Title IX is ignored. Issues of gender in relation to policy, students, curricula, and faculty are not identified nor treated as educational problems to be solved. The goal of excellence does not even have the female student in mind. (1985, p. 63)

In this chapter we will discuss gender issues in the equality of educational opportunity. We first discuss how the socialization process acts to construct gender roles in American society. Next, we present a discussion of sexism. We then describe the legislation that was designed to fight sexist practices in educational institutions. Next, we provide an overview of how sexist practices still are evident in the formal and hidden curricula of schooling. Finally we discuss how **sexism** makes the outcomes of schooling—academic achievement and occupational placement—diffferent for males and females. We argue that despite two decades of feminist activism, research detailing discriminatory practices in schools, and legislation designed to insure equality of access and treatment, females in this society do *not* have equal access to educational and economic opportunities because of their status as women.

SEX ROLE SOCIALIZATION

Children learn what it means to belong to all societies through a socialization process which begins in infancy. Children, interacting verbally and non-verbally with family members and other caretakers, learn behavior appropriate to the cultural norms. As part of this process, they learn how to be males and females (Macoby 1966; Macoby and Jacklin 1974). In a summary of research on sex role differences, Lee and Gropper (1974) report that males and females are socialized to different lifestyles through childrearing practices which involve differential expectations. Despite learning a common language, they differ in their verbal and nonverbal expressions. Males and females are socialized to belong to sex-segregated social groups, wear gender appropriate clothing, prefer activities and toys associated with one sex or another and develop different competencies based on those activities. In preschools and kindergartens, even in the 1980s, girls are more likely to be found playing in the doll corner while boys spend their time with the building blocks and trucks. Television and other forms of media play a crucial role in transmitting the culture's sex role behaviors and values. Children learn how to be men and women in American society by watching television and movies, looking at advertisements and listening to popular music (Spring 1989).

EQUALITY OF EDUCATIONAL OPPORTUNITIES FOR WOMEN

Differential socialization patterns in the society lead to differences in the goals of schooling for males and females. Since men and women are expected to play different roles in the culture, they are trained to fulfill these roles. These roles change within the social and economic context of the society. One way to examine changes in the purposes of schooling for women is to look historically at educational practices. Since the turn of the century, dramatic changes have taken place in the education provided in public schools for women. Based on actual experiences, the following fictional vignettes are presented to provide a sense of what schools were like for American women since the early part of the twentieth century. The stories, which span three generations of one family, describe school experiences for white, working class females. It is important to keep this perspective in mind while you read these accounts, since they reflect the experiences of women more privileged than those of lower social classes or minority groups.

TIME: 1912
PLACE: A SMALL RURAL HIGH SCHOOL IN EAST TENNESSEE

Emily, the fifteen year old daughter of a farmer, attends a school which was established in 1903 as a "model" rural school. The school was funded with the help of northern philanthropists for the purpose of training young men in the art of agriculture. The school is expected "to make better and wiser husbandmen of the country boys and more economical and skillful housewives of the farmers' daughters" (local newspaper, July 24, 1903). Emily is very happy attending this school which offers the skills she will need later in her role as a housewife. There is a department of domestic economy for the girls "consisting of a cooking school and instruction in good substantial and fancy needlework" and in the second year sewing classes the girls learn "the use of the needle, the highest of the feminine arts."

A U.S. Bulletin report about this school states that "if the subject to be discussed deals with technical phases of agriculture in which they are not interested, the women will meet in another room and discuss some problem of housekeeping. The discussions are made as practical as possible" (Allison, 1989).

Emily attends many classes in the department of domestic economy with her female classmates. They are becoming proficient in sewing, cooking and the general mangagement of the household. Emily hopes that soon she will meet a man who will make a good husband and provide a comfortable life for her in this community. She wants her life to revolve around the farm, the home and the children.

TIME 1956
PLACE: A NEIGHBORHOOD ELEMENTARY SCHOOL IN A SMALL NEW JERSEY TOWN

Emily's granddaughter, Jennifer, lives in a small New Jersey town across the river from Philadelphia. Emily's daughter had moved from East Tennessee with her husband looking for work in the 1940s and settled here. Jennifer is in the second grade at the elementary school just three blocks away from her home. Each day she walks back and forth from school to home twice. Like the rest of the children, she goes home at noon to eat lunch. When she arrives at the school yard in the morning and again after lunch, she uses the entry on the girl's side. The girl's playground is separate from the boys and about one third the size. The boys usually play football and baseball on their side and the girls play jump rope and hop-scotch on theirs. When the bell rings announcing the time for classes to begin, the girls line up according to classes in front of the door on their side of the school yard. The first grade girls are on the far right and sixth grade girls on the far left. The boys do the same on the other side of the building.

Jennifer is in the top reading group. She knows this because her group is always called to read first and reads more stories than the other groups. Like everyone who lives in this town, all the characters in Jennifer's reading books have white skin. The boys in the stories play outside, running, playing and building things. They often help the girls when they get in trouble. The girls tend to play inside quietly with their dolls. Jennifer and her brothers and sisters tend to play much like this at home. She likes to play school and fantasizes about being a teacher when she grows up.

TIME: 1962
PLACE: A JUNIOR HIGH SCHOOL IN A SMALL NEW JERSEY TOWN

Jennifer is now in eighth grade at the local junior high school which is about a mile from her home. In addition to her "regular" school subjects such as English, math, history and science, she takes home economics and physical education. These subjects she takes with other girls. In seventh grade the girls take cooking and in eighth grade, they take sewing. The boys take "shop" or industrial arts at this time. The males and females are separated for their gym classes with girls engaged in such activities as field hockey, lacrosse and tennis and the boys engaged in football, baseball and track. Jennifer has joined an after school club in industrial arts for girls. She has enjoyed making several projects from plastic and wood using the tools and machinery available in the shop. She feels that it isn't fair for the girls in the school to be excluded from the regular shop classes offered to the boys during the school day and petitions the administration to open these classes to both sexes. Unfortunately, despite the support of other students and the shop teacher, Jennifer's reguest is denied on the basis that females do not need to learn the skills offered in the industrial arts program.

TIME: 1966
PLACE: A HIGH SCHOOL IN THE SAME TOWN OF NEW JERSEY

Jennifer dreams of becoming an elementary school teacher. She believes that teaching and nursing are the occupations open to her. In teaching, she would be able to have a career and still marry and raise a family. Jennifer's parents, who did not attend college, have never talked with her about going on for further educational or career pursuits. They expect that she will marry and raise a family like her mother. Jennifer would like to go to a state teacher's college, but doesn't know how to begin the process. She talks with the guidence counselor at her school, Mr. Jones, who is surprised at her interest in college. He discourages her from this pursuit, knowing that her parents do not have the money to support a college education. Jennifer is surprised and hurt that Mr. Jones does not seem willing to help her. She knows that her grades are good; she has earned high scores on her SAT's and has been a member of the National Honor Society. She has not been involved in school activities because she worked four hours every day after school and six hours each Saturday. She remembers last year when her sewing teacher gave her a "D" one grading period for not modeling a knitted sweater she made in the school fashion show. It was an evening she was committed to work.

Jennifer decides to apply to college without help from the counselor. She uses the money she has saved for the five applications she sends and is pleased that spring to receive acceptances from those colleges.

TIME: 1988
PLACE: A LARGE SUBURBAN HIGH SCHOOL IN EAST TENNESSEE

Jennifer's daughter, Susan, is now a senior at a sprawling suburban high school in East Tennessee, the home of her maternal grandmother. Jennifer decided to move the family back to Tennessee following her divorce. Her love of the family's original home place precipitated this move. Susan attends the same school that her great-grandmother attended in the early part of the century, but there is now a newly built, consolidated high school in its place. Much has changed since her great-grandmother attended classes here. Unlike the curriculum at that time, Susan is offered the same choices as the male students. All students are able to take whatever subjects they choose and join whatever clubs and sports they want. Susan is the editor of the school newspaper and is also involved with a variety of school activities. She intends to go on to college, but has not decided on a field of study. She was encouraged by the recruiters at the college night to pursue studies in law, medicine, computers, veterinary science and engineering. Whatever she decides, she looks forward to a profession which will be challenging and rewarding.

These short vignettes illustrate some of the changes that have taken place for women. Does this mean that there is no more discrimination based on gender differences? **NO.** Unfortunately, although sexism is less explicitly practiced, it is still evident in American society. Often students, like Susan in the story above, *believe* that as females today they will have complete and equal access to educational and economic opportunities. Expectations about the role of men and women in American society have changed considerably from the the turn of the century. Particularly as a result of the most recent feminist movement of the 1970s and 1980s, there is greater consciousness about gender-based inequality and subsequent expansion of educational and occupational opportunities for women. However, sexism is still evident in this society; it has just become more subtle in its form.

What Is Sexism?

According to a dictionary definition of the term, sexism refers to the "discrimination by members of one sex against another, especially by men against women based on the assumption that one sex is superior" (*American Heritage Dictionary* 1983, p. 626). Sexism, analogous to racism, is the belief that one gender is inferior to the other; it justifies discrimination based on gender. Usually sexism is used to describe prejudice against females, although it "indicates any arbitrary stereotyping of males and females on the basis of their gender" (Guidelines for Equal Treatment of the Sexes in McGraw-Hill Book Company Publications 1980. p. 346).

Federal Legislation Related to Gender Discrimination

In 1972, Title IX of the Education Amendments to the Civil Rights Act was passed by Congress to address the issues of sex discrimination in educational programs that received federal financial assistance. This legislation begins by stating that

no person in the United States shall, on the basis of sex, be excluded from participation in, be denied the benefits of, or be subjected to discrimination under any education program or activity receiving federal financial assistance.

In other words, any educational institution that was the recipient of federal funds must provide equal opportunity to both sexes to participate in all programs and activities of that institution. According to Title IX, practices which were common in schools such as class segregation based on gender were no longer legal. In our story above, the policy at Jennifer's school which excluded her from participating in "male" classes like industrial arts were prohibited by federal legislation after 1972. The consequences of continuation of sexist practices such as these could result in the withdrawal of federal assistance to the institution. This legislation was an important force in changing explicit sexist practices in public schools. Consequently, students like Susan have experienced more freedom of choice in their academic and extracurricular school programs than their mothers and grandmothers.

Despite Title IX, researchers have found that sexist practices still exist in schools. Tetrault (1986) noted that research on sex-role biases in schools in combination with the movement for gender equity in the 1970s and 1980s have resulted in significant changes in the past fifteen years. These changes have been in increased enrollment of women in science and mathematics courses, increased expenditures in women's athletic programs and increases in the number of female elementary principals. The use of non-sexist language and inclusion of greater numbers of women in textbooks are also a result of a movement toward greater sex equity. However, Tetrault argues that despite equal access, separation of males or separate provisions for male activities continue to be the norm; the different educational needs of men and women are ignored and women are implicitly socialized into "the behaviors of men in the public sphere" (Tetrault 1986). Shakeshaft supports this view:

> unfortunately, few schools provide an equitable culture in which all students and faculty members can grow. Most offer white males more options in an environment that is hospitable to their needs. Females and members of minority groups, on the other hand must obtain their education in systems that are at best indifferent and at worst hostile to them. Women and members of minority groups learn that their concerns, their lives, their cultures are not the stuff of schooling. They discover that school is not a psychologically or physically safe environment for them and that they are valued neither by the system nor by society (Shakeshaft, 1986, p. 500).

GENDER DIFFERENCES IN THE FORMAL CURRICULUM

The formal school curriculum serves as the core for the daily activities of teachers and students. Earlier in this chapter we described a school in 1903 which proudly prescribed a separate curriculum for males and females so that they could be prepared for the work they would be doing after high school. Girls were taught homemaking and needlecrafts and boys were schooled in the science of agriculture. This separate curriculum reflected the needs and values of the community at that time. In today's schools, because of changed perceptions of gender roles, Title IX of the Elementary and Secondary Education Act mandates that schools must permit males and females to be able to study the same curriculum. However, in reality, gender based differential patterns of enrollment in courses, different patterns of treatment for men and women in classes, and inequities in the ways women are portrayed in the formal curricular content still exist.

Gender Identified Subject Matter

Tradition categorizes curricular content areas by gender. Math, science, and many of the vocational areas (auto shop, woodworking, drafting) historically have been considered by educators, parents and students as subjects more appropriate for males. The humanities and a few of the vocational areas (bookkeeping, typing, shorthand, cosmetology) are perceived to be more relevant for females. Fewer women than men enroll in courses in the quantitative fields of math and science. A recent report prepared for the Committee on Research in Mathematics, Science, and Technology Education (1987) reports that males spend more time with microcomputers and are more likely to participate in after-school computer related activities. More males than females take computer programming courses and go on to high paying positions in the computer industry. The authors of this report attribute these inequalities to the perception of the quantitative fields as male domains.

Sorensen and Hallinan (1987) studied 1,477 students in 48 4th–6th grade classes in ten public schools to determine the effects of gender differences on ability-grouped math classes. Based on an analysis of standardized achievement test scores, the researchers found that females are more likely to be misassigned to ability groups than males. Girls with high aptitude in math were less likely to be assigned to high-ability math groups than boys with similar aptitudes. Sorensen and Hallinan suggest that the teachers' placement decisions "may reveal" discrimination based on gender expectations. This study supports the notion that quantitative subjects "belong" to males.

Gender Based Staffing

Segregation of the curriculum along gender lines is evident in the staffing of these courses. (See Table 8.1.) Since more men than women go into quantitative subject matter teaching areas, there are more men teaching in these content areas in schools. Kelly and Nihlen (1982) report that teaching staffs are segregated by subject matter with more women teaching in language arts, foreign languages and to some extent social sciences, while men dominate the math, science, computer and engineering courses. Segregation of the teaching staff

TABLE 8.1. SUBJECTS TAUGHT BY MALE AND FEMALE TEACHERS IN PUBLIC SECONDARY SCHOOLS, UNITED STATES, 1971

Subject	% male	% female
Home economics	0.0	100.0
Foreign language	26.5	73.5
Business education	33.3	66.7
English	35.4	64.6
Health and physical education	45.8	54.2
Art	46.1	53.9
Music	70.4	29.6
Social studies	76.8	23.2
Science	85.3	14.7
Industrial arts	95.4	4.6
Agriculture	100.0	0.0

(Source: U.S. Bureau of the Census. Statistical Abstract of the United States: 1987 (107th Edition). Washington, D.C., 1986.)

along subject matter lines reinforces to students the already clear message about what is "appropriate" knowledge for males and females.

Portrayal of Women in Curricular Materials

The way in which females have been depicted in textbooks has changed over the past two decades. Feminist criticism of curricular materials has pushed publishers to portray female characters in more diverse roles. While Jennifer in the story at the beginning of this chapter was provided with a limited number of female role models in her reading texts—teachers, nurses, and housewives, her daughter Susan is more likely to read texts which depict women as doctors, telephone repair personnel and scientists.

This change in the way women are portrayed in texts is documented by Hitchcock and Tompkins (1987) in an evaluation of recent editions of six popular basal reading texts. The researchers analyzed the texts to determine the number of males and female main characters as well as the range and frequency of occupations for female characters. In an evaluation of 1121 stories, they found that females were portrayed in 37 occupations as compared with 5 occupations in 1961–63 readers and 23 occupations in 1969–71 readers. In the recent editions, males were main characters in 18 percent of stories and females in 17 percent. Surprisingly, the main characters in three times as many stories were now categorized as "other"—neutral characters such as talking trees or neutered characters such as animals. Although there has been some effort to portray women in a variety of occupational roles, Hitchcock and Tomkins argue that textbook publishers appear to be avoiding questions of sexism by creating neutral characters.

At the college level, changes in the treatment of women in textbooks is not as clearly evident. Postsecondary texts continue to ignore the roles of women and portray them in stereotypic ways. In addition, college classrooms are still predominantly taught by men, particularly at the senior ranks. Recent figures show that 90 percent of the full professors on U. S. campuses are male, as compared with 91 percent a decade ago (Sadker, Sadker, and Klein 1986). Women at the postsecondary level have fewer opportunities to find female role models in the college classroom or curriculum.

Tetrault (1986) reported that although publishers have responded to pressure to include women in textbooks, they depict "outstanding women who contributed in areas or movements traditionally dominated by men" (p. 230). She argues that women have been tacked on to a history which continues to be dominated by men's values and perspectives. She calls for a gender-balanced curriculum which also looks at ordinary women's everyday lives in traditional roles as well as their efforts to move beyond these boundaries.

Silences in the Curriculum

In an examination of the formal curriculum, the message which comes through clearly is found not in what is presented about women, but what is omitted. Curricular "silences" are revealing. In other words, what is left out of the text sends a clear message to students as to what is important and what is peripheral knowledge. Research on the portrayal of women in school texts reports that females, rather than sharing central roles with men, are either ignored or relegated to domestic roles (Kelly and Nihlen 1982).

An example of the way in which women are ignored or confined to peripheral roles is found in an analysis of texts used in social studies courses such as World and American History. Males dominate these texts. The treatment of women's contributions to the labor union or suffrage movement are minimized; females are portrayed as wives, social workers, nurses, and helpmates to men (Treckler 1973; Kelly and Nihlen 1982). Feminists critically note that the word used to describe the course is *his*-tory rather than *her*-story; they call for a rewriting of such courses to include the roles women have played (Scott 1987). Although more recent textbooks have made more efforts to incorporate women's roles, history remains the study of male military matters. Students learn American political history as a chronology of the various wars which were waged from the American Revolution through the Vietnam War. The "failure to integrate female experiences into general curriculum drives home the message that girls and their experiences are somehow "other," that they are not part of general literature and history" (Shakeshaft 1986, p. 501).

GENDER DIFFERENCES
IN THE HIDDEN CURRICULUM

The question of gender equity in the curriculum goes beyond the formal curriculum to incorporate the implicit messages we give to students. (See Chapter Six for our discussion on the hidden curriculum.) This section examines the ways in which ideas about sex roles are transmitted daily in the organizational structure and instructional techniques used in schools.

Hidden Messages in the Adminstrative Structure of Schooling

The structure of schooling has been described by educational historians as the "educational harem" (Tyack 1974) because it relies heavily on a hierarchical system in which male administrators manage female teachers and support staff. This type of structure continues to be the norm today, as we have argued in previous chapters on the organization and labor force of schools. Schools are organized so that principals dominate in policy decisions which affect the daily running of the school. Traditionally administrators have been male and consequently women in schools often find themselves in subordinate positions. This type of administrative structure clearly tells students that men hold positions of authority and power in society; women play subordinate roles in which they have control only over the children in their classrooms.

Hidden Messages in Classroom Organization

The sex of students is often used as an organizational tool for structuring activities. In elementary schools, boys and girls are called on to line up separately in order to walk to lunch or to the restrooms. Some teachers ask children to read aloud in groups according to gender. Classroom and playground games pit the girls against the boys. Although this practice may seem innocuous, separation by gender as an organizational strategy is unnecessary and results in differential treatment based on gender. The 1895 *Plessy* v. *Ferguson* "separate but equal" ruling was overturned by the Supreme Court decision in *Brown* v. *Board of Education of Topeka, Kansas* (1954), which stated that separate facilities for blacks were inherently unequal. We argue that the "separate but equal" doctrine is also inappropriate for gender.

The organization and distribution of classroom jobs may be based on teachers' perceptions of appropriate sex roles. Despite increasing awareness of sex role stereotyping, we tend to treat boys and girls differently in schools according to gender expectations. In one first grade classroom (Bennett 1986), male students were asked to perform the tasks which would take them out of the classroom, such as delivering messages to the principal's office. These jobs were highly valued by the children and considered by the teacher to be tasks requiring higher levels of responsibility. Female students were asked to perform chores inside the classroom such as picking up papers, straightening library books or erasing the blackboards—traditional roles for women. A principal who comes in to a classroom asking for "four strong boys" to carry some books, is providing a clear message about sex roles. In this case, the message is that boys play active roles and are able to handle chores which require physical strength, while girls are not.

Shakeshaft reports that research on gender and schooling provides us with two messages: "First, what is good for males is not necessarily good for females. Second, if a choice must be made, the education establishment will base policy and instruction on that which is good for males" (Shakeshaft 1986, p. 500). She argues that the school organization would better fit the needs of females if single-sex rather than coeducational situations were available. This argument is based on research which has found that females perform better in single-sex than in coeducational schools. They exhibit higher self-esteem and are more involved in the academic life of the school with increased involvement in a broad range of social and leadership activities. Males do well in coeducational schooling (Shakeshaft 1986).

Shakeshaft (1986) argues that the structure of schools as well as the curriculum mirror male rather than female development. Although females mature earlier, are ready for verbal and math skills at a younger age and have control of small motor skills sooner, classrooms are structured so as to meet the needs of males who tend to develop at a slower pace. This pattern, coupled with research that shows that male students get a larger proportion of attention from and interaction with the teacher (Sadker and Sadker 1985; Shakeshaft 1986), puts female students in difficult positions in their classrooms. "Some grow bored, others give up, but most learn to hold back, be quiet, and smile" (Shakeshaft 1986 p. 500).

Hidden Messages in Instructional Techniques

Schools rely on what Goldman and McDermott (1987) refer to as a "culture of competition." This competition can be in the form of grades, classroom games and activities or simply in the amount of time it takes to finish a task. Although there has been recent emphasis on peer tutoring and cooperative learning techniques, classrooms are usually structured so that children must work individually rather than in pairs or in groups. The stress on individual accomplishment in classrooms sets up a culture of competition where there is constant comparision of students' abilities by teachers and by students themselves. A hierarchy based upon achievement is established in the classroom as the participants develop an understanding of others' work habits, skills and abilities as they interact with each other. If you were to ask first graders to name the best and worst readers in their classroom, they would have little difficulty in so doing. As we have indicated earlier, this hierarchy is duplicated in friendship groups and the organization of high school peer structures. The use of competition in schools is taken for granted by educators as the way to "do school."

In an ethnographic study of high school extracurricular activities, Eder and Parker (1987) found that athletic programs enouraged males to be aggressive, achievement-oriented and competitive. Cheerleading, which was more highly valued for women than athletics, served to remind girls of the importance of being attractive. Traditional males and female roles—competition for men and emotional management (caretaking) for women—were the values integral to these activities.

Competition as an instructional strategy is problematic for female students who tend to prefer connection and collaboration and see relationships with others as central to their daily activities (Shakeshaft 1986). Competition is a threat to these relationships; since much of what is done in schools is based on the notion of competition, females often find themselves in uncomfortable or alienating environments. Belenky et al (1986) emphasize the need for building patterns of connection and collaboration into learning environments in order to facilitiate women's development.

Hidden Messages in Classroom Interactions

Research on gender differences in classroom interaction demonstrates that males verbally dominate classrooms at all levels of schooling, despite the gender of the classroom teacher (Martin 1972; Brophy and Good 1970; Sikes 1971). In a study by Sadker and Sadker (1985), a team of researchers observed more than 100 fourth-, sixth- and eighth- grade classes in four states and in Washington, D.C. Half of these classes were in the subject areas of English and language arts and the other half were in science and math classes. The research team found that teachers, regardless of their gender and ethnic background, asked more questions of white males. They report that male students talked more than female students at a ratio of three to one. The Sadkers found that as the school year progressed, the participation and assertiveness of the males in the classrooms increased. Males students would "grab teachers' attention" by calling out answers which then were accepted by students. When female students called out answers they were more likely to be reprimanded for inappropriate behavior, so girls were observed to sit patiently with their hands raised waiting to be called on by the teacher. The study reports that males were eight times more likely to call out answers to teachers' questions. The Sadkers argue that through this type of interaction with students, teachers socialize males to be academically assertive and girls to assume a more traditional role of sitting quietly.

The Sadkers use the term "mind sex" to describe a pattern of interaction in which teachers call on students of the same sex repeatedly. For example, if the teacher asks a question of a male student, the next several questions would also be likely to be addressed to male students. They found this pattern of same gender series of interactions is more pronounced among the male students and suggested that the self-selected sex segregation in seating patterns in more than half the classes observed may influence this practice.

Male students receive more attention of all kinds by teachers—more praise, more time, but also more reprimands and harsher discipline (Lippitt and Gold 1959; LaFrance 1985; Sikes 1971). The attention given to males is much different from that given to females. For example, the Sadkers found that teachers are more likely to assist male students in performing a task, but are more likely to do that task for the female students. Teachers give more criticism to males, so that consequently they learn to handle criticism.

Females students are neither reprimanded nor praised but tend to be ignored in classrooms, particularly high achieving females who receive the least attention of all students. Both majority and minority females learn that their opinions are not valued and their answers to questions not worthy of attention, and they come to believe they are not smart or important (Grant 1984; Hall and Sandler 1982; LaFrance 1985). If they do well in school, it is because of luck or hard work rather their own abilities as students. School interactions "reinforce societal message that females are inferior" (Shakeshaft 1986, p. 501).

There are gender differences in the ways men and women interact in social settings outside the academic world. Men speak more often than women and frequently interrupt them. Women are less active verbal participants in conversations, but they provide supportive and passive nonverbal cues by smiling and gazing at the speaker (LaFrance and Mayo 1978; Duncan and Fiske 1977). Researchers found that listeners recall more from male speakers than females even though the content is identical and the style is similar.

Women may seem unsure or less competent in their comments because they often transform declarative statements into tentative comments by adding a tag question such as "isn't it" or qualifiers such as "I guess." To listeners this signals lack of power and influence (Sadker and Sadker 1985). An interesting alternative interpretation of this practice was provided by McIntosh (1988) who argues that such a qualifier serves to signal equality and less power differential between the speaker and the listener. By avoiding the appearance of being the all knowing authority, the woman can encourage an exchange of information between the listener and the speaker.

Sexist Language in Schools

Sexist language is one way in which gender stereotypes continue to affect beliefs and attitudes about women. Although there has been an increased awareness by many educators, sexist language continues to be used in many American schools. It is not uncommon to look at elementary bulletin boards which portray pictures of community helpers as "firemen" and "policemen." Social studies courses and science talk about "mankind" or "man's contributions to science." LaFrance (1985) argues that

> one of the more subtle ways teachers contribute to female invisibility in classrooms is by reliance on the generic 'he' to refer to both men and women. . . . Theoretically, the generic 'he' includes females as well as males but recent studies show its exclusionary properties. (LaFrance 1985, p. 43)

Many institutions have written and implemented policy which discourages the use of sexist language in courses and in student writing, but these guidelines are often ignored. The use of sexist language in schools at any level is unnecessary and potentially debilitating to females. It is another way in which women are socialized to see themselves as subordinate to males.

> When a sexist word is scrawled across the lockers or when a male student uses sexist language, the silence can be deafening. Few teachers even code it as a problem, and many of the insults and put-downs of girls come from teachers and administrators themselves. After all, boys will be boys and girls will continue to receive their schooling in a hostile environment. (Shakeshaft 1986, p. 502)

GENDER BASED DIFFERENTIAL OUTCOMES IN SCHOOLING

We have presented data about the different treatment of males and females particularly as related to the organizational structure, curriculum, instructional strategies and interactions in schools. The process in which young men and women are treated differently in elementary and secondary schools leads to differential outcomes for students based on gender. In this section, we will present data on academic and occupational outcomes related to gender. There are clear differences in the academic performances of males and females as well as their later occupational attainment.

Differences in Academic Performance

What are the gender differences in student performance on academic tasks? Female students achieve higher grades throughout public schooling and do better on language related courses such as reading, writing and literature while males do better in math and science. Although high school girls make better grades than boys, males tend to elect more of the optional science and math courses which would prepare them for careers in science related areas (Ballantine 1983). Females are less likely to participate in special or gifted programs and less likely to take math and science courses—even if they are academically talented—because they are less likely to believe themselves capable of pursuing math and science in college.

Females tend to attribute their failures to internal factors such as their own lack of intellectual ability, while successes are attributed to external factors such as luck (Sadker and Sadker 1985). In a study of college retention and attrition in mathematics and science courses, McDade (1988) found differences in the ways men and women dealt with their failures in these fields. Men were more able to disengage their self images from their academic performance; rather than question their own abilities, they viewed their failures as a lack of fit with the field of study. Women internalized their failures, questioning their competence as learners in general, not specifically in this content area. Holland and Eisenhart's work with black and white college women (1988a) corroborates McDade's findings. When confronted by teachers, parents or boyfriends who told them that they lacked the drive or ability to pursue "hard" subjects, they tended to give up or lower their career aspirations, rather than to question the validity of negative judgements.

The Scholastic Achievement Test (SAT) published by the Educational Testing Service serves as a major measure of student achievement in the United States. The Project on Equal Education Rights (PEER) of the National Organization for Women is an advocacy program for equal educational opportuntities for women. The group monitors the progress of females in schools. In their 1986 Report Card, PEER found that in 1985 male SAT scores were 59 points higher than females. The national average (possible 1600) was 936 for males and 877 for females which was the largest gap in twenty years with women scoring lower on both verbal and math sections. The 1985 national average math score for men was 499 and 452 for women; the verbal score was 437 for men, 425 for women. Although the Educational Testing Service was unable to explain this discrepancy, it reported that SAT scores underpredict the grades women can expect to earn in college; the test is not an accurate predictor of women's college performance as based on grades. Researchers suggest that there is sex bias in the construction of the SAT test as well as in its content. More of the test questions are set in a science context than the humanities, where women have traditionally been encouraged to excel. The Educational Testing Service also has removed both the essay writing portion of the verbal test and the data sufficiency question on the math test—items where female students had excelled. While there is some evidence that the "gender gap" in achievement tests scores is diminishing on tests other than the SAT (the College Board achievement tests, the National Assessment of Educational Progress, graduate school admissions tests, the Armed Forces Qualification Tests, and the College Boards), it may be because while women are improving their performance in math relative to men, their verbal performance, which has been higher than men, is slipping (Kolata 1989).

The Educational Testing Service also requests that students supply information about their academic goals when they take the SAT. PEER found that in 1985, 10.6 percent of the high school senior women taking the SAT reported that their goal was to major in physical sciences as compared with 34 percent of the male seniors. In 1980–1981 (the most recent figures available according to PEER) only 3 percent of the women graduates received bachelor's degrees in physical sciences, mathematics and engineering, while 23 percent of the women graduates earned degrees in education and 11 percent graduated in nursing and health-related professions—both traditionally female professions.

Differences in Occupational Outcomes and Economic Rewards

We talked previously about equality of educational opportunities in two ways: equal access to education and equal treatment of students in schools. Women, like minority groups, have achieved equal access to educational opportuntities by law, through Title IX. However, equal treament of women in schools is not a reality. There are differences in the treatment of men and women in schools which mirror cultural beliefs about appropriate roles for males and females. The United States, like other western countries, is highly patriarchal in that men are politically, economically and socially dominant. Although there have been significant changes in both educational and economic opportuntities for women, the workforce continues to be sex-segregated with women holding subordinate positions in the economy. Kelly and Nihlen report that

> women earn less than 56 percent of male income, regardless of job categories; they are concentrated in the lowest paying jobs in both service and industrial sectors of the economy; they are segregated into occupations which permit very little upward mobility; and they are concentrated in the 'marginal' areas of the workforce (1982, p. 165).

Unequal educational treatment in schools coupled with culturally determined notions of what is appropriate women's work continue to produce inequities in the economic structure. Despite movement into traditionally male dominated fields such as science and engineering, Randour et al. (1982) found that at the bachelor's degree level, women continue to be concentrated in education, fine and applied arts, foreign languages, health professions, home economics and library science—all traditionally female professions. In addition, although greater numbers of women are now earning master's degrees and doctorates, over half of the women at the masters' level and over one third of those at the doctoral level are earning degrees in education.

SUMMARY

This chapter has addressed the major issues related to gender equity in schools. It is clear, especially after the passage of Title IX, that women have more alternatives in schools and more equitable access to educational opportunities. The gender differences are no longer as explicit as they were in the school that Emily attended in 1903. Through her schooling experience, Emily's great-granddaughter, Susan, has been given access to many educational alternatives and potential career options. However, schools continue to reproduce a patriarchal society through subtle (and often not-so subtle) messages embedded in their organizational structure, curriculum and social interaction patterns.

KEY CONCEPTS

Sex refers to the physiological traits of maleness or femaleness.

Gender in addition to physiological traits, refers to the cultural understandings and behaviors associated with maleness and femaleness. Gender is learned through a process of socialization from birth.

Sexism refers to prejudice and/or discrimination based on gender.

Sex Role Stereotyping refers to exaggerated beliefs about "appropriate" roles for males and females in a society. For example, girls are cooperative and nurturing; boys are competitive and aggressive.

EXERCISES

1. Observe a classroom. Count the number of males and females in the classroom. Note the gender of the teacher. Keep track of the number of times the teacher calls on males and females. Note the types of questions asked of male and female students. Try to document how much time is provided to students according to gender. What are some of the gender related patterns you see in this classroom? How does the content of the curriculum relate to the material presented in this chapter?

2. Select a social studies textbook at any grade level. Analyze the content of the text for gender differences. How is the text organized? What are the major topics covered? How does the text portray women and women's issues?
3. Think about your own educational experiences. How did gender play a role in these experiences? Have you had situations in schools in which you felt sexism was involved? Describe that incident.

SUGGESTED READINGS

Classic Works

Chowdorow, N. (1978). *The reproduction of mothering*. Berkeley: University of California Press.

Macoby, E., and Jacklin, C. (1974). *The psychology of sex differences*. Stanford: Stanford University Press.

Millett, K. (1977). *Sexual politics*. London: Virago Press.

Saario, T. N., Jacklin, C. N., and Tittle, C. K. (1973). Sex role stereotyping in the public schools. *Harvard Educational Review, 43* (3), pp. 386–415.

Treckler, Janice L. (1973). Women in U.S. history high school textbooks. *International Review of Education*, 19, pp. 133–139.

Modern Works

Belenky, Mary F. et al. (1986). *Women's ways of knowing.: The development of self, voice, and mind*. New York: Basic Books, Inc.

Delamont, Sara (1980). *Sex roles and the school*. London: Metheun.

Gilligan, Carol (1982). *In a different voice*. Cambridge: Harvard University Press.

Farnham, C. (1987). *The impact of feminist research in the academy*. Bloomington: Indiana University Press.

Hacker, Helen M. (1951). Women as a minority group. *Social Forces 30*, pp. 60–69.

Kelly, Gail P., and Nihlen, Ann S. (1982). Schooling and the reproduction of patriarchy: Unequal workloads, unequal rewards. In Michael W. Apple (Ed) *Cultural and economic reproduction in education: essays on class, ideology and the state*. London: Routledge & Kegan Paul, Ltd.

Klein, S. (ed.) (1985). *Handbook for achieveing sex equity through education*. Baltimore: The Johns Hopkins University Press.

Kramarae, C., and Treichler, P. (1985). *A feminist dictionary*. London: Pandora Press.

Pitman, Mary Anne, and Eisenhardt, Margaret A. (eds.). (1988). Theme issue: Women, culture, and education. *Anthropology & Education Quarterly*, Vol. 19 (2).

Randour, Mary Lou, Strasburg, Georgia L., and Lipman-Blumen, Jean. (1982). Women in higher education: Trends in enrollments and degrees earned. *Harvard Educational Review*, Vol. 52 (2), pp. 189–202.

Sadker, Myra, and Sadker, David. (1985). Sexism in the schoolroom of the '80's. *Psychology Today* (March), pp. 54–57.

Schmuck, P. A. (1987). *Women educators: Employees of schools in western countries*. Albany: State University of New York Press.

Scott, Joan Wallach. (1987). Women's history and the rewriting of history. In Christie Farnham (ed.) *The impact of feminist research in the academy*. Bloomington: Indiana Press University.

Shakeshaft, Charol. (1986). A gender at risk. *Phi Delta Kappan* (March).

Sorensen, Aage B., and Hallinan, Maureen T. (1987). Ability grouping and sex differences in mathematics achievement. *Sociology of Education*, Vol. 60 (2 April), pp. 63–72.

Tetreault, Mary Kay, and Schmuck, Patricia. (1985). Equity, educational reform and gender. *Issues in Education*, Vol. III, No. 1 (Summer), 45–67.

Walker, S., and Barton, L. (eds.) (1983). *Gender class & education*. Sussex, England: The Falmer Press.

CHAPTER 9

Alternatives to the Way We "Do School": A Critical Perspective

OVERVIEW

INTRODUCTION

What have we learned about schooling from sociology? In this text we have attempted to provide an overview of how sociologists look at students and teachers in schools. We have distinguished between the concepts of "education" and "schooling," indicating how sociological insights differ from those offered by other disciplines. In the paragraphs below, we summarize what sociologists have learned about schools and the schooling process. Following these chapter by chapter summaries, we offer alternatives to the way we "do school," based upon sociological information.

CHAPTER SUMMARIES

Theoretical and Historical Overview of the Purposes of Schooling

Sociologists have been concerned with the function schools play in society and the constant tension over how the purposes of schooling are defined. Depending upon their theoretical orientation, sociologists have argued that schools are:

1. benign agencies of social control and maintenance, acting to preserve societal equilibrium and stability;
2. mechanisms by which asymmetrical patterns of social prestige and power are reinforced so as to maintain the dominations of specific groups;
3. agencies of social transformation and change.

These arguments relate to the social value and power of various kinds of knowledge, and are played out in disagreements over what should be taught in schools to whom and who should make curricular decisions. Regardless of their formulation, sociologists place schools and the activities they encompass directly within a social context, linking individuals to social institutions and institutions to others within a given community. Sociologists all view behavior, including cognition, as socially determined, and schools as integral parts of larger social systems.

The Social Organization of Schooling

Sociologists have examined the structure and dynamics of schools as complex bureaucratic social institutions whose history and function parallel other bureaucracies in society. They tell us that schools differ from many other forms of bureaucracies in modern societies in that lines of control over various aspects of schooling are ambiguous, negotiable, and disputed. Shifts toward centralized control and standardized teaching are counterbalanced by movements toward localism and community control. Changes in the nature of the groups who control schools are reflected in curricular trends which swing between an emphasis on highly specified and technical forms of knowledge to much more diffuse, critical and literary forms. These themes are played out at every level— national, state, district, school and classroom. They are reflected in the lines of authority which govern who is responsible for what kind of work in schools, the generation and disbursement of funds as well as the physical structures and geographical arrangement of school buildings and districts. Sociologists also have noted the diffuse, open nature of patterns of control in schools. Schooling is subject to the demands of many competing and legitimate constituencies, including political and cultural factions from the community, groups of professional educators inside and outside of school: parents, taxpayers, and various levels of governmental agencies. These organizational characteristics make schools at once transparent to influence from the outside and their inhabitants zealous guardians of a fragile autonomy.

Youth Culture and the Student Peer Group

Sociologists have examined students as one of the subgroups within schools, drawing distinctions between the way student and adult participants are recruited, rewarded, evaluated and perform their tasks. They look at the roles students play and how they communicate with others. Sociologists indicate that student and adult participants articulate with school differently because the interests which link them to school differ so much that they produce "turf wars" over issues of control.

The development of an oppositional student culture is facilitated by the isolation of students from adults during the period of schooling. It is exacerbated during periods of rapid social and cultural change, when school culture, adult culture and the lived culture of youth are out of synchrony with one another. We have suggested that the further life in school and the experience of adult participants in schools lags behind what children experience in their daily life, the greater the chances are that they will become totally irrelevant to a child's life.

Contemporary problems such as poverty, homelessness, environmental degradation, teenage pregnancy, drug and alcohol abuse intensify the dysjuncture between children's lives inside and outside of school. Sociologists also have questioned the strength and significance of supposed linkages between education and future opportunities for students, given the changes in the nature of work and the labor force, the inflation of educational credentials, and the skyrocketing costs of college attendance. These issues raise questions as to whether contemporary schools have any relevance to students at all.

The Labor Force in Schooling

Sociologists have examined teacher and administrator characteristics, the roles each play, and how characteristics and roles affect the type of work they do within the school organization. Analyses tell us that teaching is a gender-stratified occupation, in that the teaching force is female-dominated, but that the actual administration of schools and school districts is dominated by males. Sociologists have suggested that schooling has a patriarchal structure which limits the control teachers exert over how they perform their work. In addition to being predominately female, the labor force consists primarily of Anglo, middle-class teachers, thus tending to reflect in the schooling process the cultural norms, values and behaviors of the dominant group.

Rationalization of the curriculum has brought increasing pressure on teachers; standardization of texts, tests, and instructional processes act to "de-skill" what teachers do and reduce their activities to mere conformity to formulaic practice. Sociologists have examined how these forces, embodied in movements like scientific management and human engineering in the 1920s and 1930s, as well as in the educational reform legislation of the 1980s, have affected teacher alienation and burnout, as measured by teacher turnover and job satisfaction.

Sociologists also have discussed the nature of professional work, questioning how closely the levels of autonomy of its practitioners, as well as their tasks, training, and governance compare with more traditional professions like law and medicine. Sociologists describe how the debate over the nature of the profession revolves around the definition of appropriate role behaviors for teachers, relative to the communities in which they teach. It involves variation in the type and length of training, the autonomy, or control individuals have over the performance of their work, and the meaning which is ascribed to it by others.

From one perspective, teachers are viewed as workers or community servants. As such, their status is like that of blue collar workers, and they are expected to act as closely supervised subordinates, public servants who are responsible for transmitting dominant cultural values to their students. Another view regards teachers as professionals and highly trained intellectuals who are charged with using their expertise to bring to the community the most enlightened pedagogy available. In this role, they are expected to be leaders and agents of social change, whose major concern is not mere transmission of the existing social order, but its transformation to a more humane and liberating way of life. The latter view, one urged by critical theorists and generally resisted by communities in the United States, justifies higher status for teachers and a shift of control of schools from local lay boards to expert teaching practitioners. The way in which teachers are viewed by the local community and the larger society to a large extent determines the role they will play in the control of public schools.

Social Class and Its Relationship to Schooling

One of the most important contributions of sociologists to our understanding of schools is their focus on the relationship between educational attainment and patterns of social class inequality in society. Sociologists tell us that societies are stratified hierarchically by social class, or access to power and material goods; higher social classes have greater ability to exercise power and to amass material goods than lower classes. Social class status is associated with educational attainment, in that the more education an individual has acquired, the higher their class status is likely to be. Sociologists have struggled to understand this relationship and how it operates. Its existence justified a great deal of hope—and educational programming—designed to improve the class status of disadvantaged students by improving the educational opportunities available to them. However, time has proven that many of our most cherished notions—such as the belief that schooling can promote social equality—were quite simplistic. To the contrary, it appears that schools actually act to reproduce the existing class structure. Sociologists suggest that this occurs because students from different social classes—including minority groups and women—are provided with very different experiences in schools. The differences parallel expectations teachers and administrators have about the status which students have when they first enroll, as well as the status they are expected to have when they finish their studies. The schooling experiences different groups have, then, are inherently unequal. Schools tend to replicate or reinforce the existing social class inequalities of people who attend them.

What Is Taught in Schools: Curriculum and the Stratification of Knowledge

Sociologists have looked at the kinds of knowledge taught in schools as well as the way information flows variably, so that different kinds of students are provided with different kinds of knowledge. They suggest that knowledge is stratified in accordance with its type and how valuable people consider it to be; that is, that types of knowledge are valued unequally, and those which are more valued are associated with possession of higher levels of power in society.

School knowledge, both formal (explicit or overt) and informal (implicit or hidden) is embodied in the curriculum. It, too, is stratified in accordance with its value and association with social power. Children are served different knowledge menus by teachers and their school experiences in accordance with what is thought to be appropriate for their different social class origins and their perceived future destinations in society. Analysis of the curriculum has permitted sociologists to attain better understanding of how schools generally act only to facilitate the mobility of *individuals*, not to reduce the poverty and inequality of disadvantaged *groups*. Hence, schools simply pass on to most individuals the status of their parents.

Ethnic Minorities and Schooling:
Equality of Education Opportunity

Having discovered the relationship between class status and educational attainment, sociologists became aware that class did not seem to be the only important factor, given the underrepresentation of minorities in the highest levels of occupational and educational attainment. Rather, the relationship was compounded by minority status. In other words, students who were disadvantaged by virtue of low socioeconomic class status were further disadvantaged if they came from a minority group. A major research effort was devoted to understanding why minority children fell so far behind their Anglo peers. Aside from pervasive patterns of racial prejudice, sociologists found that reasons for failure included institutional discrimination in the form of unequal access to academic programs and unequal treatment, overt and covert, in schools. In addition, they reported that unlike children from middle and upper class dominant culture homes, minority children faced the existence of discontinuities of language use, behavioral expectations, and attitudes between the culture of the school and that of their home. These discontinuities meant that minority children not only had to master their cognitive lessons, but that they had to learn *how* to learn them as well. Having to master a "double curriculum" is a burden which makes it difficult for minority children to be as successful in school as children from the dominant culture.

The beliefs and expectations which educators hold about minority children also lead to low expectations for their ability. They often are segregated into the lower academic and vocational curricular tracks and discouraged from aspiring to college placement. Sociologists also have identified a reciprocal response to this treatment by children; many refuse to learn or construct an inability to succeed. They do so partly in resistance to the constellation of negative pressures inflicted upon them by their teachers and counselors, and partly as a realistic appraisal of the ability of schooling to help them succeed economically, given patterns of discrimination in the labor market.

Gender: Equality of Educational Opportunity

In addition to social class and ethnic minority group membership, sociologists also have discovered that gender differences are associated with prevailing patterns of differential access to schooling, treatment once in school, and outcomes or patterns of success based on schooling. A black female from a poor home will be at a disadvantage in her schooling experiences not only because of social class and minority identification, but also because of her gender.

While affirmative action plans and enabling legislation have eliminated many of the legal barriers to the equal participation of women in education, both as students and as professionals, females still continues to receive different treatment from males in school. We have already discussed the gender-stratified nature of the teaching profession. Female students in school also experience treatment in schools which differs considerably from that of males. They receive less teacher attention, less constructive feedback, and participate less actively in the schooling process. They are discouraged from taking sufficient coursework in mathematics and the sciences to qualify them for the most prestigious career trajectories. While girls generally score higher on standardized tests in elementary school, in large part because they do better on tests of verbal skills, their scores drop below those of boys in high school; they consistently score lower on standardized tests of mathematics than boys. Information about women's lives and work, as well as women's issues play little role in the school curriculum and females continue to pursue traditional fields of study in the humanities, education, and the health professions. There they are destined for occupations enjoying less status and lower pay than that of men.

CONSTANCY IN SCHOOLING

You might wonder, since we know so much about schooling from a sociological perspective, why we still "do school" in ways which clearly contradict our research findings. Why are schools still organized and operated in much the same manner they were one hundred years ago? Why do we ignore research on individual differences and continue to educate children in batches, like cookies? Why do we say we venerate and respect teachers, and then refuse to pay them well or trust their judgement about what they teach? Why do we still believe that education is necessary in order to get ahead economically? Why, when it is clear that benefits from schooling are directly proportional to how distant one is from being white, male and middle class, do we continue to urge children who differ from middle-class white males by race, class, and gender to believe that "education pays off?" Given demographic shifts which will mean that by the year 2000, the majority of students in the public schools will come from non-European (African, Asian, or Latin American) backgrounds (Hodgkison 1985), why do those involved in planning and administration of educational programs ignore the needs of a growing multicultural student population?

Part of the answer can be found in Tom Robbins' delightful novel, *Jitterbug Perfume*. Robbins writes, "The Universe does not have laws. It has habits. And habits can be broken" (Robbins 1984, p. 283). Schools, like Robbins' universe, run on old habits. For example, when you ask teachers why they put children into three groups for reading, they may tell you that they've always done it that way. The practice is reinforced and legitimated by advice provided in the teachers' guides for basal readers. Much of what happens in and to schools is done because of habit.

Another part of the answer lies in the expectations which parents and communities hold for the practice of schooling and their resistance to new ways to organize schools and teaching procedures. Almost everyone has attended school for some long period of time. Almost everyone feels that they "know about" schools and what they are like. Parents who benefitted from school tend to want schools to be run in much the same way they were when *they* were children, and to have the same supposed effects. You might hear them say, "It was good enough for me; it ought to be good enough for my kids, too." Disadvantaged parents express the same kind of conservatism, but for different reasons: they have observed the benefits which schooling seems to have provided for the children of the middle and upper classes and fear that innovative programs will be inferior. They want their children to have the same kinds of advantages—hence the same kinds of schooling—which traditionally have benefitted the dominant groups in society.

Imagine what would happen if all schools suddenly were to discontinue compensatory education, ability grouping and academic tracking practices. Teachers would be up in arms, ignoring research findings which demonstrate that tracking actually widens the differences among children, and benefits only those in the highest tracks. They would simply feel overloaded with the wide ranges of ability in their classrooms. Middle class parents would storm the barricades, protesting to principals, school board members, and the legislatures that the life chances of their children had been impaired because teachers would be spending all their time on slow learners at the expense of the more able. Despite evidence that many so-called compensatory education programs are not targeted to instruction, that the programs often don't actually raise achievement, and that they often actually benefit students other than the target populations, disadvantaged parents would complain that without the special treatment, their children would slide even farther behind.

Imagine further, that all programs of standardized testing were eliminated. That schools were no larger than 400 students—as has been recommended by us (LeCompte and Goebel 1987; LeCompte and Dworkin, 1988; Dworkin and LeCompte 1989) and by a recent Carnegie Commission Report (1989). Imagine that the requirements for employment were demonstrated background in the arts, humanities, literature and mathematics, not a diploma. That it would not be possible to find an all-white, or even a two-thirds white, classroom.

If people, particularly teachers and administrators, were able to distance themselves personally from their long cherished notions about teaching and school organization and take a moment to contemplate the adverse consequences which their activities have for poor and minority children, they most likely would ask, "How else can you do it? What are the alternatives?" In the final portion of this text, we will engage in some intellectual play with these questions. Based upon what we have learned from the sociologists of education, we will present a few alternatives to the way we "do school." We present these alternatives in four separate categories: (1) issues which address the relationship between schools and their communities; (2) the structure of schools; (3) teacher education and classroom practice; and (4) the ideological nature of schooling, the curriculum, and instructional practices. We offer these suggestions as a mere beginning—a way for students and teachers to think in new ways about schooling and to raise questions about their own teaching and learning practices, as well as about the policies which have been implemented in their own school districts. We have tried not to be Utopian. We have restricted our own suggestions to things which are now in practice in some innovative schools or that we feel that current school districts might be able to accomplish. We hope that your thinking and questioning will not end with what we have suggested in this chapter.

SCHOOLS AND COMMUNITIES

Sociologists have been criticized for the terribly gloomy portrait they paint of the role of schools in social transformation; this is particularly true of reproduction theorists. In suggesting that the genesis of many problems which schools are called upon to solve lie outside the ability of schools to affect, sociologists seem to have left educators with little to do but wish for a more humane society. While it is true that schools are more weakly linked to the economic and social foundations of society than either educators or reformers would like to believe, it still is the case that there is much that schools can do.

School Scheduling

Perhaps the most important act schools might do is to take a serious look at the conditions in which students now live, and to arrange the schedule of the school day, the types of training, and the services available so that they more closely correspond to what students need. One consideration might be the recognition that the 12-year-limit on elementary and high school attendance—reinforced by state funding formulas—is unrealistic. Some students are slower learners, some must work for a living, or just need extra time to take on a particularly difficult program. Students who are gifted in music, the performing arts or athletics may need time off for competitions or for extra practice; they lose out when they either can't make up their classes or must give up their competitions. Often these are the students who are pushed out of school. Precedent for changing this arrangement exists; "special" or handicapped students can take additional years to finish their educational program—to age 21.

There also exists precedent for arranging the school year to correspond with the labor needs of society; the long public school summer vacations are a relic from an agricultural past, when student labor was needed on the farms during the growing season. Changes in the scheduling of the school calendar according to the needs of the community could serve to promote better working relationships between schools and parents as well as to provide for educational services unique to that community's students.

School schedules also could be re-arranged to recognize that the parents or guardians of most children work and can neither come to school during the day for conferences nor be at home after school to baby-sit or help with homework. These accommodations would help make parent involvement programs less an excuse for teachers to pass on blame and a source of guilt for parents.

Further, daycare needs to be found for the *children* of school children—the babies of teenagers who drop out of school when they can find no satisfactory or affordable child care. Currently, the majority of black babies born today are the children of unmarried adolescents. The numbers of teenaged mothers from other ethnic groups is also rising astronomically. Most teenage mothers choose to keep their babies, and most find few incentives and little assistance to remain in school (Hess and Green 1988). Programs which establish infant-care on public school campuses have been notably helpful in assuring continued school attendance and as well as better childcare among young mothers. Funds for these programs might come from re-direction of vocational education monies, about which we comment below.

Schools and the Labor Market

A closer look at the skills needed in the labor market also needs to be taken, with special emphasis on vocational training. Most public schools cannot afford to offer the state of the art training required for technical and industrial jobs. Employers often prefer to find literate job candidates and do their own training. Students in vocational programs, then, find themselves doubly short-changed; not only are they insufficiently well-trained in the basic cognitive skills to satisfy potential employers, but they also have spent years in vocational training which is outdated, obsolete, and leads only to dead-end jobs. We have argued elsewhere that the best vocational training possible is a good liberal arts education (LeCompte 1987a, 1987b; LeCompte and Dworkin 1988). A corollary is that we might recommend eliminating vocational education as a separate track altogether. In its place could be a program in which *all* students studied health, nutrition, automobile mechanics, carpentry, data processing and small engine repair as part of the skills they need for every day modern living—in addition to reading, mathematics, science, the arts, and social studies.

THE STRUCTURE OF SCHOOLS

Alternative Possibilities

How could schools be organized to better meet the needs of a diverse population? What are the issues of power in schools which need to be addressed? Who should determine how schools are structured? In this section we examine some of these questions and offer several suggestions.

As we described in Chapter Two, the most salient feature of school organization today is its size and complexity. Schools and school districts currently are organized into very large, multilayered regionally consolidated bureaucratic organizations. These complexes have replaced the smaller community schools which were the norm until the early twentieth century. It is true that the larger number of students which consolidation aggregated did facilitate the provision of more diverse curricular and extracurricular offerings. However, in schooling, big is not necessarily better. Increased size has come at the expense of the sense of community and belonging which schools often could create. They also have lost the capacity for flexibility, a characteristic which makes them able to accommodate to the varied needs and capabilities of students. Schools have, in our opinion, become so big and complex that teachers, students and administrators can no longer perform in them the work that large schools were designed to do. Recent research indicates that the bigger the school the higher are the dropout rates, especially for minority students (Turner 1989). Consistently, sociometric analysis shows that students are happier and have higher levels of participation in smaller schools. Regardless of their size, schools which, while conforming to overall structural rules, still bend them enough to facilitate increased social and academic engagement of their students tend to have reduced dropout rates, even among students who are learning disabled and from minority backgrounds (Miller, Leinhardt, and Zigmond 1988). Similarly, teachers feel more competent and more satisfied when they feel that they have some control over their work; they feel more alienated and less in control when they do not feel that they have supportive administrators and when they work in impersonal, highly bureaucratized school districts (Dworkin 1987; Dworkin, Lorence, and LeCompte 1989).

Teaching and learning are *social* acts, it is true, but they are *intimate* social acts, facilitated by the close personal attention and care of those who engage in them. As we have pointed out, intimacy and contemporary schools are virtually oxymoronic terms, made mutually exclusive by, among other things, their size. This has been a function of factors such as the school consolidation movements, urbanization, and the proliferation of tasks which schools are called upon to perform. Yet, we believe that one structural variable over which schools *do* have control is that of size. To that end, we propose that the school consolidation clock be rolled back, such that the optimum size for elementary schools be pegged at about 300 students, and for secondary schools, 200 per grade level, with a maximum of 600 students. This means that schools with four grades would have a grade level limit of 150 each. These configurations can be accomplished within existing buildings with innovative scheduling; where they exist, old buildings can be re-opened or new ones can be constructed on a much smaller scale.

Some experiments in reducing school size, particularly at the secondary level, are being attempted; one of the better known plans is in New York City. There a plan has been implemented to create "houses", or institutes for incoming freshmen in each of its 118 high schools. The aim is to reduce the potential for dropping out by providing smaller and more personal forms of organization. In one very large school of 3,330 students, nine such institutes have been formed for ninth and tenth graders, based upon themes and occupational interests. None of the themes are particularly unusual; they include law and justice, business careers, cultural arts, college bound, special education, bilingual education, English as a second language, and two others referred to as "just communities." However, the institutes or houses limit the number of students in each and provide a staff who works solely within that institute, becoming familiar and concerned with the total learning experience of their students and breaking down subject matter boundaries so that teachers become generalists. This form or organization also creates a different governance structure in which committees representing three separate interests in the school—teachers, students and the curriculum specialists—select representatives to meet with the principal on a daily basis. The organizational aim of the school is to create a more democratic governing body within the school. It

> has attacked anonymity by allowing teachers to take some initiatives, allowing some positive decision-making, and allowing kids to feel that they not

only belong to something, but they have some interest in its success (*Education Week*, March 1, 1989, p. 7)

This type of innovation illustrates the potential for large urban and suburban school districts to reorganize into smaller communities or units while staying within budget constraints and maintaining the size necessary to provide the educational alternatives offered by a consolidated high school.

Other forms of decentralization hold promise, although their claims have yet to be substantiated beyond subjective enthusiasm and they often have been clouded by scandals and charges of corruption. These include school or site-based management and the establishment of local community school boards with substantial financial and curricular control. Yet to be accomplished is a careful examination of the real impact on organizational structure of centralized systems of testing and evaluation. There is substantial evidence that these consume more than their fair share of instructional time, notwithstanding their apparent impact on teacher morale. It may be that, like the school consolidation movement, the educational testing movement may have reached the point of diminishing returns. Eliminating testing programs, as some districts have begun to do, increases instructional time and makes the curriculum more flexible.

Even more critical to overall school organization would be a radical departure from age-grading. We now "batch-process" children. From the elementary school level on, children are categorized by age and locked into movement through the grades one year at a time, with complete disregard for what we have learned from sociologists and psychologists about the most appropriate ways to organize learning for children.

The National Association for the Education of Young Children consistently has urged districts to adopt what they refer to as "developmentally appropriate practice" which gears schools to the developmental, rather than the chronological ages of children. This permits children to learn through activities appropriate for their developmental stage and to move through the curriculum in accordance with their levels of readiness. This type of teaching and learning situation has been termed a multi-graded unit, or multi-aged grouping. The emphasis is moved from didactic teaching of content to providing appropriate learning activities through which children acquire content. Not only does this arrangement change the way children learn, but it drastically alters the role of the teacher. They can no longer "rule" from the top down, but must preside over a multitude of activities, using their professional expertise to work with students in a wide range of ways.

The Problem of Power and Institutional Inertia

Where sociologists have been criticized for being too gloomy about the prospects for reform of schooling, educational researchers have been criticized for being naive or Utopian. Regardless of how insightful their work has been, much of it remains unused. As Ernest Boyer of the Carnegie Foundation for the Advancement of Teaching says:

> We've made remarkable breakthroughs in understanding the development of children, the development of learning, and the climate that enhances [them, but too often] what we know in theory and what we're doing in the classroom are very different. (Kantrowitz and Wingert 1989, p. 51)

The issue is, how does what we know get translated into what we do? How does our sociological knowledge of schooling help us to bring about change?

A key element is an understanding of how power affects processes of change in the structure of organizations. And it has been the insights of sociology which have made clear that schools and schools districts are not a-political institutions in which the exercise of power is irrelevant. People who have power are not interested in giving it away, whether they are school administrators, state bureaucrats, or old-line teachers. Many people, including school administrators and teachers, prefer to work in hierarchial structures where roles are governed by traditional habits and practice. However, despite the deeply entrenched nature of conventional practice in schooling, we believe that redistribution of power in schools is necessary for teachers to gain control over their work and their workplace. Implicit in our thinking, and that of critical theorists, is that change needs to begin at the bottom of the hierarchy. We also believe that confrontation needs to occur at the level of policy and power as well.

Unfortunately, teacher training as it currently is arranged does not prepare its students for the political arena—either on the micro or the macro level. By retaining what we call a "psycho-centric" focus on individual differences and cognition, teacher training has avoided confronting the social and political context of schooling altogether. This makes new teachers exceedingly vulnerable to pressure once they are out in the schools, prone to sliding into teaching at the lowest common denominator for survival, and to accepting the conventional wisdom of senior teachers about "how it's always been." This is why we have advocated explicit training and practice in the critical and political for preservice teachers; in-service activities for practicing teachers also could make good use of such instruction.

TEACHER EDUCATION AND CLASSROOM PRACTICE

The Teacher as Intellectual

What types of teachers are needed to provide quality schooling in a multicultural world? How should these teachers be educated? What is the role of teachers in schools today? The 1980s brought a new reform movement in teacher education calling for complete restructuring of the profession. One set of critics was based in universities and colleges of education; the other found its impetus in school districts and state legislatures. The former provided their central arguments in two documents—The Holmes Group's *Tomorrow's Teachers* (1986) and the

Carnegie Task Force on Teaching as a Profession's *A Nation Prepared: Teachers for the 21st Century* (1986). They call for a more highly educated professional teaching force.

The Holmes Group proposed a five-year program in which students would pursue a fifth year of teacher education after their completion of a liberal arts degree. The underlying assumption to this proposal is that a liberal arts degree in a particular academic field would provide preservice teachers with the knowledge base necessary to teach, while the fifth year would furnish the pedagogical knowledge and experience for successful teaching of that subject matter. These reforms leave control of entrance to the teaching profession in the hands of the university teacher training programs.

A counter proposal, calling for alternative routes to certification, has been spearheaded largely by school district personnel who feel that college teaching is out of touch with the realities of public school life, and who resent the poor preparation of many teachers. While the content of such routes to teacher certification does not differ from that proposed by the Holmes Group, the control mechanisms do. They seek to weaken or to eliminate altogether the role of colleges of education in teacher preparation. One approach places certification of teachers in the hands of school districts. It calls for the establishment of district level "teacher centers," where the methods courses and other certification requirements would be provided. People who already have degrees would enter a teacher center, take courses, and while taking them, begin an apprenticeship of teaching under the supervision of the school district. A variation calls for the teacher center to be located in a local teachers' college, but for all other activities to be carried out by the district. Still others call for centers to be established and examinations to be given under state education agency supervision, with districts again providing the supervised apprenticeships.

These plans differ substantially from traditional teacher training programs which have been in place in colleges of education throughout most of the twentieth century. The extreme case is the field of elementary education, where a teacher trainee is limited to two years of academic training, a year and a half of methods—or "Mickey Mouse—courses, and student teaching, leaving college with no real specialization whatsoever.

The demand for a more rigorously educated teaching force has gained support from both the radical left and neo-conservative right. The call for raising entrance standards, increasing the number and rigor of classes, and establishing tests for exit level competencies conforms to the neo-conservative "back to the classics" excellence movement in education as propounded by former President Reagan's Secretary of Education, William Bennett. These proposals argue from the "top down" for more centralized state control over the training and evaluation of students and teachers. They are based upon a deep suspicion that teachers cannot be trusted to work competently and the belief that only a program of tight and centralized control over teachers and their training will put things right.

On the left, critical theorists like Henry Giroux (1988) argue for the concept of "teachers as intellectuals." Contrary to the neo-conservatives, critical theorists argue for less, rather than more control over teachers. In fact, their wish is to shift the locus of power from state, university and district administrators to the classroom teacher. Giroux argues that current demands for reform in teacher education are at variance with the democratically informed schooling needed in an increasingly pluralistic society. Giroux challenges the current proposals, stating that they lead to de-skilling of teachers—the process by which teachers lose the ability to utilize professional training, judgment and autonomy in the service of their jobs. He argues that a "teacher-proof" standardized curriculum, uniform text adoptions, centralized and test-driven systems of student evaluation and placement, routinized classroom management systems, and the reduction in decision-making power—all act to reduce teachers to mere technicians. He further calls for a complete restructuring of the work of teachers so that they are viewed as valued intellectuals, not barely competent, mindless technicians. The first step in this process would be the transfer of instructional control from administrators, state bureaucrats and textbook publishers to teachers. As intellectual leaders, teachers would be responsible for determining the goals of schooling—or what knowledge should be taught, how these goals would be translated into curricular materials, and how the materials should be taught.

Central to Giroux's argument is the concept of the teacher as a critical pedagogue or transformative intellectual. To be intellectually critical educators, teachers must not only be intellectuals in the sense that they reflect seriously on the meaning and consequences of their practice, but critical in the sense that they question the taken-for-granted assumptions—the "that's the way it's always been"—of school practice and societal organization. Critical pedagogues have the *responsibility* to question political motives and social inequities with their students in an ongoing effort to create a more democratic and equitable society. Giroux is worth quoting at length on the role of teachers as transformative intellectuals:

> Transformative intellectuals need to develop a discourse that unites the language of critique with the language of possibility, so that social educators recognize that they can make changes. In doing so, they must speak out against economic, political and social injustices, both within and outside of schools. At the same time, they must work to create the conditions that give students the opportunity to become citizens who have the knowledge and courage to struggle in order to make despair unconvincing and hope practical. As difficult as this task may seem to social educators, it is a struggle worth waging. To do otherwise is to deny social educators the opportunity to assume the role of transformative intellectuals. (Giroux 1988, p. 128)

There are limitations in Giroux' critique. First, neither neo-conservatives nor critical theorists have addressed the impact of their proposals on the participation of minorities in the teaching profession. On the one hand is a concern that raising standards and increasing the length—and cost—of teacher training would make it much more difficult for minority individuals to become teachers

(Halcon and Reyes 1989). On the other is a concern that advocating radical change would threaten the legitimacy and acceptance of minority teachers. Standing too far from the standards of conventional practice might well place such teachers, already in the minority on most faculties, at risk in their districts and in danger of being fired—or at least ostracized professionally—as trouble-makers.

Another concern is that it is difficult to imagine how today's teachers could be critical, intellectual pedagogues given the limits of their preparation, the structural constraints on their activities and the oppressive working environments in which most of them work. Implicit in Giroux' notion of the teacher as transformative intellectual is a critique of the entire system of schooling. Clearly, a complete restructuring is required if teachers are to be reflective, have their skills, expertise and creativity celebrated, and work in situations which do not denigrate their sense of professionalism.

Unfortunately, both the neo-conservative right and the radical left reform calls focus primarily on teachers. This may be because blaming teachers is relatively easy; they have no powerful national association with which to mount a counterattack. It may be due to an optimistic hope that only through a "grass roots" community-based organization of teachers will significant changes in schooling be accomplished. Much more difficult is addressing the structural and political constraints which have created the radically alienating conditions prevalent in many contemporary schools. Later in this chapter, we will present alternatives for the structure of public schools which would help teachers to begin to function in the ways prescribed by critical theorists.

Teachers as Feminists

We have defined the term hegemony in the preceding chapters and shown how hegemony consists of the practices and thinking which justify existing patterns of domination and subordination in society. In this section, we begin to look at ways in which the educational system might begin to question these patterns, first by permitting teachers to become "feminists" as defined below, and second by questioning the ways minorities and poor people are treated in the schools.

We demonstrated in Chapter Four that teaching is a predominantly female activity. In fact, schools resemble "pedagogical harems," where women teach and men supervise them and administer the system. Increasing the professional status of teaching, in our view as well as that of scholars like Apple, Blau, Kelly, Lortie, Simeone, Weiler, Weis and others cited in previous chapters, cannot be discussed without considering the engendered nature and patriarchal structure of schooling. The unequal distribution of power among men and women is one of the most salient features of the profession, and it is one which undermines its status. As long as teaching is considered to be "women's work," neither it nor its participants will enjoy the power and prestige they seek. Below is defined the kind of awareness which we call feminism:

> A person, female or male, whose world view places the female in the center
> of life and society, and/or who is not prejudiced based on gender or sexual
> preference. Also, anyone in a male-dominated or patriarchal society who
> works toward the political, economic, spiritual, sexual, and social equality
> of women. (Kramarae & Treichler 1985)

Only through gaining such awareness can teachers begin to question the
legitimacy of the current male-dominated hierarchy of schools in order to gain a
voice in the decision-making process which directly affects their workplace.
Feminist teachers are those who are sensitive to and address directly issues of
gender inequality in the curricular content, instructional methods and organization of schools. Their knowledge of gender and power issues enables them to be
able to assess their own and their students experiences in schools, question the
oppressive aspects of these experiences and provide more democratic alternatives. Weiler (1988) suggests that feminist teachers, both male and female, are
more sensitive to and respectful of the racial, cultural and class identities of
their students as a consequence of having their awareness sharpened by knowledge of patterns of gender discrimination.

Recruitment to Teacher Education

What would teacher education look like from critical theoretical and feminist
perspectives? If you were to walk through the halls of most colleges of education in the United States today, you would find a fairly homogenous population
of white, middle class female students being taught by a fairly homogenous
population of white, middle class, male professors—despite an increasing number of young female and/or minority assistant professors. A salutary change
would occur if the population of colleges, among the ranks of both professors
and students, came to resemble more closely the general population of public
schools. Although minority recruitment programs have been in place in most
colleges for some years, the number of actual recruits is small and decreasing,
especially in colleges of education. The continued low status and salary of the
teaching profession as well as the lack of funds available to colleges of education for scholarships limit the number of minority students interested in pursuing
teaching as a career. In addition, as colleges move toward five year degree
plans, tuition costs soar, and the availability of financial aid continues to diminish, the actual hardships of attendance as well as the opportunity costs of
becoming a teacher become overwhelming to minority students who might wish
to become teachers.

Despite these barriers, it is essential for colleges of education to be sensitive to the type of students they are admitting into teacher education programs.
With the current reform movement's emphasis on "excellence," concerns about
race, ethnicity, class and gender balance may be obscured by concerns over
"quality." It will be easy for insensitive teacher educators to mistake being
white, middle-class, and comfortable with school culture for academic quality. A
college of education committed to preparing intellectual teachers for a multi-

cultural world will work to insure the comparable diversity of the student body. These colleges must be committed to recruiting and educating a multiethnic, gender-balanced teaching population.

THE CURRICULUM
AND INSTRUCTIONAL PRACTICE

The Multicultural Curriculum

A college committed to preparing students to teach in the multicultural schools of today also will place emphasis on courses and practical experiences which will prepare students for contact with teaching and learning among those who are ethnically, culturally and economically different from themselves. These materials should not be "ghettoized"—taught in isolated courses—or parts of courses—and only by minority faculty. The multicultural emphasis only achieves legitimacy when it ceases to be exotic, and becomes part and parcel of everyday life in every subject. Teaching in teams so that faculty become familiar with each other's subject areas and work toward integrating each—including material relevant to other races, classes and genders—into their instruction would facilitate a normalization of the currently exotic nature of both the multicultural content and the faculty who teach them. We suggest also that colleges go beyond advocating—and teaching—sensitivity to cultural differences. In addition, colleges should establish a "minimum competency" for tolerance, such that teacher candidates who demonstrate bigoted attitudes do not receive certificates to practice their trade. Such a competency is no more subjective than demonstrating competence to evaluate visual art or poetry.

An Interdisciplinary Perspective

Teachers can neither be critical, intellectuals nor competent if they have never experienced intellectual challenges nor been exposed to the world of content and ideas. With this in mind, we conform to certain aspects of the program of the neoconservative reformers, who call for basing reform of the curriculum on a liberal arts education. However, it is important to remember the multicultural curriculum we have emphasized in previous sections; liberal arts for us does not mean a return to a traditional androcentric and ethnocentric emphasis on classics of the Western European heritage. Rather, it means that students would specialize in a particular discipline of their choice for the requisite four year program, and only then enter a teacher education program which would prepare them for life and teaching in public school classrooms.

This preparation would be based upon an experiential study of schooling within its social context. Departing from the heavily cognitive orientation of contemporary teacher training programs, we propose to place greater emphasis on child and adolescent development, on the historical and philosophical antecedents of current practice, and on the social, political, and cultural context within and outside of schools and classrooms. These studies derive from what have come to be known as the foundations of education—history, philosophy, psychology, anthropology and sociology.

At the present time, despite the fact that whole children are the primary focus of what teachers do, teacher trainees take only an introductory course or two in human growth and development; their studies of psychology are narrowly limited to experimental and behavioral studies of cognition. Similarly, they get only the barest smattering of the other foundational studies, usually crammed into a single survey course covering the history, philosophy, sociology, anthropology and politics of education. Graduate programs are rarely more rigorous. The program we propose would create a much stronger emphasis on both psychological and social foundations in order to prepare teachers to examine and question current schooling practices and procedures, to analyze patterns of control and governance in education, and to provide a critique of text materials, instructional techniques, and classroom management strategies.

CREATING AN ALTERNATIVE IDEOLOGY OF SCHOOLING

The suggestions above are just a beginning. The popular press is full of other ideas; each week magazines like *Time* and *Newsweek*, *The Readers' Digest*, and nationally distributed newspapers like *The Wall Street Journal*, *USA Today*, *The New York Times*, and *The Washington Post* publish articles about the need for reform in education as well as case studies of innovative programs purporting to resolve some or all of the crisis in education. Yet the innovations, like cream, still float to the top, serving the most advantaged students, and programs for the most disadvantaged seem remarkably ineffective. We believe that the kinds of insights offered in this text provide a way of beginning a new kind of thinking about schools. What *are* the purposes of schooling in contemporary society? What *should* they be? Are the two compatible? How will the characteristics of the children enrolled in schools change in the next few years? What will the teaching force look like? How would it, and curricula, forms of control in schools, and instructional practice have to change to be congruent with the incoming population of children—and teachers? What can *you* do about it? Below are some exercises to help you begin to explore these questions.

EXERCISES

1. Find several articles in newspapers or current magazines which describe innovative educational programs. Examine the claims and counter-claims for their success. Do you think they are accurate? Are they realistic? Would they work in your home community? Why or why not? Where would they be ineffective, and why?

2. Visit a school (or classroom) in which alternative practices and structures are being used. How does this school compare to a more tradition-

ally organized school? Talk with some of the students and teachers about their experiences in this setting.

3. Watch the movie *Stand and Deliver*, an illustration of alternative teaching methods in a barrio school in Los Angeles. What worked for the teacher and students in this film? How was the teacher able to engage his students effectively? Do you think these methods would work in other settings?

4. Form small groups or committees in your class to design on paper a school based on the research knowledge presented in this text. Share your ideas in a whole group discussion. How could you incorporate some of these ideas into your real world of school practice?

SUGGESTED READINGS

Bastian, Ann et al. (1985). *Choosing equality: The ca,e for democratic schooling.* Philadelphia: Temple University Press.

Giroux, Henry. (1988). *Teachers as intellectuals: Toward a critical pedagogy of learning.* Bergin and Garvey Publishers, Inc.

Molner, Alex. (1987). *Social issues and education: A challenge and responsibility.* Alexandria, Vir.: Association for Supervision and Curriculum Development

Weiler, Kathleen. (1988). *Women Teaching for Change: Gender, Class and Power.* Bergin and Garvey Publishers, Inc.

Kramarae, C., and P. A. Treichler (Eds). (1985). *A feminist dictionary.* London: Pandora Press.

References

Abington School District v. *Schempp*, 374 U.S. 203 (1963).

Adams, R. S. & Biddle, B. J. (1970). *Realities of teaching.* New York: Holt, Rinehart & Winston.

Albjerg, P. G. (1974). *Community and class in American education.* 1865–1918. New York: John Wiley.

Allington, R. L. (1977). If they don't get to read much, how they ever gonna get good? *Journal of Reading, 21*(1), 57–61.

Allington, R. L. (1980a). Poor readers don't get to read much in reading groups. *Language Arts, 57,* 872–877.

Allington, R. L. (1980b). Teacher interruption behaviors during primary grade oral reading. *Journal of Educational Psychology, 72,* 371–377.

Allington, R. L. (1983). The reading provided readers of differing abilities. *Elementary School Journal, 83,* 548–559.

Allington, R. L. (1984). Content coverage and contextual reading in reading groups. *Journal of Reading Behavior, 16*(2), 85–96.

Allison, C. B. (1989). *Life history of MacArthur School.* Work in progress.

Allison, C. B. & Bennett, K. P. (1989). *Life in MacArthur High School: A case study.* Work in progress.

American Heritage Dictionary (1983). New York: Houghton Mifflin.

Anderson, B. D. & Mark, J. H. (1977). Teacher mobility and productivity in a metropolitan area: A seven year case study. *Urban Education, 12,* 15–36.

Anyon, J. (1983). Workers, labor and economic history, and textbook content. In M. W. Apple & L. Weis (Eds.), *Ideology and practice in schooling* (pp. 37–60). Philadelphia: Temple University Press.

Anyon, J. (1988). Schools as agencies of social legitimation. In W. F. Pinar (Ed.), *Contemporary curriculum discourses* (pp. 175–200). Scottsdale, AZ: Gorsuch Scarisbrick.

Apple, M. W. (1978). The new sociology of education: Analyzing cultural and economic reproduction. *Harvard Educational Review, 48*, 495–503.

Apple, M. W. (1979). *Ideology and curriculum*. Boston: Routledge & Kegan Paul.

Apple, M. W. (1982). *Education and power*. Boston: Routledge & Kegan Paul.

Apple, M. W. (1986). *Teachers and texts: A political economy of class & gender relations in education*. New York: Metheun.

Apple, M. W. (1988). *Teachers and texts*. New York: Routledge & Kegan Paul.

Apple, M. W. & Weis, L. (Eds.). (1983). *Ideology and practice in schooling*. Philadelphia: Temple University Press.

Aries, P. (1962). *Centuries of childhood: A social history of family life*. New York: Vintage Books.

Armor, D. (1969). *The American high school counselor*. New York: Russell Sage Foundation.

Aronowitz, S. & Giroux, H. (1985). *Education under seige*. South Hadley, MA: Bergin & Garvey.

Ashcroft, L. (1987). Diffusing "Empowering": The what and the why. *Language Arts, 64*(2), 142–156.

Au, K. H. (1979). Using the experience-text relationship with minority children. *The Reading Teacher, 32*, 677–679.

Au, K. H. (1980). Participant structures in a reading lession with Hawaiian children: Analysis of a culturally appropriate instructional event. *Anthropology and Education Quarterly, 11*, 91–115.

Au, K. H. & Jordan, C. (1981). Teaching reading to Hawaiian children: Finding a culturally appropriate solution. In H. Trueba, G. P. Guthrie & K.H. Au (Eds.). *Culture and the bilingual classroom: Studies in classroom ethnography*, 139–152. Rowley, MA: Newbury House.

Au, K. H. & Mason, J. (1981). Social organizational factors in learning to read: The balance of rights hypothesis. *Reading Research Quarterly, 17*, 139–152.

Ayella, M. E. & Williamson, J. B. (1976). The social mobility of women: A causal model of socioeconomic success. *The Sociological Quarterly, 17*, 334–354.

Ballantine, J. H. (1983). *The sociology of education: A systematic analysis*. Englewood Cliffs, NJ: Prentice-Hall.

Banks, J. A. (1979). *Teaching strategies for ethnic studies* (2nd ed.). Boston: Allyn & Bacon.

Banks, J. A. (1988). *Multiethnic education: Theory and practice* (2nd ed). Boston: Allyn & Bacon.

Baratz, S. S. & J. C. (1970). Early childhood intervention: The social science base of institutional racism. *Harvard Educational Review, 40*, 29–50.

Barker, R. G., & Gump, P. V. (1964). *Big school, small school*. Stanford, CA: Stanford University Press.

Barnhart, C. (1982). "Tuning-in": Athabaskan teachers and Athabaskan students. In R. Barnhardt (Ed.). *Cross-Cultural Issues in Alaskan Education. Vol. 2* (pp. 144–164). Fairbanks, AK: University of Alaska Center for Cross-Cultural Studies.

Barr, R. C. (1974). Instructional pace differences and their effect on reading acquisition. *Reading Research Quarterly, 9*, 526–554.

Barr, R. C. (1975). How children are taught to read: Grouping and pacing. *School Review, 83*, 479–498.

Barr, R. C. (1982). Classroom reading instruction from a sociological perspective. *Journal of Reading Behavior, 14*, 375–389.

Basso, K. H. (1984). "Stalking with stories": Names, places and moral narratives among the Western Apache. In E. M. Bruner (Ed.), *Text, play and story: The construction and reconstruction of self and society* (pp. 19–56). Washington, DC: Proceedings of the American Ethnological Society.

Bastian, A., Fruchter, N., Gittell, M., Greer, C., & Haskins, K. (1985). *Choosing equality: The case for democratic schooling.* Philadelphia: Temple University Press.

Becker, G. (1964). *Human capital: A theoretical and empirical analysis with special reference to education.* New York: Columbia University Press.

Becker, H. S. (1953). The teacher in the authority system of the public school. *Journal of Educational Sociology, 27,* 128–141.

Becker, H. S., Geer, B., Hughes, E.C. & Strauss, A.L. (1961). *Boys in white: Student culture in medical school.* Chicago: University of Chicago Press.

Belenky, M. F., Clinchy, B. M., Goldberger, N. R., & Tarule J. M. (1986). *Women's ways of knowing: The development of self, voice, and mind.* New York: Basic Books.

Bennett, E. W. (1988). *James Madison High School.* Washington, DC: U.S. Office of Education.

Bennett, K. P. (1986). *Study of reading ability grouping and its consequences for urban Appalachian first graders.* Unpublished doctoral dissertation, University of Cincinnati.

Bennett, K. P. (1988a). *Yup'ik Eskimo storyknifing: Young girls at play.* Unpublished manuscript.

Bennett, K. P. (1988b). *Yup'ik women's ways of knowing.* Charleston, WV: ERIC Clearinghouse on Rural Education and Small Schools. (Eric Document Reproduction Service No. ED 301 401)

Bensman, J., & Vidich, A. J. (1971). *The new American society: The revolution of the middle class.* Chicago: Quadrangle Books.

Benson, C. S. (1982). The deregulation of schools: Views from the federal, state and local levels. [Editor's introduction]. *Education and Urban society, 14,* 395–397.

Berger, J. (1989, June 18). New York study of welfare clients. False practices of trade schools. *New York Times,* p. A.9.

Berger, P. L., & Luckmann, T. (1967). *The social construction of reality: A treatise in the sociology of knowledge.* New York: Anchor Books.

Bernardi, B. (1952). The age system of the Nilotic Hamitic people. *Africa, 22,* 316–332.

Bernardi, B. (1985). *Age class systems, social institutions and policies based on age.* New York: Cambridge.

Bernstein, B. (1970). *Class, codes and control. Vol. I: Theoretical studies towards a sociology of language.* London: Routledge & Kegan Paul.

Bernstein, B. (1977). *Class, codes and control. Vol. III: Towards a theory of educational transmission.* London: Routledge & Kegan Paul.

Betz, M., & Garland, J. (1974). Intergenerational mobility rates of urban school teachers. *Sociology of Education, 47,* 511–522.

Bidwell, C. E. (1965). The school as a formal organization. In J. G. March (Ed.) *The handbook of organizations* (pp. 972–1022). New York: Rand McNally.

Binder, F. H. (1974). *The age of the common school, 1830–1865.* New York: John Wiley.

Blau, P. M. (1955). *The dynamics of bureaucracy.* Chicago: University of Chicago Press.

Blau, P. M., & Duncan, O. D. (1967). *The American occupational structure.* New York: John Wiley.

Blau, P. M., & Scott, W. R. (1962). *Formal organizations: A comparative approach.* San Francisco: Chandler.

Blaug, M. (1970). *An introduction to the economics of education.* London: Allen Lane.

Blaug, M. (1976). Human capital theory: A slightly jaundiced survey. *Journal of Economic Literature, 14,* 827–856.

Bloom, A. (1987). *The closing of the American mind.* New York: Simon & Schuster.

Bluestone, B., & Harrison, B. (1982). *The de-industrialization of America.* New York: Basic Books.

Blumberg, Arthur. *The school superintendent: Living with conflict.* New York: Teachers College Press, 1985, p. xiii.

Blumer, H. (1969). *Symbolic interactionism: Perspectives and method.* Englewood Cliffs, NJ: Prentice-Hall.

Bobbitt, J. F. (1912). The elimination of waste in education. *The Elementary School Teacher, 12,* 259–271.

Boehnlein, M. M. (1985). *Children, parents, and reading: An annotated bibliography.* Newark, DE: International Reading Association.

Boggs, C. (1976). *Gramsci's Marxism.* London: Pluto Press.

Boocock, S. S. (1980). *Sociology of education: An introduction* (2nd ed.). Boston: Houghton Mifflin.

Borko, H., & Eisenhart, M. (1986). Student's conceptions of reading and their reading experience in school. *The Elementary School Journal, 86,* 589–612.

Borman, K. M. (1987). Entering the workplace in the USA. In J. Mortimer & K. Borman (Eds.), *Work experience and psychological development through the lifespan* (pp. 00). Boulder, CO: Westview Press.

Borman, K. M., & Mueninghoff, E. (1982). Work roles and social roles in three elementary school settings. Paper presented at the meeting of the American Educational Research Association, New York.

Borman, K. M., & Mueninghoff, E. (1983). Lower Price Hill's children: Family, school and neighborhood. In A. Batteau (Ed.), *Appalachia and America* (pp. 210–224). Lexington, KY: University Press of Kentucky.

Borman, K. M., & Spring, J. H. (1984). *Schools in central cities.* New York: Longman.

Bossert, S. T. (1979). *Tasks and social relationships in classrooms: A study of instructional organization and its consequences.* Cambridge: Cambridge University Press.

Bottomore, T. (1984). *The Frankfurt School.* New York: Tavistock.

Boudon, R. (1974). *Education, opportunity, and social inequality: Changing prospects in western society.* New York: John Wiley.

Bourdieu, P., & Passeron, J. (1977). *Reproduction in education, society and culture.* London: Sage.

Bowers, A. W. (1965). *Hidatsa social and ceremonial organization* (Bulletin 194). Washington, DC: Smithsonian Institution Bureau of American Ethnology.

Bowles, S., & Gintis, H. (1976). *Schooling in capitalist America: Educational reform and the contradictions of economic life.* New York: Basic Books.

Boyd, W. (1966). *The history of western education* (8th ed.). New York: Barnes & Noble.

Boyd, W. L., & Crowson, R. L. (1981). The changing conception and practice of public school administration. In D. C. Berliner (Ed.) *Review of Research in Education. Vol. 9* (pp. 311–377). Washington, DC: American Educational Research Association.

Braddock, J. H., Crain, R. L., & McPartland, J. M. (1984). A long-term view of school desegregation: Some recent studies of graduates as adults. *Phi Delta Kappan*, *66*, 259–264.

Bredo, E. (1989). *After positivism, what?* Paper presented at the meeting of the American Educational Research Association, San Francisco.

Bredekamp, S. (Ed.). (1986). *Developmentally appropriate practice.* Washington, DC: National Association for the Education of Young Children.

Brenton, M. (1974). Teachers organizations: The new militancy. In E. A. Useem & M. Useem (Eds.), *The education establishment* (pp. 60–69). Englewood Cliffs, NJ: Prentice-Hall.

Brookover, W. B., & Erickson, E. L. (1975). *Sociology of education.* Homewood, IL: The Dorsey Press.

Brophy, J. E., & Good, T. L. (1970). Teachers' communication of differential expectations for children's classroom performance: Some behavioral data. *Journal of Educational Psychology*, *61*, 365–374.

Brown v. *Board of Education of Topeka*, KS, 349 U.S. 294 (1954).

Brown, R. (1986). State responsibility for at-risk youth. *Metropolitan Education*, *2*, 5–12.

Burtonwood, N. (1986). *The culture concept in educational studies.* Philadelphia, PA: Nfer-Nelson.

Butts, R. F. (1978). *Public education in the United States: From revolution to reform.* New York: Holt, Rinehart & Winston.

Butts, R. F., & Cremin, L. A. (1953). *A history of education in American culture.* New York: Holt.

Callahan, R. (1962). *Education and the cult of efficiency.* Chicago: University of Chicago Press.

Campbell, R. T. (1983). Status attainment research: End of the beginning or beginning of the end? *Sociology of Education*, *56*, 47–62.

Carnegie Task Force on Teaching as a Profession. (1986). *A nation prepared: Teachers for the 21st century.* New York: Carnegie Foundation.

Carnegie Commission Report. (1989). *Preparing American youth for the 21st century.* Washington, DC: Carnegie Council on Adolescent Development.

Carnoy, M. (Ed.). (1972). *Schooling in a corporate society: The political economy of education in America.* New York: McKay.

Carnoy, M., & Levin, H. M. (1976). *The limits of educational reform.* New York: McKay.

Carnoy, M., & Levin, H. M. (1985). *Schooling and work in the democratic state.* Stanford, CA: Stanford University Press.

Carroll, T. G. (1975). Transactions of cognitive equivalence in the domains of "work" and "play." *Anthropology and Education Quarterly*, *6*, 17–22.

Cazden, C. B., John, V. P., & Hymes, D. (Eds.). (1974). *Functions of language in the classroom.* New York: Teachers College Press.

Chafetz, J. S., & Dworkin, A. G. (1986). *Female revolt: Women's movements in world and historical perspective.* Totowa, NJ: Rowan & Allanheld.

Chandler, J. (1981). Camping for life: Transmission of values at a girls' summer camp. In R. T. Sieber & A. J. Gordon (Eds). *Children and their organizations: Investigations in American culture* (pp. 122–137). Boston: G. K. Hall.

Charters, W. W., Jr. (1970). Some factors affecting teacher survival in school districts. *American Educational Research Journal*, *7*, 1–27.

Children's Defense Fund. (1988). *A call for action to make our nation safe for children: A briefing book on the status of American children in 1988.* Washington, DC: Children's Defense Fund.

Chowdorow, N. (1978). *The reproduction of mothering.* Berkeley, CA: University of California Press.

Cicourel, A. V. (1964). *Method and measurement in sociology.* New York: The Free Press.

Cicourel, A. V., & Kituse, J. (1963). *The educational decision makers.* Indianapolis: Bobbs-Merrill.

Cleary, E. L. (1985). *Crisis and change: The church in Latin America today.* Maryknoll, NY: Orbis Books.

Cohen, J., & Rogers, J. (1983). *On democracy: Toward a transformation of American society.* Middlesex, England: Penguin Books.

Cole, M., & Griffin, P. (Eds). (1987). *Contextual factors in education: Improving science and mathematics for minorities and women.* Madison, WI: Wisconsin Center for Education Research.

Coleman, J. S. (1961). *The adolescent society.* Glencoe, IL: The Free Press.

Coleman, J. S. (1965). *Adolescents and the schools* New York: Basic Books.

Coleman, J. S. (1966). *Equality of educational opportunity.* Washington DC: U.S. Government Printing Office.

Coleman, J. S., Hoffer, T., & Kilgore, S. (1982). *High school achievement: Public, Catholic and private schools compared.* New York: Basic Books.

Coleman, J. S., & Hoffer, T. (1987). *Public and private schools: The impact of communities.* New York: Basic Books.

Collins, G. (1987, November 25). Day care for infants: Debate turns to long term effects. *The New York Times,* p. B9.

Collins, R. (1977). Functional and conflict theories of educational stratification. In J. Karabel & A. H. Kalsey (Eds.), *Power and ideology in education* (pp. 118–136). Cambridge: Oxford University Press.

Conant, J. (1988, February 15). Alaska's suicide epidemic. *Newsweek* p. 61.

Connell, R. W. (1985). *Teacher's work.* North Sydney, Australia: George Allen & Unwin.

Corwin, R. G. (1965). *Sociology of education.* New York: Appleton.

Corwin, R. G. (1970). *Militant professionalism: A study of organizational conflicts in high school.* New York: Appleton-Century-Crofts.

Coser, L. A. (1956). *The functions of social conflict.* Glencoe, IL: Free Press.

Counts, G. (1932). *Dare the school build a new social order.* New York: John Day.

Crow, M. L. (1985). The female educator at midlife. *Phi Delta Kappan, 67,* 281–284.

Cuban, L. (1984). *How teachers taught: Constancy and change in American classrooms, 1890–1980.* New York: Longman.

Cull, D. (1989, January 14). Elected officials proliferate. *New York Times,* p. 6.

Curti, M. (1971). *The social ideas of American educators.* Totowa, NJ: Littlefield, Adams & Company.

Cusick, P. A. (1983). *The egalitarian ideal and the American high school.* New York: Longman.

Dalton, G. W., Barnes, L. B., & Zaleznik, A. (1968). *The distribution of authority in formal organizations.* Boston: Harvard University, Division of Research, Graduate School of Business Administration.

D'Amato, J. D. (1987). The belly of the beast: On cultural differences, castelike status and the politics of schools. *Anthropology and Education Quarterly, 18,* 357–360.

D'Amato, J. D. (1988). "Acting": Hawaiian children's resistance to teachers. *The Elementary School Journal, 88,* 529–544.

Damico, S. B., Bell, N. A., & Green, C. (1980). Friendship in desegregated middle schools: An organizational analysis. Paper presented at the meeting of the Social Contexts of Education Conference, sponsored by Division G of the American Educational Research Association, Atlanta, GA.

Dahrendorf, R. (1959). *Class and conflict in industrial society.* Stanford, CA: Stanford University Press.

Dalton, G. W., Barnes, L. B., & Zalesnik, A. (1973). *The distribution of authority in formal organizations.* Cambridge, MA: M.I.T. Press.

Darling-Hammond, L. (1984). *Beyond the commission reports: Coming crisis in teaching.* Santa Monica, CA: Rand Corporation.

Davis, J. A. (1965). *Undergraduate career decisions.* Chicago: Aldine.

Delamont, S. (1989). *Knowledgeable women: Structuralism and the reproduction of elites.* New York: Routledge & Kegan Paul.

Delgado-Gaitan, C. (1988). The value of conformity: Learning to stay in school. *Anthropology and Education Quarterly, 19,* 354–382.

Dewey, J. (1916). *Democracy and education: An introduction to the philosophy of education.* New York: Macmillan.

Dewey, J. (1929). *The Quest for certainty.* NY: Putnam.

Dewey, J. (1938). *Experience and education.* New York: Macmillan.

Deyhle, D. (1986). Break dancing and breaking out: Anglos, Utes and Navajos in a border reservation high school. *Anthropology and Education Quarterly, 17,* 111–127.

Deyhle, D. (1987). Empowerment and cultural conflict: Navajo parents and the schooling of their children. Unpublished manuscript.

Deyhle, D. (1988, October 27). Dropouts cite reasons for leaving school [American Indian News Section]. *Farmington Daily Times.*

Deyhle, D. (1989). The Navajo dropout study. *Journal of Navajo Education.*

Domhoff, G. W. (1967). *Who rules America?* Englewood Cliffs, NJ: Prentice-Hall.

Dreeben, R. (1968). *On what is learned in school.* Reading, MA: Addison-Wesley.

Dreeben, R. (1973). The school as a workplace. In R. M. W. Travers (Ed.), *The second handbook of research on teaching* (pp. 450–473). Chicago: Rand McNally.

Dreeben, R. (1984). First grade reading groups: Their formation and change. In P. L. Peterson, L. C. Wilkinson, & M. Hallinan (Eds). *The social context of instruction: Group organization and group process* (pp. 69–83). New York: Academic Press.

Duncan, S., & Fiske, D. W. (1977). *Face-to-face interaction: Research, method and theory.* New York: John Wiley.

Durkheim, E. (1956). *The division of labor in society.* New York: The Free Press [first published in 1893].

Durkheim, E. (1961). *Moral education: A study in the theory and application of the sociology of education.* Everett K. Wilson and Herman Schnurer, trans. Everett K. Wilson (Ed.). Glencoe, IL: The Free Press.

Dworkin, A. G. (1974). Balance on the bayou: The impact of racial isolation and interaction on stereotyping in the Houston Independent School District. In A. G. Dworkin, R. G. Frankiewicz, & H. Copitka, *Intergroup Action Report* (pp. 7–51). Houston, TX: Houston Council on Human Relations.

Dworkin, A. G., Frankiewicz, R. G., & Copitka, H. (1975). Impact and assessment on stereotype reduction activities in the public schools. Paper presented at the meeting of the Southwestern Sociological Association, San Antonio.

Dworkin, A. G. (1980). The changing demography of public school teachers: Some implications for faculty turnover in urban areas. *Sociology of Education, 53,* 65–73.

Dworkin, A. G. (1985a). Ethnic bias in writing assignments. *American Sociological Association Teaching Newsletter, 10*, 15–16.

Dworkin, A. G. (1985b). *When teachers give up: Teacher burnout, teacher turnover and their impact on children.* Austin, TX: The Hogg Foundation for Mental Health.

Dworkin, A. G. (1987). *Teacher burnout in the public schools: structural causes and consequences for children.* Albany, NY: State University of New York Press.

Dworkin, A. G., & Dworkin, R. J. (1982). *The minority report: An introduction to racial, ethnic, and gender relations* (2nd ed.). New York: Holt, Rinehart & Winston.

Dworkin, A. G., Haney, C. A., & Telschow, R. L. (1988). Fear, victimization and stress among urban public school teachers. *Journal of Organizational Behavior, 9,* 159–171.

Dworkin, A. G., & LeCompte, M. D. (1989). Giving up in schools: American public education in crisis. *Houston Update, 3*(12), 1, 2,7. Houston, TX: Center for Public Policy, University of Houston.

Dworkin, A. G., Lorence, J., & LeCompte, M. D. (1989, March). *Organizational context as determinants of teacher morale.* Paper presented at the meeting of the Southwestern Social Science Association.

Ebaugh, H. R. F. (1977). *Out of the cloister: A study of organizational dilemmas.* Austin, TX: University of Texas Press.

Eder, D. (1982). The impact of management and turn allocation activities on student performance. *Discourse Processes, 5*(2), 147–159.

Eder, D. (1985). The cycle of popularity: Interpersonal relations among female adolescents. *Sociology of Education, 58*(3), 154–165.

Eder, D., & Felmlee, D. (1984). The development of attention norms in ability groups. In P. L. Peterson, L. C. Wilkinson, & M. Hallinan (Eds). *The social context of instruction: Group organization and group process* (pp. 189–207). New York: Academic Press.

Eder, D., & Parker, S. (1987). The cultural production and reproduction of gender: The effect of extracurricular activities on peer-group culture. *Sociology of Education, 60*(3), 200–213.

Education Week. (June 15, 1988). NAEP: Results of the fourth mathematics assessment, p. 29.

Education Week, March 1, 1989, p. 7.

Eisenhart, M. (1985). Women choose their careers: A study of natural decision making. *Review of Higher Education, 8*(3), 247–270.

Eisenhart, M. A. & Holland, D. C. (1988). Gender constructs and career choice: The influence of peer culture on women's commitments in college. In A. Whitehead & B. Reid (Eds.). *Cultural construction of gender.* Forthcoming 1990. Champaign, Il: Univ. of Illinois Press.

Ekstrom, R. B., Goertz, M. E., Pollack, J. M., & Rock, D. A. (1986). Who drops out of school and why?: Findings from a national study. *Teachers College Record, 87,* 356–375.

Ellsworth, E. (1988). Why doesn't this feel empowering?: Working through the repressive myths of critical pedagogy. Paper presented at the 10th Conference on Curriculum Theory and Classroom Practice, Bergamo Conference Center, Dayton, OH.

Ember, C. R., & Ember, M. (1985). *Anthropology* (4th ed.). New Jersey: Prentice Hall.

Engel v. Vitale, 370 U.S. 421 (1962).

Epstein, J. L., & Karweit, N. (Eds.). (1983). *Friends in school: Patterns of selection and influence in secondary schools.* New York: Academic Press.

Erickson, F. (1984). School literacy, reasoning and civility: An anthropologist's perspective. *Review of Educational Research*, *54*, 525–546.

Erickson, F. (1987). Transformation and school success: The politics and culture of educational achievement. *Anthropology and Education Quarterly*, *18*, 335–356.

Erickson, F., & Mohatt, G. (1982). Cultural organization of participation structures in two classrooms of Indian students. In G. Spindler (Ed.), *Doing the Ethnography of Schooling* (pp. 132–174). New York: Holt, Rinehart & Winston.

Etzioni, A. (Ed.). (1969). *The semi-professions and their organization: Teachers, nurses, social workers*. New York: The Free Press.

Evans-Pritchard, E. E. (1940). *The Nuer: A description of the modes of livelihood and political institution of a Nilotic people*. Oxford: Claridon Press.

Falk, W. W., Grimes, M. D., & Lord, G. F. (1982). Professionalism and conflict in a bureaucratic setting: The case of a teachers' strike. *Social Problems*, *29*, 551–560.

Fantini, M. D. (1975). The school-community power struggle. *National Elementary Principal*, *54*(3), 57–61.

Fantini, M., Gittell, M., & Magat, R. (1974). Local school governance. In M. Useem & E. L. Useem, (Eds.), *The education establishment* (pp. 86–98). Englewood Cliffs, NJ: Prentice-Hall.

Farnham, C. (1987). *The impact of feminist research in the academy*. Bloomington, IN: Indiana University Press.

Featherstone, H. (Ed.) (1987). Organizing classes by ability. *Harvard Education Letter*, *3*(4), 1–9.

Feinberg, W., & Soltis, J. F. (1985). *School and society*. New York: Teachers College Press.

Feistritzer, C. E. (1983). *The condition of teachers: A state by state analysis*. Princeton, NJ: Carnegie Foundation for the Advancement of Teaching.

Feldman, R. S. (1985). Nonverbal behavior, race, and the classroom teacher. *Theory Into Practice*, *24*, 45–49.

Felmlee, D., Eder, D., & Tsui, W. (1985). Peer influence on classroom attention. *Social Psychology Quarterly*, *48*(3), 215–226.

Ferrell, B. & Compton, D. (1986). The use of ethnographic techniques for evaluation in a large school district: The Vanguard case. In D. Fetterman & M.A. Pitman (Eds.). *Educational Evaluation: Ethnography in theory, practice and politics* (pp. 171–192). Beverly Hills, CA: Sage.

Fine, M. (1986). Why urban adolescents drop into and out of public high school. *Teachers College Record*, *87*, 393–410.

Fine, M. (1987). Silencing in public schools. *Language Arts*, *64*(2), 157–174.

Firestone, W. A., & Rosenblum, S. (1988). Building committment in urban high schools. *Educational Evaluation and Policy Analysis*, *10*(4), 285–299.

Fiske, E. (1986, August 30). Student debt reshaping colleges and careers [Education Life]. *New York Times*, p. 34.

Fiske, E. (1988, April 10). American test mania [Education Life]. *New York Times*, pp. 16–20.

Fordham, S., & Ogbu, J. U. (1986). Black students' school success: Coping with the "burden" of "acting white". *The Urban Review*, *18*(3), 176–206.

Fortune, R. F. (1963). *Sorcerers of Dobu*. New York: E.P. Dutton.

Freire, P. (1970). *Pedagogy of the oppressed*. New York: Continuum.

Freire, P. (1985). *The politics of education*. South Hadley, MA: Bergin & Garvey.

Freire, P. (1987). *A pedagogy for liberation*. South Hadley, MA: Bergin & Garvey.

Fuller, M. (1980). Black girls in a London comprehensive. In R. Deem (Ed.), Schooling for women's work. London: Routledge & Kegan Paul.

Furlong, V. J. (1985). *Deviant pupil: sociological perspectives*. Philadelphia: Open Univeristy Press.

Gambrell, L. B., Wilson, R. M., & Gantt, W. N. (1981). Classroom observations of task attending behaviors of good and poor readers. *Journal of Educational Research, 74*, 400–404.

Garbarino, M. S. (1983). *Sociocultural theory in anthropology*. Prospect Heights, IL: Waveland Press.

Gaertner, K. N. (1978). *Organizational careers in public school administration*. Unpublished doctoral dissertation, University of Chicago.

Gamoran, A., & Berends, M. (1987). The effects of stratification in secondary schools: A synthesis of survey and ethnographic research. *Review of Educational Research, 57*, 415–437.

Garfinkel, H. (1967). *Studies in ethnomethodology*. Englewood Cliffs, NJ: Prentice-Hall.

Geertz, C. (1973). *The interpretation of cultures*. New York: Basic Books.

Geertz, C. (1988). *Works and lives: The anthropologist as author*. Stanford, CA: Stanford University Press.

Gennep, A. van (1960). *The rites of passage*. Chicago: Chicago University Press.

Gerth, H., & Mills, C. W. (1953). *Character and social structure*. New York: Harcourt Brace & World.

Gibson, M. A. (1987a). Punjabi immigrants in an American high school. In G. Spindler & L. Spindler (Eds.), *Interpretive ethnography of education: At home and abroad* (pp. 281–310). Hillsdale, NJ: Lawrence Erlbaum Associates.

Gibson, M. A. (1987b). The school performance of immigrant minorities: A comparative view. *Anthropology and Education Quarterly, 18*, 262–276.

Gibson, M. A. (1988). *Accommodation with assimilation: Punjabi Sikh immigrants in an American high school and community*. Ithaca, NY: Cornell University Press.

Gilligan, C. (1982). *In a different voice*. Cambridge, MA: Harvard University Press.

Ginsburg, M. B. (1981). Colleague relations among middle school teachers: The Situation in two 9–13 year institutions. *British Educational Research Journal, 7*(1) 91–97.

Ginsburg, M. B. (1988). *Contradictions in teacher education and society: A critical analysis*. New York: The Falmer Press.

Giroux, H. (1983a). Theories of reproduction and resistance in the new sociology of education. *Harvard Educational Review, 53*, 257–293.

Giroux, H. (1983b). *Theory and resistance in education: A pedagogy for the opposition*. Hadley, MA: Bergin & Garvey.

Giroux, H. (1988). *Teachers as intellectuals: Toward a critical pedagogy of learning*. Hadley, MA: Bergin & Garvey.

Gitlin, A. D., Siegel, M, & Boru, K. (1988). Purpose and method: The failure of ethnography to foster school change. Paper presented at the meeting of the American Educational Research Association, New Orleans.

Gitlin, A. (forthcoming, June-September, 1989). *The politics of method: From leftist ethnography to educative research. Qualitative Studies in Education, 2*(3).

Gleick, J. (1989, May 29). After the bomb, a mushroom cloud of metaphors. *The New York Times Book Review*, p. 1.

Goetz, J. (1981). Sex-role systems in Rose Elementary School: Change and tradition in the rural transitional south. In R. T. Sieber & A. J. Gordon (Eds.), *Children and their organizations: Investigations in American culture* (pp. 58–73). Boston: G. K Hall.

Goetz, J. P., & LeCompte, M. D. (1984). *Ethnography and qualitative design in educational research.* Orlando, FL: Academic Press.

Goetz, J. P., & Breneman, E. A. (1988). Desegregation and black students' experiences in two rural southern elementary schools. *The Elementary School Journal, 88,* 503–514.

Goffman, E. (1959). *The presentation of self in everyday life.* Garden City, NY: Doubleday.

Goldman, S. V., & McDermott, R. (1987). The culture of competition in American schools. In G. Spindler (Ed.), *Education and cultural process: Anthropological approaches* (2nd ed.) (pp. 282–299). Prospect Heights, IL: Waveland Press.

Goodlad, J. I. (1984). *A place called school.* New York: McGraw-Hill.

Gordon, C. W. (1957). *The social system of the high school.* Glencoe, IL: The Free Press.

Gottlieb, D. (1964). Teaching and students: The views of Negro and White teachers. *Sociology of Education, 37,* 345–353.

Gould, S. J. (1981). *The mismeasure of man.* New York: W.W. Norton.

Graham, P. A. (1974). *Community and class in American education, 1865–1918.* New York: John Wiley.

Gramsci, A. (1971). *Selections from the prison notebooks.* In Q. Hoare & Geoff N. (Eds.) New York: International.

Grant, L. (1984). Black females "place" in desegregated classrooms. *Sociology of Education, 57* (2), 98–110.

Grant, L., & Rothenberg, J. (1986). The social enhancement of ability differences: Teacher-student interactions in first and second grade reading groups. *Elementary School Journal, 87,* 29–50.

Grant, C. A., & Sleeter, C. E. (1986). *After the school bell rings.* Philadelphia: The Falmer Press.

Greeley, A. M. (1982). *Catholic high schools and minority students.* New Brunswick, NJ: Transaction Books.

Greene, A. D. (1989, April 30). Yates valedictorian hoping success will dispel stereotype. *The Houston Chronicle,* p. 1C.

Groce, N. (1981). Growing up rural: Children in the 4-H and the Junior Granges. In R. T. Sieber & A. J. Gordon (Eds.), *Children and their organization: investigations in American culture* (pp. 106–122). Boston: G.K. Hall.

Grow, J. (Maienza). (1981). *Characteristics of access to the school superintendency for men and women.* Unpublished doctoral dissertation, University of Chicago.

Guidelines for equal treatment of the sexes in McGraw-Hill Book Company publications. (1980). In A. M. Eastman (Ed.), *The Norton reader* (5th ed.) (pp. 346–358). New York: W. W. Norton.

Gumbert, E., & Spring, J. H. (1974). *The superschool and the superstate: American education in the twentieth century.* New York: John Wiley.

Hacker, H. M. (1951). Women as a minority group. *Social Forces, 30,* 60–69.

Halcon, J. J., & Reyes, M. (1989). Trickle-down reform: Hispanics, higher education and the excellence movement. Unpublished manuscript, University of Colorado, Boulder.

Hall, G. S. (September, 1904). Quoted in "Educational questions of the day." *Current Literature,* p. 273.

Hall, R. M., & Sandler, B. R. (1982). *The classroom climate: A chilly one for women?*

Washington, DC: Project on the Status and Education of Women, Association of American Colleges.

Hammack, F. M. (1986). Large school systems; Dropout reports: An analysis of definitions, procedures and findings. *Teachers College Record, 87,* 324–342.

Hanna, J. L. (1987). *Disruptive school behavior: In a desegregated magnet school and elsewhere.* New York: Holmes & Meier.

Hare, D. (1988, November). *Teacher recruitment in three rural Louisiana parishes: The development of recruitment materials.* Paper presented at the meeting of the American Educational Studies Association. Toronto.

Hargreaves, A., & Woods, P. (1984). *Classrooms and staffrooms: The sociology of teachers and teaching.* Milton Keynes, England: Open University Press.

Hargroves, J. S. (1987). *The Boston compact: Facing the challenge of school dropouts. Education and Urban Society, 19*(3), 303–311.

Harris, M. (1981). *America now: The anthropology of a changing culture.* New York: Simon & Shuster.

Heath, S. B. (1983). *Ways with words: Language, life, and work in communities and classroom.* New York: Cambridge University Press.

Held, D. (1980). *Introduction to critical theory.* Berkeley, CA: University of California Press.

Hernstein, R. J. (1973). *IQ in the meritocracy.* Boston: Little Brown.

Hess, G. A. (1989). Panel finds school board misuses state Chapter I funds. *Newsletter of the Chigaco Panel on Public School Policy and Finance, 6*(1).

Hess, G. A. & Green, D. O. (1988). *Invisibly pregnant: A study of teenaged mothers and urban schools.* Paper presented at the meeting of the American Anthropological Association, Phoenix, AZ.

Hess, G. A., Wells, E., Prindle, C., Liffman, P., & Kaplan, B. (1987). "Where's room 185?": How schools can reduce their dropout problem. *Education and Urban Society, 19,* 320–330.

Heyns, B. J. (1974). Social selection and stratification within schools. *American Journal of Sociology, 79,* 1434–1451.

Higham, J. (1969). Origins of immigration restriction, 1882–1897: A social analysis. In S. N. Katz & S. I. Kutler (Eds.), *New perspectives on the American past: Vol. 2/1877 to the present* (pp. 82–92). Boston: Little, Brown.

Hirschman, C., & Wong, M. G. (1986). The extraordinary educational attainment of Asian-Americans: A search for historical evidence and explanations. *Social Forces, 65*(1), 1–27.

Hitchcock, M. E., & Tompkins, G. E. (1987). Are basal reading textbooks still sexist? *The Reading Teacher, 41,* 288–292.

Hodge, R. W., Siegel, P. M., & Rossi, P. H. (1966). Occupational prestige in the United States: 1925–1963. In R. Bendix & S. M. Lipset (Eds.), *Class, status and power: Social stratification in comparative perspective,* 322–335. New York: The Free Press.

Hodgkinson, H. L. (1985). *All one system: Demographics of education, kindergarten through graduate school.* Washington, DC: Institute for Educational Leadership.

Holland, D. C., & Eisenhart, M. A. (1988a). Moments of discontent: University women and the gender status quo. *Anthropology and Education Quarterly, 19,* 115–139.

Holland, D. C., & Eisenhart, M. A. (1988b). Women's ways of going to school: Cultural reproduction of women's identities as workers. In L. Weis (Ed.), *Class, race and gender in American education* (pp. 266–302). Albany, NY: State University of New York.

Holley, F. M., & Doss, D. A. (1983). *Momma got tired of takin' care of my baby.*

(Publication #82.44). Austin, TX: Office of Research and Evaluation, Independent School District.

Hollingshead, A. B. (1949). *Elmtown's youth*. New York: John Wiley.

Holmes Group, The. (1983). *Tomorrow's schools*. East Lansing, MI.

Holmes Group, The. (1986). *Tomorrow's teachers*. East Lansing, MI.

Hughes, L. W., Gordon, W. M., & Hillman, L. W. (1980). *Desegregating American's schools*. New York: Longman.

Jackson, P. (1968). *Life in classrooms*. Chicago: University of Chicago Press.

Jacob, E., & Jordan, C. (Eds.). (1987). Explaining the school performance of minority students [Theme issue]. *Anthropology and Education Quarterly*, Volume 18(4).

Jencks, C. (1972). *Inequality: A reassessment of the effect of family and schooling in America*. New York: Basic Books.

Jencks, C., Crouse, J., & Mueser, P. (1983). The Wisconsin model of status attainment: A national replication with improved measures of ability and aspiration. *Sociology of Education*, *56*, 3–19.

Jensen, A. (1969). How much can we boost I.Q. and scholastic achievement? *Harvard Educational Review*, *39*, 1–23.

Johnson, J. (1987, November 25). Death of unattended children spurs day care bills in congress. *The New York Times*, p. B9.

Joint Center for Housing Studies, Harvard University. Cited by Pamela Reeves. (March 27, 1988). Rising Rents Squeeze Lower-Income Families. *The Houston Chronicle*.

Jordan, C. (1984). Cultural compatibility and the education of ethnic minority children. *Educational Research Quarterly*, *8*(4), 59–71.

Jordan, C. (1985). Translating culture: From ethnographic information to educational program. *Anthropology and Education Quarterly*, *16*, 105–123.

Kaestle, C. F. (1983). *Pillars of the republic: Common schools and American society, 1780–1860*. New York: Hill & Wang.

Kahl, J. A. (1953). Educational and occupational aspirations of "common man" boys. *Harvard Educational Review*, *23*, 186–203.

Kantrowitz, B., & Wingert, P. (1989, April 17). How kids learn: A special report. *Newsweek*, pp. 50–56.

Karabel, J., & Halsey, A. H. (Eds.). (1977). *Power and ideology in education*. New York: Oxford University Press.

Katz, M. B. (1971). *Class, bureaucracy and the schools*. New York: Praeger.

Kaufman, Polly Welts. *Women teachers on the frontier*. New Haven, Conn.: Yale University Press, 1984.

Keddie, N. (1971). Classroom knowledge. In M. F. D. Young (Ed.), *Knowledge and control* (pp. 133–160). London: Collier-Macmillan.

Kelly, G. P., & Nihlen, A. S. (1982). Schooling and the reproduction of patriarchy: Unequal workloads, unequal rewards. In M. W. Apple (Ed.), *Cultural and economic reproduction in education: Essays on class, ideology and the state* (pp. 162–180). London: Routledge & Kegan Paul.

Keniston, K. (1968). *The young radicals*. New York: Harcourt, Brace & World.

Keniston, K. (1971). The agony of the counterculture. *Educational Record*, *52*, 205–211.

Kerr, N. (1973). The school board as an agency of legitimation. In S. D. Sieber & D. E. Wilder (Eds.), *The school in society: Studies in the sociology of education* (pp. 380–401). New York: The Free Press.

Kirby, D., Harris, T. R., & Crain, R. (1973). *Political strategies in northern school desegregation*. Lexington, MA: Lexington Books.

Klein, S. (Ed.). (1985). *Handbook for achieving sex equity through education*. Baltimore, MD: The Johns Hopkins University Press.

Kliebard, H. M. (1986). *The struggle for the American curriculum 1893–1958*. Boston: Routledge & Kegan Paul.

Knapp, M. S., & Cooperstein, R. (1986). Early research on the federal block grant: Themes and unanswered questions. *Educational Evaluation and Policy Analysis, 8*, 121–138.

Kolata, G. (1989, July 1). Gender gap in aptitude tests is narrowing, experts find. *The New York Times*, p. 1.

Kramarae, C., & Treichler, P. A. (1985). *A feminist dictionary*. London: Pandora Press.

Kunisawa, B. (1988). A nation in crisis: The dropout dilemma. *National Education Association, 6*(6), 61–65.

La Belle, T. J. (1972). An anthropological framework for studying education. *Teachers College Record, 73*, 519–538.

Labov, W. (1972). *Language in the inner city: Studies in the Black English vernacular*. Philadelphia: University of Pennsylvania Press.

LaFrance, M. (1985). The school of hard knocks: Nonverbal sexism in the classroom. *Theory Into Practice, 24*, 40–44.

LaFrance, M., & Mayo, C. (1978). *Moving bodies: Nonverbal communication in social relationships*. Monterey, CA: Brooks/Cole.

Lather, P. (1986). Research as praxis. *Harvard Educational Review, 56*, 257–277.

Lau v. Nichols, 414 U. S. 563 (1974).

LeCompte, M. D. (1972). The uneasy alliance between community action and research. *School Review, 79*(1), 123–132.

LeCompte, M. D. (1974). *Teacher styles and the development of student work norms*. Unpublished doctoral dissertation, University of Chicago.

LeCompte, M. D. (1978a). Culture shock: It happens to teachers, too. In B. Dell Felder, et. al, (Eds.), *Focus on the future: Implications for education*, (pp. 102–112). Houston, TX: University of Houston.

LeCompte, M. D. (1978b). Learning to work: The hidden curriculum of the classroom. *Anthropology and Education Quarterly, 9*, 23–37.

LeCompte, M. D. (1980). The civilizing of children: How young children learn to become students. *The Journal of Thought, 15*, 105–129.

LeCompte, M. D. (1985). Defining the differences: Cultural subgroups among mainstream children. *The Urban Review, 17*(2), 111–128.

LeCompte, M. D. (1987a). *The cultural context of dropping out: Why good dropout programs don't work*. Paper presented at the meeting of the American Association for the Advancement of Science, Chicago.

LeCompte, M. D. (1987b). The cultural context of dropping out: Why remedial programs don't solve the problems. *Education and urban society, 19*, 232–249.

LeCompte, M. D., & Bennett, K. P. (1988). *Empowerment: The once and future role of the Gringo*. Paper presented at meeting of the American Anthropological Association, Phoenix, AZ.

LeCompte, M. D., & Dworkin, A. G. (1988). Educational programs: Indirect linkages and unfulfilled expectations. In H. R. Rodgers, Jr. (Ed.), *Beyond welfare: New approaches to the problem of poverty in America* (pp. 135–167). Armonk, NY: M. E. Sharpe.

LeCompte, M. D., & Goebel, S. G. (1985, June 6). *Issues in defining and enumerating dropouts* [HISD dropout report #1]. Houston, TX: Department of Planning, Research and Evaluation, Houston Independent School District.

LeCompte, M. D., & Goebel, S. G. (1987). Can bad data produce good program planning?: An analysis of record-keeping on school dropouts. *Education and Urban Society*, *19*, 250–268.

Lee, P. C., & Gropper, N. B. (1974). Sex-role culture and educational practice. *Harvard Educational Review*, *44*, 369–409.

Lee, V. E., & Bryk, A. S. (1988). Curriculum tracking as mediating the social distribution of high school achievement. *Sociology of Education*, *61*, 78–94.

Lee, E. S., & Rong, X. (1988). The educational and economic achievement of Asian-Americans. *The Elementary School Journal*, *88*, 545–560.

Lever, J. (1976). Sex differences in the games children play. *Social Problems*, *23*, 479–488.

Liebow, E. (1969). *Tally's corner: A study of Negro streetcorner men.* Boston: Little, Brown.

Linton, R. (1945). *The cultural background of personality.* New York: Appleton-Century.

Lippitt, R., & Gold, M. (1959). Classroom social structure as a mental health problem. *Journal of Social Issues*, *15*, 40–49.

Littwin, J. (1987). *The postponed generation: Why America's grown-up kids are growing up later.* New York: Morrow.

Lortie, D. (1969). The balance of control and autonomy in elementary school teaching. In A. Etzioni (Ed.), *The semi-professions and their organization: Teachers, nurses, social workers* (pp. 1–53). New York: The Free Press.

Lortie, D. (1973). Observations on teaching as work. In R. M. W. Travers (Ed.), *The second handbook of research on teaching*, (pp. 474–496). Chicago: Rand-McNally.

Lortie, D. (1975). *Schoolteacher: A sociological study.* Chicago: The University of Chicago Press.

Maccoby, E. (1966). *The development of sex differences.* Stanford Ca: Stanford University Press.

Maccoby, E., & Jacklin, C. (1974). *The psychology of sex differences.* Stanford, CA: Stanford University Press.

Main, J. T. (1966). The class structure of revolutionary America. In R. Bendix & S.M. Lipset, *Class, status and power: Social stratification in comparative perspective* (pp. 111–121). New York: The Free Press.

Maloney, M. E. (1985). *School dropouts: Cincinnati's challenge in the eighties* (Working Paper #15). Cincinnati, OH: Urban Appalachian Council.

Mann, H. (1842). *Fifth annual report of the secretary of the board.* Boston: Board of Education.

Mark, J. H., & Anderson, B. D. (1978). Teacher survival rates—A current look. *American Educational Research Journal*, *15*, 379–383.

Marotto, R. A. (1986). "Posin' to be chosen": An ethnographic study of in-school truancy. In D. A. Fetterman & M. A. Pitman (Eds.), *Educational evaluation: Ethnography in theory, practice and politics* (pp. 193–214). Beverley Hills, CA: Sage Publications.

Marrou, H. I. (1956). *A history of education in antiquity.* Madison, WI: University of Wisconsin Press.

Martin, R. (1972) Student sex and behavior as determinents of the type and frequency of teacher-student contacts. *Journal of School Psychology, 10,* 339–347.

Marx, K. (1959). *Basic writings on politics and philosophy.* L. Feuer (Ed.). Garden City, NY: Anchor Books.

Marx, K. (1955). *The communist manifesto.* Chicago: H. Regney.

Marx, K. (1971). *Economy, class and social revolution.* New York: Scribner.

Marx, K. (1973) *On society and social change.* Chicago: University of Chicago Press.

Mason, W. F. (1961). *The beginnng teacher: Status and career orientations.* Washington, DC: Department of Health, Education and Welfare, U. S. Government Printing Office.

Massachusetts teacher, The. (1851). *Immigration, 4,* 289–291.

McCarthy, C. (1988). Rethinking liberal and radical perspectives on racial inequality in schooling: Making the case for nonsynchrony. *Harvard Educational Review, 58,* 265–279.

McDade, L. (1988). Knowing the "right stuff": Attrition, gender, and scientific literacy. *Anthropology & Education Quarterly, 19,* 93–114.

McDermott, R. P. (1976). *Kids make sense: An ethnographic account of the instructional management of success and failure in a first grade classroom.* Unpublished doctoral dissertation, Stanford University, CA.

McDermott, R. P. (1977). Social relations as contexts for learning in school. *Harvard Educational Review, 47,* 198–213.

McDill, E. L., Pallas, A. M., & Natriello, G. (1985, February). *Uncommon sense: School administrators, school reform, and potential dropouts.* Paper presented at the meeting of the National Invitational Conference on Holding Power and Dropouts, Columbia University, NY.

McGivney, J. H., & Haught, J. M. (1972). The politics of education: A view from the perspective of the central office staff. *Educational Administrative Quarterly, 8*(3), 35.

McIntosh, P. M. (1988, November). Feeling a fraud [Keynote address]. American Educational Studies Association, Toronto.

McLaren, P. (1980). *Cries from the corridor: The new suburban ghettos.* Toronto: Metheun.

McLaren, P. (1986). *Schooling as a ritual performance.* Boston: Routledge & Kegan Paul.

McLaren, P. (1989). *Life in schools.* New York: Longman.

McLeod, J. (1987). *Ain't no makin' it: Leveled aspirations in a low-income neighborhood.* Boulder, CO: Westview Press.

McNeil, J. D. (1985). *Curriculum: A comprehensive introduction* (3rd ed.). Boston: Little, Brown.

McNeil, L. (1983). Defensive teaching and classroom control. In M. W. Apple & L. Weis (Eds.), *Ideology and practice in schooling* (pp. 114–142). Philadelphia: Temple University Press.

McNeil, L. M. (1986). *Contradictions of control: School structure and school knowledge.* New York: Routledge.

McNeil, L. M. (1988a). Contradictions of control, Part I: Administrators and teachers. *Phi Delta Kappan, 69*(5), 333–339.

McNeil, L. M. (1988b). Contradictions of control, Part II: Teachers, students and curriculum. *Phi Delta Kappan, 69*(6), 432–438.

McNeil, L. M. (1988c). Contradictions of control, Part III: Contradictions of reform. *Phi Delta Kappan, 69*(7), 478–485.

McRobbie, A. (1978). Working class girls and the culture of femininity. In Women's Studies Group, Centre for Contemporary Cultural Studies (Ed.), *Women take issue: Aspects of women's subordination* (pp. 96–108). London: Hutchinson.

Mechling, J. (1981). Male gender display at a boy scout camp. In R. T. Sieber & A. J. Gordon (Eds.), *Children and their organizations: Investigations in American culture* (pp. 138–160). Boston: G. K. Hall.

Merton, R. K. (1967). *Social theory and social structure.* New York: Free Press.

Mertz, N. T., & McNeely, S. R. (1988). Secondary schools in transition: A study of the emerging female administrator. *American Secondary Education, 17*(2), 10–14.

Metz, M. H. (1978). *Classrooms and corridors: The crisis of authority in desegregated secondary schools.* Berkeley, CA: University of California Press.

Miles, M. W. (1977). The student movement and the industrialization of higher education. In J. Karabel & A. H. Halsey (Eds.), *Power and ideology in education* (pp. 432–456). Cambridge, MA: Oxford University Press.

Mills, C. W. (1956). *The power elite.* New York: Oxford University Press.

Miller, S. E., Leinhardt, G., & Zigmond, N. (1988). Influencing engagement through accommodation: An ethnographic study of at-risk students. *American Educational Research Journal, 25*, 465–489.

Millett, K. (1977). *Sexual politics.* London: Virago Press.

Mohatt, G. V., & Erickson, F. (1981). Cultural differences in teaching styles in an Odawa school: A sociolinguistic approach. In H. Trueba, G. P. Guthrie, & K. H. Au (Eds.), *Culture and the bilingual classroom* (pp. 105–119). Rowley, MA: Newbury House.

Moll, L. C., & Diaz, R. (1987). Teaching writing as communication: The use of ethnographic findings in classroom practice. In D. Broome (Ed.). *Literacy and schooling* (pp. 193–221). Norwood, NJ: Ablex Press.

Molner, A. (1987). *Social issues and education: A challenge and responsibility.* Alexandria, VA: Association for Supervision and Curriculum Development.

Morgenstern, J. (1989, January 1). Can "USA Today" be saved? *New York Times Magazine,* section 6, p. 13.

Morrow, G. (1986). Standardizing practice in analysis of school dropouts. *Teachers College Record, 87,* 342–356.

Murnane, R. J. (1975). *The impact of school resources on the learning of inner-city children.* Cambridge, MA: Ballinger.

Nadel, S. F. *The theory of social structure.* Glencoe, IL: The Free Press, 1957, pp. 35–41. Quoted in Bidwell, Charles E. The school as a formal organization. In James G. March, ed. *The handbook of organizations.* New York: Rand McNally, 1965.

Nash, R. (1976). Pupil expectations of their teachers. In M. Stubbs & S. Delamont (Eds.). *Explorations in classroom observation* (pp. 83–101). New York: John Wiley.

National Assessment of Educational Progress (NAEP) Report. (1988). *Science and engineering indicators—1987* (N.S.B. 87-1). Washington, DC: U.S. Government Printing Office.

National Commission on Excellence in Education. (1983). *A nation at risk.* Washington, DC: U.S. Government Printing Office.

NEA Today, March 1988, pp. 14–15.

National Education Association. (1963). Teachers in public schools. *NEA Research Bulletin, 41,*(1) 23–26.

National Education Association. (1970). Teacher strikes. 1960–61 to 1970–71. *National Education Association Bulletin, 48*(1).

National Education Association (1972). The American public school teacher, 1970–1971: More highlights from the preliminary report. *NEA Research Bulletin, 50*(1), 3–8.

National Institute of Education. (1978). *Violent schools—safe schools: The safe school study report to congress* (Vol. 1). Washington DC: Department of Health, Education & Welfare, U.S. Government Printing Office.

Needle, R. H., Griffin, T., Svendsen, R., & Berney, C. (1980, February). Teacher stress: Sources and consequences. *The Journal of School Health,* 96–99.

Oakes, J. (1985). *Keeping track: How schools structure inequality.* New Haven: Yale University Press.

Obermiller, P. J. (1981). The question of urban appalachian ethnicity. In W. W. Philliber (Ed.), *The invisible minority.* Lexington, KY: University of Kentucky Press.

Ogbu, J. U. (1978). *Minority education and caste: The American system in cross-cultural perspective.* New York: Academic Press.

Ogbu, J. U. (1983). Minority status and schooling in plural societies. *Comparative Education Review, 27*(2), 168–190.

Ogbu, J. U. (1987). Variability in minority school performance: A problem in search of an explanation. *Anthropology and Educational Quarterly, 18,* 312–335.

O'Neill, D. M., & Sepielli, P. (1985). *Education in the United States: 1940–1983* [CDS-85-1]. Washington, DC: U.S. Department of Commerce, Bureau of the Census.

Ortiz, F. I. (1981). *Career patterns in education: Men, women and minorities in public school administration.* New York: Praeger.

Ortiz, F. I. (1988). Hispanic-American children's experiences in classrooms: A comparison between Hispanic and non-Hispanic children. In L. Weis (Ed.), *Race, class and gender in American education* (pp. 63–87). Albany, NY: State University of New York Press.

Orum, L. (1984). *Hispanic dropouts: Community responses.* Washington, DC: Office of Research, Advocacy and Legislation, National Council of La Raza.

Page, R. (1987). Lower-track classes at a college-preparatory high school: A caricature of educational encounters. In G. Spindler & L. Spindler (Eds.), *Interpretive ethnography of education at home and abroad.* Hillsdale, NJ: Lawrence Erlbaum.

Page, R. (1988). *Interpreting curriculum differentiation.* Unpublished manuscript, University of California, Riverside.

Parsons, T. (1951). *The social system* Glencoe, IL: The Free Press.

Parsons, T. (1959). The school class as a social system: Some of its functions in American society. *Harvard Educational Review, 29,* 297–319.

Pavalko, R. M. (1970). Recruitment to teaching: Patterns of selection and retention. *Sociology of Education, 43,* 340–353.

Perrillo, V. (1980). *Strangers to these shores.* Boston: Houghton Mifflin.

Persell, C. H. (1977). *Education and inequality: The roots and results of stratification in America's schools.* New York: The Free Press.

Peterson, K. S. (1987, November 17). School cost can cut doubly deep: Scholarship meets hardship. *USA Today,* p. 1[Section D].

Peterson, P. E. (1976). *School politics Chicago style.* Chicago: University of Chicago Press.

Pettigrew, T. F., & Green, R. L. (1976). School desegregation in large cities: A critique of the Coleman "white flight" thesis. *Harvard Educational Review report series No. 11. School desegregation: The continuing challenge* (pp. 17–69). Cambridge, MA.

Phillips, D. C. (1987). *Philosophy, science and social inquiry.* New York: Pergamon Press.

Philips, S. U. (1972). Participant structures and communicative competence: Warm Springs Indian children in community and classroom. In C. B. Cazden, V. John & D. Hymes (Eds.), *Functions of language in the classroom* (pp. 370–394). NY: Teachers College Press.

Phillips, B. N., & Lee, M. (1980). The changing role of the American teacher: Current and future sources of stress. In C.L. Cooper & J. Marshall (Eds.), *White collar and professional stress* (pp. 93–111). New York: John Wiley.

Piestrup, A. (1973). Black dialect interference and accommodation in first grade [Monograph No. 4]. Berkeley, CA: Language Behavior Research Laboratory.

Pinar, W. F. (Ed.). (1988). *Contemporary curriculum discourses*. Scottsdale, AZ: Gorsuch Scarisbrick.

Pinar, W. F. (1989). A reconceptualization of teacher education. *Journal of Teacher Education, 40*(1), 9–12.

Pitman, M. A. (1987). Compulsory education and home schooling: Truancy or prophecy? *Education and Urban Society, 19*, 280–290.

Pitman, M. A. & Eisenhardt, M. A. (Eds.). (1988). Women, culture, and education [Theme issue]. *Anthropology & Education Quarterly, 19*(2).

Plessy v. *Ferguson*, 163 U.S. 537 (1895).

Popper, K. R. (1968). *The logic of scientific discovery*. New York: Harper & Row.

Powell, A. G., Farrar, E., & Cohen, D. K. (1985). *The shopping mall high school: Winners and losers in the educational marketplace*. Boston: Houghton Mifflin.

Project on Equal Education Rights. (1986). *1986 PEER report card: A state-by-state survey of the status of women and girls in American's schools* [PEER Policy Paper #5]. Washington, DC.

Psacharaopoulos, G. (1973). *Returns to education: An international comparison*. San Francisco, CA: Jossey-Bass.

Randour, M. L., Strasburg, G. L., & Lipman-Blumen, J. (1982). Women in higher education: Trends in enrollments and degrees earned. *Harvard Educational Review, 52*, 189–202.

Ravitch, D. ,& Finn, C. E. (1987). *What seventeen year olds don't know*. New York: Harper & Row.

Reeves, P. (1988, March 27). Rising rents squeeze lower-income families. *The Houston Chronicle*, p. 6.

Reisler, R., Jr., & Friedman, M. S. (1978). Radical misfits? How students from an alternative junior high school adapted to a conventional high school. *Educational Theory, 28*(1), 17–82.

Report of the Massachusetts senate committee on establishing a reform school. (1984). Commonwealth of Massachusetts, Senate. (Doc. No. 86, 1846)

Resnick, D. P., & Resnick, L. B. (1985). Standards, curriculum and performance: A historical and comparative perspective. *Educational Researcher, 14*(4), 5–20.

Reyes, M., & Halcon, J. J. (1988). Racism in Academic: The old wolf revisited. *Harvard Educational Review, 58*, 299–314.

Reynolds, W. B. (1986). Education alternatives to transportation failures: The desegregation response to a resegregation dilemma. *Metropolitan Education* (1), 3–15.

Rist, R. C. (1970). Student social class and teacher expectations: The self-fulfilling prophecy in ghetto education. *Harvard Educational Review, 40*, 411–451.

Rist, R. C. (1973). *The urban school: A factory for failure*. Cambridge, MA: The MIT Press.

Robbins, T. (1984) *Jitterbug perfume*. New York: Bantam.

Robinson, V., & Pierce, C. (1985). *Making do in the classroom: A report on the misassignment of teachers.* Washington, DC: Council for Basic Education in Cooperation with the American Federation of Teachers.

Rogers, D. (1968). *110 Livingston Street: Politics and bureaucracy in the New York City schools.* New York: Random House.

Rose, R. (1988). *"Syntactic styling" as a means of linguistic empowerment: Illusion or reality?* Paper presented at the meeting of the American Anthropological Association, Phoenix, AZ.

Rosenfeld, G. (1971). *Shut those thick lips.* New York: Holt, Rinehart & Winston.

Rosenfeld, R. A. (1980). Race and sex differences in career dynamics. *American Sociological Review, 45,* 583–609.

Ross, E. A. (1901) *Social control: A survey of the foundations of order.* New York: Macmillan.

Rudolph, L., & Rudolph, S. (1967). *The modernity of tradition.* Chicago: University of Chicago Press.

Rumberger, R. W. (1987). High school dropouts: A review of issues and evidence. *Review of Educational Research, 57,* 101–122.

Ryan, W. (1976). *Blaming the victim.* New York: Random House.

Saario, T. N., Jacklin, C. N., & Tittle, C. K. (1973). Sex role stereotyping in the public schools. *Harvard Educational Review, 43,* 386–415.

Sadker, M. P., & Sadker, D. M. (1985, March). Sexism in the schoolroom of the '80's. *Psychology Today* pp. 54–57.

Sadker, M. P. & Sadker, D. M. (1988). *Teachers, schools, and society.* New York: Random House.

Sadker, M. P., Sadker, D. M., & Klein, S. S. (1986). Abolishing misperceptions about sex equity in education. *Theory Into Practice, 25,* 219–226.

Sarason, S. B. (1971). *The culture of the school and the problem of change.* Boston: Allyn & Bacon.

Schildkrout, E. (1984). Young traders of Northern Nigeria. In J. P. Spradley & D. W. McCurdy (Eds.), *Conformity and conflict: Readings in cultural anthropology* (pp. 246–253). Boston: Little, Brown.

Schmuck, P. A. (Ed.). (1987). *Women educators: Employees of schools in western countries.* Albany, NY: Statue University of New York Press.

Schofield, J. (1982). *Black and white in school: Trust, tension or tolerance?* New York: Praeger.

Schultz, T. W. (1961). Investment in human capital. *American Economic Review, 51,* 1–17.

Scimecca, J. A. (1980). *Education and society.* New York: Holt Rinehart & Winston.

Scott, J. W. (1987). Women's history and the rewriting of history. In C. Farnham (Ed.), *The impact of feminist research in the academy* (pp. 34–50). Bloomington, IN: Indiana Press University.

Sege, I. (1989, June 27). Children in poverty, Part three. The inner city: Streets of children begetting children. *The Oregonian,* p. A2. Reprinted from *The Boston Globe*

Sennett, R., & Cobb, J. (1973). *The hidden injuries of class.* New York: Vintage Books.

Sewell, W. H., & Shah, V. P. (1977). Socioeconomic status, intelligence and the attainment of higher education.

Sewell, W. H., Haller, A. 0., & Portes, A. (1969). The educational and early occupational attainment process. *American Sociological Review, 34,* 82–92.

Sewell, W. H., Haller, A. 0., & Ohlendorf, G. W. (1970). The educational and early occupational attainment process: Replication and revision. *American Sociological Review, 34,* 82–92.

Sewell, W. H., & Shah, V. P. (1967). Socioeconomic status, intelligence, and the attainment of higher education. *Sociology of Education, 40,* 1–23.

Shaker, P., & Kridel, C. (1989). The return to experience: A reconceptualist call. *Journal of Teacher Education, 40*(1), 2–8.

Shakeshaft, C. (1986). A gender at risk. *Phi Delta Kappan. 67,* 449–503.

Shavelson, R. J., & Stern, P. (1981). Research on teachers' pedagogical thoughts, judgments, decisions and behavior. *Review of Educational Research, 51,* 455–498.

Shultz, J., & Erickson, F. (1982). *The counselor as gatekeeper.* New York: Academic Press.

Sieber, R. T. (1981). Socialization implicatons of school discipline, or how first-graders are taught to "listen". In R. T. Sieber & A. J. Gordon, (Eds.), *Children and their organization* (pp. 18–44). Boston: G. K. Hall.

Sikes, J. (1971). Differential behavior of male and female teachers with male and female students. Unpublished doctoral dissertation, University of Texas, Austin.

Silberman, C. E. (1973). *The open classroom reader.* New York: The Free Press.

Sills, D. L. (1970). Perserving organizational goals. In O. Grusky & G. A. Miller (Eds.), *The sociology of organizations: Basic studies* (pp. 227–236). New York: The Free Press.

Simeone, A. (1986). *Academic women: Working towards equality.* South Hadley, MA: Bergin & Garvey.

Simmel, G. (1955). *Conflict.* Glencoe, IL: Free Press.

Simmel, G. (1968). *The conflict in modern culture and other essays.* New York: Teachers College.

Simpson, R. L., & Simpson, I. H. (1969). Women and bureaucracy in the semi-professions. In A. Etzioni (Ed.), *The semi-professions and their organization: Teachers, nurses, social workers* (pp. 196–266). New York: The Free Press.

Sizer, T. (1984). *Horace's compromise: The dilemma of the American high school.* Boston: Houghton Mifflin.

Smith, A. L. (1905) quoted in J. S. Haller Jr. & R. M. Haller (Eds.) (1974). *The physician and sexuality in Victorian America.* NY: W. W. Norton, p. 59.

Smith, L. M., & Geoffrey, W. (1968). *The complexities of an urban classroom: An analysis toward a general theory of teaching.* New York: Holt, Rinehart & Winston.

Smith v. School Commissioners of Mobile Alabama, 827 F.2d 684 (1987).

Sorensen, A. B., & Hallinan, M. T. (1987). Ability grouping and sex differences in mathematics achievement. *Sociology of Education, 60*(2), 63–72.

Spencer, DeeAnn. (1986). *Contemporary women teachers: Balancing school and home.* New York: Longman Inc.

Spencer, H. (1967). The evolution of society: Selections from Herbert Spencer's principles of sociology (R. L. Carneiro, Ed.). Chicago: University of Chicago Press. (First printed 1898 as *First Principles.* New York: Appleton.)

Spencer, H. (1851). *Social Statics.* London: Chapman.

Spindler, G. D. (1987). Beth-Ann: A Case Study of Culturally Defined Adjustment and Teacher Perceptions. In G. D. Spindler (Ed.) *Education and Cultural Process: Anthropological Approaches* (2nd Edition). Prospect Heights, IL: Waveland Press.

Spradley, J. P., & McCurdy, D. W. (Eds.). (1972). *The cultural experience: Ethnography in complex society.* Chicago: Science Research Associates.

Spring, J. H. (1976). *The sorting machine.* New York: David McKay.

Spring, J. H. (1985). *American education* (3rd ed.). New York: Longman.

Spring, J. H. (1988a). *Conflict of interests: The politics of American education*. New York: Longman.

Spring, J. H. (1988b). The political structure of popular culture. Paper presented at the 10th Conference on Curriculum Theory and Classroom Practice, Bergamo Conference Center, Dayton, OH.

Spring, J. H. (1989). *American education* (4th ed.). New York: Longman.

Srinivas, M. N. (1965). *Religion and society among the Coorgs of South India*. New York: Asia.

St. John, N. H. (1975). *School desegregation: Outcomes for children*. New York: Wiley-Interscience.

Steinberg, L., Blinde, P., & Chan, K. (1984). Dropping out among language minority youth. *Review of Educational Research, 54*(1), 113–132.

Steinberg, L. D., Greenberger, E., Garduque, L., & McAuliffe, S. (1982). High school students in the labor force: Some costs and benefits to schooling and learning. *Educational Evaluation and Policy Analysis, 4*(3), 363–372.

Stern, S. P. (1987, November). *Black parents: Drop-outs or push-outs from school participation*. Paper presented at the meeting of the American Anthropological Association, Chicago.

Stinchcome, A. (1964). *Rebellion in a high school*. Chicago: Quadrangle Press.

Suarez-Orozco, M. M. (1987). "Becoming somebody": Central American immigrants in U.S. inner-city schools. *Anthropology and Education Quarterly, 18*, 287–300.

Sumner, W. G. (1883). *What the social classes owe to each other*. New York: Harper Brothers.

Sykes, G. (1958). *The society of captives*. Princeton, NJ: Princeton University Press.

Tar, Z. (1985). *The Frankfurt School*. New York: Schocken Books.

Tatel, D. S., Lanigan, K. J., & Sneed, M. F. (1986). The fourth decade of Brown: Metropolitan desegregation and quality education. *Metropolitan Education*,(1), 15–36.

Tedford, D. (1988, October 16). Making the grade at HISD: It helps being white, well-off. *The Houston Chronicle*, p. 1.

Tetreault, M. K., & Schmuck, P. (1985). Equity, educational reform and gender. *Issues in Education, 3*(1), 45–67.

Tetreault, M. K. (1986). The journey from male-defined to gender-balanced education. *Theory Into Practice, 25*, 227–234.

Tiedt, S. W. (1966). *The role of the federal government in education*. New York: Oxford University Press.

Tinker v. Des Moines School District, 393 U.S. 503 (1969).

Tobier, E. (1984). *The changing face of poverty: Trends in New York City's population in poverty, 1960–1990*. New York: Community Service Society.

Today's numbers, tomorrow's nation. (1986, May 14). *Education Week*, p. 14.

Treckler, J. L. (1973). Women in U.S. history high school textbooks. *International Review of Education, 19*, 133–139.

Turner, J. H. (1978). The structure of sociological theory (rev. ed.). Homewood, IL: The Dorsey Press.

Turner, R. L. (1989, April). *Organizational size effects at different levels of schooling*. Paper presented at the meeting of the American Educational Research Association, New Orleans.

Turner, V. (1969). *The ritual process: Structure and anti-structure*. Ithaca, NY: Cornell University Press.

Turner, V. (1974). *Dramas, fields and metaphors: Symbolic action in human society*. Ithaca, NY: Cornell University Press.

Tyack, D. (1974). *The one best system*. Cambridge, MA: Harvard University Press.

Tylor, E. B. (1958). *Primitive culture*. New York: Harper Torchboks (originally published in 1871).

U. S. Bureau of the Census. (1986). *Statistical Abstract of the United States: 1987* (107th edition). Washington, DC.

Useeem, E. L. & Useem, M. (Eds.). (1974). *The educational establishment*. Englewood Cliffs: NJ: Prentice Hall.

Valentine, C. A. (1968). *Culture and poverty: Critique and counter proposals*. Chicago: University of Chicago Press.

Valli, L. (1983). Becoming clerical workers: Business education and the culture of femininity. In M. W. Apple & L. Weis (ed.). *Ideology and practice in schooling*, (pp. 213–234). Philadelphia: Temple University Press.

Valli, L. (1988). *The parallel curriculum at Central Catholic High School*. Paper presented at the American Educational Research Association, New Orleans, LA.

Valverde, S. A. (1987). A comparative study of Hispanic dropouts and graduates Why do some leave school early and some finish? *Education and Urban Society, 19*, 311–320.

Van Galen, J. (1987). Maintaining Control. The Structuring of parent involvement. In. G. W. Noblit & W. T. Pink (Eds.), *Schooling in social context* (pp. 78–90). Norwood, NJ: Ablex Publishing.

Van Ness, H. (1981). Social control and social organization in an Alaskan Athabaskan classroom: A microethnography of getting ready for reading. In H. Trueba, Guthrie, G. P. & Au, K. H. (eds.). *Culture and the bilingual classroom* (pp. 120–138). Rowley, MA: Newbury House.

Vogt, L. (1985). *Rectifying the school performance of Hawaiian and Navajo students*. Paper presented at the meeting of the American Anthropological Association, Washington, DC.

Walker, S., & Barton, L. (1983). *Gender class & education*. Sussex, England: The Falmer Press.

Waller, W. (1932). *The sociology of teaching*. New York: John Wiley.

Warren, M. A. (1980). The nature of woman: An encyclopedia and guide to the literature. Inverness, CA: Edgepress, p. 181. Quoted in C. Kramarae & P. A. Treichler (Eds.) (1985). *A feminist dictionary*. London: Pandora Press.

Wax, M. (Ed.). (1980). *When schools are desegregated: Problems and possibilities for students, educators, parents and the community*. NJ: Transaction Books.

Weber, M. (1947). *The theory of social and economic organizations*. (A. M. Henderson & T. Parsons, Trans.). New York: Oxford University Press.

Weber, M. (1958). *From Max Weber: Essays in sociology*. (H. Gerth and C. W. Mills, Eds. and Trans.). New York: Oxford University Press.

Weber, M. (1962). *Basic concepts in sociology*. New York: Philosophical Library.

Wehlage, G. G., & Rutter, R. A. (1986) Dropping out: What do schools contribute to the problem? *Teachers College Record, 87*, 374–392.

Weiler, K. (1988). *Women teaching for change*. South Hadley, MA: Bergin & Garvey.

Weis, L. (Ed.). (1988). *Class, race and gender in American education*. Albany, NY: State University of New York Press.

Weis, L. High school girls in a de-industrializing society. In L. Weis (Ed.), *Class, race and gender in American education* (pp. 183–209). Albany, NY: State University of New York Press.

Whitty, G. (1985). *Sociology and school knowledge: Curriculum theory, research and politics*. London: Metheun.

Williams, S. B. (1987). A comparative study of Black dropouts and Black high school graduates in an urban public school system. *Education and Urban Society, 19*, 303–311.

Willis, P. (1977). *Learning to labour*. Lexington, MA: D. C. Heath.

Wilson, M. (1963). *Good company: A study of Nyakyusa age villages*. Boston: Beacon.

Wilson, W. J. (1987). *The truly disadvantaged*. Chicago: University of Chicago Press.

Wirt, F. M., & Kirst, M. W. (1974). State politics of education. In E. L. Useem & M. Useem (Eds.), *The education establishment* (pp. 69–86). Englewood, NJ: Prentice-Hall.

Wolcott, H. (1973). *The man in the principal's office*. Prospect Heights, IL: Waveland Press.

Woo, L. C. (1985). Women administrators: Profiles of success. *Phi Delta Kappan, 67*, 285–288.

Woodhouse, L. (1987). The culture of the 4-year-old in day care: Impacts on social, emotional and physical health. Unpublished doctoral dissertation, University of Cincinnati.

Wright, E. O. (1978). *Class, crisis and the state*. London: New Left Books.

Wright, E. O., & Perrone, L. (1977). Marxist class categories and income inequality. *American Sociological Review, 42*, 32–55.

Young, M. F. D. (1958). *The rise of the meritocracy*. London: Thames & Hudson.

Young, M. F. D. (1971). *Knowledge and control: New directions for the sociology of education*. London: Collier-Macmillan.

Ziegler, S., Hardwick, N., & McGreath. (1989). *Academically successful inner city children: What they can tell us about effective education*. Paper presented at the meeting of the American Educational Research Association, San Francisco.

Zigli, B. (1981). A distinctive culture, but an identity crisis. In G. Blake (Ed.), *The urban Appalachians*. Cincinnati: The Cincinnati Enquirer.

Index